the weinstock edition

ArtScroll Mesorah Series®

R' Elchonon Bunim Wasserman
Rosh Yeshivah, Ohel Torah, Baranowitz
d. 13 Tammuz 5701

R' Yisrael Meir Kagan
The Chafetz Chaim
Radin
d. 24 Elul 5693

R' Naftali Tzvi Yehudah Berlin
The Netziv
Rosh Yeshivah, Volozhin
d. 29 Av 5653

R' Yosef Chaim Shneur Kotler
Rosh Yeshivah,
Beth Medrash Govoha
d. 3 Tammuz 5742

R' Zalman Sorotzkin
Rav of Lutzk
d. 8 Tammuz 5726

R' Gedaliah Schorr
Rosh Yeshivah,
Torah Vodaath
and Beth Medrash Elyon
d. 7 Tammuz 5739

הגדה של פסח בית וויינשטאק

OF THE ROSHEI YESHIVAH

GREAT TORAH LEADERS

BOOK THREE

Adapted by
Rabbi Yaakov Blinder
from the Hebrew,
compiled by Rabbi Asher Bergman

the weinstock edition

THE HAGGADAH

ILLUMINATING THOUGHTS FROM

Published by
Mesorah Publications, ltd

A PROJECT OF THE

ARTSCROLL MESORAH SERIES®

"THE HAGGADAH OF THE ROSHEI YESHIVAH" — BOOK THREE

© Copyright 2001 by Mesorah Publications, Ltd.
First edition – First impression: March, 2001

ALL RIGHTS RESERVED

No part of this book may be reproduced **in any form,** photocopy, electronic media, or otherwise – even FOR PERSONAL, STUDY GROUP, OR CLASSROOM USE – without **written** permission from the copyright holder, except by a reviewer who wishes to quote brief passages in connection with a review written for inclusion in magazines or newspapers.

THE RIGHTS OF THE COPYRIGHT HOLDER WILL BE STRICTLY ENFORCED.

Published by **MESORAH PUBLICATIONS, LTD.**
4401 Second Avenue / Brooklyn, NY 11232 / (718) 921-9000 / Fax: (718) 680-1875
www.artscroll.com / e-mail: artscroll@mesorah.com

Distributed in Israel by SIFRIATI / A. GITLER
6 Hayarkon Street / Bnei Brak 51127 / Israel

Distributed in Europe by LEHMANNS
Unit E, Viking Industrial Park, Rolling Mill Road / Jarrow, Tyne and Wear, NE32 3DP / England

Distributed in Australia and New Zealand by GOLDS WORLD OF JUDAICA
3-13 William Street / Balaclava, Melbourne 3183, Victoria / Australia

Distributed in South Africa by KOLLEL BOOKSHOP
Shop 8A Norwood Hypermarket/ Norwood 2196 / Johannesburg, South Africa

Printed in the United States of America by
Noble Book Press Corp.
Custom bound by Sefercraft, Inc. / 4401 Second Avenue / Brooklyn NY 11232

ISBN: 1-57819-552-7 (Hard Cover)
ISBN: 1-57819-553-5 (Paperback)

This Haggadah — the story of redemption — is dedicated in honor of our beloved parents

Morris and Sara Weinstock עמו״ש

in this, their **50**th year of marriage.

Our ancestors were redeemed from Egypt because they were ready to accept the Torah and devote themselves to its fulfillment. Our parents had their own redemption, and they, too, strive to bring the Torah alive in themselves, their children, and their communities.

At an age when others were enjoying childhood, they were struggling, surviving and taking responsibility for others — developing strengths and learning lessons they never forgot. From the ashes of Poland, they came to America, married, and became builders of the fledgling Orthodox life that was beginning to emerge.

Loving and devoted to one another, no sacrifice was too great to make for their children. Their unassuming manner of giving tzedakah has made them pillars of their community. Yet, they consider the "Yiddish nachas" they enjoy from their children, grandchildren and great grandchildren as their crowning achievement and their greatest source of pride.

May הקב״ה give them the years and health to enjoy all that they have built, and may He give us the wisdom and strength to continue building on their foundation עד מאה ועשרים שנה.

Benjamin and Eileen Weinstock
Daniel, Etan and Suzi, Allon, Ariel, and Liat

David and Mindy Weinstock
Zachary, Rachel, Joshua, and Jacob

Aryeh and Shirley Rendel
Rivka and Noam Fix & Aharon Yehuda
Yocheved and Davy Dombrowsky
Shoshana, Deena, Michael, and Dovid
Yudit

The Order of the Seder

The Seder ritual contains fifteen observances, which have been summarized in the familiar rhyme Kaddesh, Urechatz, Karpas, Yachatz, and so on. Aside from its convenience as a memory device, the brief formula has been given various deeper interpretations over the years. Accordingly, many people recite the appropriate word from the rhyme before performing the mitzvah to which it applies — קדש, *Kaddesh*, before Kiddush, ורחץ, *Urechatz*, before washing hands, and so on.

KADDESH	**Sanctify** the day with the recitation of Kiddush.	קדש
URECHATZ	**Wash** the hands before eating Karpas.	ורחץ
KARPAS	Eat a **vegetable** dipped in salt water.	כרפס
YACHATZ	**Break** the middle matzah. Put away larger half for Afikoman	יחץ
MAGGID	**Narrate** the story of the Exodus from Egypt.	מגיד
RACHTZAH	**Wash** the hands prior to the meal.	רחצה
MOTZI	Recite the blessing, **Who brings forth**, over matzah as a food.	מוציא
MATZAH	Recite the blessing over **Matzah**.	מצה
MAROR	Recite the blessing for the eating of the **bitter herbs**.	מרור
KORECH	Eat the **sandwich** of matzah and bitter herbs	כורך
SHULCHAN ORECH	The **table prepared** with the festive meal.	שלחן עורך
TZAFUN	Eat the afikoman which had been **hidden** all during the Seder.	צפון
BARECH	Recite Bircas Hamazon, the **blessings** after the meal.	ברך
HALLEL	Recite the **Hallel** Psalms of praise.	הלל
NIRTZAH	Pray that God **accept** our observance and speedily send the Messiah.	נרצה

◆§ Publisher's Preface

To understand our pride at bringing this Haggadah to the English-speaking public, one need merely look at the cover. Presented in this work are the comments of *gedolei Yisrael* who taught, led, and inspired countless thousands, in Europe, Israel and America, before and after the Holocaust. They were architects of the rebirth of Torah life and institutions after the *churban*. In a very real sense, much of today's Torah world sprang from the seeds they lovingly and laboriously planted. All were legends in their lifetimes, and their words and teachings still resonate. It is a privilege, therefore, to make their sensitivity and genius, their pure faith and incisive comments available to the audience that thirsts for their wisdom.

The story of the Exodus is a cornerstone of our *emunah*, the public demonstration that nature is God's tool, not His master, and that He can change it at will. The Seder is a major vehicle to inculcate this belief in young and old — but especially in the young, to whom the commandment of וְהִגַּדְתָּ לְבִנְךָ , *and you shall tell your son*, is directed. In this work, we read how great Torah leaders carried out that commandment, with their families and with their extended families of students.

The material in this Haggadah was compiled by **Rabbi Asher Bergman.** We speak for thousands of readers in expressing gratitude for his skill, perseverance, and dedication to the cause of presenting Torah to a wide audience.

This volume has been dedicated by the **Weinstock** and **Rendel** families in honor of their parents, **Morris** and **Sara Weinstock.** Mr. & Mrs. Weinstock survived the Holocaust with a burning conviction that they must build family life and Torah life. With love, sincerity and dedication they raised a model family and did more than their share to mold their broader family — the community — in the image of pre-War devotion to Torah.

We are very thankful to the **Mesorah Heritage Foundation** for its support of the scholars who enable us to produce a wide variety of distinguished Torah publications.

We express our gratitude to **Rabbi Yaakov Blinder**, a scholar of note and a fine writer, for his illuminating translation. **Rabbi Chaim Kaisman** read the manuscript and made important comments.

Rabbi Sheah Brander designed the book in the stunning fashion that has become his hallmark.

[ix] *Publisher's Preface*

Eli Kroen designed and executed the stunning cover. **Avrohom Biderman** shepherded all aspects of the production on two continents. **Shmuel Blitz**, director of ArtScroll Jerusalem, was heavily involved from the outset. We are grateful to them all.

We extend our thanks to **Chumie Zaidman** who corrected and formatted the manuscript, and to **Mrs. Faigie Weinbaum** who proofread.

We are confident that this Haggadah will be a valuable addition to the Pesach Seder of countless people and that it will stand the test of time.

Rabbi Meir Zlotowitz
Rabbi Nosson Scherman

Adar 5761 / February 2001

עֶרֶב פֶּסַח — Erev Pesach

Laws of the Search for *Chametz*

1. One must begin the search immediately at the beginning of the night of the fourteenth of Nisan. It is proper for one to begin just after *tzeis hakochavim*, even before the light of day has completely subsided, so that he not delay the search or forget about it (*Orach Chayim* 431:1 and *Mishnah Berurah* §1).

2. It is forbidden to begin a meal or to begin a bath or to do any kind of work starting from a half-hour before nighttime. However, a snack — that is, a *k'beitzah* or less of bread, or fruit in any amount — is permitted at this time. When the actual time for the search arrives one should not spend much time eating even a snack, as this would cause a delay in the start of the search (432:2 and *Mishnah Berurah* §2, 5-6).

3. It is also forbidden to engage in Torah study once the time for the search has arrived. (There are those who forbid this also during the half-hour *before* nightfall. This applies only in private, however, and not, for instance, to someone who gives a short *shiur* in a *beis midrash* after Ma'ariv. If someone asks a person who is not learning to remind him about the search when the proper time comes, he may also learn during this half-hour interval) (ibid. *Mishnah Berurah* §7).

4. Any place into which it is possible that *chametz* might have been brought must be searched. Even places not normally used for *chametz*, but where there is a reasonable possibility that *chametz* may happen to have been brought there, require a search. This includes houses, yards (except in cases where one can assume that leftover food is eaten by animals or birds), nooks and crevices as far as the hand can reach, and whatever containers might have once been used for holding *chametz*. In a situation where a search in a particular place would entail great difficulty, it is possible to be lenient and sell that place to a non-Jew, so that it would not require a search. The details of these rules may be found in *Orach Chayim* 433:3,5 and *Mishnah Berurah* §23.

5. Pockets of garments must be searched, even if one feels confident that he has never put any *chametz* in them, because one often does so without realizing it (433:11 and *Mishnah Berurah* §47).

6. One should clean up the house before the search is begun. It is customary to clean the whole house on or before the 13th of Nisan, so that the search can be started without delay at nightfall of the 14th. It is also customary to take a feather with which to dust out the *chametz* from holes and crevices (ibid. and *Mishnah Berurah* §46).

7. It is preferable to use a single wax candle for the search. A search done by the light of a torch is not valid at all, but one done using a candle made of tallow is valid. The validity of a search done by the light of an oil candle is a matter of dispute between halachic authorities (433:2 and *Mishnah Berurah* §10). Contemporary authorities rule that one may use a flashlight for the search.

Note: Source references within the laws refer to *Shulchan Aruch Orach Chayim*, unless otherwise noted.

8. It is customary to place several pieces of bread (taking care that they should not crumble) in safe places around the house, where they may be found by the person conducting the search. (The *Arizal* wrote that *ten* pieces should be used.) Some halachic authorities write that this practice is not obligatory, and the *Taz* in fact advises against it, lest the pieces become lost. (The *Pischei Teshuvah*, however, notes that nowadays, when the entire house is rid of *chametz* before the search, there is a sound halachic basis for the practice of placing some *chametz* around the house to provide something for which to search.) (432:2, *Mishnah Berurah* §13 and *Shaar Hatziun* ad loc.)
9. There is a controversy as to whether one must search those rooms which are to be sold to a non-Jew with the *chametz*. The custom is to be lenient in this regard, although it would be preferable that in this circumstance the *chametz* be sold *before* the search (436, *Mishnah Berurah* §32).

Laws of the *Berachah* over the Search

1. Some say that it is proper to wash the hands before reciting the *berachah* for the search, but this is only for the sake of cleanliness (432, *Mishnah Berurah* §1).
2. One must not speak between the *berachah* and the onset of the search. If he spoke about matters unrelated to the search, he must repeat the *berachah* (432:1, *Mishnah Berurah* §5).
3. One should not speak about matters unrelated to the search until he completes the search, so that one may devote his entire concentration to the task at hand. If he did, however, speak about unrelated matters after beginning the search, he need not repeat the *berachah*. Furthermore, it is altogether permitted to speak about any matters related to the search at this point (ibid.).
4. Immediately after the search one should recite the כָּל חֲמִירָא declaration, annulling all the *unknown chametz* in his possession. If one does not understand the Aramaic content of this declaration, he should say it in Hebrew or English or whatever language he does understand. If one said it in Aramaic, so long as he has a basic understanding of what the declaration means, though he may not understand the translation of every word, the annulment is valid. One who does not understand the content at all, and thinks he is reciting a prayer of some sort, has not annulled his *chametz* (434:2 and *Mishnah Berurah* §8).

Laws of *Erev Pesach*

1. Prayers are held early on *erev Pesach* in order to allow people to finish eating before the end of the fourth hour of the day (*Mishnah Berurah* 429:13).
2. אֵל אֶרֶךְ אַפַּיִם, לַמְנַצֵּחַ, and מִזְמוֹר לְתוֹדָה are not said on *erev Pesach* (*Orach Chayim* 429:2).
3. It is forbidden to eat *chametz* after a third of the halachic day has passed. The duration of the day can be calculated in various ways. One should consult a competent Halachic authority or a reliable Jewish calendar (443:1 and *Mishnah Berurah* §8).

4. The deadline for ridding one's property of *chametz* and deriving benefit from the *chametz* is at the end of the *fifth* hour of the halachic day (*Mishnah Berurah* §9).
5. Immediately after a third of the day has passed, one should burn the remaining *chametz* and then recite the second כָּל חֲמִירָא declaration, annulling *all* the *chametz* in his possession. This declaration must not be delayed past the start of the sixth hour, for at that time the annulment no longer has any validity (434:2). See **"Burning the *Chametz*"** below.
6. If *erev Pesach* falls on a Shabbos, the *chametz* should be burned on the day before *erev Pesach* (Friday) in the morning, at the same time as other years. However, the כָּל חֲמִירָא declaration should not be said until the 14th of Nisan, i.e. Shabbos morning, after the last *chametz* meal has been eaten (444:2).
7. One should take care that all food utensils not *kashered* for Pesach have been thoroughly cleaned, so that they do not contain any *chametz* residue, and they should be placed out of reach for the duration of Pesach (440:2; end of 442, *Mishnah Berurah* 433:23).
8. Those utensils too hard to clean from *chametz* residue should be sold together with the *chametz*. (Only the *residue itself* should be sold, not the utensil, so as to avoid the necessity of immersing the utensil in a *mikveh* when it is repurchased from the non-Jew.) These utensils should also be placed in a room where they are out of reach, or together with the *chametz* that is being sold (ibid.).
9. After halachic noon it is forbidden to do any work (מְלָאכָה). If someone's clothing tore at that time, and he needs that article of clothing for *Yom Tov,* he may make a minor repair for himself, even if it involves expert workmanship. Someone else may also do it for him at no charge (*Orach Chayim* 468, *Mishnah Berurah* §5).
10. Any manner of work which is forbidden on *Chol Hamoed* is also forbidden on *erev Pesach* afternoon, although it is permissible for one to have a non-Jew do these things for him (*Mishnah Berurah* §7).
11. One should cut his nails and have his hair cut before noon. If, however, he neglected to do so, he may have his hair cut by a non-Jew even after noon, and he may cut his own nails (*Mishnah Berurah* §5).
12. Any matzah which one could use for fulfilling the mitzvah of matzah at the Seder may not be eaten all day on *erev Pesach,* even if that matzah has been crumbled or ground into flour and mixed with water or juices. Some people have a custom not to eat matzah from *Rosh Chodesh* Nisan (471:2, *Mishnah Berurah* §10).
13. A child who is too young to understand the story of the Exodus may be fed matzah on *erev Pesach* (471:2 and *Mishnah Berurah* §13).
14. Although we consider matzah with folds or bubbles to be unfit for Pesach use, these may also not be eaten on *erev Pesach* (*Mishnah Berurah* §12).
15. Matzah that has been prepared by adding juices into the dough (such as egg matzah or fruit-juice matzah) may be eaten on *erev Pesach.* (Note: It is the Ashkenazi practice to avoid such matzos whenever the eating of *chametz* is forbidden, except for the sick or elderly.)
16. From the beginning of the *halachic* tenth hour of the day, only snacks such as

הגדה של פסח

fruits and vegetables may be eaten. One should be careful, however, not to fill himself up on these either, to preserve one's appetite for the matzah at the Seder (471:1 and *Mishnah Berurah* 7).

17. The Gemara says that a small amount of wine can also cause satiety, but a large amount stimulates the appetite. *Be'ur Halachah* concludes that the amount of wine one may drink depends on his individual nature, and that a person should not drink (after the tenth hour) an amount of wine that he feels may make him feel sated (471:1 and *Be'ur Halachah* ad loc.).

Fast of the Firstborn

1. There is a custom for firstborn males to fast on *erev Pesach*, even if they are firstborn to only one of their parents. If the firstborn son is a minor, the father fasts in his place. If the father is a firstborn himself (and thus has to fast in his own right), the mother fasts for the child. (See *Orach Chayim* 270 and *Mishnah Berurah* ad loc. for the details of this law.)
2. If the firstborn has a headache or similar infirmity he does not have to fast. Similarly, if the fast is likely to cause him to be unable to fulfill the evening's mitzvos of matzah, *maror*, and the four cups of wine properly, it is better for him not to fast. In either of these cases, however, he should limit his eating to small amounts rather than eating full meals (470 and *Mishnah Berurah* ad loc.).
3. There is a controversy among the halachic authorities as to whether a firstborn may eat at a meal served in honor of a mitzvah, and this issue depends on the local custom. The generally accepted practice is to permit eating at a festive meal at the completion of a *mesechta*, even if the firstborn himself did not participate in the learning (*Mishnah Berurah* §10).

Burning the *Chametz*

1. The *chametz* should preferably not be burned until the day of the 14th of Nisan, after the last *chametz* meal has been eaten. If someone is concerned that the *chametz* found in the search may become lost or find its way back into the rest of the house if it is left too long, he should burn it at night, and he is considered to have fulfilled the Torah commandment to destroy *chametz* on *erev Pesach* (תַּשְׁבִּיתוּ) (*Orach Chayim* 445:1, *Mishnah Berurah* §6).
2. If one has *hoshanos* which had been used on Sukkos, he should use them to feed the flame burning the *chametz*, so that they may be used for yet another mitzvah (*Mishnah Berurah* §7).
3. The *chametz* must be burned (until it is completely charred) before the beginning of the sixth hour, and thereupon the declaration of annulment (כָּל חֲמִירָא) is recited. The annulment is ineffective if it is recited once the sixth hour has begun (*Mishnah Berurah* §1,6).
4. One should not recite the annulment declaration before his *chametz* has been fully burned, so that he will be able to fulfill the mitzvah of תַּשְׁבִּיתוּ (burning the *chametz*) with *chametz* that still belongs to him (443:2).

בדיקת חמץ

The *chametz* search is initiated with the recitation of the following blessing:

בָּרוּךְ אַתָּה יהוה אֱלֹהֵינוּ מֶלֶךְ הָעוֹלָם, אֲשֶׁר קִדְּשָׁנוּ בְּמִצְוֹתָיו, וְצִוָּנוּ עַל בִּעוּר חָמֵץ.

Upon completion of the *chametz* search, the *chametz* is wrapped well and set aside to be burned the next morning and the following declaration is made. The declaration must be understood in order to take effect; one who does not understand the Aramaic text may recite it in English, Yiddish or any other language. Any *chametz* that will be used for that evening's supper or the next day's breakfast or for any other purpose prior to the final removal of *chametz* the next morning is not included in this declaration.

כָּל חֲמִירָא וַחֲמִיעָא דְּאִכָּא בִרְשׁוּתִי, דְּלָא חֲמִתֵּהּ וּדְלָא בְעַרְתֵּהּ וּדְלָא יָדַעְנָא לֵהּ, לִבָּטֵל וְלֶהֱוֵי הֶפְקֵר כְּעַפְרָא דְאַרְעָא.

ביעור חמץ

The following declaration, which includes all *chametz* without exception, is to be made after the burning of leftover *chametz*. It should be recited in a language which one understands. When *Pesach* begins on *Motzaei Shabbos*, this declaration is made on *Shabbos* morning. Any *chametz* remaining from the *Shabbos* morning meal is flushed down the drain before the declaration is made.

כָּל חֲמִירָא וַחֲמִיעָא דְּאִכָּא בִרְשׁוּתִי, דַּחֲזִתֵּהּ וּדְלָא חֲזִתֵּהּ, דַּחֲמִתֵּהּ וּדְלָא חֲמִתֵּהּ, דְּבִעַרְתֵּהּ וּדְלָא בִעַרְתֵּהּ, לִבָּטֵל וְלֶהֱוֵי הֶפְקֵר כְּעַפְרָא דְאַרְעָא.

עירוב תבשילין

It is forbidden to prepare on *Yom Tov* for the next day even if that day is the Sabbath. If, however, Sabbath preparations were started before *Yom Tov* began, they may be continued on *Yom Tov*. *Eruv tavshilin* constitutes this preparation. A matzah and any cooked food (such as fish, meat or an egg) are set aside on the day before *Yom Tov* to be used on the Sabbath and the blessing is recited followed by the declaration [made in a language understood by the one making the *eruv*].

If the first days of Pesach fall on Thursday and Friday, an *eruv tavshilin* must be made on Wednesday.

[In *Eretz Yisrael*, where only one day *Yom Tov* is in effect, the *eruv* is omitted.]

בָּרוּךְ אַתָּה יהוה אֱלֹהֵינוּ מֶלֶךְ הָעוֹלָם, אֲשֶׁר קִדְּשָׁנוּ בְּמִצְוֹתָיו, וְצִוָּנוּ עַל מִצְוַת עֵרוּב.

SEARCH FOR CHAMETZ

The *chametz* search is initiated with the recitation of the following blessing:

Blessed are You, HASHEM, our God, King of the universe, Who has sanctified us with His commandments, and commanded us concerning the removal of chametz.

Upon completion of the *chametz* search, the *chametz* is wrapped well and set aside to be burned the next morning and the following declaration is made. The declaration must be understood in order to take effect; one who does not understand the Aramaic text may recite it in English, Yiddish or any other language. Any *chametz* that will be used for that evening's supper or the next day's breakfast or for any other purpose prior to the final removal of *chametz* the next morning is not included in this declaration.

Any chametz which is in my possession which I did not see, and remove, nor know about, shall be nullified and become ownerless, like the dust of the earth.

BURNING THE CHAMETZ

The following declaration, which includes all *chametz* without exception, is to be made after the burning of leftover *chametz*. It should be recited in a language which one understands. When *Pesach* begins on *Motzaei Shabbos*, this declaration is made on *Shabbos* morning. Any *chametz* remaining from the *Shabbos* morning meal is flushed down the drain before the declaration is made.

Any chametz which is in my possession which I did or did not see, which I did or did not remove, shall be nullified and become ownerless, like the dust of the earth.

ERUV TAVSHILIN

It is forbidden to prepare on *Yom Tov* for the next day even if that day is the Sabbath. If, however, Sabbath preparations were started before *Yom Tov* began, they may be continued on *Yom Tov*. *Eruv tavshilin* constitutes this preparation. A matzah and any cooked food (such as fish, meat or an egg) are set aside on the day before *Yom Tov* to be used on the Sabbath and the blessing is recited followed by the declaration [made in a language understood by the one making the *eruv*].
If the first days of Pesach fall on Thursday and Friday,
an *eruv tavshilin* must be made on Wednesday.

[In *Eretz Yisrael*, where only one day *Yom Tov* is in effect, the *eruv* is omitted.]

Blessed are You, HASHEM, our God, King of the universe, Who sanctified us with His commandments and commanded us concerning the commandment of eruv.

בְּהָדֵין עֵרוּבָא יְהֵא שָׁרֵא לָנָא לַאֲפוּיֵי וּלְבַשּׁוּלֵי וּלְאַצְלוּיֵי וּלְאַטְמוּנֵי וּלְאַדְלוּקֵי שְׁרָגָא וּלְתַקָּנָא וּלְמֶעְבַּד כָּל צָרְכָּנָא, מִיּוֹמָא טָבָא לְשַׁבַּתָּא לָנָא וּלְכָל יִשְׂרָאֵל הַדָּרִים בָּעִיר הַזֹּאת.

הדלקת נרות

The candles are lit and the following blessings are recited.
When *Yom Tov* falls on *Shabbos*, the words in parentheses are added.

בָּרוּךְ אַתָּה יהוה אֱלֹהֵינוּ מֶלֶךְ הָעוֹלָם, אֲשֶׁר קִדְּשָׁנוּ בְּמִצְוֹתָיו, וְצִוָּנוּ לְהַדְלִיק נֵר שֶׁל [שַׁבָּת וְשֶׁל] יוֹם טוֹב.

בָּרוּךְ אַתָּה יהוה אֱלֹהֵינוּ מֶלֶךְ הָעוֹלָם, שֶׁהֶחֱיָנוּ וְקִיְּמָנוּ וְהִגִּיעָנוּ לַזְּמַן הַזֶּה.

אֲשֶׁר קִדְּשָׁנוּ בְּמִצְוֹתָיו,
Who has sanctified us with His commandments,

A Prerequisite for Attaining Sanctity

The **Chafetz Chaim** writes that although we state in this blessing, and in dozens of others like it, that God's commandments endow us with sanctity, this is only so if the person performing the mitzvah sanctifies *himself* first. The Torah tells us, "You shall make yourselves holy, and you will be holy" (Vayikra 11:44). The Talmud (*Yoma* 39a) explains: "If a person sanctifies himself a little bit, [God] will sanctify him even more." One cannot hope to achieve a state of holiness through external actions if he does not begin by purifying himself from within.

How is this initial purification process to be undertaken? The Torah writes (in *Bamidbar* 15:39-40), "And it shall be *tzitzis* for you, and you will see it and remember all the mitzvos of Hashem and do them, and you will not go astray after your heart and after your eyes... In order that you remember and do all My mitzvos and be holy to your God." The second part of this excerpt (*In order that you remember and do all My mitzvos and be holy to your God*) seems to be totally extraneous; the Torah has already said that the function of the *tzitzis* is that we should "see it and remember all the mitzvos of Hashem and do them." What is

Through this eruv may we be permitted to bake, cook, fry, insulate, kindle flame, prepare for, and do anything necessary on the festival for the sake of the Sabbath — for ourselves and for all Jews who live in this city.

LIGHTING THE CANDLES

*The candles are lit and the following blessings are recited.
When Yom Tov falls on Shabbos, the words in parentheses are added.*

Blessed are You, HASHEM, our God, King of the universe, Who has sanctified us with His commandments, and commanded us to kindle the flame of the (Sabbath and the) festival.

Blessed are You, HASHEM, our God, King of the universe, Who has kept us alive, sustained us, and brought us to this season.

---

the point of this repetition?

In order to answer this question let us first consider what the Torah means by "not going astray after your hearts and eyes." The Talmud (*Berachos* 12b) elaborates on these terms and explains that "going astray after one's heart" refers to allowing oneself to foster heretical thoughts, and "going astray after one's eyes" refers to improper sexual thoughts.

Now we can understand the apparent repetitiousness noted in the verses cited above. First the Torah tells us that the *tzitzis* is intended to lead us to remembrance and performance of God's mitzvos. But the Torah immediately cautions us that first we must rid ourselves of all types of sinful thoughts, and only then can the performance of the mitzvos achieve its goal — that "we should become holy to our God." Without this initial step on our part the mitzvos cannot work to imbue us with sanctity.

The Chafetz Chaim illuminated this point more clearly through a parable: Once there was a poor family who lived in a broken-down hovel in the poorest section of town. The walls were full of soot from the faulty fireplace, and the floor was made of loose dirt, which more often than not was a muddy mess. The sanitary conditions and the general state of disrepair in the house were disgraceful and embarrassing.

One day the man, who had a beautiful and charming young daughter, heard that a fine boy from a respectable family was interested in asking for her hand in

It is customary to recite the following prayer after the kindling.
The words in brackets are included as they apply.

יְהִי רָצוֹן לְפָנֶיךָ, יהוה אֱלֹהַי וֵאלֹהֵי אֲבוֹתַי, שֶׁתְּחוֹנֵן אוֹתִי [וְאֶת אִישִׁי, וְאֶת בָּנַי, וְאֶת בְּנוֹתַי, וְאֶת אָבִי, וְאֶת אִמִּי] וְאֶת כָּל קְרוֹבַי; וְתִתֶּן לָנוּ וּלְכָל יִשְׂרָאֵל חַיִּים טוֹבִים וַאֲרוּכִים; וְתִזְכְּרֵנוּ בְּזִכְרוֹן טוֹבָה וּבְרָכָה; וְתִפְקְדֵנוּ בִּפְקֻדַּת יְשׁוּעָה וְרַחֲמִים; וּתְבָרְכֵנוּ בְּרָכוֹת גְּדוֹלוֹת; וְתַשְׁלִים בָּתֵּינוּ; וְתַשְׁכֵּן שְׁכִינָתְךָ בֵּינֵינוּ. וְזַכֵּנִי לְגַדֵּל בָּנִים וּבְנֵי בָנִים חֲכָמִים וּנְבוֹנִים, אוֹהֲבֵי יהוה, יִרְאֵי אֱלֹהִים, אַנְשֵׁי אֱמֶת, זֶרַע קֹדֶשׁ, בַּיהוה דְּבֵקִים, וּמְאִירִים אֶת הָעוֹלָם בַּתּוֹרָה וּבְמַעֲשִׂים טוֹבִים, וּבְכָל מְלֶאכֶת עֲבוֹדַת הַבּוֹרֵא. אָנָּא שְׁמַע אֶת תְּחִנָּתִי בָּעֵת הַזֹּאת, בִּזְכוּת שָׂרָה וְרִבְקָה וְרָחֵל וְלֵאָה אִמּוֹתֵינוּ, וְהָאֵר נֵרֵנוּ שֶׁלֹּא יִכְבֶּה לְעוֹלָם וָעֶד, וְהָאֵר פָּנֶיךָ וְנִוָּשֵׁעָה. אָמֵן.

---

marriage. When the poor man came home at night he told his wife the exciting news, and informed her that the family of the prospective groom would be calling the following evening to discuss the matter. He asked her to tidy up the house and make it presentable, so as to make a favorable first impression for this crucial meeting.

The woman, who worked as a cleaning lady for one of the richest families in town, had an idea. She told her employer about her situation and persuaded him to loan her a beautiful golden fruit bowl and a large, precious mirror, with an ornamental gilded frame. She brought the objects home and set them in place in anticipation of her meeting.

It is customary to recite the following prayer after the kindling. The words in brackets are included as they apply.

May it be Your will, HASHEM, my God and God of my forefathers, that You show favor to me [my husband, my sons, my daughters, my father, my mother] and all my relatives; and that You grant us and all Israel a good and long life; that You remember us with a beneficent memory and blessing; that You consider us with a consideration of salvation and compassion; that You bless us with great blessings; that You make our households complete; that You cause Your Presence to dwell among us. Privilege me to raise children and grandchildren who are wise and understanding, who love HASHEM and fear God, people of truth, holy offspring, attached to HASHEM, who illuminate the world with Torah and good deeds and with every labor in the service of the Creator. Please, hear my supplication at this time, in the merit of Sarah, Rebecca, Rachel, and Leah, our mothers, and cause our light to illuminate that it not be extinguished forever, and let Your countenance shine so that we are saved. Amen.

When the guests arrived, the woman's efforts proved to be in vain, of course. Rather than impressing her company with the expensive articles, these inappropriate objects only served to underscore, by contrast, the squalor and poverty that pervaded the house.

The Jewish soul has the tremendous potential to achieve the highest levels of sanctity, to serve as a sanctuary for the *Shechinah,* as it is written, "I am Hashem, Who dwells in the midst (or *inside*) of the Children of Israel" (*Bamidbar* 35:34). But it is possible to set up this sanctuary only if the filth and impurities of the *yetzer hara* (man's evil inclinations) have first been cleaned out of that soul.

סדר אמירת קרבן פסח

After *Minchah*, many customarily recite the following passages that describe the קָרְבַּן פֶּסַח, *pesach* offering:

רִבּוֹן הָעוֹלָמִים, אַתָּה צִוִּיתָנוּ לְהַקְרִיב קָרְבַּן הַפֶּסַח בְּמוֹעֲדוֹ בְּאַרְבָּעָה עָשָׂר יוֹם לַחֹדֶשׁ הָרִאשׁוֹן, וְלִהְיוֹת כֹּהֲנִים בַּעֲבוֹדָתָם וּלְוִיִּים בְּדוּכָנָם וְיִשְׂרָאֵל בְּמַעֲמָדָם קוֹרְאִים אֶת הַהַלֵּל. וְעַתָּה בַּעֲוֹנוֹתֵינוּ חָרַב בֵּית הַמִּקְדָּשׁ וּבָטֵל קָרְבַּן הַפֶּסַח, וְאֵין לָנוּ לֹא כֹהֵן בַּעֲבוֹדָתוֹ וְלֹא לֵוִי בְּדוּכָנוֹ וְלֹא יִשְׂרָאֵל בְּמַעֲמָדוֹ, וְלֹא נוּכַל לְהַקְרִיב הַיּוֹם קָרְבַּן פֶּסַח. אֲבָל אַתָּה אָמַרְתָּ וּנְשַׁלְּמָה פָרִים שְׂפָתֵינוּ. לָכֵן יְהִי רָצוֹן מִלְּפָנֶיךָ יהוה אֱלֹהֵינוּ וֵאלֹהֵי אֲבוֹתֵינוּ שֶׁיִּהְיֶה שִׂיחַ שִׂפְתוֹתֵינוּ חָשׁוּב לְפָנֶיךָ כְּאִלּוּ הִקְרַבְנוּ אֶת הַפֶּסַח בְּמוֹעֲדוֹ וְעָמַדְנוּ עַל מַעֲמָדוֹ, וְדִבְּרוּ הַלְוִיִּים בְּשִׁיר וְהַלֵּל לְהוֹדוֹת לַיהוה. וְאַתָּה תְּכוֹנֵן מִקְדָּשְׁךָ עַל מְכוֹנוֹ, וְנַעֲשֶׂה וְנַקְרִיב לְפָנֶיךָ אֶת הַפֶּסַח בְּמוֹעֲדוֹ, כְּמוֹ שֶׁכָּתַבְתָּ עָלֵינוּ בְּתוֹרָתֶךָ עַל יְדֵי מֹשֶׁה עַבְדֶּךָ כָּאָמוּר:

שמות יב:א-יא

וַיֹּאמֶר יהוה אֶל מֹשֶׁה וְאֶל אַהֲרֹן בְּאֶרֶץ מִצְרַיִם לֵאמֹר. הַחֹדֶשׁ הַזֶּה לָכֶם רֹאשׁ חֳדָשִׁים רִאשׁוֹן הוּא לָכֶם לְחָדְשֵׁי הַשָּׁנָה. דַּבְּרוּ אֶל כָּל עֲדַת יִשְׂרָאֵל לֵאמֹר בֶּעָשֹׂר לַחֹדֶשׁ הַזֶּה וְיִקְחוּ לָהֶם אִישׁ שֶׂה לְבֵית אָבֹת שֶׂה לַבָּיִת. וְאִם יִמְעַט הַבַּיִת מִהְיוֹת מִשֶּׂה וְלָקַח הוּא וּשְׁכֵנוֹ הַקָּרֹב אֶל בֵּיתוֹ בְּמִכְסַת נְפָשֹׁת אִישׁ לְפִי אָכְלוֹ תָּכֹסּוּ עַל הַשֶּׂה. שֶׂה תָמִים זָכָר בֶּן שָׁנָה יִהְיֶה לָכֶם מִן הַכְּבָשִׂים וּמִן הָעִזִּים תִּקָּחוּ. וְהָיָה לָכֶם לְמִשְׁמֶרֶת עַד אַרְבָּעָה עָשָׂר יוֹם לַחֹדֶשׁ הַזֶּה וְשָׁחֲטוּ אֹתוֹ כֹּל קְהַל עֲדַת יִשְׂרָאֵל בֵּין הָעַרְבָּיִם.

RECITAL OF THE KORBAN PESACH

After Minchah, many customarily recite the following passages that describe the קָרְבַּן פֶּסַח, pesach offering:

Master of the universe, You commanded us to bring the pesach offering at its set time, on the fourteenth day of the first month; and that the Kohanim be at their assigned service, the Levites on their platform, and the Israelites at their station reciting the Hallel. But now, through our sins, the Holy Temple is destroyed, the pesach offering is discontinued, and we have neither Kohen at his service, nor Levite on his platform, nor Israelite at his station. So we are unable to bring the pesach offering today. But You said: "Let our lips compensate for the bulls" — therefore, may it be Your will, HASHEM, our God and the God of our forefathers, that the prayer of our lips be considered by You as if we had brought the pesach offering at its set time, had stood at its station, and the Levites had uttered song and Hallel, to thank HASHEM. And may You establish Your sanctuary on its prepared site, that we may ascend and bring the pesach offering before You at its set time — as You have prescribed for us in Your Torah, through Moshe, Your servant, as it is said: in Your Torah, through Moshe, Your servant, as it is said:

Shemos 12:1-11

And HASHEM said to Moshe and Aharon in the land of Egypt, saying: This month shall be for you the beginning of the months, it shall be for you the first of the months of the year. Speak to the entire assembly of Israel saying: On the tenth of this month, they shall take for themselves — each man — a lamb or kid for each fathers' house, a lamb or kid for the household. But if the household will be too small for a lamb or kid, then he and his neighbor who is near his house shall take according to the number of people; everyone according to what he eats shall be counted a lamb/kid. An unblemished lamb or kid, a male, within its first year shall it be for you; from the sheep or goats shall you take it. It shall be yours for examination until the fourteenth day of this month; the entire congregation of the assembly of Israel shall slaughter it in the afternoon.

וְלָקְחוּ מִן הַדָּם וְנָתְנוּ עַל שְׁתֵּי הַמְּזוּזֹת וְעַל הַמַּשְׁקוֹף עַל הַבָּתִּים אֲשֶׁר יֹאכְלוּ אֹתוֹ בָּהֶם. וְאָכְלוּ אֶת הַבָּשָׂר בַּלַּיְלָה הַזֶּה צְלִי אֵשׁ וּמַצּוֹת עַל מְרֹרִים יֹאכְלֻהוּ: אַל תֹּאכְלוּ מִמֶּנּוּ נָא וּבָשֵׁל מְבֻשָּׁל בַּמָּיִם כִּי אִם צְלִי אֵשׁ רֹאשׁוֹ עַל כְּרָעָיו וְעַל קִרְבּוֹ. וְלֹא תוֹתִירוּ מִמֶּנּוּ עַד בֹּקֶר וְהַנֹּתָר מִמֶּנּוּ עַד בֹּקֶר בָּאֵשׁ תִּשְׂרֹפוּ. וְכָכָה תֹּאכְלוּ אֹתוֹ מָתְנֵיכֶם חֲגֻרִים נַעֲלֵיכֶם בְּרַגְלֵיכֶם וּמַקֶּלְכֶם בְּיֶדְכֶם וַאֲכַלְתֶּם אֹתוֹ בְּחִפָּזוֹן פֶּסַח הוּא לַיהוה.

Some recite the following ten Scriptural passages as part of the recital of the *korban pesach*. Others continue on p. 28.

שמות יב:כא-כח

וַיִּקְרָא מֹשֶׁה לְכָל זִקְנֵי יִשְׂרָאֵל וַיֹּאמֶר אֲלֵיהֶם מִשְׁכוּ וּקְחוּ לָכֶם צֹאן לְמִשְׁפְּחֹתֵיכֶם וְשַׁחֲטוּ הַפָּסַח.

וְנָתְנוּ עַל שְׁתֵּי הַמְּזוּזֹת וְעַל הַמַּשְׁקוֹף
and they shall place it on the two doorposts and on the lintel

"Reach for the Stars" — Here (*Shemos* 12:7), where God spells out the instructions for performing the first *pesach* sacrifice in Egypt and the smearing of its blood on the doors of the Jewish homes, the Torah writes, "And they shall place it on the two doorposts and on the lintel." But later, where Moshe repeats God's commandments to the people (12:22), we read, "You shall apply it to the lintel and to the two doorposts." **R' Gedaliah Schorr** noted that there are two differences between the statements: First, in God's command the *lintel* is mentioned before the *doorposts*, while in Moshe's words the order is reversed. Second, in the former verse the verb "to place" (וְנָתְנוּ) is used, while in the latter the verb "to apply" (וְהִגַּעְתֶּם, lit., "to cause to reach") is written. What is the significance of these differences?

The Midrash (*Shemos Rabbah* 17:3) teaches that the application of the blood onto these three places of the people's doorways represented the three Patriarchs, for it would be through their merit that God would redeem His people from exile and servitude. The lintel, the Midrash explains, represented the merits of Avraham, and the two doorposts stood for those of Yitzchak and Yaakov.

Based on this Midrash, we may suggest an explanation for the two differences in language noted above. Moshe was intimating to the people that they had to strive to emulate the faith and deeds of their forefathers, as indicated by his choice of the word וְהִגַּעְתֶּם — suggesting reaching out and striving. This is why he mentioned the lintel, representing the highest level of achievement, before the doorposts. This is because when one strives and toils towards a goal he must "reach for the stars" and fix his sights on the highest possible aspirations. In God's words, however, the command

They shall take some of its blood and they shall place it on the two doorposts and on the lintel of the houses in which they will eat it. They shall eat the meat on that night — roasted over the fire — and matzos; with bitter herbs shall they eat it. You shall not eat it partially roasted or cooked in water; only roasted over fire — its head, its legs, with its innards. You shall not leave any of it until morning; any of it that is left until morning you shall burn in the fire. So shall you eat it: your loins girded, your shoes on your feet, and your staff in your hand; you shall eat it in haste — it is a pesach offering to HASHEM.

Some recite the following ten Scriptural passages as part of the recital of the korban pesach. Others continue on p. 29.

Shemos 12:21-28

Moshe called to all the elders of Israel and said to them, "Draw forth or buy yourselves sheep for your families, and slaughter the pesach

---

relates to the actual placement of the blood — not to the effort and attitude involved in placing it. In that case, the doorposts, which are closer to the ground, are specified first. This is because when it comes to actual implementation of one's goals he must proceed slowly, step by step, until he reaches the desired aim.

This lesson applies to Torah learning as much as to any other endeavor in life. The Talmud (*Berachos* 50a) tells us that although it is generally appropriate to pray to God only for minimal, humble requests, when it comes to Torah knowledge the rule is "Open up your mouth wide (i.e., with large requests) and I will fill it!" (*Tehillim* 81:11). With Torah, even more than with any other activity of life, the proper attitude is to strive for the maximum possible accomplishments. But when it comes to putting these aspirations into action, we are cautioned not to proceed too speedily: "If a person acquires Torah in large bundles, he will lessen [his final accomplishment]; if he gathers up little by little, he will achieve much" (*Eruvin* 54b).

מִשְׁכוּ וּקְחוּ לָכֶם צֹאן לְמִשְׁפְּחֹתֵיכֶם
Draw forth or buy yourselves sheep for your families,

The Pesach Sacrifice — Renouncing Idolatry

What is meant by "draw forth"? The Midrash interprets this homiletically, "Draw yourselves away from your idolatrous practices, and then get yourselves sheep and prepare yourselves for the *pesach* sacrifice." The *pesach* sacrifice, then, was meant to be a medium through which the people were to distance themselves from the idolatrous practices to which they had accustomed themselves until that time. **R' Gedaliah Schorr** noted that this underlying theoretical theme of the *pesach* sacrifice can be applied to account for a concrete halachic application.

According to the halachah, a non-Jew who wishes to become a member of the Jewish nation must undergo three steps — immersion in a mikveh, circumcision (for males), and the bringing of a sacrifice (specifically, a fowl for a burnt-offering)

[15] THE HAGGADAH OF THE ROSHEI YESHIVAH

וּלְקַחְתֶּם אֲגֻדַּת אֵזוֹב וּטְבַלְתֶּם בַּדָּם אֲשֶׁר בַּסַּף וְהִגַּעְתֶּם אֶל הַמַּשְׁקוֹף וְאֶל שְׁתֵּי הַמְּזוּזֹת מִן הַדָּם אֲשֶׁר בַּסָּף וְאַתֶּם לֹא תֵצְאוּ אִישׁ מִפֶּתַח בֵּיתוֹ עַד בֹּקֶר. וְעָבַר יהוה לִנְגֹּף אֶת מִצְרַיִם וְרָאָה אֶת הַדָּם עַל הַמַּשְׁקוֹף וְעַל שְׁתֵּי הַמְּזוּזֹת וּפָסַח יהוה עַל הַפֶּתַח וְלֹא יִתֵּן הַמַּשְׁחִית לָבֹא אֶל בָּתֵּיכֶם לִנְגֹּף. וּשְׁמַרְתֶּם אֶת הַדָּבָר הַזֶּה לְחָק לְךָ וּלְבָנֶיךָ עַד עוֹלָם.

וְהָיָה כִּי תָבֹאוּ אֶל הָאָרֶץ אֲשֶׁר יִתֵּן יהוה לָכֶם כַּאֲשֶׁר דִּבֵּר וּשְׁמַרְתֶּם אֶת הָעֲבֹדָה הַזֹּאת. וְהָיָה כִּי יֹאמְרוּ אֲלֵיכֶם בְּנֵיכֶם מָה הָעֲבֹדָה הַזֹּאת לָכֶם. וַאֲמַרְתֶּם זֶבַח פֶּסַח הוּא לַיהוה אֲשֶׁר פָּסַח עַל בָּתֵּי בְנֵי יִשְׂרָאֵל בְּמִצְרַיִם בְּנָגְפּוֹ אֶת מִצְרַיִם וְאֶת בָּתֵּינוּ הִצִּיל וַיִּקֹּד הָעָם וַיִּשְׁתַּחֲווּ. וַיֵּלְכוּ וַיַּעֲשׂוּ בְּנֵי יִשְׂרָאֵל כַּאֲשֶׁר צִוָּה יהוה אֶת מֹשֶׁה וְאַהֲרֹן כֵּן עָשׂוּ.

שמות יב:מג-נ

וַיֹּאמֶר יהוה אֶל מֹשֶׁה וְאַהֲרֹן זֹאת חֻקַּת הַפָּסַח כָּל בֶּן נֵכָר לֹא יֹאכַל בּוֹ. וְכָל עֶבֶד אִישׁ מִקְנַת כֶּסֶף וּמַלְתָּה אֹתוֹ אָז יֹאכַל בּוֹ. תּוֹשָׁב וְשָׂכִיר לֹא יֹאכַל בּוֹ. בְּבַיִת אֶחָד יֵאָכֵל לֹא תוֹצִיא מִן הַבַּיִת מִן הַבָּשָׂר חוּצָה וְעֶצֶם לֹא תִשְׁבְּרוּ בוֹ. כָּל עֲדַת יִשְׂרָאֵל יַעֲשׂוּ אֹתוֹ. וְכִי יָגוּר אִתְּךָ גֵּר וְעָשָׂה פֶסַח לַיהוה הִמּוֹל לוֹ כָל זָכָר וְאָז יִקְרַב לַעֲשֹׂתוֹ וְהָיָה כְּאֶזְרַח הָאָרֶץ וְכָל עָרֵל לֹא יֹאכַל בּוֹ. תּוֹרָה אַחַת יִהְיֶה לָאֶזְרָח וְלַגֵּר הַגָּר בְּתוֹכְכֶם. וַיַּעֲשׂוּ כָּל בְּנֵי יִשְׂרָאֵל כַּאֲשֶׁר צִוָּה יהוה אֶת מֹשֶׁה וְאֶת אַהֲרֹן כֵּן עָשׂוּ.

---

in the Temple. Nowadays, of course, the third step is impossible to implement, but the law is that a conversion without this act is also valid (except that a convert who has not brought his sacrifice may not partake of other sacrificial foods). The *Meshech Chochmah* presents the possibility that the requirement of bringing this "conversion-sacrifice" is applicable only before the convert's first Pesach has passed by. But once he has brought a *pesach* sacrifice, this obviates the need for him to bring a conversion-sacrifice subsequently. The *Meshech Chochmah* bases this ruling on the the Torah's words: "If a stranger should live among you and he makes a *pesach* sacrifice to Hashem... he shall be like a native of the land" (*Shemos* 12:48) — implying that after the offering of the *pesach* sacrifice, the stranger gains complete equality with the born Jew.

According to the principle established above, we can understand the *Meshech Chochmah's* novel interpretation quite well. The conversion process is one through which the prospective convert renounces his previously held beliefs and embraces the Torah as his way of life. While it is true that the Torah requires him to bring a special sacrifice as part of this process, it is quite feasible that the offering of a *pesach* offering. You shall take a bundle of hyssop and dip it into the blood that is in the basin, and touch the lintel and the two doorposts with some of the blood that is in the basin, and as for you, you shall not leave the entrance of your house until morning. HASHEM will pass through to smite Egypt, and He will see the blood that is on the lintel and the two doorposts; and HASHEM will pass over the entrance and He will not permit the destroyer to enter your homes to smite. You shall observe this matter as a decree for yourself and for your children forever.

"It shall be that when you come to the land that HASHEM will give you, as He has spoken, you shall observe this service. And it shall be that when your children say to you, 'What is this service to you?' You shall say, 'It is a pesach feast-offering to HASHEM, Who passed over the houses of the Children of Israel in Egypt when He smote the Egyptians, but He saved our households,' " and the people bowed their heads and prostrated themselves. The Children of Israel went and did as HASHEM commanded Moshe and Aharon, so did they do.

Shemos 12:43-50

HASHEM said to Moshe and Aharon, "This is the decree of the pesach offering: no alienated person may eat from it. Every slave of a man, who was bought for money, you shall circumcise him; then he may eat from it. A sojourner and a hired laborer may not eat from it. In one house shall it be eaten; you shall not remove any of the meat from the house to the outside, and you shall not break a bone in it. The entire assembly of Israel shall perform it.

"When a proselyte sojourns among you he shall make the pesach offering for HASHEM; each of his males shall be circumcised, and then he may draw near to perform it and he shall be like the native of the land; no uncircumcised male may eat from it. One law shall there be for the native and the proselyte who lives among you." All the Children of Israel did as HASHEM had commanded Moshe and Aharon, so did they do.

---

sacrifice — which itself symbolizes the casting off of idolatrous beliefs and subjecting oneself to the yoke of Heaven — can take the place of this conversion-sacrifice.

This idea may be used to shed light on a difficult statement of the Sages as well. The Torah writes, "If a stranger should live among you and he makes a *pesach* sacrifice to Hashem..." (*Bamidbar* 9:14). The verse could also be translated as follows, however: "If a stranger should live among you he shall make a *pesach* sacrifice to Hashem." The Talmud poses this as a possible interpretation of the verse and, based on this, entertains the possibility that every stranger who seeks entry to the Jewish nation must bring a *pesach* sacrifice immediately, regardless of the time of year, as it says, "He shall make a *pesach* sacrifice to Hashem." This interpretation

ויקרא כג:ד-ה

אֵלֶּה מוֹעֲדֵי יהוה מִקְרָאֵי קֹדֶשׁ אֲשֶׁר תִּקְרְאוּ אֹתָם בְּמוֹעֲדָם. בַּחֹדֶשׁ הָרִאשׁוֹן בְּאַרְבָּעָה עָשָׂר לַחֹדֶשׁ בֵּין הָעַרְבָּיִם פֶּסַח לַיהוה.

במדבר ט:א-יד

וַיְדַבֵּר יהוה אֶל מֹשֶׁה בְמִדְבַּר סִינַי בַּשָּׁנָה הַשֵּׁנִית לְצֵאתָם מֵאֶרֶץ מִצְרַיִם בַּחֹדֶשׁ הָרִאשׁוֹן לֵאמֹר. וְיַעֲשׂוּ בְנֵי יִשְׂרָאֵל אֶת הַפָּסַח בְּמוֹעֲדוֹ. בְּאַרְבָּעָה עָשָׂר יוֹם בַּחֹדֶשׁ הַזֶּה בֵּין הָעַרְבַּיִם תַּעֲשׂוּ אֹתוֹ בְּמוֹעֲדוֹ כְּכָל חֻקֹּתָיו וּכְכָל מִשְׁפָּטָיו תַּעֲשׂוּ אֹתוֹ. וַיְדַבֵּר מֹשֶׁה אֶל בְּנֵי יִשְׂרָאֵל לַעֲשֹׂת הַפָּסַח. וַיַּעֲשׂוּ אֶת הַפֶּסַח בָּרִאשׁוֹן בְּאַרְבָּעָה עָשָׂר יוֹם לַחֹדֶשׁ בֵּין הָעַרְבַּיִם בְּמִדְבַּר סִינָי כְּכֹל אֲשֶׁר צִוָּה יהוה אֶת מֹשֶׁה כֵּן עָשׂוּ בְּנֵי יִשְׂרָאֵל. וַיְהִי אֲנָשִׁים אֲשֶׁר הָיוּ טְמֵאִים לְנֶפֶשׁ אָדָם וְלֹא יָכְלוּ לַעֲשֹׂת הַפֶּסַח בַּיּוֹם הַהוּא וַיִּקְרְבוּ לִפְנֵי מֹשֶׁה וְלִפְנֵי אַהֲרֹן בַּיּוֹם הַהוּא. וַיֹּאמְרוּ הָאֲנָשִׁים הָהֵמָּה אֵלָיו אֲנַחְנוּ טְמֵאִים לְנֶפֶשׁ אָדָם לָמָּה נִגָּרַע לְבִלְתִּי הַקְרִב אֶת קָרְבַּן יהוה בְּמֹעֲדוֹ בְּתוֹךְ בְּנֵי יִשְׂרָאֵל.

---

is rejected because of the following phrase in the verse: "One law shall be for you, for both the stranger and the native of the land," which implies that the law of the *pesach* sacrifice is exactly the same, both for native Jews and converts — it is to be brought on the fourteenth of Nisan, and not at any other time.

The difficulty with this Talmudic discussion is: How can the Sages even consider the possibility that a convert should bring a *pesach* sacrifice when it is not Pesach? What would be the logic behind such a strange requirement? According to the concept introduced above, however, we can understand the passage very well. The underlying principle of the *pesach* sacrifice is, after all, a form of renouncement of idolatry and the acceptance of the mastery of God, and such a sacrifice is obviously quite appropriate for a convert, regardless of the season in which he converts.

וַיֹּאמְרוּ הָאֲנָשִׁים הָהֵמָּה אֵלָיו אֲנַחְנוּ טְמֵאִים לְנֶפֶשׁ אָדָם לָמָּה נִגָּרַע לְבִלְתִּי הַקְרִב אֶת קָרְבַּן ה' בְּמֹעֲדוֹ

And those men said to him, "We are unclean through contact with a dead person; why should we be deprived of offering Hashem's sacrifice in its time . . .?"

The Burning Desire to Do a Mitzvah

When presented with this argument Moshe turned to God for guidance and was taught the laws of the "second Pesach," to be held a month after the regular *pesach* sacrifice for the benefit of those who could not participate the first time. Rashi quotes the comment of the Sages: "This section of the Torah (i.e., the laws

הגדה של פסח [18]

Vayikra 23:4-5

These are the appointed festivals of HASHEM, the holy convocations, which you shall designate in their appropriate time. In the first month on the fourteenth of the month in the afternoon is the time of the pesach offering to HASHEM.

Bamidbar 9:1-14

HASHEM spoke to Moses, in the Wilderness of Sinai, in the second year from their exodus from the land of Egypt, in the first month, saying: "The Children of Israel shall make the pesach offering in its appointed time. On the fourteenth day of this month in the afternoon shall you make it, in its appointed time; according to all its decrees and laws shall you make it."

Moshe spoke to the Children of Israel to make the pesach offering. They made the pesach offering in the first [month], on the fourteenth day of the month, in the afternoon, in the Wilderness of Sinai; according to everything that HASHEM had commanded Moses, so the Children of Israel did.

There were men who had been contaminated by a human corpse and could not make the pesach offering on that day; so they approached Moshe and Aharon on that day. And those men said to him, "We are unclean through contact with a dead person; why should we be deprived of offering Hashem's sacrifice in its time among the Children of Israel?"

---

of the second Pesach) should by right have been said by Moshe like the rest of the Torah (directly, without being prompted by the 'unclean men'). But these men merited to have this portion of the Torah written through them, for God sees to it that good people serve as the medium for good things and bad people serve as the medium for bad things."

The entire question of the unclean men seems to be inappropriate, noted **R' Gedaliah Schorr**: "Why should we be deprived of offering Hashem's sacrifice in its time?" If the law says that unclean people may not offer the *pesach* sacrifice, then that is the end of the discussion. There is no room for such questions in Torah law. What would be our response if an uncircumcised person would ask, "Why should I be deprived of participating in the *pesach* sacrifice?" We would answer him simply, "Because that is the law!"

In order to explain this dialogue R' Gedaliah set forth an important principle and provided several examples to illustrate it. In the *Zohar* the story is told that a young boy once encountered several Tannaim (Sages of the period of the Mishnah) on their way back from performing the mitzvah of *pidyon shevuyim* (ransoming captives), and he was able to discern on their faces that they had not recited the *Shema* that morning. They explained to the child that they had been involved in an important mitzvah, a matter of life and death, and that in such cases one is exempt from reciting the *Shema* — and, for that matter, from all other mitzvos. The explanation of the Tannaim was certainly halachically correct, but the fact remains

[19] THE HAGGADAH OF THE ROSHEI YESHIVAH

וַיֹּאמֶר אֲלֵהֶם מֹשֶׁה עִמְדוּ וְאֶשְׁמְעָה מַה יְצַוֶּה יהוה לָכֶם. וַיְדַבֵּר יהוה אֶל מֹשֶׁה לֵּאמֹר. דַּבֵּר אֶל בְּנֵי יִשְׂרָאֵל לֵאמֹר אִישׁ אִישׁ כִּי יִהְיֶה טָמֵא לָנֶפֶשׁ אוֹ בְדֶרֶךְ רְחֹקָה לָכֶם אוֹ לְדֹרֹתֵיכֶם וְעָשָׂה פֶסַח לַיהוה. בַּחֹדֶשׁ הַשֵּׁנִי בְּאַרְבָּעָה עָשָׂר יוֹם בֵּין הָעַרְבַּיִם יַעֲשׂוּ אֹתוֹ עַל מַצּוֹת וּמְרֹרִים יֹאכְלֻהוּ. לֹא יַשְׁאִירוּ מִמֶּנּוּ עַד בֹּקֶר וְעֶצֶם לֹא יִשְׁבְּרוּ בוֹ כְּכָל חֻקַּת הַפֶּסַח יַעֲשׂוּ אֹתוֹ: וְהָאִישׁ אֲשֶׁר הוּא טָהוֹר וּבְדֶרֶךְ לֹא הָיָה וְחָדַל לַעֲשׂוֹת הַפֶּסַח וְנִכְרְתָה הַנֶּפֶשׁ הַהִוא מֵעַמֶּיהָ כִּי קָרְבַּן יהוה לֹא הִקְרִיב בְּמֹעֲדוֹ חֶטְאוֹ יִשָּׂא הָאִישׁ הַהוּא. וְכִי יָגוּר אִתְּכֶם גֵּר וְעָשָׂה פֶסַח לַיהוה כְּחֻקַּת הַפֶּסַח וּכְמִשְׁפָּטוֹ כֵּן יַעֲשֶׂה חֻקָּה אַחַת יִהְיֶה לָכֶם וְלַגֵּר וּלְאֶזְרַח הָאָרֶץ.

במדבר כח:טז

וּבַחֹדֶשׁ הָרִאשׁוֹן בְּאַרְבָּעָה עָשָׂר יוֹם לַחֹדֶשׁ פֶּסַח לַיהוה.

דברים טז:א-ח

שָׁמוֹר אֶת חֹדֶשׁ הָאָבִיב וְעָשִׂיתָ פֶּסַח לַיהוה אֱלֹהֶיךָ כִּי בְּחֹדֶשׁ הָאָבִיב הוֹצִיאֲךָ יהוה אֱלֹהֶיךָ מִמִּצְרַיִם לָיְלָה. וְזָבַחְתָּ פֶּסַח לַיהוה אֱלֹהֶיךָ צֹאן וּבָקָר בַּמָּקוֹם אֲשֶׁר יִבְחַר יהוה לְשַׁכֵּן שְׁמוֹ שָׁם. לֹא תֹאכַל עָלָיו חָמֵץ שִׁבְעַת יָמִים תֹּאכַל עָלָיו מַצּוֹת לֶחֶם עֹנִי כִּי בְחִפָּזוֹן יָצָאתָ מֵאֶרֶץ מִצְרַיִם לְמַעַן תִּזְכֹּר אֶת יוֹם צֵאתְךָ מֵאֶרֶץ מִצְרַיִם כֹּל יְמֵי חַיֶּיךָ.

---

that the child was able to discern that they had missed the *Shema* that day. They were justified — and even *required* — to forgo the recitation of *Shema* in their situation, but it was somehow still held against them in a certain sense. The principle we may derive from here is that even when a situation calls for a mitzvah to be pushed aside, fully within the realm of halachah, the person involved is considered to have "omitted" that mitzvah. Apparently there is some reason why God chose this particular person to enter into that predicament in the first place; if he would have been completely virtuous and blameless he would have been spared the emergency situation and been allowed to fulfill the mitzvah unhindered.

Another application of this principle may be found in the Talmud (*Megillah* 16b), where the Gemara comments on the Megillah's description of Mordechai as being "acceptable to most of his brethren" (Esther 10:3). Some of the members of the Sanhedrin, the Gemara tells us, distanced themselves from Mordechai, for he had stopped his full-time Torah scholarship after he was appointed to a high government post by Achashverosh. What was Mordechai's task in Achashverosh's government? The Talmud (ibid.) explains that it involved the saving of Jewish lives. There is no doubt about the fact that when faced with the opportunity to save a

Moshe said to them, "Stand and I will hear what HASHEM will command you."

HASHEM spoke to Moshe, saying, "Speak to the Children of Israel, saying: If any man will become contaminated through a human corpse or on a distant road, whether you or your generations, he shall make the pesach offering for HASHEM, in the second month, on the fourteenth day, in the afternoon, shall they make it; with matzos and bitter herbs shall they eat it. They shall not leave over from it until morning nor shall they break a bone of it; like all the decrees of the pesach offering shall they make it. But a man who is pure and was not on the road and had refrained from making the pesach offering, that soul shall be cut off from its people, for he had not offered HASHEM's offering in its appointed time; that man will bear his sin. When a convert shall dwell with you, and he shall make a pesach offering to HASHEM, according to the decree of the pesach offering and its law, so shall he do; one decree shall be for you, for the proselyte and the native of the Land."

Bamidbar 28:16

In the first month, on the fourteenth day of the month, shall be a pesach offering to HASHEM.

Devarim 16:1-8

You shall observe the month of springtime and perform the pesach offering for HASHEM, your God, for in the month of springtime HASHEM, your God, took you out of Egypt at night. You shall slaughter the pesach offering to HASHEM, your God, from the flock, [and also offer] cattle, in the place where HASHEM will choose to rest His Name. You shall not eat leavened bread with it, for seven days you shall eat matzos because of it, bread of affliction, for you departed from the land of Egypt in haste — so that you will remember the day of your departure from the land of Egypt all the days of your life.

---

life — and certainly many lives — the Torah scholar must close his books and turn his attention to the task at hand. And yet — some of the members of the Sanhedrin did not approve. How can this be? How could they not approve of Mordechai's actions if he only did what he was obligated to do? The answer is that, as explained above, they felt that if Mordechai had not had some sort of spiritual imperfection God would have seen to it that this governmental position would not have landed in Mordechai's lap in the first place.

These unclean men who were barred from offering the *pesach* sacrifice were, as Rashi notes, "good men." One opinion in the Talmud has it that they were Aharon's cousins, who had attended to the bodies of Nadav and Avihu after they were killed in the Mishkan; according to another opinion they were the bearers of Yosef's coffin. They could not understand why they were now being deprived of participating in this awesome mitzvah. They realized that they were excluded from the sacrifice by virtue of their having carried out the mitzvah of caring for the dead, but they could not understand *why* God had brought it about that they should be

וְלֹא יֵרָאֶה לְךָ שְׂאֹר בְּכָל גְּבֻלְךָ שִׁבְעַת יָמִים וְלֹא יָלִין מִן הַבָּשָׂר אֲשֶׁר תִּזְבַּח בָּעֶרֶב בַּיּוֹם הָרִאשׁוֹן לַבֹּקֶר. לֹא תוּכַל לִזְבֹּחַ אֶת הַפָּסַח בְּאַחַד שְׁעָרֶיךָ אֲשֶׁר יהוה אֱלֹהֶיךָ נֹתֵן לָךְ. כִּי אִם אֶל הַמָּקוֹם אֲשֶׁר יִבְחַר יהוה אֱלֹהֶיךָ לְשַׁכֵּן שְׁמוֹ שָׁם תִּזְבַּח אֶת הַפֶּסַח בָּעָרֶב כְּבוֹא הַשֶּׁמֶשׁ מוֹעֵד צֵאתְךָ מִמִּצְרָיִם. וּבִשַּׁלְתָּ וְאָכַלְתָּ בַּמָּקוֹם אֲשֶׁר יִבְחַר יהוה אֱלֹהֶיךָ בּוֹ וּפָנִיתָ בַבֹּקֶר וְהָלַכְתָּ לְאֹהָלֶיךָ. שֵׁשֶׁת יָמִים תֹּאכַל מַצּוֹת וּבַיּוֹם הַשְּׁבִיעִי עֲצֶרֶת לַיהוה אֱלֹהֶיךָ לֹא תַעֲשֶׂה מְלָאכָה.

יהושע ה:י-יא

וַיַּחֲנוּ בְנֵי יִשְׂרָאֵל בַּגִּלְגָּל וַיַּעֲשׂוּ אֶת הַפֶּסַח בְּאַרְבָּעָה עָשָׂר יוֹם לַחֹדֶשׁ בָּעֶרֶב בְּעַרְבוֹת יְרִיחוֹ. וַיֹּאכְלוּ מֵעֲבוּר הָאָרֶץ מִמָּחֳרַת הַפֶּסַח מַצּוֹת וְקָלוּי בְּעֶצֶם הַיּוֹם הַזֶּה.

מלכים ב כג:כא-כב

וַיְצַו הַמֶּלֶךְ אֶת כָּל הָעָם לֵאמֹר עֲשׂוּ פֶסַח לַיהוה אֱלֹהֵיכֶם כַּכָּתוּב עַל סֵפֶר הַבְּרִית הַזֶּה. כִּי לֹא נַעֲשָׂה כַּפֶּסַח הַזֶּה מִימֵי הַשֹּׁפְטִים אֲשֶׁר שָׁפְטוּ אֶת יִשְׂרָאֵל וְכֹל יְמֵי מַלְכֵי יִשְׂרָאֵל וּמַלְכֵי יְהוּדָה: כִּי אִם בִּשְׁמֹנֶה עֶשְׂרֵה שָׁנָה לַמֶּלֶךְ יֹאשִׁיָּהוּ נַעֲשָׂה הַפֶּסַח הַזֶּה לַיהוה בִּירוּשָׁלָם:

דברי הימים ב ל:א-כ

וַיִּשְׁלַח יְחִזְקִיָּהוּ עַל כָּל יִשְׂרָאֵל וִיהוּדָה וְגַם אִגְּרוֹת כָּתַב עַל אֶפְרַיִם וּמְנַשֶּׁה לָבוֹא לְבֵית יהוה בִּירוּשָׁלָם לַעֲשׂוֹת פֶּסַח לַיהוה אֱלֹהֵי יִשְׂרָאֵל. וַיִּוָּעַץ הַמֶּלֶךְ וְשָׂרָיו וְכָל הַקָּהָל בִּירוּשָׁלָם לַעֲשׂוֹת הַפֶּסַח בַּחֹדֶשׁ הַשֵּׁנִי. כִּי לֹא יָכְלוּ לַעֲשֹׂתוֹ בָּעֵת הַהִיא כִּי הַכֹּהֲנִים לֹא הִתְקַדְּשׁוּ לְמַדַּי וְהָעָם לֹא נֶאֶסְפוּ לִירוּשָׁלָם. וַיִּישַׁר הַדָּבָר בְּעֵינֵי הַמֶּלֶךְ וּבְעֵינֵי כָּל הַקָּהָל: וַיַּעֲמִידוּ דָבָר לְהַעֲבִיר קוֹל בְּכָל יִשְׂרָאֵל מִבְּאֵר שֶׁבַע וְעַד דָּן לָבוֹא לַעֲשׂוֹת פֶּסַח לַיהוה אֱלֹהֵי יִשְׂרָאֵל בִּירוּשָׁלָם כִּי לֹא לָרֹב עָשׂוּ כַּכָּתוּב: וַיֵּלְכוּ הָרָצִים בָּאִגְּרוֹת מִיַּד הַמֶּלֶךְ וְשָׂרָיו בְּכָל יִשְׂרָאֵל וִיהוּדָה

---

in this position in the first place. They therefore came before Moshe and asked, "Why should we be deprived of offering Hashem's sacrifice in its time?" They did not mean to argue with the law; they simply wanted to know what they had done to warrant having this law apply to them.

But there was a surprise answer to their question. They were in fact fully virtuous, and they were *not* going to be excluded from the *pesach* sacrifice after all, for there

No leaven of yours shall be seen throughout your boundary for seven days, nor shall any of the flesh that you offer on the afternoon before the first day remain overnight until morning. You may not slaughter the pesach offering in one of your cities that Hashem, your God, gives you; except at the place that Hashem, your God, will choose to rest His Name, there shall you slaughter the pesach offering in the afternoon, when the sun descends, the appointed time of your departure from Egypt. You shall roast it and eat it in the place that Hashem, your God, will choose, and in the morning you may turn back and go to your tents. For a six-day period you shall eat matzos and on the seventh day shall be an assembly to Hashem, your God; you shall not perform any labor.

Yehoshua 5:10-11

The Children of Israel encamped at Gilgal and performed the pesach offering on the fourteenth day of the month in the evening, in the plains of Yericho. They ate from the grain of the land on the day after the pesach offering, matzos and roasted grain, on this very day.

II Melachim 23:21-22

The king then commanded the people, saying, "Perform the pesach offering unto Hashem your God, as written in this Book of the Covenant." For such a pesach offering had not been celebrated since the days of the Judges who judged Israel, and all the days of the kings of Israel and the kings of Yehudah; but in the eighteenth year of King Yoshiyahu this Pesach was celebrated unto Hashem in Yerushalayim.

II Divrei Hayamim 30:1-20

Chizkiyahu then sent word to all of Israel and Yehudah, and also wrote letters to Ephraim and Menasheh to come to the Temple of Hashem in Yerushalayim to perform the pesach offering to Hashem, God of Israel. For the king and his officers and all the congregation had conferred and decided to perform the pesach offering in the second month, for they had not been able to perform it at its [proper] time, for the Kohanim had not yet sanctified themselves in sufficient numbers, and the people had not been gathered to Yerushalayim by then. The matter was deemed proper by the king and all of the congregation. They established the matter to make an announcement throughout all of Israel, from Beer-sheva to Dan, to come and perform the pesach offering unto Hashem, God of Israel, in Yerushalayim, because for a long time they had not done in accordance with what was written.

The runners went throughout all of Israel and Yehudah with the

---

would be a second Pesach for people in situations such as theirs. This is what the Sages meant when they used the expression "God sees to it that good people serve as the medium for good things" in this case. They were so righteous that God wanted their zeal to participate in the *pesach* sacrifice to come out into the open and be the medium through which the laws of the second Pesach became recorded in the Torah.

וּכְמִצְוַת הַמֶּלֶךְ לֵאמֹר בְּנֵי יִשְׂרָאֵל שׁוּבוּ אֶל יהוה אֱלֹהֵי אַבְרָהָם יִצְחָק וְיִשְׂרָאֵל וְיָשֹׁב אֶל הַפְּלֵיטָה הַנִּשְׁאֶרֶת לָכֶם מִכַּף מַלְכֵי אַשּׁוּר. וְאַל תִּהְיוּ כַּאֲבוֹתֵיכֶם וְכַאֲחֵיכֶם אֲשֶׁר מָעֲלוּ בַּיהוה אֱלֹהֵי אֲבוֹתֵיהֶם וַיִּתְּנֵם לְשַׁמָּה כַּאֲשֶׁר אַתֶּם רֹאִים: עַתָּה אַל תַּקְשׁוּ עָרְפְּכֶם כַּאֲבוֹתֵיכֶם תְּנוּ יָד לַיהוה וּבֹאוּ לְמִקְדָּשׁוֹ אֲשֶׁר הִקְדִּישׁ לְעוֹלָם וְעִבְדוּ אֶת יהוה אֱלֹהֵיכֶם וְיָשֹׁב מִכֶּם חֲרוֹן אַפּוֹ: כִּי בְשׁוּבְכֶם עַל יהוה אֲחֵיכֶם וּבְנֵיכֶם לְרַחֲמִים לִפְנֵי שׁוֹבֵיהֶם וְלָשׁוּב לָאָרֶץ הַזֹּאת כִּי חַנּוּן וְרַחוּם יהוה אֱלֹהֵיכֶם וְלֹא יָסִיר פָּנִים מִכֶּם אִם תָּשׁוּבוּ אֵלָיו: וַיִּהְיוּ הָרָצִים עֹבְרִים מֵעִיר לָעִיר בְּאֶרֶץ אֶפְרַיִם וּמְנַשֶּׁה וְעַד זְבֻלוּן וַיִּהְיוּ מַשְׂחִיקִים עֲלֵיהֶם וּמַלְעִגִים בָּם. אַךְ אֲנָשִׁים מֵאָשֵׁר וּמְנַשֶּׁה וּמִזְּבֻלוּן נִכְנְעוּ וַיָּבֹאוּ לִירוּשָׁלָיִם. גַּם בִּיהוּדָה הָיְתָה יַד הָאֱלֹהִים לָתֵת לָהֶם לֵב אֶחָד לַעֲשׂוֹת מִצְוַת הַמֶּלֶךְ וְהַשָּׂרִים בִּדְבַר יהוה. וַיֵּאָסְפוּ יְרוּשָׁלַיִם עַם רָב לַעֲשׂוֹת אֶת חַג הַמַּצּוֹת בַּחֹדֶשׁ הַשֵּׁנִי קָהָל לָרֹב מְאֹד. וַיָּקֻמוּ וַיָּסִירוּ אֶת הַמִּזְבְּחוֹת אֲשֶׁר בִּירוּשָׁלָיִם וְאֵת כָּל הַמְקַטְּרוֹת הֵסִירוּ וַיַּשְׁלִיכוּ לְנַחַל קִדְרוֹן. וַיִּשְׁחֲטוּ הַפֶּסַח בְּאַרְבָּעָה עָשָׂר לַחֹדֶשׁ הַשֵּׁנִי וְהַכֹּהֲנִים וְהַלְוִיִּם נִכְלְמוּ וַיִּתְקַדְּשׁוּ וַיָּבִיאוּ עֹלוֹת בֵּית יהוה: וַיַּעַמְדוּ עַל עָמְדָם כְּמִשְׁפָּטָם כְּתוֹרַת מֹשֶׁה אִישׁ הָאֱלֹהִים הַכֹּהֲנִים זֹרְקִים אֶת הַדָּם מִיַּד הַלְוִיִּם. כִּי רַבַּת בַּקָּהָל אֲשֶׁר לֹא הִתְקַדָּשׁוּ וְהַלְוִיִּם עַל שְׁחִיטַת הַפְּסָחִים לְכֹל לֹא טָהוֹר לְהַקְדִּישׁ לַיהוה. כִּי מַרְבִּית הָעָם רַבַּת מֵאֶפְרַיִם וּמְנַשֶּׁה יִשָּׂשכָר וּזְבֻלוּן לֹא הִטֶּהָרוּ כִּי אָכְלוּ אֶת הַפֶּסַח בְּלֹא כַכָּתוּב כִּי הִתְפַּלֵּל יְחִזְקִיָּהוּ עֲלֵיהֶם לֵאמֹר יהוה הַטּוֹב יְכַפֵּר בְּעַד. כָּל לְבָבוֹ הֵכִין לִדְרוֹשׁ הָאֱלֹהִים יהוה אֱלֹהֵי אֲבוֹתָיו וְלֹא כְּטָהֳרַת הַקֹּדֶשׁ. וַיִּשְׁמַע יהוה אֶל יְחִזְקִיָּהוּ וַיִּרְפָּא אֶת הָעָם.

דברי הימים ב לה:א-יט

וַיַּעַשׂ יֹאשִׁיָּהוּ בִירוּשָׁלַיִם פֶּסַח לַיהוה וַיִּשְׁחֲטוּ הַפֶּסַח בְּאַרְבָּעָה עָשָׂר לַחֹדֶשׁ הָרִאשׁוֹן: וַיַּעֲמֵד הַכֹּהֲנִים עַל מִשְׁמְרוֹתָם וַיְחַזְּקֵם לַעֲבוֹדַת בֵּית יהוה: וַיֹּאמֶר לַלְוִיִּם הַמְּבִינִים לְכָל יִשְׂרָאֵל הַקְּדוֹשִׁים לַיהוה תְּנוּ אֶת אֲרוֹן הַקֹּדֶשׁ בַּבַּיִת אֲשֶׁר בָּנָה שְׁלֹמֹה בֶן דָּוִיד מֶלֶךְ יִשְׂרָאֵל אֵין לָכֶם מַשָּׂא בַּכָּתֵף עַתָּה עִבְדוּ אֶת יהוה אֱלֹהֵיכֶם וְאֵת עַמּוֹ יִשְׂרָאֵל.

letters from the hand of the king and his leaders, and by order of the king, saying, "Return to Hashem, the God of Avraham, Yitzchak and Yisrael, and He will return to the remnant of you that still remains from the hands of the kings of Ashur. Do not be like your fathers and brothers who betrayed Hashem, the God of their forefathers, so that He made them into a desolation, as you see. Do not stiffen your necks now as your fathers did! Reach out to Hashem and come to His Sanctuary, which He has sanctified forever, and worship Hashem, your God, so that His burning wrath may turn away from you! For when you return to Hashem, your brothers and sons will be regarded with mercy by their captors, and [will be allowed] to return to this land, for Hashem your God is gracious and merciful, and He will not turn His face away from you if you return to Him!"

The runners passed from city to city in the land of Ephraim and Menasheh up to Zevulun but people laughed at them and mocked them. However, some people from Asher, Menasheh and Zevulun humbled themselves and came to Yerushalayim. Also in Yehudah the hand of God was upon them, instilling them all with a united heart to follow the commandment of the king and the leaders regarding the word of Hashem.

So a great crowd assembled in Jerusalem to observe the Festival of Matzos in the second month — a very large congregation. They got up and removed the altars that were in Yerushalayim, they also removed all the incense altars and threw them into the Kidron Ravine. They slaughtered the pesach offering on the fourteenth of the second month, and the Kohanim and Levites felt humiliated and sanctified themselves and brought burnt-offerings to the Temple of Hashem. They stood at their ordained positions, in accordance with the Torah of Moshe, the man of God — the Kohanim threw the blood [on the Altar], [taking it] from the hands of the Levites. For there were many in the congregation who had not sanctified themselves, and the Levites took charge of slaughtering the pesach offering for anyone who was not pure, to sanctify it to Hashem. For many of the people — many from Ephraim, Menasheh, Yissachar and Zevulun — had not purified themselves, and they ate the pesach offering not in accordance with that which is written; but Chizkiyahu prayed for them, saying, "May the benevolent Hashem grant atonement for whoever sets his heart to seek out God, Hashem, the God of his forefathers, though without the purity required for the sacred." Hashem listened to Chizkiyahu and absolved the people.

II Divrei Hayamim 35:1-19

Yoshiyahu made the pesach offering to Hashem. They slaughtered the pesach offering on the fourteenth day of the first month.

He set up the Kohanim according to their divisions, and he encouraged them in the service of the Temple of Hashem. He then said to the Levites, who taught all of Israel, who were consecrated to Hashem, "Place the Holy Ark in the Temple that Shlomo son of David, the king of Israel, built. Then you will no longer have any carrying on your shoulder; so now serve Hashem your God and His people Israel.

וְהָכִינוּ לְבֵית אֲבֹתֵיכֶם כְּמַחְלְקוֹתֵיכֶם בִּכְתָב דָּוִיד מֶלֶךְ יִשְׂרָאֵל וּבְמִכְתַּב שְׁלֹמֹה בְנוֹ. וְעִמְדוּ בַקֹּדֶשׁ לִפְלֻגּוֹת בֵּית הָאָבוֹת לַאֲחֵיכֶם בְּנֵי הָעָם וַחֲלֻקַּת בֵּית אָב לַלְוִיִּם. וְשַׁחֲטוּ הַפָּסַח וְהִתְקַדְּשׁוּ וְהָכִינוּ לַאֲחֵיכֶם לַעֲשׂוֹת כִּדְבַר יְהוָה בְּיַד מֹשֶׁה. וַיָּרֶם יֹאשִׁיָּהוּ לִבְנֵי הָעָם צֹאן כְּבָשִׂים וּבְנֵי עִזִּים הַכֹּל לַפְּסָחִים לְכָל הַנִּמְצָא לְמִסְפַּר שְׁלֹשִׁים אֶלֶף וּבָקָר שְׁלֹשֶׁת אֲלָפִים אֵלֶּה מֵרְכוּשׁ הַמֶּלֶךְ. וְשָׂרָיו לִנְדָבָה לָעָם לַכֹּהֲנִים וְלַלְוִיִּם הֵרִימוּ חִלְקִיָּה וּזְכַרְיָהוּ וִיחִיאֵל נְגִידֵי בֵּית הָאֱלֹהִים לַכֹּהֲנִים נָתְנוּ לַפְּסָחִים אַלְפַּיִם וְשֵׁשׁ מֵאוֹת וּבָקָר שְׁלֹשׁ מֵאוֹת. וְכָנַנְיָהוּ וּשְׁמַעְיָהוּ וּנְתַנְאֵל אֶחָיו וַחֲשַׁבְיָהוּ וִיעִיאֵל וְיוֹזָבָד שָׂרֵי הַלְוִיִּם הֵרִימוּ לַלְוִיִּם לַפְּסָחִים חֲמֵשֶׁת אֲלָפִים וּבָקָר חֲמֵשׁ מֵאוֹת. וַתִּכּוֹן הָעֲבוֹדָה וַיַּעַמְדוּ הַכֹּהֲנִים עַל עָמְדָם וְהַלְוִיִּם עַל מַחְלְקוֹתָם כְּמִצְוַת הַמֶּלֶךְ. וַיִּשְׁחֲטוּ הַפָּסַח וַיִּזְרְקוּ הַכֹּהֲנִים מִיָּדָם וְהַלְוִיִּם מַפְשִׁיטִים. וַיָּסִירוּ הָעֹלָה לְתִתָּם לְמִפְלַגּוֹת לְבֵית אָבוֹת לִבְנֵי הָעָם לְהַקְרִיב לַיהוָה כַּכָּתוּב בְּסֵפֶר מֹשֶׁה וְכֵן לַבָּקָר. וַיְבַשְּׁלוּ הַפֶּסַח בָּאֵשׁ כַּמִּשְׁפָּט וְהַקֳּדָשִׁים בִּשְּׁלוּ בַּסִּירוֹת וּבַדְּוָדִים וּבַצֵּלָחוֹת וַיָּרִיצוּ לְכָל בְּנֵי הָעָם. וְאַחַר הֵכִינוּ לָהֶם וְלַכֹּהֲנִים כִּי הַכֹּהֲנִים בְּנֵי אַהֲרֹן בְּהַעֲלוֹת הָעוֹלָה וְהַחֲלָבִים עַד לָיְלָה וְהַלְוִיִּם הֵכִינוּ לָהֶם וְלַכֹּהֲנִים בְּנֵי אַהֲרֹן. וְהַמְשֹׁרְרִים בְּנֵי אָסָף עַל מַעֲמָדָם כְּמִצְוַת דָּוִיד וְאָסָף וְהֵימָן וִידֻתוּן חוֹזֵה הַמֶּלֶךְ וְהַשֹּׁעֲרִים לְשַׁעַר וָשָׁעַר אֵין לָהֶם לָסוּר מֵעַל עֲבֹדָתָם כִּי אֲחֵיהֶם הַלְוִיִּם הֵכִינוּ לָהֶם. וַתִּכּוֹן כָּל עֲבוֹדַת יְהוָה בַּיּוֹם הַהוּא לַעֲשׂוֹת הַפֶּסַח וְהַעֲלוֹת עֹלוֹת עַל מִזְבַּח יְהוָה כְּמִצְוַת הַמֶּלֶךְ יֹאשִׁיָּהוּ. וַיַּעֲשׂוּ בְנֵי יִשְׂרָאֵל הַנִּמְצְאִים אֶת הַפֶּסַח בָּעֵת הַהִיא וְאֶת חַג הַמַּצּוֹת שִׁבְעַת יָמִים. וְלֹא נַעֲשָׂה פֶסַח כָּמֹהוּ בְּיִשְׂרָאֵל מִימֵי שְׁמוּאֵל הַנָּבִיא וְכָל מַלְכֵי יִשְׂרָאֵל לֹא עָשׂוּ כַּפֶּסַח אֲשֶׁר עָשָׂה יֹאשִׁיָּהוּ וְהַכֹּהֲנִים וְהַלְוִיִּם וְכָל יְהוּדָה וְיִשְׂרָאֵל הַנִּמְצָא וְיוֹשְׁבֵי יְרוּשָׁלָיִם. בִּשְׁמוֹנֶה עֶשְׂרֵה שָׁנָה לְמַלְכוּת יֹאשִׁיָּהוּ נַעֲשָׂה הַפֶּסַח הַזֶּה.

Organize yourselves by your fathers' families, according to your divisions, in accordance with the written instructions of David king of Israel and the written instructions of his son Shlomo. Stand in the Sanctuary according to the groupings of your fathers' families near your kinsmen, the populace, and the Levites' fathers' family division. Slaughter the pesach offering; sanctify yourselves and prepare your kinsmen to act in accordance with the word of HASHEM, through Moshe."

Yoshiyahu donated animals of the flock — sheep and goats — to the populace, all of them for pesach offerings for those who were present, in the amount of thirty thousand, in addition to three thousand [head of] cattle; all this was from the personal property of the king. His officers also contributed voluntarily to the populace, to the Kohanim and to the Levites. Chilkiyah, Zecharyahu and Yechiel, the managers of the Temple of God, gave two thousand six hundred [sheep] to the Kohanim for pesach offerings, and three hundred [head of] cattle. Cananyahu, together with his brethren Shemaiah and Nesanel, and Chashavyahu, Yeiel and Yozabad, officers of the Levites, donated five thousand [sheep] for pesach [offerings] for the Levites, and five hundred [head of] cattle.

Thus the service was in order. The Kohanim were stationed at their positions and the Levites in their divisions, in accordance with the king's orders. They slaughtered the pesach offering, and the Kohanim threw [the blood, which they had taken] from their hands, while the Levites were flaying. They removed the parts that were to be offered up — in order to give [flesh of the pesach offering] to the family groups of the populace — to offer them up before HASHEM, as is written in the Book of Moshe; and similarly for the cattle. They cooked the pesach offering over the fire according to the law, and they cooked the [other] sacrificial meat in pots and cauldrons and pans, and distributed it quickly to all the populace. Afterwards they prepared [the pesach offering] for themselves and for the Kohanim, because the Kohanim — the descendants of Aharon — were busy burning burnt-offerings and fats until nighttime, so now the Levites prepared for themselves and for the Kohanim, the descendants of Aharon.

The singers, the descendants of Asaf, stood at their positions — according to the decree of David, Asaf, Heiman and Yedusun the king's seer — with the gate-keepers at every gate; they did not have to leave their own tasks, for their brother Levites had prepared for them. The entire service of HASHEM was thus well organized on that day, to perform the pesach offering and to bring up burnt-offerings upon the Altar of HASHEM, in accordance with the command of King Yoshiyahu. So the Children of Israel who were present performed the pesach offering at that time, and then the Festival of Unleavened Bread for seven days. Such a pesach offering had not been celebrated since the days of Shmuel Hanavi. None of the kings of Israel performed like the pesach offering that Yoshiyahu did with the Kohanim, the Levites, all of Yehudah and Israel who were present, and the inhabitants of Yerushalayim. It was in the eighteenth year of Yoshiyahu's reign that this pesach offering was performed.

כָּךְ הָיְתָה עֲבוֹדַת קָרְבַּן הַפֶּסַח בְּבֵית אֱלֹהֵינוּ בְּיוֹם אַרְבָּעָה עָשָׂר בְּנִיסָן:

אֵין שׁוֹחֲטִין אוֹתוֹ אֶלָּא אַחַר תָּמִיד שֶׁל בֵּין הָעַרְבַּיִם. עֶרֶב פֶּסַח, בֵּין בְּחֹל בֵּין בְּשַׁבָּת, הָיָה הַתָּמִיד נִשְׁחָט בְּשֶׁבַע וּמֶחֱצָה וְקָרֵב בִּשְׁמוֹנֶה וּמֶחֱצָה. וְאִם חָל עֶרֶב פֶּסַח לִהְיוֹת עֶרֶב שַׁבָּת הָיוּ שׁוֹחֲטִין אוֹתוֹ בְּשֵׁשׁ וּמֶחֱצָה וְקָרֵב בְּשֶׁבַע וּמֶחֱצָה. וְהַפֶּסַח אַחֲרָיו.

כָּל אָדָם מִיִּשְׂרָאֵל, אֶחָד הָאִישׁ וְאֶחָד הָאִשָּׁה, כָּל שֶׁיָּכוֹל לְהַגִּיעַ לִירוּשָׁלַיִם בִּשְׁעַת שְׁחִיטַת הַפֶּסַח הָיָב בְּקָרְבַּן פֶּסַח.

מְבִיאוֹ מִן הַכְּבָשִׂים אוֹ מִן הָעִזִּים, זָכָר תָּמִים בֶּן שָׁנָה, וְשׁוֹחֲטוֹ בְּכָל מָקוֹם בָּעֲזָרָה, אַחַר גְּמַר עֲבוֹדַת תָּמִיד הָעֶרֶב וְאַחַר הֲטָבַת הַנֵּרוֹת.

וְאֵין שׁוֹחֲטִין הַפֶּסַח, וְלֹא זוֹרְקִין הַדָּם, וְלֹא מַקְטִירִין הַחֵלֶב, עַל הֶחָמֵץ.

שָׁחַט הַשּׁוֹחֵט, וְקִבֵּל דָּמוֹ שֶׁבְּרֹאשׁ הַשּׁוּרָה בִּכְלִי שָׁרֵת, וְנוֹתֵן לַחֲבֵרוֹ, וַחֲבֵרוֹ לַחֲבֵרוֹ. כֹּהֵן הַקָּרוֹב אֵצֶל הַמִּזְבֵּחַ זוֹרְקוֹ זְרִיקָה אַחַת כְּנֶגֶד הַיְסוֹד, וְחוֹזֵר הַכְּלִי רֵיקָן לַחֲבֵרוֹ, וַחֲבֵרוֹ לַחֲבֵרוֹ. מְקַבֵּל אֶת הַמָּלֵא וּמַחֲזִיר אֶת הָרֵיקָן. וְהָיוּ הַכֹּהֲנִים עוֹמְדִים שׁוּרוֹת וּבִידֵיהֶם בָּזִיכִין שֶׁכֻּלָּן כֶּסֶף אוֹ כֻּלָּן זָהָב. וְלֹא הָיוּ מְעֹרָבִים. וְלֹא הָיוּ לַבָּזִיכִין שׁוּלַיִם, שֶׁלֹּא יַנִּיחוּם וְיִקְרַשׁ הַדָּם.

אַחַר כָּךְ תּוֹלִין אֶת הַפֶּסַח בְּאֻנְקְלָיוֹת, וּמַפְשִׁיט אוֹתוֹ כֻּלּוֹ, וְקוֹרְעִין בִּטְנוֹ וּמוֹצִיאִין אֵמוּרָיו – הַחֵלֶב שֶׁעַל הַקֶּרֶב, וְיוֹתֶרֶת הַכָּבֵד, וּשְׁתֵּי הַכְּלָיוֹת, וְהַחֵלֶב שֶׁעֲלֵיהֶן, וְהָאַלְיָה לְעֻמַּת הָעָצֶה. נוֹתְנָן בִּכְלִי שָׁרֵת וּמוֹלְחָן וּמַקְטִירָן הַכֹּהֵן עַל הַמַּעֲרָכָה, חֶלְבֵי כָּל

הגדה של פסח [28]

This was the service of the pesach offering on the fourteenth of Nisan:

We may not slaughter it until after the afternoon tamid offering. On the eve of Pesach, whether on a weekday or on Shabbos, the tamid offering would be slaughtered at seven and a half hours [after daybreak], and offered at eight and a half hours. But when erev Pesach fell on Friday, they would slaughter it at six and a half hours, and offer it at seven and a half. [In either case] the pesach offering [was slaughtered] after it.

Every Jew, male or female, whoever is able to reach Yerushalayim in time to slaughter the pesach, is obligated to bring the pesach offering.

It may be brought from sheep or from goats, an unblemished male in its first year. It may be slaughtered anywhere in the Temple Courtyard, after the completion of the afternoon tamid offering, and after the kindling of the Menorah's lamps.

We may not slaughter the pesach, nor throw its blood [onto the Altar], nor burn its fats [on the Altar], if chametz is in our possession.

Someone [even a non-Kohen] would slaughter [the animal]. The Kohen at the head of the line [closest to the animal] would receive its blood in a sanctified vessel and pass it to his colleague, and he to his colleague. The Kohen closest to the Altar would throw it, with one throwing, at the base [of the Altar], then return the vessel to his colleague, and he to his colleague. He would first accept the full one, then return the empty one. The Kohanim would stand in lines, [all the Kohanim of each line] holding either silver or golden vessels. But they would not mix [two types of vessels in one line]. The vessels did not have flat bottoms, lest one would put down a vessel [and forget it], thus causing the blood to congeal.

Following this, they would suspend the pesach from hooks. They would skin it completely, tear open its stomach and remove the organs ordained for the Altar — the suet covering the stomach, the diaphragm with the liver, the two kidneys and the suet upon them, and [in the case of a lamb] the tail opposite the kidneys. They would place [these organs] in a sanctified vessel and salt them, then a Kohen would burn them on the Altar fire. The portions of each

זֶבַח וָזֶבַח לְבַדּוֹ. בַּחֹל, בַּיּוֹם וְלֹא בַּלַּיְלָה שֶׁהוּא יוֹם טוֹב. אֲבָל אִם חָל עֶרֶב פֶּסַח בַּשַּׁבָּת, מַקְטִירִין וְהוֹלְכִין כָּל הַלַּיְלָה. וּמוֹצִיא קְרָבָיו וּמְמַחֶה אוֹתָן עַד שֶׁמֵּסִיר מֵהֶן הַפֶּרֶשׁ.

שְׁחִיטָתוֹ וּזְרִיקַת דָּמוֹ וּמִחוּי קְרָבָיו וְהֶקְטֵר חֲלָבָיו דּוֹחִין אֶת הַשַּׁבָּת, וּשְׁאָר עִנְיָנָיו אֵין דּוֹחִין.

בְּשָׁלֹשׁ כִּתּוֹת הַפֶּסַח נִשְׁחָט. וְאֵין כַּת פְּחוּתָה מִשְּׁלֹשִׁים אֲנָשִׁים. נִכְנְסָה כַּת אַחַת, נִתְמַלְּאָה הָעֲזָרָה, נוֹעֲלִין אוֹתָהּ. וּבְעוֹד שֶׁהֵם שׁוֹחֲטִין וּמַקְרִיבִין, הַכֹּהֲנִים תּוֹקְעִין, הֶחָלִיל מַכֶּה לִפְנֵי הַמִּזְבֵּחַ, וְהַלְוִיִּים קוֹרְאִין אֶת הַהַלֵּל. אִם גָּמְרוּ קֹדֶם שֶׁיַּקְרִיבוּ כֻּלָּם, שָׁנוּ; אִם שָׁנוּ, שִׁלֵּשׁוּ. עַל כָּל קְרִיאָה תָּקְעוּ הֵרִיעוּ וְתָקְעוּ. גָּמְרָה כַּת אַחַת לְהַקְרִיב, פּוֹתְחִין הָעֲזָרָה, יָצְאָה כַּת רִאשׁוֹנָה, נִכְנְסָה כַּת שְׁנִיָּה, נָעֲלוּ דַּלְתוֹת הָעֲזָרָה. גָּמְרָה, יָצְאָה שְׁנִיָּה וְנִכְנְסָה שְׁלִישִׁית. כְּמַעֲשֵׂה הָרִאשׁוֹנָה כָּךְ מַעֲשֵׂה הַשְּׁנִיָּה וְהַשְּׁלִישִׁית.

אַחַר שֶׁיָּצְאוּ כֻּלָּן רוֹחֲצִין הָעֲזָרָה מִלִּכְלוּכֵי הַדָּם, וַאֲפִלּוּ בַּשַּׁבָּת. אַמַּת הַמַּיִם הָיְתָה עוֹבֶרֶת בָּעֲזָרָה, שֶׁכְּשֶׁרוֹצִין לְהָדִיחַ הָרִצְפָּה סוֹתְמִין מְקוֹם יְצִיאַת הַמַּיִם וְהִיא מִתְמַלֵּאת עַל כָּל גְּדוֹתֶיהָ, עַד שֶׁהַמַּיִם עוֹלִין וְצָפִין וּמְקַבְּצִין אֲלֵיהֶם כָּל דָּם וְלִכְלוּךְ שֶׁבָּעֲזָרָה. אַחַר כָּךְ פּוֹתְחִין הַסְּתִימָה וְיוֹצְאִין הַמַּיִם עִם הַלִּכְלוּךְ, נִמְצֵאת הָרִצְפָּה מְנֻקָּה, זֶהוּ כְּבוֹד הַבַּיִת.

יָצְאוּ כָּל אֶחָד עִם פִּסְחוֹ וְצָלוּ אוֹתָם. כֵּיצַד צוֹלִין אוֹתוֹ? מְבִיאִין שַׁפּוּד שֶׁל רִמּוֹן, תּוֹחֲבוֹ מִתּוֹךְ פִּיו עַד בֵּית נְקוּבָתוֹ, וְתוֹלֵהוּ לְתוֹךְ הַתַּנּוּר וְהָאֵשׁ לְמַטָּה, וְתוֹלֶה כְּרָעָיו וּבְנֵי מֵעָיו חוּצָה לוֹ, וְאֵין מְנַקְּרִין אֶת הַפֶּסַח כִּשְׁאָר בָּשָׂר.

בְּשַׁבָּת אֵינָן מוֹלִיכִין אֶת הַפֶּסַח לְבֵיתָם, אֶלָּא כַּת הָרִאשׁוֹנָה יוֹצְאִין בְּפִסְחֵיהֶן וְיוֹשְׁבִין בְּהַר הַבַּיִת, הַשְּׁנִיָּה יוֹצְאִין עִם פִּסְחֵיהֶן וְיוֹשְׁבִין בַּחֵיל, וְהַשְּׁלִישִׁית בִּמְקוֹמָהּ

offering [would be placed on the fire] separately. On a weekday, [this would be done] by day and not at night when the festival had already begun. But when erev Pesach fell on Shabbos, they would burn [the organs] during the entire night. They would remove the innards and squeeze them until all their wastes were removed.

Slaughtering it, throwing its blood, squeezing out its innards, and burning its fats [on the Altar] supersede Shabbos; but its other requirements do not supersede [Shabbos].

The pesach is slaughtered in three groups, no group comprising less than thirty men. The first entered, filling the Courtyard; then they closed the gates. For as long as they slaughtered and offered [the pesach], the Kohanim would blow the shofar, the flute would play before the Altar, and the Levites would recite Hallel. If they completed [Hallel] before all had brought their offerings, they repeated it. If they completed [Hallel] a second time, they would recite it a third time. For each recitation, they blew tekiah, teruah, tekiah. When the first group was done offering, they opened the Courtyard [gates]. The first group left, the second group entered, and the Courtyard gates were closed. When they were done, the second group left and the third group entered. Like the procedure of the first, so was the procedure of the second and third.

After all [three groups] had left, they [the Kohanim] would wash the [stone] Courtyard [floor] of the blood, even on Shabbos. A channel of water passed through the Courtyard. When they wished to wash the floor, they would block the outlet, causing the water to overflow and gather all the bloods and other waste matter in the Courtyard. Then they would remove the blockage and the water with the waste would run out. Thus, the floor would be clean. And this is the manner of cleansing the Temple.

They left, each with his pesach, and roasted them. In what manner was it roasted? They would bring a pomegranate wood spit, thrust it through its mouth to its anus and suspend it inside the oven with the fire below it. Its legs and innards were suspended outside [its body cavity]. They would not purge the pesach in the same manner as other meat.

On Shabbos they would not carry the pesach [meat] to their homes. Rather, the first group would go out [of the Courtyard] with their pesach offerings and remain on the Temple Mount. The second group would go out and remain within the Cheil [a ten-cubit-wide area, just outside the Courtyard walls]. The third group would remain where they were.

עוֹמֶדֶת. חָשְׁכָה, יָצְאוּ וְצָלוּ אֶת פִּסְחֵיהֶן.

כְּשֶׁמַּקְרִיבִין אֶת הַפֶּסַח בָּרִאשׁוֹן מַקְרִיבִין עִמּוֹ בְּיוֹם אַרְבָּעָה עָשָׂר זֶבַח שְׁלָמִים, מִן הַבָּקָר אוֹ מִן הַצֹּאן, גְּדוֹלִים אוֹ קְטַנִּים, זְכָרִים אוֹ נְקֵבוֹת, וְהִיא נִקְרֵאת חֲגִיגַת אַרְבָּעָה עָשָׂר, עַל זֶה נֶאֱמַר בַּתּוֹרָה, וְזָבַחְתָּ פֶּסַח לַיהוה אֱלֹהֶיךָ צֹאן וּבָקָר.[1] וְלֹא קְבָעָהּ הַכָּתוּב חוֹבָה אֶלָּא רְשׁוּת בִּלְבָד, מִכָּל מָקוֹם הִיא כְּחוֹבָה מִדִּבְרֵי סוֹפְרִים, כְּדֵי שֶׁיְּהֵא הַפֶּסַח נֶאֱכָל עַל הַשֹּׂבַע. אֵימָתַי מְבִיאִין עִמּוֹ חֲגִיגָה? בִּזְמַן שֶׁהוּא בָא בְחֹל, בְּטָהֳרָה וּבְמוּעָט. וְנֶאֱכֶלֶת לִשְׁנֵי יָמִים וְלַיְלָה אֶחָד, וְדִינָהּ כְּכָל תּוֹרַת זִבְחֵי שְׁלָמִים, טְעוּנָה סְמִיכָה וּנְסָכִים וּמַתַּן דָּמִים שְׁתַּיִם שֶׁהֵן אַרְבַּע וּשְׁפִיכַת שִׁירַיִם לַיְסוֹד.

זֶהוּ סֵדֶר עֲבוֹדַת קָרְבַּן פֶּסַח וַחֲגִיגָה שֶׁעָמּוֹ בְּבֵית אֱלֹהֵינוּ שֶׁיִּבָּנֶה בִּמְהֵרָה בְיָמֵינוּ, אָמֵן. אַשְׁרֵי הָעָם שֶׁכָּכָה לּוֹ, אַשְׁרֵי הָעָם שֶׁיהוה אֱלֹהָיו.[2]

אֱלֹהֵינוּ וֵאלֹהֵי אֲבוֹתֵינוּ, מֶלֶךְ רַחֲמָן רַחֵם עָלֵינוּ, טוֹב וּמֵיטִיב הִדָּרֶשׁ לָנוּ. שׁוּבָה אֵלֵינוּ בַּהֲמוֹן רַחֲמֶיךָ בִּגְלַל אָבוֹת שֶׁעָשׂוּ רְצוֹנֶךָ. בְּנֵה בֵיתְךָ כְּבַתְּחִלָּה וְכוֹנֵן מִקְדָּשְׁךָ עַל מְכוֹנוֹ. וְהַרְאֵנוּ בְּבִנְיָנוֹ וְשַׂמְּחֵנוּ בְּתִקּוּנוֹ. וְהָשֵׁב שְׁכִינָתְךָ לְתוֹכוֹ, וְהָשֵׁב כֹּהֲנִים לַעֲבוֹדָתָם וּלְוִיִּים לְשִׁירָם וּלְזִמְרָם, וְהָשֵׁב יִשְׂרָאֵל לִנְוֵיהֶם. וְשָׁם נַעֲלֶה וְנֵרָאֶה וְנִשְׁתַּחֲוֶה לְפָנֶיךָ. וְנֹאכַל שָׁם מִן הַזְּבָחִים וּמִן הַפְּסָחִים אֲשֶׁר יַגִּיעַ דָּמָם עַל קִיר מִזְבַּחֲךָ לְרָצוֹן. יִהְיוּ לְרָצוֹן אִמְרֵי פִי וְהֶגְיוֹן לִבִּי לְפָנֶיךָ, יהוה צוּרִי וְגֹאֲלִי.[3]

---

(1) *Devarim* 16:2. (2) *Tehillim* 144:15. (3) 19:15.

When it became dark, they would leave [for their homes] and roast their pesach offerings.

When they would bring the pesach offering, they would bring with it — on the fourteenth of Nisan — a peace-offering, either from the cattle herd or from the flock, old or young, male or female. This is called "the festive offering of the fourteenth." Regarding this the Torah states: And you shall slaughter the pesach offering to HASHEM, your God, from the flock and cattle.[1] Yet the Torah did not establish this as an obligation, but only as a voluntary offering. Nevertheless, it was made obligatory by the Rabbis, in order that the pesach offering be eaten in satiety. When may the festive-offering be brought with it [the pesach]? When it [the pesach] is brought on a weekday, in purity and there are few. It may be eaten for two days and the included night, its laws being the same as the laws of other peace-offerings. It requires semichah, libations, two [Altar] applications of blood that are equivalent to four, and pouring the remainder [of the blood] at the [Altar's] base.

This is the order of the pesach offering and the festive-offering brought with it in the Temple of our God — may it be rebuilt speedily, in our days — Amen. Praiseworthy is the people for whom this is so; praiseworthy is the people whose God is HASHEM.[2]

Our God and the God of our forefathers, O merciful King, have mercy on us; O good and beneficent One, let Yourself be sought out by us; return to us in Your yearning mercy for the sake of the forefathers who did Your will. Rebuild Your House as it was at first, and establish Your Sanctuary on its prepared site; show us its rebuilding and gladden us in its perfection. Return Your Shechinah to it; restore the Kohanim to their service, the Levites to their song and music; and restore Israel to their dwellings. And there may we ascend and appear and prostrate ourselves before You. There we shall eat of the peace offerings and pesach offerings whose blood will gain the sides of Your Altar for favorable acceptance. May the expressions of my mouth and the thoughts of my heart find favor before You, HASHEM, my Rock and my Redeemer.[3]

הַהֲכָנוֹת לַסֵּדֶר – Preparing for the Seder

Preparing Wine for the Four Cups

1. It is preferable to use red wine, if it is not inferior in quality to the white wine available (472:11).

2. One may use boiled wine or wine to which flavoring has been added, although it is preferable to use pure, unboiled wine so long as it is not of inferior quality (472:2 and *Mishnah Berurah* 39-40).

Karpas

1. One should use the vegetable called *karpas,* because this word is an anagram of the words ס׳, 60 (referring to the 600,000 Jews), and פֶּרֶךְ, *worked hard.* However, any vegetable may be used other than those which may be used for *maror*.

2. One should prepare salt water or Kosher for Pesach vinegar in which to dip the *karpas*. (If the Seder night falls on Shabbos, the salt water should be made beforehand. If one forgot to do so, he may prepare the minimum amount of salt water on Shabbos, immediately prior to the meal, making sure that he puts less than 66 percent salt in the mixture.) (473:4 and *Mishnah Berurah* 19, 21).

Maror

1. There are five vegetables which the Mishnah (*Pesachim* 2:6) mentions which may be used for *maror*: *chazeres* (lettuce), *ulshin* (endives), *tamcha* (horseradish), *charchavinah* and *maror.* One may use either the leaves or the stalks of these species. While one may not use their roots, the thick, hard part of the root (as the horseradish root) has the same status as the stalk. The leaves may not be used after they have dried out, but the stalk may be used when dry. Neither may be used if it has been soaked in water or any other liquid for 24 hours.

    Since the Mishnah lists the varieties in order of preference, and *chazeres* precedes *tamcha,* it should be more preferable to use lettuce than horseradish. However, since lettuce is extremely hard to rid of all the bugs that infest it, if one is unable to check and cleanse the lettuce thoroughly he should use horseradish instead (473:5, *Mishnah Berurah* ad loc.).

2. The horseradish should be ground, as eating a whole piece of horseradish constitutes a danger to one's well-being and is not a fulfillment of the mitzvah. However, the ground horseradish should not be left open for a long time after, as this causes all its bitterness to dissipate (ibid.).

3. The *Mishnah Berurah* records that the *Gra* used to leave the grinding of the horseradish until after he came home from shul on the Seder night, and then left it covered until the beginning of the Seder. (Note: The grinding of these vegetables on *Yom Tov* should be done differently than usual. See *Orach Chayim* 504.) When the Seder night comes out on Shabbos, when such grinding is forbidden, the horseradish should be prepared before Shabbos and left covered until the beginning of the Seder. (Nowadays many people prepare the

horseradish before *Yom Tov* even when it is not Shabbos, since its sharpness can be preserved quite well in a closed container. This is the practice of *Maran R' Schach* as well.) (ibid.)

4. If someone is too ill or delicate to eat the entire *k'zayis* of horseradish at one time, he may spread it out over a period of *Kedei Achilas Peras* (approx. 2-9 minutes).

Charoses

1. *Charoses* should be prepared with fruits which are used in *Tanach* as metaphors for Israel — such as figs (see *Shir Hashirim* 2:13), nuts (ibid., 6:11) and apples (ibid., 8:5). It is also customary to use almonds, because the Hebrew word for almond (שָׁקֵד) also means *swift*, and is thus a reminder of God's speedy deliverance of the Jews from Egypt. One should also put in pieces of ginger and cinnamon, to symbolize the straw that was used by the Jewish slaves to prepare bricks. The *charoses* should have a thick consistency, as a reminder of the mortar that the Egyptians forced the Jews to prepare. However, just before it is used (to dip the *maror*) some wine should be poured into it, as a remembrance of the blood that played an important role in the Exodus (and also to make it more usable as a dip). When the Seder is held on Shabbos the wine should be put into the *charoses* before Shabbos. If one forgot to do so, he may do it differently than usual, and should add enough wine to made a loose consistency (504).

Two Cooked Foods

1. After the destruction of the Temple the Sages instituted the practice of placing two kinds of cooked foods on the Seder table, one to commemorate the meat of the *pesach* offering and the other to commemorate the meat of the *chagigah* offering — both of which were sacrificed in the Temple on the fourteenth of Nisan and eaten at the Seder. The custom has developed that one of the two foods should be meat, customarily a shankbone (corresponding to the human arm, symbolizing the "outstretched arm" of Hashem) that has been roasted on the fire (as the *pesach* meat was). The second food is customarily an egg, because the Aramaic word for egg (בֵּיעָא) is related to the Aramaic word for *desire* — God *desired* (בָּעָא) to take us out of Egypt with an outstretched *arm*. The egg can be cooked or roasted in any way (as the *chagigah* was), although some have the custom to roast it specifically.

    Rema writes that many have the custom to eat eggs at the Seder. He explains that eggs are traditionally eaten by mourners, and they are eaten at this time as a commemoration of the destruction of the Temple. The *Mishnah Berurah*, citing *Gra*, says that we eat the egg of the Seder plate, since, as noted above, it symbolizes the *chagigah* offering. (According to this explanation, only the egg on the Seder plate needs to be eaten, but this custom subsequently became popularly extended to include the eating of eggs in general.) (473:4, *Mishnah Berurah* ad loc.; 470:2, *Mishnah Berurah* 11.)

2. It is best to boil or roast these two foods before *Yom Tov*. If this was neglected, they may be prepared on *Yom Tov*. If they were prepared on *Yom Tov*, the foods must be eaten on that day of *Yom Tov*, as one may only cook food on *Yom Tov* if it will be eaten that same day. The two foods will thus have to be prepared anew for the second Seder (ibid.).

Making Arrangements for Reclining

1. The seats of those who must recline while drinking the wine and eating the matzah should be prepared in a manner that will enable comfortable reclining on one's left side (472:2).

Preparing the Cups

1. The cups should be whole (not chipped or broken) and clean, and should be able to hold at least a *revi'is*. Since it is preferable to drink a majority of the wine in the cup for each of the four cups, it is advisable not to use a very large cup. This applies to the cups used by all the participants in the Seder, including women and children (who have reached the age of training in mitzvos). (472:14, 15; *Mishnah Berurah* 33.)

Preparing the Table

1. The table should be set with elegant and luxurious articles according to one's means. Although it is usually proper to use moderation in this regard out of mourning for the Temple, on Pesach it is encouraged, as this serves as yet another demonstration of our freedom. The table should be set in advance so that the Seder can get underway without delay (so the children should not become too tired) (472:1,2; *Mishnah Berurah* 6).

The Beginning of the Seder

1. Although, as mentioned above, the Seder should begin as promptly as possible, *Kiddush* should not be said before dark (*tzeis hakochavim*) (472:1).
2. It is customary for the leader to wear a *kittel* for the Seder (ibid., *Mishnah Berurah* 12).
3. Only one Seder plate is set, before the leader of the Seder. There are several different opinions as to how the Seder plate should be arranged (see diagrams on page 40).
4. The children should be kept awake at least until after reciting עֲבָדִים הָיִינוּ, so that they should hear the basic story of the Exodus. Children who have reached the age of training in mitzvos must participate in all the practices of the entire Seder. (However they must only consume a cheekful of wine, according to the size of their own mouths, for each required cup. Furthermore, there is an opinion that holds that they need not drink the four cups of wine at all.) (472:15; *Mishnah Berurah* §46, 47.)

Reclining

1. One should not recline on his back or stomach, but only on his left side. This

applies to left-handed people as well (472:3, *Mishnah Berurah* ad loc.).

2. Someone who is in mourning for a relative should also recline, although he should do so in a less luxurious manner than usual. It is also customary for a mourner not to wear a *kittel* for the Seder, although some opinions permit it (*Mishnah Berurah* 13).

3. The custom is that women do not recline (472:4).

4. A student in the presence of his *rebbi* — or any person in the presence of a great, recognized rabbinical figure — should not recline. This holds true only if they are seated at the same table. (According to some opinions, a student in the presence of his *rebbi* should ask for permission to recline even if he is sitting at a separate table.) (472:5, *Mishnah Berurah* 18.)

5. A son must recline in the presence of his father, even if his father is also his *rebbi* (472:5).

6. If one forgot to recline for any of the places in the Seder which call for reclining, he has not fulfilled that mitzvah, and it must be performed again. *Raaviah* maintains, however, that since eating in a reclining position is not a sign of freedom and leisure in our culture, the practice need not be followed. Although we do not follow the *Raaviah's* opinion, when redoing one of the mitzvos might lead to a halachic complication, this opinion is adopted and the mitzvah in question is not done over. These exceptions will be noted in appropriate places in the Haggadah (472:7, *Mishnah Berurah* 20).

Drinking the Four Cups

1. Even if one dislikes wine or suffers discomfort when drinking it, he should force himself to drink the four cups (unless it will actually make him ill). The wine may be diluted, as long as it remains fit to be used as *Kiddush* wine.

2. It is preferable to drink the entire cup of wine each time. The minimum amount that *must* be consumed is a majority of a *revi'is*, although there is an opinion that one must drink most of the wine in the cup, if the cup is larger than a *revi'is*. The requisite amount of wine should be drunk all at once, or at the very most within a time span of *kedei achilas pras* (approx. 2-9 minutes) (472:9, *Mishnah Berurah* 30, 33, 34).

3. The four cups must be drunk in their appropriate places in the Seder: one for *Kiddush*, one after *Maggid*, one for *bentching*, and one for *Hallel* (472:8).

THE SEDER PLATE

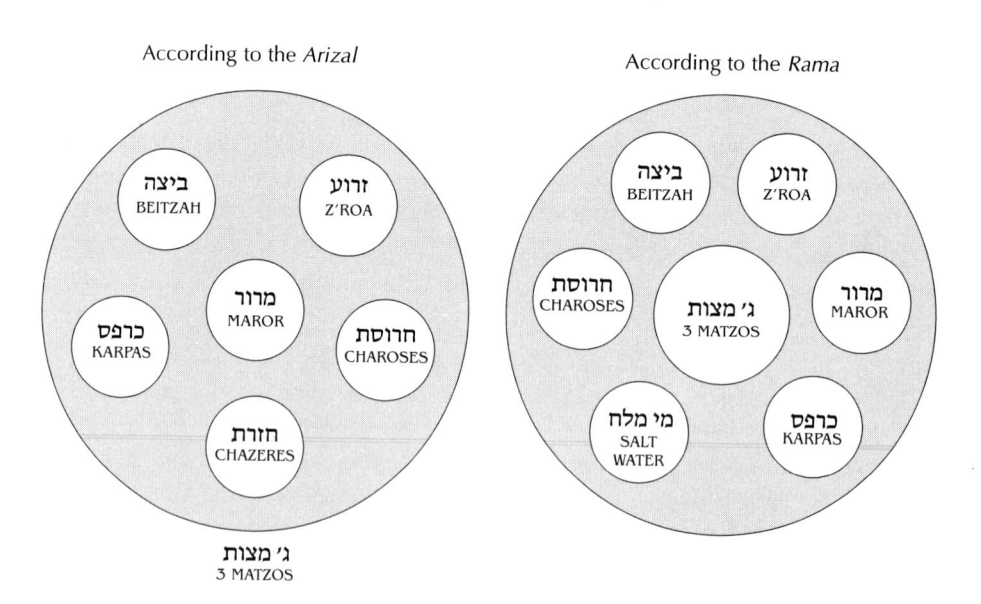

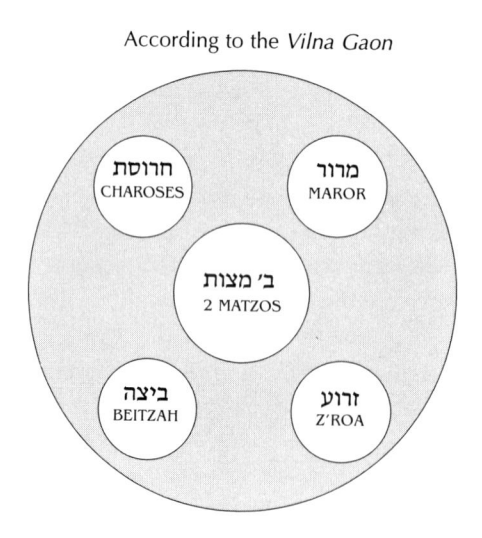

According to the *Arizal*

- ביצה / BEITZAH
- זרוע / Z'ROA
- כרפס / KARPAS
- מרור / MAROR
- חרוסת / CHAROSES
- חזרת / CHAZERES

ג' מצות / 3 MATZOS

According to the *Rama*

- ביצה / BEITZAH
- זרוע / Z'ROA
- חרוסת / CHAROSES
- ג' מצות / 3 MATZOS
- מרור / MAROR
- מי מלח / SALT WATER
- כרפס / KARPAS

According to the *Vilna Gaon*

- חרוסת / CHAROSES
- מרור / MAROR
- ב' מצות / 2 MATZOS
- ביצה / BEITZAH
- זרוע / Z'ROA

סִימָנֵי הַסֵּדֶר – The Order of the Seder

kaddesh	**Sanctify** the day with the recitation of Kiddush.	קדש
urechatz	**Wash** the hands before eating Karpas.	ורחץ
karpas	Eat a **vegetable** dipped in salt water.	כרפס
yachatz	**Break** the middle matzah. Put away larger half for Afikoman	יחץ
maggid	**Narrate** the story of the Exodus from Egypt.	מגיד
rachtzah	**Wash** the hands prior to the meal.	רחצה
motzi	Recite the blessing, **Who brings forth**, over matzah as a food.	מוציא
matzah	Recite the blessing over **Matzah**.	מצה
maror	Recite the blessing for the eating of the **bitter herbs**.	מרור
korech	Eat the **sandwich** of matzah and bitter herbs	כורך
shulchan orech	The **table prepared** with the festive meal.	שלחן עורך
tzafun	Eat the afikoman which had been **hidden** all during the Seder.	צפון
barech	Recite Bircas Hamazon, the **blessings** after the meal.	ברך
hallel	Recite the **Hallel** Psalms of praise.	הלל
nirtzah	Pray that God **accept** our observance and speedily send the Messiah.	נרצה

קַדֵּשׁ — Kaddesh

Laws of Kiddush

1. If someone forgot to say שֶׁהֶחֱיָנוּ in *Kiddush* he may say it at any time during the duration of the holiday, until the end of the last day of Pesach. (If one remembered after he has said שֶׁהֶחֱיָנוּ in *Kiddush* on the second night in *Chutz La'aretz* he should not say it again.) (*Mishnah Berurah* 473:1.)

2. If someone forgot to say *Havdalah* in *Kiddush* when the Seder is on *Motzaei Shabbos*, he should say *Havdalah* on the second cup of wine (after *Maggid*). If he remembered his mistake only after the second cup, see the details in *Mishnah Berurah* 473:5.

3. When drinking the *Kiddush* wine, one should have in mind that he is doing so for the sake of fulfilling the mitzvah of drinking the first of the four cups of wine of the Seder. Many people have the custom to recite a verbal declaration to this effect before *Kiddush* (הֲרֵינִי מוּכָן וּמְזוּמָן) (*Mishnah Berurah* 473:1).

4. Even those who have the custom to wash their hands for *Hamotzi* before saying *Kiddush* during the rest of the year should not do so on the Seder night. Similarly, the washing for the *karpas* should not be done before *Kiddush*, even if this is more convenient for some reason (*Mishnah Berurah* 473:6).

5. The master of the house should not pour his own wine, but should be served by someone else, as an expression of freedom and nobility (473:1).

6. One must drink the wine while reclining on his left side (see above, p. 38). If he forgot to recline, the *Rema* writes that he should drink another cup of wine while reclining. The *Mishnah Berurah*, however, notes that others contend that a new *berachah* would have to be recited over this additional cup of wine, and this would thus give the appearance of adding on to the ordained number of four cups. According to them, then, the wine should not be drunk again (see above, p. 39).

7. There are differing opinions as to whether one may drink between the first and second cup, so this should be avoided unless absolutely necessary. This, however, applies only to wine or other alcoholic beverages; other kinds of drinks may be drunk at this point (473:3, *Mishnah Berurah* §16).

קדש

Kiddush should be recited and the Seder begun as soon after synagogue services as possible — however, not before nightfall. Each participant's cup should be poured by someone else to symbolize the majesty of the evening, as though each participant had a servant.

Some recite the following before *Kiddush*:

הֲרֵינִי מוּכָן וּמְזוּמָּן לְקַדֵּשׁ עַל הַיַּיִן, וּלְקַיֵּם מִצְוַת כּוֹס רִאשׁוֹן מֵאַרְבַּע כּוֹסוֹת. לְשֵׁם יִחוּד קֻדְשָׁא בְּרִיךְ הוּא וּשְׁכִינְתֵּיהּ, עַל יְדֵי הַהוּא טָמִיר וְנֶעְלָם, בְּשֵׁם כָּל יִשְׂרָאֵל. וִיהִי נֹעַם אֲדֹנָי אֱלֹהֵינוּ עָלֵינוּ, וּמַעֲשֵׂה יָדֵינוּ כּוֹנְנָה עָלֵינוּ, וּמַעֲשֵׂה יָדֵינוּ כּוֹנְנֵהוּ.

On Friday night begin here:

(וַיְהִי עֶרֶב וַיְהִי בֹקֶר)

יוֹם הַשִּׁשִּׁי. וַיְכֻלּוּ הַשָּׁמַיִם וְהָאָרֶץ וְכָל צְבָאָם. וַיְכַל אֱלֹהִים בַּיּוֹם הַשְּׁבִיעִי מְלַאכְתּוֹ אֲשֶׁר עָשָׂה, וַיִּשְׁבֹּת בַּיּוֹם הַשְּׁבִיעִי מִכָּל מְלַאכְתּוֹ אֲשֶׁר עָשָׂה. וַיְבָרֶךְ אֱלֹהִים אֶת יוֹם הַשְּׁבִיעִי וַיְקַדֵּשׁ אֹתוֹ, כִּי בוֹ שָׁבַת מִכָּל מְלַאכְתּוֹ אֲשֶׁר בָּרָא אֱלֹהִים לַעֲשׂוֹת.[1]

וַיְבָרֶךְ אֱלֹהִים אֶת יוֹם הַשְּׁבִיעִי
God blessed the seventh day

The Financial Reward of Keeping the Shabbos

One time the **Chafetz Chaim** had occasion to travel to Moscow on yeshivah business. While he was there he heard about one of the wealthy businessmen in the city who was keeping his factory open late on Friday afternoons past sunset, thus encroaching upon the early Shabbos hours, and then opening it up again the next day before Shabbos was over. The next day this businessman was among the throngs of people who had come to see the famous *tzaddik* and seek his blessing.

"If it is a blessing that you seek," the Chafetz Chaim told the businessman, "let me tell you a story:

"Once there was a poor, uneducated farmer, who would come into town to sell his wheat to the local grain dealer. A price was agreed upon, such and such a number of rubles for each bushel of wheat. The dealer used to count the number of bushels being delivered to him as he poured it into his storage area, and make a mark on the wall behind him with a piece of coal for each bushel.

"But this farmer was so simple minded that he found it difficult to keep track of the count in this manner. It was so hard to count up all those little marks! Each time he did so he would come up with a different total! He therefore requested that a different system be used for him, and the merchant made the following suggestion. Instead of making confusing marks on the wall, the dealer would put a kopek

הגדה של פסח   [44]

KADDESH

Kiddush should be recited and the Seder begun as soon after synagogue services as possible — however, not before nightfall. Each participant's cup should be poured by someone else to symbolize the majesty of the evening, as though each participant had a servant.

Some recite the following before Kiddush:

Behold, I am prepared and ready to recite the Kiddush over wine, and to fulfill the mitzvah of the first Four Cups. For the sake of unification of the Holy One, Blessed is He, and His Presence, through Him Who is hidden and inscrutable — [I pray] in the name of all Israel. May the pleasantness of my Lord, our God, be upon us — may He establish our handiwork for us; our handiwork may He establish.

On Friday night begin here:
(And there was evening and there was morning)

The sixth day. Thus the heaven and the earth were finished, and all their array. On the seventh day God completed His work which He had done, and He abstained on the seventh day from all His work which He had done. God blessed the seventh day and hallowed it, because on it He abstained from all His work which God created to make.[1]

---
1. *Bereishis* 1:31-2:3.

(penny) on the counter for each bushel. When the measuring was finished there would be a concrete, tangible pile of coins on the countertop which could be easily counted. The farmer approved of the new method, and the measuring process began. The merchant would scoop out a bushel of grain into a measuring basket, place the kopek on the table, and go to pour the wheat into the storage bin, the pile of coins mounting higher and higher all the time.

"At one point during the lengthy process the growing pile of glistening coins began to look very attractive indeed to the farmer, and after a while his greed got the better of him. He succumbed to temptation and surreptitiously swiped some of the dealer's coins, slipping them into his pocket while the merchant was going back and forth in the warehouse. As the process proceeded the farmer's heart began to pound harder and harder within him. Did someone see him take the money? Was the dealer somehow keeping track of the bushels and would therefore notice at the end of the measuring that some coins were missing?

"Finally the merchant finished his measurements and he and the farmer began to count the kopeks. A total was arrived at and the merchant handed over to the farmer the corresponding amount of money.

"How relieved the farmer was that he had not been caught! He had lined his pockets with a good ten kopeks and had gotten away with it!

"Of course the farmer was nothing but a fool," continued the Chafetz Chaim. "If he had left the ten kopeks on the counter he would have made much more than that

On all nights continue here:

סַבְרִי מָרָנָן וְרַבָּנָן וְרַבּוֹתַי:

בָּרוּךְ אַתָּה יהוה אֱלֹהֵינוּ מֶלֶךְ הָעוֹלָם, בּוֹרֵא פְּרִי הַגָּפֶן:

[On Friday night include all passages in parentheses.]

בָּרוּךְ אַתָּה יהוה אֱלֹהֵינוּ מֶלֶךְ הָעוֹלָם, אֲשֶׁר בָּחַר בָּנוּ מִכָּל עָם, וְרוֹמְמָנוּ מִכָּל לָשׁוֹן, וְקִדְּשָׁנוּ בְּמִצְוֹתָיו. וַתִּתֶּן לָנוּ יהוה אֱלֹהֵינוּ בְּאַהֲבָה [שַׁבָּתוֹת לִמְנוּחָה וּ]מוֹעֲדִים לְשִׂמְחָה, חַגִּים וּזְמַנִּים

---

amount, for each kopek was nothing more than a token to represent a bushel of wheat, worth many hundreds of kopeks!"

"Your situation," said the Chafetz Chaim to the businessman, "is analogous to that of the farmer. The *Zohar* teaches that Shabbos is the source of all goodness that we receive in life, for the merit for observing this great mitzvah is enough to supply blessing sufficient for the whole week. When a Jew tries to 'steal' a few hours or a few minutes away from Shabbos it is as if he is stealing something from God, as it were, to line his pockets. But in reality, just like the farmer in the story, he is only a fool, for in the end the theft of the few rubles earned in that amount of time would be offset many, many times by the amount of blessing he would receive for keeping the Shabbos. By 'stealing' from Shabbos he is in reality stealing from himself!

"So," concluded the Chafetz Chaim, "if it is a blessing you have come to seek, why get it from me? Take the blessing of Shabbos, and that of the One Who sanctified it!"

וַתִּתֶּן לָנוּ . . . מוֹעֲדִים לְשִׂמְחָה
And You have given us . . . holidays for rejoicing,

The Joy of Yom Tov — R' Gedaliah Schorr called attention to an apparent difficulty with the wording of this phrase. It would have been smoother and more accurate, he asserted, to have said, "holidays *in which* to rejoice." "Holidays for rejoicing" seems to imply that the holidays are associated with rejoicing in general, and not specifically with the joy of the festivals themselves.

The explanation for this idea is as follows. Each one of the mitzvos contains within it a microcosm of all 613 mitzvos of the Torah, as indicated by the prayer recited by some before the performance of a mitzvah (וְתַרְיַ"ג מִצְוֹת הַתְּלוּיִם בָּהּ). In other words, each mitzvah contains some lesson that can be applied to the performance of all other mitzvos. For instance, the mitzvah of eating matzah, with its exhortation to "guard the matzos (from leavening)," teaches us the universal lesson that we must hasten to perform God's will, with enthusiasm and zeal. In the words of the Sages,

הגדה של פסח [46]

On all nights continue here:
By your leave, my masters and teachers:

Blessed are You, HASHEM, our God, King of the universe, Who creates the fruit of the vine.

[On Friday night include all passages in parentheses.]

Blessed are You, HASHEM, our God, King of the universe, Who has chosen us from all nations, exalted us above all tongues, and sanctified us with His commandments. And You, HASHEM, our God, have lovingly given us (Sabbaths for rest,) holidays for rejoicing, feasts and seasons

---

we learn from the precept of matzah that "When a mitzvah comes your way, do not allow it to 'ferment.' "

The same may be said of the mitzvah to rejoice on the festivals. The Rambam writes (*Hil. Lulav* 8:15), "The joy that a person should experience in doing a mitzvah and in his love of God Who commanded its performance is an important form of service of God, and whoever removes himself from this joy deserves to be punished, as it says (*Devarim* 28:47), '... because you did not serve Hashem your God with joy and with gladness of heart.' " The joy that we are enjoined to experience during the festivals is thus a source from which is derived our joy in serving God in general — in the performance of *all* 613 mitzvos.

מוֹעֲדִים לְשִׂמְחָה
holidays for rejoicing,

The Song of Rosh Chodesh

True joy, **R' Shneur Kotler** used to say, is experienced only when one rejoices in the presence of the *Shechinah*, as it is written, "And you shall rejoice *before Hashem your God*" (*Devarim* 12:12). But how exactly does one achieve this state of "standing before Hashem"? This can be accomplished in one of two ways. There are certain times of the year when the Jew experiences a closeness with Hashem which does not exist on a regular basis — namely, the festivals, when we are commanded, "You shall rejoice on your holiday" (ibid., 16:14). The second way one can be considered to be in God's presence is by being physically situated in the Temple, the dwelling-place (as it were) of the *Shechinah*.

In the *Mussaf* prayer for *Rosh Chodesh* we say, "May we all rejoice in the service of the Temple and in the songs of Your servant David, which are... recited before Your Altar." It is interesting to note that there is no mention of the songs sung in the Temple in any other *Mussaf* prayer (Shabbos, Festivals, Rosh Hashanah, Yom Kippur), although every *mussaf* sacrifice in the Temple was in fact accompanied by songs sung by the Levites. Why did the Sages see fit to make mention of this song specifically in the *Mussaf* of *Rosh Chodesh*? Another question that is asked is: What

לְשָׂשׂוֹן, אֶת יוֹם [הַשַּׁבָּת הַזֶּה וְאֶת יוֹם] חַג הַמַּצּוֹת הַזֶּה,
זְמַן חֵרוּתֵנוּ [בְּאַהֲבָה] מִקְרָא קֹדֶשׁ, זֵכֶר לִיצִיאַת

is meant by the phrase "the songs... which are recited before Your Altar"? Why is the specific location of the singing mentioned? It is well known that the Temple songs were recited before the Altar!

In order to answer these questions let us examine the words of the Ramban, in his critique on the Rambam's *Sefer Hamitzvos* (*Shoresh* 1). The issue under discussion there is whether the obligation to recite *Hallel* should be considered to be of Biblical origin, or is it only a later rabbinical enactment? The Ramban writes that "it is possible to consider the recitation of songs of praise to God, whether in conjunction with the sacrificial service or independent of it (i.e., *Hallel*), to be an expression of joy, and hence an application of the Torah's commandment to be joyful on the festivals. *Rosh Chodesh* (when *Hallel* is not recited — except by a post-Mishnaic custom) is excluded from this rule outside of the Temple service, however, because it is not a festival, and therefore does not require joyousness."

The Ramban's words may be explained as follows. The festivals are times which (as explained above) are intrinsically suited for closeness with God, and as such it is possible to experience true joy on these days even in a situation which is unrelated to the Temple service. On *Rosh Chodesh*, however, which is not a full-fledged holiday, this unique condition does not exist temporally, and the only joyousness that can exist on that day is spatially, through the service in the Temple. Therefore, the Ramban writes, the joy of song expresses itself on *Rosh Chodesh* only in the Temple (through the songs of the Levites), but not outside of it (in the form of *Hallel*). This, then, is why in the *Rosh Chodesh* liturgy we find a prayer to "rejoice in the service of the Temple and in the songs of Your servant David, which are... recited before Your Altar." On *Rosh Chodesh* it is only through the Temple service that we can experience the closeness to God that is the true source of joy.

In a similar vein, the Midrash relates that there was a certain spot outside Jerusalem called "the rock of calculations," where people would go and work out their monetary calculations. What was the purpose of this arrangement? The Midrash explains that since Jerusalem is called "the joy of all the land" (*Tehillim* 48:3), this area was set aside so as not to spoil the sense of joy that Jerusalem was to impart to all those who lived there or visited there. This Midrash makes even clearer the idea that closeness to God and a sense of tremendous inner joy are closely related.

מִקְרָא קֹדֶשׁ
a holy convocation,

Making the Most of Shabbos

The Torah, referring to the festivals of the Jewish year, writes, "The holidays of Hashem, which you shall declare holy convocations — these are My holidays" (*Vayikra* 23:2). *Sforno* explains the meaning of the verse as follows:

for joy, (this Sabbath and) this Feast of Matzos, the season of our freedom (in love,) a holy convocation in commemoration of the Exodus from

> Together with the physical rejoicing of the day. . . part of one's time should be occupied on these days with holy matters. . ... The Torah tells us here that holidays which you make into "holy convocations" — meaning that people get together to involve themselves with sacred matters — these are *My* holidays. But if you do not do this, but make them instead into convocations of profane, mundane matters and of physical pleasures, these are not *My* holidays, but *your* holidays (i.e., celebrated only for your own pleasure), as in the verse, "My soul despises *your* holidays" (*Yeshayahu* 1:14).

The **Chafetz Chaim** reminds us that the Sages of the Midrash portrayed the Torah as expressing its concern before God: "When the Jews enter the Land of Israel, this one will run to tend his olive orchard and that one will run to care for his vineyard. What will become of *me* then?" God reassured the Torah, "Do not worry. Shabbos will be your companion!" Shabbos is thus supposed to be a time that is dedicated to the study of Torah. In a similar vein, the *Talmud Yerushalmi* states: "Shabbos and the holidays were given only so that people should engage in studying the Torah during these times." As *Sforno* explained, if we do not utilize these days of rest to nurture the spirit and to draw ourselves closer to God and His service, we have missed the main point of these days.

The Chafetz Chaim expanded further on this concept. In *Mishlei* (3:6) we read, "In all your ways know Him, and He will straighten your paths." The meaning of this verse, the Chafetz Chaim explained, is that if a person goes through his daily routine in life with the attitude that he desires to serve God with all his ability, but must unfortunately take time out from this ideal pursuit in order to make a living, raise a family, etc. — then God will consider his paths "straight" and grant him reward accordingly.

How can it be determined whether a person indeed has this attitude, or whether he really considers his work and responsibilities to be the main focus of his life? It is when a time arises during which there is no work and all mundane responsibilities are set aside — such as Shabbos and *Yom Tov*. Does the person take this fabulous opportunity and run to the *beis midrash* to spend his hours of free time engaging in Torah study? Or does he waste the day with idle chatter and frivolous entertainment? If he takes advantage of his lack of work-related responsibilities to serve God and become closer to Him, this testifies clearly that even during the week, when he is totally preoccupied with mundane pursuits, his priority really lies in the spiritual realm. The six days between one Shabbos and the next might represent a vast majority of his life in terms of quantity of time, but in terms of focus and relative importance these weekdays are simply interruptions in the pursuit of his true objective in life. Despite the length of time involved in this interruption of six days, the verse in *Mishlei* cited above tells us that God considers the person's

מִצְרָיִם, כִּי בָנוּ בָחַרְתָּ וְאוֹתָנוּ קִדַּשְׁתָּ מִכָּל הָעַמִּים, [וְשַׁבָּת] וּמוֹעֲדֵי קָדְשֶׁךָ [בְּאַהֲבָה וּבְרָצוֹן] בְּשִׂמְחָה וּבְשָׂשׂוֹן הִנְחַלְתָּנוּ. בָּרוּךְ אַתָּה יהוה, מְקַדֵּשׁ [הַשַּׁבָּת וְ]יִשְׂרָאֵל וְהַזְּמַנִּים.

On Saturday night, add the following two paragraphs:

בָּרוּךְ אַתָּה יהוה אֱלֹהֵינוּ מֶלֶךְ הָעוֹלָם, בּוֹרֵא מְאוֹרֵי הָאֵשׁ.

בָּרוּךְ אַתָּה יהוה אֱלֹהֵינוּ מֶלֶךְ הָעוֹלָם, הַמַּבְדִּיל בֵּין קֹדֶשׁ לְחֹל, בֵּין אוֹר לְחֹשֶׁךְ, בֵּין יִשְׂרָאֵל לָעַמִּים, בֵּין יוֹם הַשְּׁבִיעִי לְשֵׁשֶׁת יְמֵי הַמַּעֲשֶׂה. בֵּין קְדֻשַּׁת שַׁבָּת לִקְדֻשַּׁת יוֹם טוֹב הִבְדַּלְתָּ, וְאֶת יוֹם הַשְּׁבִיעִי מִשֵּׁשֶׁת יְמֵי הַמַּעֲשֶׂה קִדַּשְׁתָּ, הִבְדַּלְתָּ וְקִדַּשְׁתָּ אֶת עַמְּךָ יִשְׂרָאֵל בִּקְדֻשָּׁתֶךָ. בָּרוּךְ אַתָּה יהוה, הַמַּבְדִּיל בֵּין קֹדֶשׁ לְקֹדֶשׁ.

On all nights conclude here:

בָּרוּךְ אַתָּה יהוה אֱלֹהֵינוּ מֶלֶךְ הָעוֹלָם, שֶׁהֶחֱיָנוּ וְקִיְּמָנוּ וְהִגִּיעָנוּ לַזְּמַן הַזֶּה.

The wine should be drunk without delay while reclining on the left side. It is preferable to drink the entire cup, but at the very least, most of the cup should be drained.

---

entire week to be built around the spiritual ideal that he so espouses. (He "straightens his path.") If, on the other hand, a person does not apply himself to spiritual endeavors on Shabbos, not only does he lose the reward for engaging in such spiritual activities on Shabbos itself, but he loses thereby the reward that God might have given him for his activities during the other six days of the week as well!

The Chafetz Chaim illustrated the idea with a parable. Once there was an entrepreneur who bought a parcel of real estate for 30,000 gold pieces, intending to build a large apartment complex on the site. He hired architects and builders and spent two years of his life overseeing the project until every detail of the project was finally finished to his satisfaction.

Now that the venture was completed, he could rent out the apartments for a total of 3000 gold pieces. But suddenly he came to a strange decision — that the apartments should stand empty. An acquaintance of his approached him and asked, "What's happened to your project? Why did you decide not to rent out the apartments?"

The businessman answered, "There is a great deal of bother involved with finding suitable tenants, collecting rents, maintaining the apartments, keeping books, etc. I decided that 3000 gold pieces is not worth the bother."

The man's friend could not believe his ears. "First of all," he explained to the entrepreneur, "even 3000 gold pieces is no paltry sum, and it is worthwhile to put

Egypt. For You have chosen and sanctified us above all peoples, (and the Sabbath) and Your holy festivals (in love and favor), in gladness and joy have You granted us as a heritage. Blessed are You, HASHEM, Who sanctifies (the Sabbath,) Israel, and the festive seasons.

On Saturday night, add the following two paragraphs:

Blessed are You, HASHEM, our God, King of the universe, Who creates the illumination of the fire.

Blessed are You, HASHEM, our God, King of the universe, Who distinguishes between sacred and secular, between light and darkness, between Israel and the nations, between the seventh day and the six days of activity. You have distinguished between the holiness of the Sabbath and the holiness of a Festival, and have sanctified the seventh day above the six days of activity. You distinguished and sanctified Your nation, Israel, with Your holiness. Blessed are You, HASHEM, Who distinguishes between holiness and holiness.

On all nights conclude here:

Blessed are You, HASHEM, our God, King of the universe, Who has kept us alive, sustained us, and brought us to this season.

The wine should be drunk without delay while reclining on the left side. It is preferable to drink the entire cup, but at the very least, most of the cup should be drained.

---

in the effort to earn it when the opportunity is there. Secondly, it is not 3000 gold pieces that you are forfeiting, but more like 50,000, because if you do not rent out the apartments it will turn out that your original investment and two years of effort and toil will have been wasted!"

The lesson of the parable is that once a person has put so much effort into the pursuit of his livelihood and his other obligations, he has the opportunity on Shabbos to show that deep in his heart his priorities lie in spiritual matters. By forfeiting this opportunity, it is not only the spiritual "earnings" of Shabbos itself that are wasted, but those of the other six days of the week as well.

בֵּין אוֹר לְחֹשֶׁךְ בֵּין יִשְׂרָאֵל לָעַמִּים
between light and darkness, between Israel and the nations,

A Nation Apart From Others On a visit to the United States in 1938, **R' Elchanan Wasserman** delivered an address, in which he discussed several points, among them the following:

In the last few years, our people have been plagued by many grave troubles and misfortunes. Many people ask, "Why have all these terrible tragedies befallen us? What has aroused God's wrath so severely?"

The answer to this question is quite clear to anyone who looks into the relevant Biblical verses and understands their implications.

Our period is called "the prelude to the Messianic era" (עִקְבָתָא דִמְשִׁיחָא). The prophets clearly predicted what would occur at this time, as it says, "That which you plan in your minds, it shall not be; that which you say, 'We will be like all the nations.' As I live... I shall rule over you with a strong hand and an outstretched arm and with poured-out wrath" (*Yechezkel* 20:32-33). The Jewish people must fulfill their destiny prescribed for them in the Torah: "I have separated you from the nations" (*Vayikra* 20:26); "You shall be for me a treasured nation from among all the nations" (*Shemos* 19:5). This distinction should express itself in all walks of life — in our speech, in our dress, etc. It is well known that in certain countries our brethren have abandoned this time-honored practice of deliberate separation and seek to emulate their non-Jewish neighbors in all their mannerisms, even to the point of total assimilation to them. It is for this reason that all these sufferings and misfortunes are coming upon us at this time, for as the prophet warned us centuries ago, "It shall not be!" It cannot be possible for the Jewish people to breach the barrier between themselves and the other nations; if they do not see to it that these boundaries are observed then God will see to it for them — "with a strong hand and an outstretched arm and with poured-out wrath."

Rav Chaim (Brisker) Soloveitchik once noted that in *Havdalah* we compare the distinction between "Israel and the nations" to that between "light and darkness" (referring to "day and night" — *Bereishis* 1:4). We find that sometimes the night "encroaches" upon the territory of the day, as in the winter, when night begins in the midafternoon hours, and that at times the day lingers on into what we consider to be night hours, during the summer. But regardless of the shift in hours, there is always a clear, substantial barrier that stands as a divider between the two entities — namely, twilight. The same unbreakable buffer zone must exist between Israel and the other nations — whether we ourselves observe it or it is forced upon us.

- וּרְחַץ – Urechatz

- כַּרְפַּס – Karpas

- יַחַץ – Yachatz

וּרְחַץ

The head of the household — according to many opinions, all participants in the Seder — washes his hands as if to eat bread, [pouring water from a cup, twice on the right hand and twice on the left] but without reciting a blessing.

כַּרְפַּס

All participants take a vegetable other than *maror* and dip it into salt water. A piece smaller in volume than half an egg should be used. The following blessing is recited [with the intention that it also applies to the *maror* which will be eaten during the meal] before the vegetable is eaten.

בָּרוּךְ אַתָּה יהוה אֱלֹהֵינוּ מֶלֶךְ הָעוֹלָם, בּוֹרֵא פְּרִי הָאֲדָמָה.

יַחַץ

The head of the household breaks the middle matzah in two. He puts the smaller part back between the two whole matzos, and wraps up the larger part for later use as the *afikoman*. Some briefly place the *afikoman* portion on their shoulders, in accordance with the Biblical verse recounting that Israel left Egypt carrying their matzos on their shoulders, and say בְּבֶהָלוּ יָצְאנוּ מִמִּצְרָיִם, "*In haste we went out of Egypt.*"

URECHATZ

The head of the household — according to many opinions, all participants in the Seder — washes his hands as if to eat bread, [pouring water from a cup, twice on the right hand and twice on the left] but without reciting a blessing.

KARPAS

All participants take a vegetable other than *maror* and dip it into salt water. A piece smaller in volume than half an egg should be used. The following blessing is recited [with the intention that it also applies to the *maror* which will be eaten during the meal] before the vegetable is eaten.

Blessed are You, Hashem, our God, King of the universe, Who creates the fruits of the earth.

YACHATZ

The head of the household breaks the middle matzah in two. He puts the smaller part back between the two whole matzos, and wraps up the larger part for later use as the *afikoman*. Some briefly place the *afikoman* portion on their shoulders, in accordance with the Biblical verse recounting that Israel left Egypt carrying their matzos on their shoulders, and say בְּבְהִלוּ יָצְאנוּ מִמִּצְרָיִם, *"In haste we went out of Egypt."*

מַגִּיד — Maggid

Laws of *Maggid*

1. Men and women alike are obligated to recite the Haggadah (or hear it recited by someone else). The absolute minimum requirement in this regard is listening to *Kiddush* (and drinking the wine, as well as the other three cups of wine) and the recitation of the passage רַבָּן גַּמְלִיאֵל הָיָה אוֹמֵר וכו׳ (*Mishnah Berurah* 473:64).

2. The main parts of the Haggadah should be translated or explained in the vernacular if there are people present who do not understand Hebrew (473:6).

3. One should not recite the Haggadah in the reclining position assumed for the wine and matzah; rather, it should be recited with a feeling of reverence and awe.

4. The matzah should be at least partly visible during the recitation of the Haggadah. The Gemara explains that matzah is called לֶחֶם עוֹנִי (*Devarim* 16:3) because it is the bread over which many words are recited (עוֹנִין) (473:7, *Mishnah Berurah* §76).

5. While reciting the Haggadah, one should bear in mind that he is doing so in order to fulfill the Torah's mitzvah to recount the story of the Exodus. Many people have the custom to recite a verbal declaration to this effect before *Maggid* (הִנְנִי מוּכָן וּמְזוּמָן) (*Mishnah Berurah* 473:1).

6. The second cup of wine, which follows *Maggid*, must be consumed while reclining. If one forgot to recline while drinking it, he should drink another cup afterwards (without a *berachah*) (472:7).

מגיד

Some recite the following before Maggid:

הִנְנִי מוּכָן וּמְזֻמָּן לְקַיֵּם הַמִּצְוָה לְסַפֵּר בִּיצִיאַת מִצְרָיִם. לְשֵׁם יִחוּד קֻדְשָׁא בְּרִיךְ הוּא וּשְׁכִינְתֵּיהּ, עַל יְדֵי הַהוּא טָמִיר וְנֶעְלָם, בְּשֵׁם כָּל יִשְׂרָאֵל. וִיהִי נֹעַם אֲדֹנָי אֱלֹהֵינוּ עָלֵינוּ, וּמַעֲשֵׂה יָדֵינוּ כּוֹנְנָה עָלֵינוּ, וּמַעֲשֵׂה יָדֵינוּ כּוֹנְנֵהוּ:

The broken matzah is lifted for all to see as the head of the household begins with the following brief explanation of the proceedings.

הָא לַחְמָא עַנְיָא דִי אֲכָלוּ אַבְהָתָנָא בְּאַרְעָא דְמִצְרָיִם. כָּל דִּכְפִין יֵיתֵי וְיֵכוֹל, כָּל דִּצְרִיךְ יֵיתֵי וְיִפְסַח.

כָּל דִּכְפִין יֵיתֵי וְיֵכוֹל, כָּל דִּצְרִיךְ יֵיתֵי וְיִפְסַח
Whoever is hungry — let him come and eat; whoever is in need — let him come and partake of the pesach.

Matzah and the Needy

The repetitiousness of this passage is problematic: What is the difference between "Let anyone who is hungry come and eat" and "Let anyone who is in need come and partake of the pesach"? A further question, posed by many Haggadah commentators, is: If the word יִפְסַח is to be understood literally as, "Let him partake of the meat of the *pesach* sacrifice," how can we explain the inclusion of such a declaration in the הָא לַחְמָא עַנְיָא prayer, which, as the commentators assume, was added to the Haggadah text in Babylonia after the destruction of the Temple, when the *pesach* sacrifice was no longer practiced altogether?

R' Zalman Sorotzkin explained the difficult passage as follows. It is forbidden to eat certain filling foods in the late afternoon preceding the Seder (*Pesachim* 99b, *Shulchan Aruch*, O.C. 471:1). The reason for this rabbinical prohibition is to ensure that one should have a hearty appetite when matzah is first eaten at the Seder. It is this matzah (that eaten at the beginning of the meal) to which we refer when we declare, "Let anyone who is *hungry* come and eat," for this matzah is supposed to be eaten when one is hungry. The piece of matzah eaten at the end of the meal (commonly referred to as the *afikoman*), on the other hand, is eaten nowadays as a commemoration of the meat of the *pesach* sacrifice, which had to be eaten at the end of the meal (*Pesachim* 119b). This *afikoman*, like the *pesach* meat it represents, is supposed to be eaten while one is *not* ravenously hungry, but is already somewhat satiated (עַל הַשֹּׂבַע). It is to this second serving of matzah that we refer when we announce, "Let anyone who is *in need* come and partake of the *pesach*" — alluding not to the *pesach* sacrifice itself, but to the *afikoman* which substitutes for it, and for which the term דִּכְפִין ("one who is hungry") is totally inappropriate.

כָּל דִּכְפִין יֵיתֵי וְיֵכוֹל
Whoever is hungry — let him come and eat;

Feeling the Pain of Others

This declaration seems to have no particular relevance to Pesach. We are, after all, commanded

הגדה של פסח [58]

MAGGID

Some recite the following before Maggid:

Behold, I am prepared and ready to fulfill the mitzvah of telling of the Exodus from Egypt. For the sake of the unification of the Holy One, Blessed is He, and His presence, through Him Who is hidden and inscrutable — [I pray] in the name of all Israel. May the pleasantness of my Lord, our God, be upon us — may He establish our handiwork for us; our handiwork may He establish.

The broken matzah is lifted for all to see as the head of the household begins with the following brief explanation of the proceedings.

This is the bread of affliction that our fathers ate in the land of Egypt. Whoever is hungry — let him come and eat; whoever is in need — let him come and partake of the pesach.

---

to care for the poor on *all* the festivals, as the Torah tells us: "And you shall rejoice (on the holiday) before Hashem your God, you. . . and the stranger and the orphan and the widow who are in your midst. . . ." (*Devarim* 16:11). Why, then, is this invitation issued only on Pesach, but not on Sukkos and Shavuos?

The answer to this question, **R' Zalman Sorotzkin** suggested, becomes apparent if we look at the verse that follows the quote in the previous paragraph: "Remember that you were a slave in Egypt, and observe and do these statutes" (ibid., 16:12). The Torah explains the reason why it is so insistent that we not neglect the less fortunate elements of society who live among us: It is because we ourselves should identify with these unfortunate people based on our own past history. By remembering our own humble origins we will no longer be able to allow any feelings of superiority to induce us to remain apathetic to their plight. Although all the festivals are related to the idea of the Exodus from Egypt to one degree or another, it is only Pesach that focuses entirely on that theme. That this is so may be seen in the liturgy for the various holidays. Shavuos is described as "the time of the giving of our Torah," and Sukkos as "the time of our rejoicing." It is only Pesach that is given the title of "the time of our freedom (i.e., from Egyptian bondage)." It is therefore especially important on this festival, when we focus on the miracle of our redemption from slavery and oppression, that we remember the poor and unfortunate among us.

כָּל דִּכְפִין יֵיתֵי וְיֵכוֹל, כָּל דִּצְרִיךְ יֵיתֵי וְיִפְסַח

Whoever is hungry — let him come and eat; whoever is in need — let him come and partake of the pesach.

The Matzah/Sacrifice Connection

Several very strong questions are posed by the commentators in connection with this passage. The first, mentioned previously, is: Why does this introductory paragraph, which was quite clearly added to the Haggadah after the Jews were exiled from their land, mention "partaking of *the pesach*," that is, the paschal sacrifice, which was discontinued after the destruction of the Temple? Indeed, how can one

הָשַׁתָּא הָכָא, לְשָׁנָה הַבָּאָה בְּאַרְעָא דְיִשְׂרָאֵל. הָשַׁתָּא עַבְדֵי, לְשָׁנָה הַבָּאָה בְּנֵי חוֹרִין.

invite participants to join with him in his paschal sacrifice altogether at this late hour; the law requires that the list of participants be finalized before the lamb is slaughtered, on the afternoon preceding the Seder! Another question is: What is the connection between this line and the sentence that follows it: "Now we are here (in exile)..." And finally, what is the significance behind the seemingly repetitious ending of the paragraph: "Now we are here; next year may we be in the Land of Israel. Now we are slaves; next year may we be free men"?

The **Netziv** proposed an approach that answers all of these questions. This paragraph, he asserts, serves as a *preamble* to the exile-era Haggadah. The beginning of the paragraph notes that the focus of the story of the Haggadah revolves around the "bread of affliction," a term which, the Netziv maintains, describes matzah only when it is not eaten in conjunction with the *pesach* meat. The paragraph announces that although in years gone by the focus of the Seder and its discussion of the Exodus was the *pesach* sacrifice, nowadays it is this "bread of affliction" which is the center of our attention.

At this point, the Netziv continues, the paragraph announces that nowadays the Sages instituted that, wherever possible, the matzah eaten at the Seder — which is a substitute for the *pesach* meat — should be governed by the same set of halachos that used to apply to the *pesach* sacrifice, as a sort of commemoration of the *pesach* sacrifice which is no longer practiced. For instance, the halachah forbids eating any food after the meat of the *pesach* sacrifice so that the taste of that meat might linger on in one's mouth long after its actual consumption; nowadays this law is applied to matzah, and no food may be eaten after the last bit of matzah eaten at the end of the meal (*Pesachim* 119b). Similarly, just as the sacrifice had to be eaten before midnight (according to some Tannaim), so too with matzah. Furthermore, just as the *pesach* sacrifice was not allowed to be eaten in two different places, so too with the last piece of matzah at the end of the meal (known popularly as the *afikoman*). And just as the eating of the *pesach* meat could not continue if all those participating happened to doze off, so too with the *afikoman*.

However, the Haggadah points out, in this respect the Sages did *not* extend the laws of the *pesach* sacrifice to the matzah of the Seder: When it comes to matzah, unlike the sacrifice, people may be invited to join even at the last minute. They did not wish to eliminate or hamper the tremendous mitzvah of taking in needy guests, so in this case they did not apply the stringencies of the *pesach* sacrifice to the matzah. "Let *anyone* who is hungry come and eat!" As regards other laws, however, "Let anyone who needs come and celebrate the *pesach* " — meaning that the eating of the "bread of affliction" (which is the topic of this paragraph) is intended to be carried out in a manner which parallels the eating of the *pesach* in the days of the Temple.

The question that presents itself at this point is: Why indeed did the Sages see fit

> Now, we are here; next year may we be in the Land of Israel! Now, we are slaves; next year may we be free men!

to graft the Torah's laws of eating the *pesach* meat onto the eating of matzah? What did they seek to accomplish by instituting these parallels?

To this question the Haggadah gives two answers: First, "This year we are here; next year may we be in the Land of Israel." We must remember that the eating of the paschal sacrifice is not only an event that took place in the distant past; we constantly hope and pray that the Temple will be rebuilt "speedily in our days" and that all sacrifices will be practiced once again. In order to keep the basic laws of the *pesach* sacrifice fresh in the collective minds of the people of Israel, the Sages decreed that instead of falling into disuse along with the sacrifice itself, they should be practiced in connection with the matzah. In that way, when the Temple is rebuilt people will be somewhat familiar with the laws of the *pesach*. "This year we are here" — but who knows? It is very possible that "next year we will be in the Land of Israel," offering the paschal sacrifice once again.

The second explanation given by the Haggadah for applying the laws of the *pesach* sacrifice to the matzah is, "This year we are enslaved; next year may we be free men." The Midrash tells us that the reason the commandments of the *pesach* sacrifice were given to the Israelites even before the Exodus was in order to supply them with a source of merit by which they could be deemed worthy of redemption, for the spiritual state of the people had fallen drastically. We hope and pray then, that just as the laws of the *pesach* sacrifice helped our ancestors merit deliverance from bondage to freedom, so too may these laws — although they unfortunately cannot be applied to the sacrifice itself — serve as a source of merit for us today, and allow us to emerge from our present state of enslavement to the other nations to freedom!

> כָּל דִּכְפִין יֵיתֵי וְיֵכוֹל . . . לְשָׁנָה הַבָּאָה בְּנֵי חוֹרִין
> *Whoever is hungry — let him come and eat*
> *. . . next year may we be free men!*

Finding Favor in the Eyes of Hashem

The question is asked by the commentators (as mentioned above): Why are these two topics juxtaposed? What is the relevance of inviting guests to our prayer for deliverance from exile?

The answer to this question may be learned from a story that happened with the **Chafetz Chaim**. It was during World War I, when thousands of Jews, including the Chafetz Chaim and his yeshivah, were forced to flee from the countryside to the main cities. The times were very difficult; the economy had come to a standstill, and people were literally starving to death. One day a well-dressed, wealthy-looking man came to see the Chafetz Chaim in his home.

The Chafetz Chaim greeted the man warmly. "*Shalom Aleichem!* Where are you from?"

The Seder plate is removed and the second of the four cups of wine is poured. The youngest present asks the reasons for the unusual proceedings of the evening.

מַה נִּשְׁתַּנָּה הַלַּיְלָה הַזֶּה מִכָּל הַלֵּילוֹת?

שֶׁבְּכָל הַלֵּילוֹת אָנוּ אוֹכְלִין חָמֵץ וּמַצָּה, הַלַּיְלָה הַזֶּה – כֻּלּוֹ מַצָּה.

"From Minsk," came the answer.

"And what is your occupation?" asked the Rabbi.

"I deal in leather," the man replied.

"And how is business these days? Are you managing?" asked the Chafetz Chaim, always concerned for the welfare of a fellow Jew.

"*Baruch Hashem*, I am doing well. I lack nothing."

"Even during wartime?!" the Rabbi asked incredulously.

"*Especially* during wartime," the businessman explained. "You see, I supply shoes to the Russian army, and the quantity of orders is immense. I am therefore managing quite comfortably."

"I see," said the Chafetz Chaim. "You are very lucky that the war has not affected your line of business. But it is still somewhat amazing that you manage to emerge unharmed from dealing with the representatives of Czar Nikolai, that arch anti-Semite, who will do anything to impede the advancement and prosperity of any Jew!"

"What you say is true," the businessman confessed. "But thank God these men have one passion that is even greater than their anti-Semitism — greed! A little bribe here and there, and all goes well in the end."

"How exactly does that work?" asked the Chafetz Chaim curiously.

"Well, you see, Rebbe, there is practically no such thing as a perfect piece of leather. There is always a small hole, a crack or some other imperfection; one hide is too tough and another is too soft. There are enough excuses for any batch delivered to the army to be rejected. But if the right people are 'shmeered' at the right times, the order is accepted without problems — and everyone is happy."

"Ah, now I see!" exclaimed the Chafetz Chaim. You have enlightened me, my friend!"

"*I* have enlightened the *Rebbe*?" asked the man, somewhat bewildered.

The Chafetz Chaim explained what exactly he had learned from the words of the leather merchant. "The spiritual world works along the same lines as the earthly world (*Berachos* 58a). When our souls go to Heaven to be judged after our lives have come to an end, we will present to the Heavenly Judge all of our "merchandise" — the Torah and mitzvos that we have accomplished throughout our lifetimes. Each deed will be carefully scrutinized and many faults will be found: This one was performed without intent, that one was carried out without joy, this one was implemented with ulterior motives, etc. All these mitzvos will be disqualified. Maybe, if we are lucky, one percent of our deeds will be judged to be a source of merit for us. How ashamed we will be when we see all that we have accomplished wiped away before our eyes!

The Seder plate is removed and the second of the four cups of wine is poured. The youngest present asks the reasons for the unusual proceedings of the evening.

Why is this night different from all other nights?

1. For on all other nights we may eat chametz and matzah, but on this night — only matzah.

"But now, I have learned from your words that there is a course of action that can alleviate this dire situation — giving a bribe. 'A bribe?!' you are certainly asking yourself. Does the Torah not say that 'God does not show favorites or take bribes' (*Devarim* 10:17)? Yet there is a way by which we can hope that God will judge us with His attribute of mercy, and that is if we ourselves act with mercy towards others. The Sages say, 'If someone has mercy on his fellow men, [God] shows mercy toward him from Heaven' (*Shabbos* 151b). If we are kind and patient to other people, God will be lenient when he looks over our 'merchandise'; otherwise, if God judges us strictly, we have no hope.

"There are some people," the Chafetz Chaim concluded, "who spend all their time learning Torah, but are stingy with their time when it comes to dedicating an hour a day to performing acts of kindness to others less fortunate than they. If only they would realize that that one hour might save their entire day!"

The merchant understood the Chafetz Chaim's message and applied it to himself. His brethren were in such dire straits at this time and in such desperate need of assistance. How could he sit back and enjoy the comforts of life when there is so much he could do for others? He gave the Chafetz Chaim a large sum of money to be distributed to the needy.

The concept discussed by the Chafetz Chaim concerning the individual and his judgment before God can be applied to the nation as a whole as well. We hope and pray every day that this day might be the one when the *Mashiach* will come and redeem us. But the redemption is, of course, dependent upon the state of our merit as a nation. How can we hope to be found worthy in light of all the imperfections found in our deeds? It is only if we extend a helping hand toward others in need that we can have the slightest chance of being judged favorably sufficiently to bring the Messianic redemption. This is why, immediately after issuing our invitation to the poor and unfortunate among us by announcing . . . כָּל דִכְפִין ("Whoever is hungry. . ."), we pray that in consideration of such acts of kindness we might soon be the beneficiaries of God's kindness and be led from servitude to eternal liberation.

שֶׁבְּכָל הַלֵּילוֹת אָנוּ אוֹכְלִין חָמֵץ וּמַצָּה, הַלַּיְלָה הַזֶּה – כֻּלּוֹ מַצָּה
For on all other nights we may eat chametz and matzah, but on this night — only matzah.

Why Not Chametz *and* Matzoh?

This question seems quite difficult to understand, coming as it does immediately following the paragraph of הָא לַחְמָא עַנְיָא, where the reason for eating matzah on this night

[63] THE HAGGADAH OF THE ROSHEI YESHIVAH

שֶׁבְּכָל הַלֵּילוֹת אָנוּ אוֹכְלִין שְׁאָר יְרָקוֹת, הַלַּיְלָה הַזֶּה – מָרוֹר.
שֶׁבְּכָל הַלֵּילוֹת אֵין אָנוּ מַטְבִּילִין אֲפִילוּ פַּעַם אֶחָת, הַלַּיְלָה הַזֶּה – שְׁתֵּי פְעָמִים.
שֶׁבְּכָל הַלֵּילוֹת אָנוּ אוֹכְלִין בֵּין יוֹשְׁבִין וּבֵין מְסֻבִּין, הַלַּיְלָה הַזֶּה – כֻּלָּנוּ מְסֻבִּין.

---

is clearly indicated: "This is the bread of our affliction that our forefathers ate in the land of Egypt." What further explanation does the child seek beyond what has already been stated?

R' Zalman Sorotzkin explained that the child's question is more than simply, "Why do we eat matzah?" Rather, the child is responding to what he has just heard about the matzah serving as a reminder of our enslavement to the Egyptians. He now understands why we eat matzah at the Seder; however, this being a celebration of our *liberation* from bondage, would it not be more appropriate if we would eat both *chametz and* matzah? In this manner we would be able to show the contrast between our situation prior to our emancipation and that following redemption — a sort of demonstration of "before" and "after," as it were. After all, the Seder is full of such contrasting themes — the *maror* and *charoses* representing bitterness and slavery versus the four cups of wine and the reclining posture representing freedom and leisure, etc. To this the Haggadah supplies the answer (below, p. 158, after some digression): "This matzah that we eat. . . represents the fact that the dough of our ancestors did not have time to rise, for they were driven out of Egypt and could not delay. . . ." In other words, we explain to the child that matzah in fact has a dual symbolism. In addition to being the bread of affliction, reminiscent of slavery and adversity, it also recalls the sudden haste of God's delivery of our ancestors from bondage. It is not necessary, then, to eat matzah *and chametz* in order to illustrate the "before and after" effect; this is accomplished through the eating of matzah all by itself!

כֻּלָּנוּ מְסֻבִּין
we all recline.

A Source for Reclining at the Seder — Although the practice of reclining at the Seder is of rabbinic origin, the Sages of the Midrash find an allusion to it in the Torah: "God did not lead the people (out of Egypt) by the way of the Philistines . . . but He led the people round about, by the way of the wilderness, toward the Reed Sea" (*Shemos* 13:17-18). The word וַיַּסֵּב (*He led them round about*), the Midrash notes, closely resembles the word for

2. For on all other nights we eat many vegetables, but on this night — we eat maror.
3. For on all other nights we do not dip even once, but on this night — twice.
4. For on all other nights we eat either sitting or reclining, but on this night — we all recline.

"reclining" (לְהָסֵב). But surely the Midrash intends more than a mere play on words; what is the deeper intention behind this comment of the Sages?

R' Zalman Sorotzkin explained the connection between the cited verse and the concept of reclining at the Seder as follows. Moshe had always asked Pharaoh not for total release from slavery, but for a three-day holiday, during which the people might "go into the wilderness and worship Hashem their God" (*Shemos* 3:18). When Pharaoh, after suffering all the plagues, finally released the Jews, it is unclear whether he did so based on this original understanding, or whether he completely relinquished any and all claims of mastery or authority over the people permanently. Indeed, Rashi tells us that the reason Pharaoh gave chase after his former slaves (*Shemos* 14:5) after they left was because he realized that the Jews were not going to return after three days as planned.

If the former possibility is the correct one — and the Israelites were released on Pesach for only a three-day reprieve — then our liberation from Egyptian bondage should not be celebrated on the first day of Pesach, but on the seventh day, which is the anniversary of the drowning of Pharaoh's army in the Reed Sea. This, after all, was the point at which the Jews were truly freed from servitude to the Egyptians, for until then they had been expected to ultimately return to Egypt.

Now let us return to the verse cited above: "God did not lead the people by the way of the Philistines. . . but He led the people round about, by the way of the wilderness." This verse is the first clear indication that God's intention was from the outset to lead the people directly to Eretz Yisrael, and not to have them return to Egypt under any circumstances; the only question involved was the matter of which route to take to the Promised Land. Pharaoh may have had second thoughts subsequently, but the fact of the matter, as this verse makes clear, is that when he released the people on the night of the fifteenth of Nisan he did so totally and unconditionally, disregarding the original meager request of a three-day holiday in the desert in favor of total emancipation. Thus, the key to understanding that it is the fifteenth of Nisan — the Seder night — that marks the anniversary of our deliverance from Egypt, and not the seventh day of Pesach, lies in this verse, and this is why the Midrash sees a connection between these words and the practice of reclining at the Seder.

The Seder plate is returned. The matzos are kept uncovered as the Haggadah is recited in unison. The Haggadah should be translated if necessary, and the story of the Exodus should be amplified upon.

עֲבָדִים הָיִינוּ לְפַרְעֹה בְּמִצְרַיִם, וַיּוֹצִיאֵנוּ יהוה אֱלֹהֵינוּ מִשָּׁם בְּיָד חֲזָקָה

עֲבָדִים הָיִינוּ לְפַרְעֹה בְּמִצְרַיִם
We were slaves to Pharaoh in Egypt,

Thanking God for All Our Successes

The Mishnah (*Pesachim* 116a) teaches that the recounting of the story of the Exodus at the Seder should be done in a manner that begins by describing the initial indignity of the Jews in Egypt and ends with their subsequent prestige. There is a dispute in the Gemara as to what this statement means. According to Shmuel, the Mishnah refers to *physical* indignity and prestige: "We were slaves to Pharaoh in Egypt (*indignity*) and Hashem our God took us out from there with a strong hand and an outstretched arm (*prestige*)." Rav, however, holds that the Mishnah is speaking of *spiritual* indignity and prestige: the fact that our distant ancestors were originally idolaters (*indignity*), until Avraham discovered the path to the true God (*prestige*). In practice, both versions have been incorporated into the Haggadah text.

At first glance it would seem that Rav's interpretation is more appropriate. After all, the ultimate goal of the Exodus was not mere physical emancipation from the bonds of Egyptian slavery; as stated numerous times in the Torah, God's purpose in taking the Jews out of Egypt was to take them to Himself as His people. God's revelation and the giving of the Torah on Mount Sinai were seen as the culmination of the Exodus process begun fifty days earlier (see *Shemos* 3:12). Why, then, should the recounting of the Exodus at the Seder not center around the spiritual aspect of our birth as a people?

The answer to this question, **R' Zalman Sorotzkin** suggested, is that the Seder celebration is supposed to be an occasion for expression of thanksgiving to God for all the wonders He has done for us in taking us out of Egypt and making us His people. In this connection it is important to bear in mind the saying of the Sages (*Berachos* 33b): "Everything is in the hands of Heaven except for the fear of Heaven." That is, all the events in man's life are controlled by God except for his spiritual state; this area of life is left completely up to the individual himself to take command. God may determine if a person should be healthy or ill, rich or poor, happy or depressed — but He will never decide for him whether he will be good or bad. We may therefore suggest that Shmuel believes it is inappropriate to give thanks to God for our *spiritual* well-being, for any advantage we might have in this area, in accordance with the aforementioned dictum, is a result of our own accomplishments — or those of our ancestors — and should not be regarded as blessings from God.

This appears to be a cogent argument. What, then, would Rav reply to this objection? R' Sorotzkin explained that while it is true that God does not determine a person's spiritual choices in life, nevertheless the Sages tell us (*Yoma* 38b) that

The Seder plate is returned. The matzos are kept uncovered as the Haggadah is recited in unison. The Haggadah should be translated if necessary, and the story of the Exodus should be amplified upon.

We were slaves to Pharaoh in Egypt, but HASHEM our God took us out from there with a mighty hand

"If a person is interested in purifying himself, [God] helps him." It seems, then, that although God does not *cause* a person to choose good or evil, He does *assist* a person who has undertaken to choose the proper path of his own accord. The same principle may be applied to Avraham. According to the Midrash (*Bereishis Rabbah* 39) Avraham realized the existence of God on his own, and subsequently God revealed Himself to the patriarch and thus facilitated his process of awareness of Him. Besides this, of course, God commanded Avraham to leave his country of origin and settle in Eretz Yisrael, so as to escape the negative influences of his family and former acquaintances, and to better be in a position to galvanize the spiritual revolution that he had begun. There were others who recognized the existence of God, such as Noach, Shem, Ever, the "souls that [Avraham and Sarah] made" (*Bereishis* 12:5), etc. But since these people did not merit the same kind of Divine intervention that Avraham did, they were not able to keep the faith that they had developed in themselves through their offspring. The Haggadah alludes to this idea when it cites the verse from *Yehoshua* (24:2-4): "Your fathers always lived beyond the Euphrates River — Terach, the father of Avraham and Nachor — and they served other gods. Then I took your father Avraham from beyond the River and led him through all the land of Canaan." The implication is that the fact that God "took Avraham and led him through the land of Canaan" enabled him to completely sever his ties with his previous idolatrous milieu.

Similarly, the Rambam writes (*Hil. Avodah Zarah* 1:17-18): "The 'root' that Avraham 'planted' was almost uprooted, and the children of Yaakov were about to turn to the mistaken ways of the nations. But God, out of His love for us, and in keeping with the oath He had sworn to our forefather Avraham, established Moshe. . . and sent him [to the Jewish people to teach them the proper path]." In light of this Divine intervention in our forefather's spiritual destiny, Rav believes that it is entirely appropriate for us to give thanks and praises to God for allowing us to thrive and to survive as a people — in the spiritual sense — to the present day.

עֲבָדִים הָיִינוּ לְפַרְעֹה בְּמִצְרָיִם
We were slaves to Pharaoh in Egypt,

Twofold Slavery — Why does the Haggadah explicitly mention both Pharaoh and Egypt? **R' Zalman Sorotzkin** noted that the Egyptian populace themselves were in servitude to the king of the country (as recounted in *Bereishis* 47:25). Furthermore, the Egyptians were descended from Mitzrayim, a son of Cham, whose descendants Noach cursed to be "slaves of slaves" (ibid., 9:25). What the Haggadah is alluding to with these words, therefore, is that not only were our ancestors enslaved, which would have been bad enough, but they were in servitude to the *Egyptians* — of all nations — thus increasing their indignity even more.

R' Zalman suggested another explanation for the double expression "to Pharaoh in Egypt," as well. Our ancestors' servitude to the Egyptians was twofold in nature. On one hand, it consisted of difficult physical labor — but it also included a sort of cultural servitude, for, as the Midrashim tell us, the Jews had sunk to a deplorably low level of impurity and immorality as a result of their extensive contact with the predominant Egyptian culture. This twofold servitude is alluded to by the double expression used by the Haggadah: We were slaves "in Egypt," referring to the physical, laborious aspect of the servitude. And furthermore, we were slaves "to Pharaoh" — who was deified by his countrymen and actually believed himself to be divine (see *Yechezkel* 29:3). We, too, were influenced by these corrupt, idolatrous ideologies.

This theme is reflected further as the paragraph proceeds: "Had not the Holy One, Blessed is He, taken our fathers out from Egypt, then we, our children, and our children's children would have remained subservient to Pharaoh in Egypt." It is interesting to note the change in expression from the beginning of the paragraph, where the Haggadah said "We were *slaves* to Pharaoh in Egypt," whereas at this point the language is changed to "we would have remained *subservient* to Pharaoh in Egypt." What the Haggadah means to say is that if God had not taken us out of Egypt with His "mighty hand and outstretched arm" — but we would have been liberated from slavery in some other, natural manner, such as revolution, reconciliation, foreign intervention, etc. — we might have rid ourselves of the physical type of servitude, acquiring civil rights, freedom, etc., but we should still be *subservient* — in the moral, spiritual sense — to the Egyptians, for their culture and ideas would have remained entrenched in our minds forever. The Jews would have become a nation of "Hebraic Egyptians," a far cry from the glory and sanctity that God chose to bestow upon them.

It is also noteworthy that the Haggadah speaks of "we, our children, and our children's children" being subservient to the Egyptians if not for the Exodus. It does not suffice with "we would have remained subservient," nor does it go so far as to say, "we and all our descendants. . . ." Why does the Haggadah use this particular expression, which refers to precisely three generations, no more and no less?

R' Zalman continued explaining this point along the same lines as what we have been discussing all along. According to the Talmud (*Kiddushin* 30a) a person has an obligation to provide a Torah education not only to his sons (and himself, of course), but to his grandsons as well (based on *Devarim* 4:9). Thus, what the Haggadah intimates is that if not for the Exodus and God's personal redemption of the Jewish people, "we, our children, and our children's children" — the three parties to whom we are obligated to teach the Torah — instead of being imbued with the values of Torah and purity, would be "subservient to the idolatrous 'Torah' of Pharaoh in Egypt."

הגדה של פסח

עֲבָדִים הָיִינוּ לְפַרְעֹה בְּמִצְרָיִם, וַיּוֹצִיאֵנוּ
ה' אֱלֹהֵינוּ מִשָּׁם בְּיָד חֲזָקָה וּבִזְרוֹעַ נְטוּיָה
We were slaves to Pharaoh in Egypt, but Hashem our God took us out from there with a mighty hand and an outstretched arm.

The Might of Hashem's Hand

This line is a paraphrase of *Devarim* 6:21, which reads exactly: "We were slaves to Pharaoh in Egypt, but Hashem took us out from Egypt with a mighty hand." The most striking difference between the Biblical verse and the Haggadah's version is perhaps the addition of the words "and with an outstretched arm." What was the Haggadah's purpose in introducing these words here? If it sought to amplify the depiction of God's might as it was manifested in the deliverance of our ancestors from Egypt, it could have added other, more dramatic descriptions of God's power and the wonders and miracles of the Exodus. The **Netziv** suggested that the addition was intended to be in line with the requirement that the recounting of the Exodus should be done in a manner in which the narrator "begins with (Israel's) initial indignity and ends with their subsequent prestige" (Mishnah, *Pesachim* 116a), as follows.

The *Mechilta* comments on the words, "God saved Israel on the that day *from the hand* of Egypt" (*Shemos* 14:30): "The situation was like a man who holds a bird in his hand; if he wants to he can kill the bird in an instant. And it was like pulling an embryo out of its mother's womb. . ." What message is the *Mechilta* trying to impart to us with these two comparisons?

The Netziv explains that the *Mechilta* means to tell us that the Torah in this verse is not trying to depict God's might, that it was "so great that He was even able to save Israel from the Egyptians." God is all-powerful, and such a statement would be unnecessary. Rather, the Torah is trying to show the difficulty of the situation at the time. Let us imagine that a big, muscular man has just had his bird stolen by a scrawny weakling. It is no problem for the bird's owner to apprehend the crook and overpower him — but if the robber puts his fingers around the bird's neck and threatens to kill it, all of the muscular man's might will be of no avail. The more force he tries to use, the greater the chance that his bird will be slaughtered. The Jews in Egypt, the *Mechilta* tells us, were in a similar situation. The Talmud tells us that it is for the Jews' own good that God has dispersed them to every corner of the globe, for this way if the Jews in one country are annihilated, there are always more Jews somewhere else (*Pesachim* 87a). But at this time, of course, the entire Jewish people lived in one country — Egypt — and they were held under such total control by the Egyptians that they were in dire danger of instant, total annihilation. It was no problem, of course, for God to rain down plagues and punishments upon the Egyptians, but what was even more amazing was that He was able to do so without allowing the Egyptians to "strangle the bird that was in their hand."

The second metaphor expressed by the *Mechilta* is that of the fetus in its mother's womb. A man might be very strong indeed, but he can hit a pregnant cow on the back as much as he wants and he will not be able to dislodge its fetus before

וּבִזְרֹעַ נְטוּיָה. וְאִלּוּ לֹא הוֹצִיא הַקָּדוֹשׁ בָּרוּךְ הוּא אֶת אֲבוֹתֵינוּ מִמִּצְרַיִם, הֲרֵי אָנוּ וּבָנֵינוּ וּבְנֵי בָנֵינוּ מְשֻׁעְבָּדִים הָיִינוּ לְפַרְעֹה בְּמִצְרָיִם. וַאֲפִילוּ כֻּלָּנוּ חֲכָמִים, כֻּלָּנוּ נְבוֹנִים, כֻּלָּנוּ זְקֵנִים, כֻּלָּנוּ יוֹדְעִים אֶת הַתּוֹרָה, מִצְוָה עָלֵינוּ לְסַפֵּר בִּיצִיאַת מִצְרָיִם.

---

the calf is good and ready to leave the womb. What the analogy means, the Netziv explains, is that just as a fetus is attached (literally) to its mother and has no desire whatsoever to be removed from its womb, so too the Jewish people had many members who wished to remain in Egypt rather than venture forth into the desert towards an unknown promised land. Many Jews, after all, had senior positions with powerful and wealthy men in Egypt, and they themselves led comfortable, contented lives. It was in order to eliminate this class of people, the Midrash tells us, that God brought about the plague of Darkness, so that these men could be stricken down without the Egyptians witnessing it. As powerful and tough as a man might be, he will not be able to rescue a captive from his captors if the prisoner himself does not want to go free! This, then, is the second message that the Torah is alluding to with these words: God delivered the Jews from Egypt despite the resistance of a good many of their number to being rescued.

In what manner did God manage to free the Jews despite these two difficulties mentioned by the *Mechilta*? He did so "with a mighty hand and an outstretched arm."

The "mighty hand," as the Haggadah explains below, refers to the "pestilence," which the Netziv understands to be a reference to the pestilence which God inflicted upon the huge number of Jews who did not want to leave Egypt, during the three days of darkness.

The "outstretched arm" is explained by the Haggadah below as being an allusion to God's "sword." This interpretation put forth by the Haggadah is quite mysterious, as the commentators note, for no sword is mentioned anywhere in the Torah in connection with the Exodus! The Netziv explains that this "sword" was an additional punishment which, according to the Midrash, accompanied each of the ten plagues. The role of this extra punishment, the Netziv writes, was to strike down specific individuals among Pharaoh's advisers who advocated annihilating the Jews ("strangling the bird") as a result of the plague. The only way for the mighty man in the parable to save his bird is to ensure that the robber is constantly overwhelmed and disoriented by blow after blow so that he is unable to muster up enough concentration for even the one second that it takes to kill the defenseless bird.

The Haggadah begins its answer to the child by citing a verse from *Devarim* 6:21: "We were slaves to Pharaoh in Egypt." But in these words the Haggadah sees an allusion to the two obstacles cited by the *Mechilta*. "We were slaves *to Pharaoh*" — most Jews were not slaves to the lower classes, but to powerful government

and an outstretched arm. Had not the Holy One, Blessed is He, taken our fathers out from Egypt, then we, our children, and our children's children would have remained subservient to Pharaoh in Egypt. Even if we were all men of wisdom, understanding, experience, and knowledge of the Torah, it would still be an obligation upon us to tell about the Exodus from Egypt.

---

officials, or even directly *to Pharaoh* himself. This was enough to make them unwilling to leave their comfortable positions and participate in the Exodus. And "we were slaves . . . in Egypt": Unlike today's exiles, the entire Jewish nation lived under the jurisdiction of one extremely powerful and violent country — and were thus under an immediate threat of total annihilation, like the bird in the *Mechilta's* analogy.

These two facts depict quite vividly the indignity of the Jewish people at the time, in two different respects. Spiritually, they had sunk to such a level that they preferred servitude to rich and powerful Egyptian lords over independence and the opportunity of becoming God's chosen nation through the acceptance of the Torah. And physically, their situation was so precarious that they were in imminent danger of perishing completely. Thus, it is an appropriate fulfillment of the Mishnah's requirement to "begin with the initial indignity (of the Jews)."

The Haggadah at this point adds one phrase to the Torah's verse which it had begun to cite, in order to explain how each of these impediments to deliverance were overcome by God. The problem of "We were slaves to Pharaoh" — of masses of people who were unwilling to give up the good life in the palace — was overcome through "the mighty hand," when these individuals were struck down during the plague of Darkness. And the difficulty of "We were slaves. . . in Egypt" — of being as vulnerable as a bird in a villain's grip — was solved through the medium of "the outstretched arm," which delivered constant blows to Pharaoh that were so thorough as to distract him from utilizing his option of annihilating the Jews at once.

וַאֲפִילוּ כֻּלָּנוּ חֲכָמִים, כֻּלָּנוּ נְבוֹנִים, כֻּלָּנוּ זְקֵנִים, כֻּלָּנוּ יוֹדְעִים אֶת הַתּוֹרָה
Even if we were all men of wisdom, understanding, experience, and knowledge of the Torah,

Even a Simple Torah Scholar Is Great

The implication of this statement is that it is possible to have "knowledge of the Torah," and at the same time not to be wise or intelligent. The **Chafetz Chaim** cautioned that although a true Torah scholar must, of course, possess intelligence and wisdom, one should be careful not to scorn those who have gained Torah knowledge without being blessed with these traits.

He recounted that in Volozhin there was a Jew who worked very hard to make a living, but devoted every spare moment to learning Gemara, although not very

וְכָל הַמַּרְבֶּה לְסַפֵּר בִּיצִיאַת מִצְרַיִם, הֲרֵי זֶה מְשֻׁבָּח.

deeply, and after a while he went through the entire *Shas* several times, and would often quote passages from it. The man's understanding of the material left something to be desired, to say the least, but he did go through it nonetheless. When he would enter the *beis midrash*, the Chafetz Chaim related, R' Chaim Volozhiner (the famed disciple of the Vilna Gaon and founder of the Volozhin Yeshivah) would rise from his seat as a sign of respect for the man. His closest students were taken aback by this practice, and they asked him, "Rebbe, before whom are you standing? This man might be familiar with the words of the Talmud, but he does not have a deep understanding of the matters discussed, and he often doesn't understand even the simple meaning of the passage!"

R' Chaim countered their argument with an allegory. "There are many different editions of the Talmud. There is the beautiful Amsterdam edition, renowned for its fine quality, accuracy, and beauty. And then there is the Sulzbach edition, which is infamous for its inferior printing and typographical errors. Should we say that only the Amsterdam *Shas* has the sanctity of being called a holy book, while the Sulzbach *Shas* may be treated like an ordinary secular book? Certainly not! Mistakes or no mistakes, a *Shas* is still a *Shas*. The same applies here as well," R' Chaim concluded. "It is true that this man's knowledge of the Talmud is inferior and wanting in many respects, and even downright wrong in many cases. But this does not take away the fact that he still knows *Shas*!"

The Chafetz Chaim used to apply this lesson on the congregational level as well as the personal level. There are certain groups of Jews with whom we do not agree. We find their methods or deeds to be deficient and lacking in propriety. But as long as they are faithful to the principles of Judaism, and observe all the laws of the Torah, we must accord them due respect for what they do accomplish.

וְכָל הַמַּרְבֶּה לְסַפֵּר בִּיצִיאַת מִצְרַיִם, הֲרֵי זֶה מְשֻׁבָּח
The more one elaborates upon (lit., "enlarges") the discussion of the Exodus, the more he is praiseworthy.

Elaborating on the Exodus

By "enlarging" the discussion of the Exodus, the Haggadah apparently refers to spending more time than the minimum few minutes it takes to simply recite the basic Exodus story. The more time one devotes to this effort the more praiseworthy he is.

However, notes the **Netziv**, this statement of the Haggadah presents a problem. There is a *Baraisa* (Tannaitic dictum) in the *Tosefta* (*Pesachim* 10:8) that states that one is *obligated* to discuss the Exodus, to the best of his ability, all night long (see also *Shulchan Aruch*, O.C. 481:2). This seems to stand in direct contradiction to the assertion of the Haggadah that it is deemed *praiseworthy* — but not obligatory — to "enlarge" the discussion of the Exodus!

The Netziv answered that there is indeed room for "enlarging" this mitzvah beyond its minimum parameters. This is because, as the Haggadah states below, the

The more one elaborates upon the discussion of the Exodus, the more he is praiseworthy.

time frame for fulfilling the mitzvah of recounting the Exodus is specifically "when [*pesach,*] matzah and *maror* are lying before you." The time for eating of the *pesach* sacrifice and of the matzah is clearly delineated, although it is a matter of dispute — according to some Tannaim it ceases at midnight, while according to others it continues until daybreak. If one eats matzah after the appropriate time period has lapsed (for example, after midnight according to the first opinion), he has accomplished nothing at all (and, in fact, may find himself in violation of בַּל תּוֹסִיף, the prohibition to add on to the Torah's delineations of the mitzvos). The mitzvah of recounting the Exodus, the Haggadah informs us here, is unlike that of eating matzah. The required time frame for recounting the Exodus expires, as explained above, at the same time as that for eating matzah — at midnight or at daybreak — but it is not considered to be a meaningless and futile exercise to continue one's discussion of the Exodus even beyond this time; on the contrary, to do so is praiseworthy.

That this is so is borne out by an analysis of the story presented in the next paragraph of the Haggadah. We know that R' Eliezer and R' Elazar ben Azaryah both maintained that the deadline for eating the *pesach* meat (and hence that for eating matzah) is at midnight (*Berachos* 9a). According to the equation laid out by the Haggadah below, that the time frame for recounting the Exodus corresponds to the time frame for eating [*pesach,*] matzah and *maror,* we should expect that these two Sages would maintain that the mitzvah of recounting the Exodus should come to an end at midnight. And in fact, this is exactly what we find in the *Mechilta* (*Bo*): "R' Eliezer says: If the group (assembled at the Seder) is made up of scholars or their students, they must occupy themselves with discussing the laws of Pesach *until midnight.*" Yet in the narrative in the Haggadah, we find R' Eliezer and R' Elazar ben Azaryah themselves participating in the Sages' discussion of the Exodus *all night long*! Why did they not stop at midnight and go to bed? Furthermore, even R' Akiva (another participant at this all-night discussion), who maintains that the time for eating the pesach meat (and matzah) continues until morning, should have stopped his discussion at the first light of day, at which time eating the *pesach* or matzah is no longer permissible. Yet we find that the discussion continued until the time for the recitation of the *Shema*, which is some time after the break of day! These facts show clearly there are two separate issues involved in determining the time frame for recounting the Exodus: It is *obligatory* to discuss the Exodus (or the laws of the *pesach,* etc.) until midnight or daybreak (depending on one's position in that dispute), but it is considered *praiseworthy* to continue this discussion (to "enlarge" it) even beyond this time.

One may ask at this point: Why indeed is it permissible (and even praiseworthy) to "enlarge" this particular mitzvah beyond its defined boundaries, while generally such expansion of a mitzvah's delineated framework is forbidden? Why is it, for instance, that continuing to dwell in the sukkah after the end of Sukkos is prohibited, while carrying on discussing the Exodus beyond midnight (or daybreak) is

מַעֲשֶׂה בְּרַבִּי אֱלִיעֶזֶר וְרַבִּי יְהוֹשֻׁעַ וְרַבִּי אֶלְעָזָר בֶּן עֲזַרְיָה וְרַבִּי עֲקִיבָא וְרַבִּי טַרְפוֹן שֶׁהָיוּ מְסֻבִּין בִּבְנֵי בְרַק, וְהָיוּ מְסַפְּרִים בִּיצִיאַת מִצְרַיִם כָּל אוֹתוֹ הַלַּיְלָה. עַד שֶׁבָּאוּ תַלְמִידֵיהֶם וְאָמְרוּ לָהֶם, רַבּוֹתֵינוּ הִגִּיעַ זְמַן קְרִיאַת שְׁמַע שֶׁל שַׁחֲרִית.

---

countenanced and encouraged? The answer to this question, the Netziv writes, is that besides the mitzvah of *recounting* the Exodus on Pesach night, there is another mitzvah to *recall* the Exodus every single day and every single night of the year. (This mitzvah is accomplished through the recitation of the third paragraph of the *Shema* and the blessing that follows it, in the morning and evening prayers.) Although the daily recalling of the Exodus is a short and simple affair, there is certainly nothing wrong with elaborating upon this recollection and discussing it in greater detail. Thus, if the discussion of the Exodus that begins as a fulfillment of the Pesach mitzvah to recount the Exodus is extended a bit, it can always be seen as an augmentation of the daily mitzvah of recalling the Exodus (which does not cease to apply at midnight).

Using the explanation laid out above, we can suggest an answer to another question, which has been asked concerning the paragraph after the next one: אָמַר רַבִּי אֶלְעָזָר בֶּן עֲזַרְיָה הֲרֵי אֲנִי וכו׳ ("R' Elazar ben Azaryah said: I am like a seventy-year-old man. . ."). This story, quoted from the Mishnah in *Berachos* (12b), deals not with the *Pesach* mitzvah of recounting the story of the Exodus, but with the *daily* mitzvah of recalling the Exodus, and, as such, it has absolutely no relevance to the Haggadah. This enigma has been raised and discussed by nearly every Haggadah commentator. According to what has been explained above, however, we can offer a simple solution to this problem. The Haggadah has just asserted that it is considered meritorious to "enlarge" the recounting of the Exodus, which, as we have explained, means that one should seek to prolong the discussion of the Exodus even beyond its required time frame. But normally the "enlargement" of mitzvos is forbidden! The only reason it is permitted here is that there is another, independent mitzvah that is applicable every day — and every night — which enables us to continue the discussion of the Exodus after midnight (according to R' Elazar ben Azaryah, or after daybreak according to R' Akiva) without fear of impropriety. It is in order to establish this fact that the Haggadah cites the Mishnah from *Berachos*, which speaks of the mitzvah of recalling the Exodus daily, and of its applicability to nights as well as days.

הִגִּיעַ זְמַן קְרִיאַת שְׁמַע
It is time for the reading of the morning Shema.

Saying Shema in Its Proper Time — These great Sages were so engrossed in their discussions that they did not even notice that the time for *Shema* had arrived until their students reminded them.

The **Chafetz Chaim** used to caution people to be careful about not letting the time for *Shema* — which is often rather early in the day — pass them by. This exhortation

It happened that Rabbi Eliezer, Rabbi Yehoshua, Rabbi Elazar ben Azaryah, Rabbi Akiva, and Rabbi Tarfon were gathered (at the Seder) in Bnei Brak. They discussed the Exodus from Egypt all that night until their students came and said to them: "Our teachers, it is [daybreak] time for the reading of the morning Shema."

---

was aimed not only at those who do not get around to saying *Shema* at the proper time out of laziness or lack of care, but also at those who take great care to prepare themselves for their prayers and spend a good deal of time learning or meditating to achieve the proper frame of mind for *davening* (as mentioned in *Berachos* 30b) — if as a result of these preparations the time for *Shema* is missed, that person has lost more than he has gained.

The Chafetz Chaim illustrated this point by way of a parable. Once there was an unsophisticated villager who had an only daughter, whom he loved dearly. He decided during her early childhood that he would begin to set aside a dowry for her so that he would be able to marry her off in style, to a fine young man. He made himself a box, in which he intended to save up the money for the dowry. Whenever he would be paid for his work he would take some of the bills and slip them into the "dowry box," and over the years quite a nice bundle of bills accumulated.

When the girl came of age the villager decided it was time to break open the box and begin to buy the things his daughter would need to prepare herself for marriage. He took several of the finely preserved bills to the local stores and tried to make purchases with them. But the village store owners did not recognize the bills. The man was shocked. "But I worked hard for these bills! I earned them fair and square. Surely they must be legal tender!"

The store owners suggested that the man go to the big city, where he might find a bank that would take the bills and exchange them for something they could accept.

The man obliged and went to the nearest city that same day. As he stood in line he saw that people in front of him were presenting tattered, faded bills to the clerks, who would occasionally scold the owners for their lack of care in preserving the money, but would eventually redeem every bill that they could identify and piece together. The villager was relieved at this sight. Surely his fine, crisp bills, that had been preserved in the box would present no problem at all!

The man's turn finally came. He placed his wad of bills on the countertop and asked the clerk to exchange them for others that would be more acceptable in his village. The clerk took the pile of bills and sifted through them. He then declared to the villager, "These bills are worthless, Mister!"

The villager was dumbfounded. "But I earned them with the sweat of my brow!" he protested. "I preserved them in a box with great care! I saw how you exchanged all those torn, damaged bills for the men before me in line. Yet these fine, shiny bills you reject!"

אָמַר רַבִּי אֶלְעָזָר בֶּן עֲזַרְיָה, הֲרֵי אֲנִי כְּבֶן שִׁבְעִים שָׁנָה, וְלֹא זָכִיתִי שֶׁתֵּאָמֵר יְצִיאַת מִצְרַיִם בַּלֵּילוֹת, עַד שֶׁדְּרָשָׁהּ בֶּן זוֹמָא, שֶׁנֶּאֱמַר, לְמַעַן

The clerk explained the difference to the villager. "Those bills of the customers before you, tattered though they were, are still legal tender in this country. Your bills, however, were disqualified by the government many years ago. They have passed the date of redemption, and are quite worthless!"

The lesson of the parable is that when a person recites the *Shema* and says his prayers during the prescribed times, these prayers may be somewhat "tattered" and deficient in their quality, and it is quite feasible that in Heaven there are complaints and criticisms heard because of these shortcomings — but it is still a valid *Shema* and a valid prayer (as long as the minimum standard of concentration was met). But if someone spends so much time preparing himself to offer a more perfect *Shema* or a more meaningful prayer that he misses the deadline, even if his prayers come out being "fine and crisp" they are no longer acceptable.

אָמַר ר' אֶלְעָזָר בֶּן עֲזַרְיָה וכו'
R' Elazar ben Azaryah said, etc.

Reciting the Haggadah Even if One Is Alone

As discussed above, there are two separate mitzvos in the Torah: (1) to *recall* the Exodus from Egypt every single day; and (2) to *recount* the story of the Exodus on the first night of Pesach. The passage here is quoted from the Mishnah in *Berachos* (12b), which deals not with the mitzvah of *recounting* the story of the Exodus on Pesach, but with the daily mitzvah of *recalling* the Exodus, and as such has no apparent relevance to the Haggadah. We have already cited one possible answer to this difficulty above; here we will cite another solution given by the same Sage, the **Netziv**, which provides insight into some interesting issues regarding this section.

The Netziv begins by asking a very basic question: It is taken for granted that there is a mitzvah to recount the story of the Exodus on the first night of Pesach, as explained in the previous paragraph. But what is the source in the Torah for this mitzvah? The usual verse adduced as a source is, "You shall tell your son on that day, saying: Because of this did Hashem do for me when I went out of Egypt" (*Shemos* 13:8). But using this verse as a source for the mitzvah is problematic, for the following reason.

The Mishnah (*Pesachim* 116a) describes the mitzvah of recounting of the Exodus at the Seder as being carried out through a question-and-answer process: The son asks and the father answers. However, a *Baraisa* (ibid.) teaches that even if one has no son present at the Seder, or is not asked any questions by his son — and even if he is all by himself — he must recount the story of the Exodus nevertheless. Now, all the verses in the Torah that deal with recounting the Exodus speak specifically of a father responding to the queries of his son ("When your son asks you. . ." — *Shemos*

Rabbi Elazar ben Azaryah said: I am like a seventy-year-old man, but I could not succeed in having the Exodus from Egypt mentioned every night, until Ben Zoma expounded it, as it says: "In order that

13:14, ibid., 12:26, *Devarim* 6:20). On what basis, then, does the halachah determine that one is obligated to recount the Exodus even when there are no questions posed by a son? True, there is a fourth verse — the one cited above, in the previous paragraph, from *Shemos* 13:8 — that does not mention a response to a question (this is the verse that the Haggadah assigns to the son "who does not know how to ask questions"), but even in this verse it is a father who is relating the story to his son. We still have no source that covers a situation for a person who has no son at his Seder.

A glance at the words of the Rambam (*Hil. Chametz U'matzah* 7:1-2) will shed light on this question:

> It is a positive commandment to recount the miracles and wonders of the Exodus on the night of the fifteenth of Nisan, as it is written, "Remember this day, on which you went out of Egypt" (*Shemos* 13:3), just as it is written, "Remember the Sabbath day" (ibid., 20:8). And how do we know that this verse refers specifically to the night of the fifteenth (of Nisan)? Because the Torah says, "You shall tell your son on that day, saying, Because of this, etc." — [implying that the verse refers to] a time when matzah and *maror* are lying before you. Even if one has no son, and even if [the assembled] are all great scholars, they are obligated to recount the story of the Exodus.

The Rambam derives the general obligation to recount the story of the Exodus from a completely different source: "Remember this day, on which you went out of Egypt" (*Shemos* 13:3). He mentions the familiar verse ("You shall tell your son on that day. . .") only in order to determine the prescribed *time* for "remembering this day" — namely, at the same time when matzah and *maror* are eaten. For the exhortation to "remember this day," at first glance, could easily be taken to indicate a requirement to remember this day of the Exodus forever, continuously, every day.

But how indeed does the Rambam know that the commandment of "Remember this day" refers to the *Pesach* mitzvah of recounting the Exodus and not to a *daily* mitzvah to recall the Exodus? Another question that is often asked in regard to this passage from the Rambam is: What point is he trying to make by bringing in the verse about Shabbos, by saying, "just as it is written, 'Remember the Sabbath day' "?

The Netziv explained the Rambam's words as follows. There is yet another verse in the Torah that speaks of remembering the Exodus, namely, the verse cited by R' Elazar ben Azaryah in the name of Ben Zoma: "In order that you remember the day when you left Egypt all the days of your life" (*Devarim* 16:3). Now, this verse explicitly calls for remembering the Exodus every day (*all the days of your life*). If so, *Shemos* 13:3 ("Remember this day. . .") cannot be referring to the daily mitzvah of recalling the Exodus, for this is already mandated in *Devarim* 16:3. This is what forced the Rambam to interpret *Shemos* 13:3 as referring to a single, particular time in the year,

תִּזְכֹּר אֶת יוֹם צֵאתְךָ מֵאֶרֶץ מִצְרַיִם כֹּל יְמֵי חַיֶּיךָ.[1] יְמֵי חַיֶּיךָ הַיָּמִים, כֹּל יְמֵי חַיֶּיךָ הַלֵּילוֹת. וַחֲכָמִים אוֹמְרִים, יְמֵי חַיֶּיךָ הָעוֹלָם הַזֶּה, כֹּל יְמֵי חַיֶּיךָ לְהָבִיא לִימוֹת הַמָּשִׁיחַ.

---

just as the word זָכוֹר (*Remember*) is used in the context of Shabbos to indicate a remembrance which takes place not constantly but at a specific time. And when is this specific time for recalling the Exodus? "When matzah and *maror* are lying before you."

To sum up briefly, the derivation of the mitzvah for *all* people (even those without children and even those who are very wise) to recount the Exodus on Pesach night is from *Shemos* 13:3 ("Remember this day. . ."), for all the other, more obvious sources in the Torah speak only of fathers responding to their children's questions. And the only reason we are able to apply this verse to the Pesach mitzvah (as opposed to its more apparent application to the *daily* mitzvah) is that there is already another verse (*Devarim* 16:3, ". . . that you remember the day when you left Egypt all the days of your life") that establishes the requirement for a daily remembrance. Thus, it is *Devarim* 16:3 that begins the whole process of derivation through which we learn that the recounting of the Exodus at the Seder is obligatory for one and all.

The Haggadah has just asserted that, "Even if we were all men of wisdom, understanding, experience, and knowledge of the Torah, it would still be an obligation upon us to tell about the Exodus from Egypt." It is in order to back up that assertion that the Haggadah now cites the discussion between Ben Zoma and the other Sages concerning *Devarim* 16:3, from which it is seen clearly that this verse refers to the daily mitzvah, forcing us to interpret *Shemos* 13:3 (which applies to all situations, even when there are no children or questioners) as a reference to Pesach night.

לְמַעַן תִּזְכֹּר אֶת יוֹם צֵאתְךָ מֵאֶרֶץ מִצְרַיִם כֹּל יְמֵי חַיֶּיךָ
In order that you may remember the day
you left Egypt all the days of your life.

Doing It Right — The Exodus is such an important event in our history that we must recall it every day, twice a day. As the *Chinuch* explains, "[The Exodus] is a major element and a strong pillar in our Torah and in our faith, for it is a sign and an affirmation of God's creation of the world and His continued supervision of it, and that He is able to change whatever forces of nature He desires at any time, as He did in Egypt. . .. By constantly remembering this event we silence any possible doubts that might spring up in our minds concerning the creation of the world, and we strengthen our faith in God and our knowledge of Him. . .."

The moral lesson to be learned from reflection on this matter is expanded upon by *Sefer Chareidim*: "The result of this remembrance is that a person should not think that he is free to do as he wishes, but should be aware that he is a servant to God, Who redeemed him from Egypt for this purpose."

If someone simply recites the words describing the Exodus each morning and

you may remember the day you left Egypt all the days of your life."[1] The phrase "the days of your life" would have indicated only the days; the addition of the word "all" includes the nights as well. But the [other] Sages declare that "the days of your life" would mean only the present world; the addition of "all" includes the days of Mashiach.

---

1. *Devarim* 16:3.

---

night, without attempting to learn their message and instill these ideas in his mind, he is missing a major ingredient in the mitzvah. The **Chafetz Chaim** elucidates this point with a parable:

There was once a poor, unemployed man who was desperate to find some way to earn a living. He approached one of the wealthy men in town and offered his services as an attendant. The rich man informed him, however, that he did not require this man's services. The poor man pleaded with the rich man to reconsider.

The pauper's predicament was so pitiful that it moved the wealthy man to tears. "Very well," he finally agreed. "I will employ you. But under one condition — that you show me complete loyalty and follow my orders with strict precision."

The poor man was delighted at the job offer, and eagerly agreed to this reasonable condition. Over the weeks and months he indeed proved himself to be a most loyal and obedient servant.

One day the rich man told his attendant that he had to go out of town on business for several days. "I made a list of all the things you must do to keep the house in order in my absence," he informed him. "You must follow the instructions to the letter. Every morning and evening look the list over again so that you do not forget any of its details."

"You can rely on me!" the servant reassured him. "You have seen by now that I am trustworthy."

When the wealthy man returned to his house the following week he was shocked to see the house in an utter shambles. The food in the kitchen had rotted, his pet canary had died of neglect, and filth and stench were everywhere. "You have betrayed my trust in you!" the man exclaimed angrily. "You were supposed to have followed my orders!"

"Oh, but I *did* do as you said," said the attendant defensively. "I read the list of instructions carefully every morning and evening, just as you told me to!" To prove his point, the man began to recite the contents of the list by heart: "Clean up the leftover food, feed the canary, wash the floors, dust the furniture, etc."

"Bungling fool!" exclaimed the rich man, now even more annoyed at the servant's ineptness. "Did you really think that reading the list was the main point of my instructions to you? The list was only intended to remind you of the *actions* that you were supposed to take. The constant reading and rereading were only to be an assurance against forgetting what you were to *do*!"

בָּרוּךְ הַמָּקוֹם, בָּרוּךְ הוּא. בָּרוּךְ שֶׁנָּתַן תּוֹרָה לְעַמּוֹ יִשְׂרָאֵל, בָּרוּךְ הוּא. כְּנֶגֶד אַרְבָּעָה בָנִים דִּבְּרָה תוֹרָה – **אֶחָד חָכָם, וְאֶחָד רָשָׁע, וְאֶחָד תָּם, וְאֶחָד שֶׁאֵינוֹ יוֹדֵעַ לִשְׁאוֹל.**

כְּנֶגֶד אַרְבָּעָה בָנִים דִּבְּרָה תוֹרָה
Concerning four sons does the Torah speak —

The Cynic Reacts Instantly

It is interesting to note that the word "tomorrow" appears only in the Torah's description of the dialogue with the wise son ("When your son will ask you *tomorrow*, saying, 'What are the testimonies and decrees. . . that Hashem our God has commanded you?'") and the simple son ("And it shall be that when your son will ask you *tomorrow*, 'What is this?'"). The word does not appear in regard to the wicked son ("And it shall be that when your sons will say to you [not *tomorrow*], 'Of what purpose is this service to you?'") and the son who cannot ask questions ("You shall tell your son on that day [not *tomorrow*]. . ."). What is the significance of this distinction? asked **R' Zalman Sorotzkin**.

R' Zalman began his discussion of this issue by noting that some of the commentators divide the four sons into two basic groups: The first is the "virtuous group," consisting of the wise, righteous son, who displays the proper attitude in his question and receives the most cordial answer, and the simple son who, though lacking the erudition and clarity of the wise son, nevertheless faithfully follows along with the righteous elements of society. The second group is the "corrupt group," consisting of the wicked son, who "removes himself from the community," and the son who is unable to ask, who, though not sharp enough to disparage the service he sees, but is nevertheless drawn after the negative and skeptical outlook of the wicked son. (This is why the wicked son and the son who does not know how to ask are both given the same answer by the Haggadah — וְהִגַּדְתָּ לְבִנְךָ. . . בַּעֲבוּר זֶה עָשָׂה ה' לִי בְּצֵאתִי מִמִּצְרָיִם.)

With this in mind we can now approach the question posed above: Why does the word "tomorrow" appear in connection with the wise son and the simple son (the "virtuous group"), but not in the context of the the "corrupt group"? The answer is that the members of the second group, the bad sons, do not wait to ask their questions until some distant date ("tomorrow," meaning "in the distant future" — *Rashi* to *Shemos* 13:14), many years after the Exodus. Rather, they demonstrate their negative attitudes even while the Exodus is still fresh in their minds. Such is the power of cynicism that one who possesses this trait is capable of detracting from even the most manifest miracle, even while it is happening before his eyes! It is not beyond such people to worship a golden calf right at the foot of Mount Sinai, even as the Torah is being given!

The wise and simple sons, however, ask their questions in the future ("tomor-

> Blessed is the Omnipresent; Blessed is He. Blessed is the One Who has given the Torah to His people Israel; Blessed is He. Concerning four sons does the Torah speak — one is wise, one is wicked, one is simple, and one is unable to ask.

row"), when the Exodus is a distant, dim memory in the minds of the nation. They long to understand the traditions that connect them to generations past, ultimately stretching back to the time of the Exodus from Egypt, and to relate to them and participate in them.

> כְּנֶגֶד אַרְבָּעָה בָנִים דִּבְּרָה תוֹרָה – אֶחָד חָכָם,
> וְאֶחָד רָשָׁע, וְאֶחָד תָּם, וְאֶחָד שֶׁאֵינוֹ יוֹדֵעַ לִשְׁאוֹל
> Concerning four sons does the Torah speak — one is wise,
> one is wicked, one is simple, and one is unable to ask

A Father's Obligation Extends to All of His Sons

The Haggadah's presentation of the four sons seems a bit longwinded on account of the fourfold repetition of the word "one is" (אֶחָד). It would have been so much less complicated to say, כְּנֶגֶד אַרְבָּעָה בָנִים דִּבְּרָה תוֹרָה – חָכָם, רָשָׁע, תָּם, וְשֶׁאֵינוֹ יוֹדֵעַ לִשְׁאוֹל. (Although the English translation would come out more or less the same — "The Torah speaks of four different children — a wise one, a wicked one, a simple one, and one who is unable to ask," the Hebrew would be reduced from 10 words to 6!) What is the reason for the Haggadah's use of this mode of expression? This question was raised by **R' Zalman Sorotzkin**.

The word אֶחָד, R' Zalman notes, besides its basic meaning of "one," is also sometimes used in the sense of "whether X or Y," or "not only X, but even Y." This is in fact the most common meaning of the word when it is repeated several times in a sentence in consecutive phrases (see *Tosafos*, *Berachos* 11a). For instance, the Mishnah (*Shabbos* 20b) teaches that one may not light a Shabbos candle made of animal fats, "whether the fat has been cooked (melted) or has not been cooked" (אֶחָד מְבֻשָּׁל וְאֶחָד שֶׁאֵינוֹ מְבֻשָּׁל), or, more precisely, "not only when it has not been cooked (for solid fat does not make good fuel for a candle), but even when it has been cooked (and liquefied fat does make good fuel)."

This is how the word should be understood in this context in the Haggadah as well, R' Zalman asserted. One might have reasoned that if one's son is wise and well versed in the Torah there is no need to relate the story of the Exodus to him. After all, he has been taught this material in school so many times, and his A+ average shows that he has certainly learned the lesson well. On the other hand, one might have adopted the opposite position: A wise son can always gain an added insight to what he knows already when he reviews it yet again — "Give [knowledge] to the wise man and he will become even wiser" (*Mishlei* 9:9). But when confronted with the hostility and cynicism of the wicked son, what is the

חָכָם מָה הוּא אוֹמֵר? מָה הָעֵדֹת וְהַחֻקִּים וְהַמִּשְׁפָּטִים אֲשֶׁר צִוָּה יהוה אֱלֹהֵינוּ אֶתְכֶם?[1] וְאַף אַתָּה אֱמָר לוֹ כְּהִלְכוֹת הַפֶּסַח, אֵין מַפְטִירִין אַחַר הַפֶּסַח אֲפִיקוֹמָן.

---

point of telling him the story of the Exodus? He will in any event not believe or accept what we relate to him! Similar arguments might be advanced for the simple son and the son who does not know how to ask questions: What is the use of explaining anything to these dullards; they will not understand the point in any event! The Haggadah therefore tells us that the Torah rejects all these approaches; a father's obligation to relate the story of the Exodus to his children applies *whether* (אֶחָד) the son is wise, whether he is wicked, whether he is simple, or is incapable of asking questions. There is always some advantage (albeit a different one in each of the four cases) to be gained in relating the story of the Exodus, for any son, in any generation.

מָה הָעֵדֹת וְהַחֻקִּים וְהַמִּשְׁפָּטִים אֲשֶׁר צִוָּה ה' אֱלֹהֵינוּ אֶתְכֶם
What are the testimonies, decrees, and ordinances which Hashem, our God, has commanded you?

It All Depends on Who Is Talking

The wicked son was chastised for his use of the word "to you," from which we inferred that he himself is not interested in participating in the Pesach celebration and that he has thereby separated himself from the community. But the wise son also says "that Hashem, our God, has commanded *you*"! Why do we not criticize him for his choice of words as well? The **Chafetz Chaim** answered this question by means of a parable.

Once there was a businessman who owned a small glassware store. As the years went by he began to do quite well and was able to invest a respectable sum of money into his store. He enlarged the showroom, expanded and upgraded his stock, refurbished the store inside and out, and built two large, stunning display windows at the storefront. Meanwhile, his less successful competitor across the street watched jealously as improvement after improvement proceeded, and after this he stood by helplessly as a steady stream of customers frequented the other store as they walked right by his. He was green with envy, but powerless to do anything about the situation.

One day a favored customer came to the big store to place a large order for a huge amount of money. On the way out of the store he slipped on the marble floor and fell right onto the display window, smashing it and breaking many of the items in the window as well. The storeowner and his employees rushed out to help the man to his feet and brush him off. They examined him carefully to ensure that he had not incurred any injury as a result of all the broken glass. They calmed him down from the shock of the fall and reassured him that he need not concern

The wise son — what does he say? "What are the testimonies, decrees, and ordinances which HASHEM, our God, has commanded you?"[1] Therefore explain to him the laws of the pesach offering: that one may not eat dessert after the final taste of the pesach offering.

---

1. *Devarim* 6:20.

---

himself over the damaged goods. "These things happen; we must do something about that floor; we will fix the window and replace the broken items; don't worry about a thing; etc."

The competitor watched the whole sequence of events from his store across the street, and came up with a "brilliant" idea. . ..

The next day the competitor crossed the street and passed by the big store. Suddenly he "accidentally" slipped on the same flooring, smashing the other display window, by which he "happened" to destroy a large amount of merchandise. To his shock, however, he was not as lucky as the customer who had fallen the previous day. He was cut badly by the shards of glass and bled extensively. He waited there for the storekeeper and his assistants to come to his aid and hurry to forgive him for the "accident." But instead they came over and reprimanded him with shouts and curses, informing him that he would be charged for every last penny of the damage he caused. The police were summoned immediately.

"I don't understand," he said, still dripping with blood. "Yesterday a man broke the other window and was not even hurt, and yet you ran over to comfort him and ensure him that all would be taken care of. Here I have undergone the identical fall as he did, and you are shouting curses at me, and charging me for damages to boot! This is simply unfair!"

"Nonsense!" answered the other storekeeper angrily. "The man who fell yesterday was an established customer, who brings me large volumes of business, and will hopefully continue to do so in the future. For such a person it is appropriate and wise to overlook his clumsiness. But you are a jealous competitor, and all the evidence points to the likelihood that you staged your fall deliberately! And anyway, even if you did fall by accident, you are legally bound to pay for damages, and I have no reason whatsoever to waive this substantial debt."

This story may be compared to the case of the wise son versus the wicked son. The wise son was not born yesterday. We are familiar with him and his behavior patterns for several years. He basically upholds the mitzvos and conducts himself with fear of God. Even if he occasionally "slips" and uses a word which can be construed as conveying negative overtones we are prepared to overlook the choice of words and assume that no harm was intended. But when the wicked son, who shows scorn and contempt for his heritage and is known to have a negative outlook, uses the same expression, we are justified in interpreting his words according to their negative insinuation and in holding him fully responsible for this.

רָשָׁע מָה הוּא אוֹמֵר? מָה הָעֲבֹדָה הַזֹּאת לָכֶם? —[1]

רָשָׁע מַה הוּא אוֹמֵר? מָה הָעֲבוֹדָה הַזֹּאת לָכֶם
The wicked son — what does he say?
"Of what purpose is this service to you?"

A Question or a Rejection

The wicked son expresses his wonderment over the ritual of the *pesach* sacrifice, as the context of this verse (*Shemos* 12:26) makes clear. Actually, the wicked son poses a decent question, the **Netziv** pointed out. Sacrifices are generally intended to achieve atonement for sin. Even the so-called "peace-offering" effects atonement in a certain sense (as the Netziv explained in his commentary on the Torah, *Ha'amek Davar*). The *Ma'aser Beheimah* (animal-tithe) sacrifice, and the offering of firstborn animals, although not intended for atonement, also have a clear rationale behind them. Rendering the firstborn of one's cattle to God is an expression of the appreciation and acceptance of the fact that God is the first Being of the Universe, both in the temporal and causal sense. And by designating *Ma'aser Beheimah* for God we recognize our indebtedness to Him for all the bounty with which He has blessed us. Thanksgiving offerings are, of course, intended to show our gratitude to God for some specific incident where we have benefited from His grace in a particularly manifest manner.

But what is the point of the *pesach* sacrifice? the wicked son wonders. What is it supposed to accomplish? As far as the very first *pesach* sacrifice, offered in Egypt, is concerned, its purpose was understandable. As the Midrash tells us, when the time came for the Jews to be liberated from Egypt they were found to be totally devoid of merit that might justify God's intervention on their behalf, and He therefore gave the people two mitzvos — circumcision and the *pesach* sacrifice — with which to occupy themselves in order to "earn" their deliverance. Alternatively, the original *pesach* sacrifice can be seen as a sort of thanksgiving offering, as the Rosh mentions (*Pesachim* 10:30, in explaining why we use three matzos at the Seder; the thanksgiving sacrifice was accompanied by three types of unleavened bread.) After all, one of the occasions for which one is supposed to bring a thanksgiving offering is when he is released from imprisonment (*Berachos* 54b), and the Exodus from Egypt is a prime example of this sort of situation. But expressions of thanksgiving are appropriate only at the time of the salvation involved, not as a yearly commemoration thereafter (as the Netziv showed in his commentary to the *She'iltos, Ha'amek She'alah, Hil. Chanukah*). It is for this reason that the wicked son asks, "Of what purpose is this sacrificial service *to you*?" In other words, "As far as the original *pesach* sacrifice that the Jews brought in Egypt is concerned, I can understand the reason of that offering *for them,* but what is its point *for you,* nowadays?

Having explained the wicked son's question so clearly and insightfully, a problem arises at this point: Why is this son called "wicked" if all he did was to ask a good question? The answer, as the Haggadah notes, is that his choice of the words "to you" shows that he excludes himself from participation in the mitzvah with the rest of the community. He could have made the same point by saying, "What is this

The wicked son — what does he say? "Of what purpose is this service to you?"[1] — [implying]

1. *Shemos* 12:26.

sacrificial service for *us* nowadays?" There is a great difference between *questioning* and *rejecting,* and the use of the word "you" shows clearly that it is the latter that this son intends to do. This is what brands him as a wicked son, for while it is acceptable, and even commendable, to seek the explanations and symbolisms behind the Torah's mitzvos, it is unacceptable to reject any part of the Torah simply because it does not appeal to our own intellectual disposition.

מָה הָעֲבֹדָה הַזֹּאת לָכֶם? – לָכֶם וְלֹא לוֹ
"Of what purpose is this service to you?" —
[implying] "to you," but not "to him."

In Proper Context

The wicked son is taken to task because of his use of the expression "to you." Reading into his words, we detect a note of detachment from and disinterest in the observances of Pesach. But elsewhere in the Torah we find similar expressions, **R' Zalman Sorotzkin** noted, and no sinister insinuation is attached to those words. When a farmer harvests his crops (of one of the seven species listed in *Devarim* 8:8) he is supposed to take the first-ripening specimens of those crops (which he had identified at the beginning of the growing season) to the Temple and announce to the Kohen, "I declare this day, before Hashem, *your* God. . . ." In this case the Sages do not disapprove of the choice of words, objecting to, " '*your* God,' but not '*my* God'!?" And similarly in *Bereishis* 27:20, Yaakov tells his father, "Hashem, *your* God, made it available for me."

R' Zalman answered this question by noting that each of these verses must be examined in its own context. When the farmer brings his first-ripened crops to Jerusalem, he stands in awe before the officiating Kohen (in fact according to *Targum Yonasan,* the verse is speaking of the *Kohen Gadol*) in the magnificent and awe-inspiring atmosphere of the Temple courtyard, and phrases his words with the utmost reverence and deference. He turns to this representative of God and declares, "You spend your days and nights in the Temple, totally immersed in the service of God. I, who spend my days and nights tilling the soil and performing other mundane tasks, have come here to thank God for his beneficence, and to learn from you how to worship Him in the most proper manner." In this context it is indeed appropriate to refer to God as "your God," without implying any negative connotations whatsoever. Similarly, when Yitzchak asked his son to bring him meat to eat as a prelude to the blessings he sought to bestow upon him, it was no ordinary culinary feast in which Yitzchak was interested in indulging himself. Eating this meat was a form of service before God (the Sages tell us that it was a *pesach* sacrifice), through which Yitzchak would be able to muster up the spiritual powers necessary to confer the awesome blessings of Avraham upon his son and successor. In this situation as well, it was entirely fitting for Yaakov to tell him,

לָכֶם וְלֹא לוֹ, וּלְפִי שֶׁהוֹצִיא אֶת עַצְמוֹ מִן הַכְּלָל,

"*Your* God made it available for me, to bring to you for His service." But the wicked son, when he asks (or, more precisely, "declares" — כִּי יֹאמְרוּ אֲלֵיכֶם בְּנֵיכֶם; see following piece), "What is this service to you," he is addressing himself to his father and brothers (who are apparently in one of the other categories of sons), and everyone else who has gathered together to participate in this *pesach* ceremony. It is not out of deference, then, that he chooses this expression, but out of contempt and derision.

מָה הָעֲבֹדָה הַזֹּאת לָכֶם? — לָכֶם וְלֹא לוֹ
"Of what purpose is this service to you?" —
[implying] "to you," but not to him.

The Wicked Son — The first of the four times the Torah deals with the obligation of fathers to teach their children about the Exodus we read: "And it shall be that when your sons will say to you, 'Of what purpose is this service to you?' you shall say, 'It is a *pesach* sacrifice unto Hashem, Who passed over the houses of the Children of Israel when he struck the Egyptians and saved our houses'" (*Shemos* 12:26-27). The Haggadah determines that this passage relates to the wicked son, based on the inference of "to *you*," but not "to *me*." But there are several other factors present in this verse that indicate this as well, **R' Zalman Sorotzkin** noted.

First, this is the only one of the four parallel passages that says, "When your sons will *say* to you," rather than, "When your sons will *ask* you." The other sons are interested in hearing an answer to their question; this son has no such concern. He already knows all the answers. He wants *us* to hear *his* opinion, not vice versa. Therefore he does not ask his father anything; rather, he *states* his rhetorical "question" to all those around him: "Of what purpose is this service to you?"

Second, this is the only one of the four selections that refers to "sons" in the plural, as opposed to "your son." Unfortunately, the Torah foresaw that the time would come when the masses of people would fit into this category more than into any of the others.

Third, this question is the one that will be posed "when you come to the land that God will give you" (ibid., 12:25). When the Jews are in exile from their homeland we might be able to condone questions concerning the appropriateness of celebrating our freedom from Pharaoh's bondage at a time when we have so many other "Pharaohs" ruling over us — some of them being much worse than the original one! We can understand the resistance of the son who expresses astonishment over the Pesach celebrations in such situations. But "when you come to the land that God will give you," when you are still enjoying complete, obvious benefit from your miraculous Exodus from Egypt, when you have so much to be thankful for — if your son puts forth this question under *those* circumstances, this is nothing but a sign of ungratefulness and irreverence toward God.

"to you," but not to him. By excluding himself from the community of believers, he denies the basic

מָה הָעֲבדָה הַזֹּאת לָכֶם
"Of what purpose is this service to you?"

Never Discard a Mitzvah

Why is the wicked son's question considered so improper? After all, he is only trying to reduce the yoke of Torah observance by concentrating more on the underlying concept and less on the ritualistic details.

The **Chafetz Chaim** illustrated the problem behind the wicked son's statement with a parable:

A man walked into a store and began hauling away loads of merchandise and throwing it into a nearby river. Those who witnessed the man's odd behavior looked on with pity. "The poor man. He must have lost his mind!" they thought.

There was one wise man among them who corrected their oversimplified conclusion. "It is not absolutely certain that the man is insane," he remarked. "But one thing is for sure — the man who is throwing the merchandise into the river is not the owner of the store!"

This is how we look at the wicked son's attitude as well. When someone shows a willingness to do away with even one of the mitzvos of the Torah he shows clearly that this "merchandise" is not his; with his words he betrays his attitude that this service is "yours," not his.

וּלְפִי שֶׁהוֹצִיא אֶת עַצְמוֹ מִן הַכְּלָל, כָּפַר בְּעִקָּר
By excluding himself from the community of believers he denies the basic principle of Judaism.

On Leaving the Community

The Haggadah makes two assertions here in connection with the wicked son: (1) He has removed himself from the community, and (2) he has denied a basic principle of Judaism. What is the basis for this harsh verdict? All this son did was to express cynicism about the *pesach* sacrifice; why does this remove him from the community of Israel and make him a denier of a basic principle of faith?

R' Zalman Sorotzkin addressed the first difficulty as follows. Sacrifices may be divided into two categories — public offerings and private offerings. Usually it is quite clear to which category a given sacrifice belongs. A private offering is one undertaken by an individual (or a group of individuals), at their own expense. A public offering, on the other hand, is one that is offered on behalf of the nation at large, and bought at public expense (paid for by the money of the *"Terumas Halishkah,"* that fund that contained the annual half-shekel donations of each and every Jewish man). One practical difference between the two classes of offerings is that public sacrifices are generally (see, however, *Yoma* 50a) permitted on Shabbos and are permitted to be carried out even when the individuals involved

כָּפַר בְּעִקָּר – וְאַף אַתָּה הַקְהֵה אֶת שִׁנָּיו וֶאֱמָר לוֹ,

are ritually impure, while private sacrifices do not have these two leniencies. The *pesach* sacrifice is unique in that it is considered a public sacrifice (for every eligible Jew must participate in it), as evidenced by the fact that it is offered even on Shabbos and even when a majority of the congregation has become ritually defiled — yet it is brought on an individual basis, at the individual's expense. By not participating in the *pesach* sacrifice, then, the wicked son is doing much more than simply adopting a personal stance regarding a particular observance in Judaism; he is affecting the community as a whole, for through his lack of participation he causes this "public sacrifice" to apply to less than the entire community, thus detracting from its overall quality.

As far as the Haggadah's second charge against the wicked son, that he has denied a basic principle of Judaism, R' Zalman explained that by withdrawing from participation in the *pesach* sacrifice the wicked son puts himself in the company of those mentioned in the Torah's exhortation: "Any alien shall not partake of [the *pesach* sacrifice]," which, as the Sages tell us, means to exclude "any person whose ideas are alien before God," i.e., a heretic. Furthermore, one of the basic foundations of the Jewish faith is the belief in the fact that God took us out of Egypt (hence the first of the Ten Commandments: "I am Hashem, your God, Who took you out of the land of Egypt"). By refusing to be involved with the *pesach* sacrifice — and scoffing at others who do perform this precept — the wicked son is indirectly denying this basic principle.

וּלְפִי שֶׁהוֹצִיא אֶת עַצְמוֹ מִן הַכְּלָל וְכוּ' וְאַף אַתָּה הַקְהֵה אֶת שִׁנָּיו
By excluding himself from the community . . .
Therefore, blunt his teeth

Beyond Rehabilitation — Many people ask: Is it proper to simply abandon the wicked son and to deal with him with hostility? Perhaps a little warmth would bring him back into the fold.

The **Chafetz Chaim** explained this situation with an analogy to a cholera epidemic. Cholera is an extremely contagious disease, but fortunately there are those who are willing to risk their own health to care for those are stricken by the debilitating illness, although this care involves extensive physical contact with the affected person. But this is only as long as the patient is still alive. Once he has breathed his last breath, however, his body is hurriedly and unceremoniously disposed of, so as to avoid the spread of the epidemic.

The same applies to our care for the spiritually ill among us. It is a great and holy obligation for us to attempt to reach out to those who have become distanced from the ways of Torah and Judaism, and to try to show them the true path. But once a person has reached the level of "removing himself from the community" and "denying the basic principles of Judaism," he is to be shunned and ostracized, for the dangers of working with such a person outweigh the chances of success.

principle of Judaism. Therefore, blunt his teeth and tell him:

וְאַף אַתָּה הַקְהֵה אֶת שִׁנָּיו וֶאֱמָר לוֹ
Therefore, blunt his teeth and tell him . . .

Remove the Alluring Forbidden Fruits

The Torah says simply, "And you shall tell your son on that day, saying. . .." On what does the Haggadah base the need to "blunt his teeth"? Furthermore, what sort of punishment or action is "blunting his teeth," and what is it supposed to accomplish?

R' Zalman Sorotzkin explained the idea behind this difficult passage. A heretic who denies the Torah is of course free (in his own eyes) from all restrictions imposed by the Torah. This obviously allows him to lead a much easier lifestyle. The question that always arises in such cases is: Did this person arrive at his ideological position based on sound logical premises and then, as a result of his beliefs, adopt a Torah-free lifestyle? Or perhaps the sequence was the other way around: The person, tempted by all the pleasures that could be his if he would only reject the Torah, saw to it that the appropriate ideological position be arrived at that might enable him to partake of those forbidden pleasures.

Experience teaches us that usually it is the latter scenario that is the accurate depiction of events; the ideology is invented to justify the desired goal. The Haggadah teaches us the remedy for this kind of heretical outlook: "Blunt his teeth." Taking away the person's teeth, thus robbing him of the ability to enjoy those forbidden fruits that lured him away from his religion in the first place, will enable the wicked son to reconsider matters from a more unbiased, rational point of view. Thus, although the Torah does not explicitly call for this action, the Haggadah informs us that *before* we can hope to deal with the wicked son's problem with his faith, before we can even begin to tell him, "Because of this Hashem did for me when I went out of Egypt," we must first strike at the root of this individual's problem and "blunt his teeth" (a metaphor for the removal of physical temptation).

הַקְהֵה אֶת שִׁנָּיו
blunt his teeth

Teaching a Lesson

This violent reaction seems to be a bit extreme. What of the verse that states, "The words of the wise are heard through gentleness" (*Koheles* 9:17)? Wouldn't gentle persuasion be more effective than such unremitting harshness?

The **Chafetz Chaim** answered this question with the following parable. A man was once passing by the back entrance of a large wedding hall. The rear service door was wide open, and the man happened to cast a glance into the large, bustling kitchen. "What a large banquet this must be!" he thought to himself, marveling at the huge amount of food being prepared for serving. Just then he saw a horrifying sight that shocked him thoroughly. There was a poisonous snake

בַּעֲבוּר זֶה עָשָׂה יהוה לִי בְּצֵאתִי מִמִּצְרָיִם. לִי וְלֹא לוֹ, אִלּוּ הָיָה שָׁם לֹא הָיָה נִגְאָל.

perched over the huge vat of soup sitting on the stove. The man wasted no time and ran around to the main entrance of the hall, ran inside, and ascended the podium. "I have an important announcement to make!" he shouted urgently. "I was just in the kitchen and I saw a poisonous snake poised right above one of the pots! Everyone must refrain from eating the soup, for it may contain some of the animal's deadly venom!"

A commotion stirred among the startled guests. The band stopped playing, the people stopped dancing, and everyone paused to assess the situation. No one dared to touch the soup that had just been brought to the table. The man was very pleased with himself, realizing that he had saved the large gathering from illness or even death.

Suddenly, however, one of the guests, a cynical type who liked to take life easy and did not bother with extraneous matters such as safety precautions, approached the podium and, with a calm look on his face, reprimanded this "intruder" for ruining the party. "Why are you frightening the guests?" he demanded. Then, turning to the people in the hall, he announced, "There is no cause for alarm. This man was only kidding! What a joke! A snake in the kitchen, of all things!"

The people in the hall began to laugh. It was a party, after all, and sometimes people make jokes at parties. Calm was restored, the band resumed its playing, and the guests began reaching for the soup once again.

The man who had come in from outside was astounded. What was he to do now? How could he convince the guests of his sincerity after this other man had rendered his warning meaningless? He quickly realized that he had no choice but to smack the man squarely in the face. This would prove to everyone conclusively that this was no joke. He did exactly that, and the lives of the guests were saved.

The situation with the wicked son is analogous to that of the man in the parable. Sometimes, unfortunately, we find ourselves in a situation where we must act with force in order to counter the dangerous statements made by malicious or irresponsible individuals, who endanger the health — physical or spiritual — of others.

לִי וְלֹא לוֹ
"To me," but not for him

Reinforcing the Righteous

The wording of the Haggadah seems to be inexact. Since we are discussing the answer given to the wicked son's question, it would have been more accurate to have said, " 'To me,' but not 'to *you*.' " Why does the Haggadah tell us to speak of the wicked son in the third person (*him*), rather than address him directly in the second person (*you*)? The same question may be asked concerning the next phrase: "Had *he* been there *he* would not have been redeemed." The commentators explain that the

> "It is because of this that HASHEM did so for me when I went out of Egypt."[1] "To me," but not for him — had he been there, he would not have been redeemed.

1. *Shemos* 13:8.

---

wicked son is not interested in hearing answers to his "questions"; he simply registers his grievances and goes on his way. Listening to arguments and challenges to his position, however truthful they may be, does not concern him.

A story is told concerning the **Chafetz Chaim** that illustrates this point.

There was a learned, pious man in Radin (the Chafetz Chaim's village), named R' Moshe Binyamin, who worked for the Chafetz Chaim, traveling from town to town selling the sage's books. The Chafetz Chaim made a special request of R' Moshe Binyamin — that besides simply selling the books he should address the public wherever he goes and try to instill within his audience the importance of studying the Torah and keeping its mitzvos. R' Moshe Binyamin was a salesman, and was not thrilled about taking on the role of itinerant preacher as well, but he of course honored the Chafetz Chaim's wishes.

One time R' Moshe Binyamin returned to Radin from one of his excursions and went to report to the Chafetz Chaim. "I sold this many *Chafetz Chaims,* and that many *Mishnah Berurahs,*" he told him. "But I would like to request of the Rebbe that I be relieved of the duty to preach as I travel. I see that these speeches make no effect upon the populace in any event!"

"Words of Torah are compared to the rain and the dew," the Chafetz Chaim told him. "There is no doubt that they are beneficial, but the results are not seen immediately. It takes time for such messages to sink in."

"I understand your point, Rebbe," answered R' Moshe Binyamin. "But this is only true when the people who are weak in their commitment to Torah and mitzvos are at least present in the audience to benefit from the life-giving 'rain'! But these days such people don't even go near a synagogue; my words don't reach them at all.

"I'll give you an example," R' Moshe Binyamin continued. "Last week I arrived at a certain place and was told by the residents that there was a terrible breach in Shabbos observance in town. A local chemist, a Jew, would light his furnaces on Shabbos — in public. I spent the following Shabbos in that town and admonished the congregation concerning the severity of Shabbos desecration. I explained to them that someone who violated the Shabbos publicly was deemed to be a complete denier of Judaism. The audience was very moved, and I thought for a while that I had actually accomplished something. But then I learned that the man in question never comes to the synagogue. All my words were not even heard by the one for whom they were intended."

"R' Moshe Binyamin, may you be blessed for your accomplishments!" the Chafetz Chaim declared comfortingly. "You are under the impression that when I asked you to speak to the communities in which you visit that I wish you to influence people such as that chemist and his likes. But this is not so! I am well

תָּם מָה הוּא אוֹמֵר? מַה זֹּאת? וְאָמַרְתָּ אֵלָיו, בְּחֹזֶק יָד הוֹצִיאָנוּ יהוה מִמִּצְרַיִם מִבֵּית עֲבָדִים.¹

וְשֶׁאֵינוֹ יוֹדֵעַ לִשְׁאוֹל, אַתְּ פְּתַח לוֹ. שֶׁנֶּאֱמַר, וְהִגַּדְתָּ לְבִנְךָ בַּיּוֹם הַהוּא לֵאמֹר, בַּעֲבוּר זֶה עָשָׂה יהוה לִי בְּצֵאתִי מִמִּצְרָיִם.²

---

aware of the fact that such people are not to be found in audiences that come to hear itinerant preachers! My intention is rather that you should have an influence upon the other people in town, to strengthen their resolve so they are not adversely influenced by such acts of impiety."

The same applies to the wicked son in the Haggadah. He is not even present to hear our "speech"; we therefore address ourselves to those who *are* assembled here and have heard his sacrilegious pronouncements, to protect them from his negative influence. "If *he* were there," we assure them, "*he* would not have been redeemed."

וְשֶׁאֵינוֹ יוֹדֵעַ לִשְׁאוֹל, אַתְּ פְּתַח לוֹ

As for the son who is unable to ask, you must initiate the subject for him (lit., you open up for him).

Encourage Your Child

What does the Haggadah mean by the odd expression "opening up for him"? The **Netziv** explained that this expression is based on *Mishlei* 31:8: "Open up your mouth for the mute one." That verse employs a figure of speech, and refers to someone who is unaware of his options ("mute") in the face of legal proceedings. We are enjoined to speak with *our* mouths to him so that he may learn how to present his position with *his* mouth. Here too, the Haggadah intimates to us that we should try to engage the "son who is unable to ask" in conversation and try to prod him into asking the questions that he has not been able to formulate on his own.

But how does the Haggadah know that this is the approach to be taken with the "son who is unable to ask"? Where does it see this idea insinuated in the words of the Torah?

The Netziv answers that the Haggadah derives this outlook from the word וְהִגַּדְתָּ (and you shall tell). The three-letter root of the word is נגד, meaning "to draw something out." The fact that the Torah uses this word rather than the more common וְאָמַרְתָּ ("and you shall say"), as it does for the other three sons (*Shemos* 12:27, ibid., 13:14, *Devarim* 6:21), alludes to the fact that we are expected to "draw out" words from his mouth, encouraging him to ask questions to which we can respond.

The simple son — what does he say? "What is this?" Tell him: "With a strong hand did HASHEM take us out of Egypt, from the house of bondage."[1]

And as for the son who is unable to ask, you must initiate the subject for him, as it says: You shall tell your son on that day, saying: "It is because of this that HASHEM did so for me when I went out of Egypt."[2]

---

1. *Shemos* 13:14. 2. Ibid. v. 8.

וְשֶׁאֵינוֹ יוֹדֵעַ לִשְׁאוֹל, אַתְּ פְּתַח לוֹ
And as for the one who is unable to ask,
you must initiate the subject for him,

The Teacher's Obligation

The commentators note that the word the Haggadah uses here for "you" is אַתְּ, which is usually the form used when speaking to a woman, rather than the usual masculine form, אַתָּה. **R' Zalman Sorotzkin** accounted for this anomaly as follows. One might have supposed that when dealing with a dull child, one who is not even on the level that he can ask questions, it is sufficient to "initiate the subject" on a very superficial level. The Haggadah therefore uses the word אַתְּ, which consists of the first and last letters of the alphabet, in order to intimate that this sort of approach is inadequate, and that the entire story with all of its implications must be set before him, "from A to Z," even though this may involve a more challenging and time-consuming task than with a son of greater intelligence.

וְהִגַּדְתָּ לְבִנְךָ בַּיּוֹם הַהוּא
You shall tell your son on that day. . ..

The Exodus and the Final Redemption

The Rambam writes in *Hil. Chametz U'matzah* (7:1): "It is a positive commandment to relate the miracles and wonders that were done for our forefathers in Egypt on the night of the fifteenth of Nisan, as it says, 'Remember this day on which you went out of Egypt' (*Shemos* 13:3), just as it says, 'Remember the Sabbath day' (ibid., 20:8)." The Rambam thus cites two Biblical verses in connection with this mitzvah — one referring to the Exodus and the other concerning the Sabbath day. **R' Shneur Kotler** addressed the question asked by numerous commentators: Why does the Rambam cite the verse about the Sabbath day altogether? What deeper insight are we supposed to gain from this second verse beyond what is seen plainly in the first verse?

In dealing with this question, R' Shneur began by noting a curious line in the *Yotzros* prayers for *Shabbos Hagadol*: "My lips will sing out with a new song and with uttering midrashic explanations, when I see the 'four craftsmen' (who will herald in the Messianic era — *Zechariah* 2:3ff)." The "new song" to be sung on the day of the Messianic redemption is mentioned in the Haggadah as well (below, p. 165). But what exactly is meant by "the uttering of midrashic explanations"? We know of the central role played by midrashic explanations in the recounting of the Exodus, for such discussions fill the bulk of the Haggadah text. But how can the expounding of Biblical verses be relevant to the Messianic era? The miracles involved in that process will be beheld by our very eyes; what need will there be to derive them from Biblical allusions?

A further question raised by R' Shneur relates to the argument between Ben Zoma and the other Sages, recorded in *Berachos* 12b and cited in the Haggadah above (p. 78). Ben Zoma held that the miracles of the future redemption will so dwarf the miracles of the Exodus from Egypt that the latter will not be mentioned at all anymore at that time. This he derives from the verse, "Behold, days are coming, says Hashem, when it will no longer be said, 'As Hashem lives, Who took us out of the land of Egypt,' but rather, 'As Hashem lives, Who took out the Children of Israel from the lands of the north and from all the lands where He had scattered them' " (*Yirmiyahu* 16:14-15). The other Sages, however, were of the opinion that although the future miracles would overshadow those of the Exodus, the daily recollection of the Exodus which is mandated by the Torah in the present will not be discontinued at that time; rather, it will become of secondary importance. The question is: According to the other Sages, how can it be possible that the daily recollection of the Exodus — which is a Torah commandment, and will always remain so — be of secondary importance in comparison to the remembrance of events of the Messianic era, which is not a commandment at all?

To answer all these questions, we must realize that within Moshe's mission to go to Pharaoh and free the Jews from Egypt lay the seeds of all future deliverances and salvations, down to the final redemption in Messianic times. In fact, the Rambam explains that the reason Moshe was so hesitant to accept the task God assigned to him (*Shemos* 4:10ff) was that he realized that he would not be able to accomplish the goal — namely, absolute deliverance — to the fullest extent. (This was not due to any shortcoming on the part of Moshe; rather, it was the people who were undeserving of complete redemption at that time, for they had already sunk almost to the lowest possible rung of impurity at that point.)

This explains why God revealed Himself to Moshe at the burning bush with the Name "I Will Be What I Will Be" (*Shemos* 3:14), which, as the Talmud (*Berachos* 9b) interprets, is an allusion to calamities that the Jewish people would suffer in the future. Of what relevance were these future misfortunes to Moshe's mission to Pharaoh? According to what we have explained, the answer to this question becomes clear, for Moshe's assignment contained within it the germ of all future redemptions from all future calamities.

We can also better understand now why God told Moshe at this point, "This is My Name forever (לעולם)" (ibid., 3:15) which the Sages (*Pesachim* 50a) interpret to mean: "This is My Name, being concealed (לעלם)," because God's Name is not pronounced the way it is written. As the Talmud (ibid.) explains, in the Messianic future, when our perceptions of Godliness will become clearer and more refined, this will not be the case, for the Name will be pronounced as it is written. Why did God give Moshe all this information at this time? Because, as explained above, Moshe's task represented not only the liberation of the Jews from Egypt, but was the beginning of a lengthy and complicated process of deliverance, which would ultimately end in the Final Redemption of Messianic times.

Now we can return to answer some of the questions posed earlier. How can the Talmud say that the commemoration of the Exodus, which is a mitzvah, will become secondary to the commemoration of the miracles of the dawn of the Messianic era? The answer is that the Future Redemption should not be viewed as an isolated historical event, but as the continuation and the climax of the process that began with the Exodus. The miracles of the Future Redemption will thus not be in competition with those of the Exodus; they will simply provide us with a refined vision and understanding of what the redemption of the Exodus was all about. In this sense the memory of the Exodus will be subordinate to that of the events of the Messianic future.

Why will there be an "utterance of midrashic explanations" at that time? The answer is that the same verses and interpretations that have always been applied to the Exodus will take on new, expanded meanings when viewed in light of the events that will come to pass in the days of the *Mashiach*.

As the *Meshech Chochmah* points out, the *pesach* sacrifice is a type of conversion-sacrifice. Each year, when offering this sacrifice, we are symbolically "converting" ourselves anew, revitalizing our commitment to God and strengthening our dedication to His service. This is also the underlying principle behind the Haggadah's exhortation that "in every generation a person must view himself as if he himself had gone out of Egypt." This does not mean that we should transport ourselves in our imaginations back to the days of Pharaoh and Moshe. Rather, the opposite is true; we are to take the events of the past and realize that they are relevant to us today, for the process of redemption and spiritual refinement that was set into motion at the time of the Exodus continues in our own day, and will ultimately lead to the Final Redemption.

Now we can return to the question that we originally asked: What is the point behind the Rambam's analogy between remembering the Exodus and "Remembering the Sabbath" (*Shemos* 20:8)? The answer is that just as the observance of the Sabbath is not intended to be a dry ritualistic exercise, but is intended to instill within us an awareness "that in six days God made the heavens, the earth, the sea, and all that is in them, and He rested on the seventh day" (ibid., 20:11), so too the mitzvos performed on Pesach night must inculcate within us the realization that the lessons of the Exodus of old are still operative for us today, and that the process of deliverance is still very much alive, leading eventually to the ultimate Messianic redemption.

יָכוֹל מֵרֹאשׁ חֹדֶשׁ, תַּלְמוּד לוֹמַר בַּיּוֹם הַהוּא. אִי בַּיּוֹם הַהוּא, יָכוֹל מִבְּעוֹד יוֹם, תַּלְמוּד לוֹמַר בַּעֲבוּר זֶה. בַּעֲבוּר זֶה לֹא אָמַרְתִּי אֶלָּא בְּשָׁעָה שֶׁיֵּשׁ מַצָּה וּמָרוֹר מֻנָּחִים לְפָנֶיךָ.

מִתְּחִלָּה, עוֹבְדֵי עֲבוֹדָה זָרָה הָיוּ אֲבוֹתֵינוּ, וְעַכְשָׁו קֵרְבָנוּ הַמָּקוֹם לַעֲבוֹדָתוֹ. שֶׁנֶּאֱמַר, וַיֹּאמֶר יְהוֹשֻׁעַ אֶל כָּל הָעָם, כֹּה אָמַר יהוה אֱלֹהֵי יִשְׂרָאֵל, בְּעֵבֶר הַנָּהָר יָשְׁבוּ אֲבוֹתֵיכֶם מֵעוֹלָם, תֶּרַח אֲבִי אַבְרָהָם וַאֲבִי נָחוֹר, וַיַּעַבְדוּ אֱלֹהִים אֲחֵרִים.

לֹא אָמַרְתִּי אֶלָּא בְּשָׁעָה שֶׁיֵּשׁ מַצָּה וּמָרוֹר מֻנָּחִים לְפָנֶיךָ
Only when matzah and maror lie before you

Seeing Is Believing

One time a man came to the **Chafetz Chaim** to receive his blessing.

"Tell me," the Rabbi asked his visitor. "Where do you send your children to school?"

"To the local secular Jewish school," came the answer.

"How can it be that a believing Jew would send his son to such an institution?" asked the Chafetz Chaim, astonished.

"But Rebbe," the man protested. "Part of the curriculum in this school is Bible studies, where the boys are taught all the teachings of the *Chumash* and *Tanach*!"

"And the teachers — do they cover their heads?" inquired the Chafetz Chaim.

"No," admitted the man, "but they do teach *Chumash*. They instill in the children belief in the Creator."

"Let me explain something to you," the Chafetz Chaim responded. "The Torah says that we should dwell in the sukkah for seven days 'so that your future generations should know that I caused the Children of Israel to dwell in booths when I took them out of Egypt' (*Vayikra* 23:43). Now, if God wanted to ensure that our children would know about the miracles of the Exodus, why didn't He just command us to tell them about it? Why do we have to bother to go out of our comfortable homes into a shabby, cold hut? The answer is that a mere story heard from a father would not have an impact upon the next generation. The child has to see his parent or teacher actually taking the lesson they desire to impart and putting it into action. Even when the Torah does indeed command us, 'You shall tell your son on that day [about the Exodus],' this is only to be done when 'matzah and *maror* are placed before us,' as the Haggadah derives.

"So it is in this situation. The instructor can teach all he wants about the *Chumash* and its stories and laws, but if he himself does not put these lessons into action, it will have no effect whatsoever on the children's minds and souls."

One might think [that the obligation to discuss the Exodus commences] with the first day of the month of Nisan, but the Torah says: "You shall tell your son on that day." But the expression "on that day" could be understood to mean only during the daytime; therefore the Torah adds: "It is because of this that HASHEM did so for me when I went out of Egypt." The pronoun "this" implies something tangible, thus, "You shall tell your son" applies only when matzah and maror lie before you — at the Seder.

Originally our ancestors were idol worshipers, but now the Omnipresent has brought us near to His service, as it says: Yehoshua said to all the people, "So says HASHEM, God of Israel: Your fathers always lived beyond the Euphrates River, Terach the father of Avraham and Nachor, and they served other gods.

וְעַכְשָׁו קֵרְבָנוּ הַמָּקוֹם לַעֲבוֹדָתוֹ
But now the Omnipresent has brought us near to His service,

The Need to Grow Spiritually

Many people believe that the purpose for being placed on this earth is to spend one's life refraining from sin. We were supplied with a pure soul, they reason, and we must strive to prevent it from becoming defiled. While it is true that sin contaminates the soul and the punishment for transgressing is harsh and bitter, wrote the **Chafetz Chaim,** avoiding wrongdoing is not the *goal* of our existence. It is unacceptable to simply fold our hands, stand in the corner, and evade the temptation to sin. Rather, our purpose in life is to *serve* God, in the positive sense — by accomplishing good deeds and fulfilling the mitzvos of the Torah.

The Chafetz Chaim illustrated the point with a parable:

Once there was a well-to-do businessman who had suffered a reversal of fortune, and lost his money. A friend of his offered to help him out by lending him 500 rubles — a considerable sum of money — to build his business up again.

A year later the lender came to visit his friend to see how his business was doing and to ask when he thought he might be able to repay the loan.

"I can give it to you right now if you want!" the borrower proudly declared to his surprised friend. He took out a wad of bills from the drawer and gave it back to his friend — in the original package in which he had received it.

The lender looked at the money and quickly realized that these were the exact same bills he had lent his friend a year ago. They had not been touched! He was upset at what he saw, and told his friend, "Why did I go to the trouble of lending you such a large amount of money? So that it should sit idle in your drawer for a

וָאֶקַּח אֶת אֲבִיכֶם אֶת אַבְרָהָם מֵעֵבֶר הַנָּהָר,
וָאוֹלֵךְ אוֹתוֹ בְּכָל אֶרֶץ כְּנָעַן, וָאַרְבֶּה אֶת זַרְעוֹ,

year? I could have made much better use of the money myself! It was supposed to be of benefit to you, to help you improve your financial situation!"

If someone goes through life and returns his soul to its Maker pure and unsullied — but untouched, in its original "wrapper" — this is considered to be a tremendous waste of opportunity.

The Chafetz Chaim interpreted a verse in *Tehillim* (24:3-4) in a manner that reflects this concept: "Who will go up to the mountain of Hashem? (i.e., Who will receive eternal reward in the World to Come?). . . He who did not carry My soul in vain." (This is the literal translation, although it is usually rendered as ". . . He who did not swear falsely.") A person who wastes the soul that God has given him does not merit to "go up to the mountain of Hashem"; this privilege is reserved for those who did not "carry their souls" through life in vain, without purpose.

וָאוֹלֵךְ אוֹתוֹ בְּכָל אֶרֶץ כְּנָעַן
And I had him travel through all the land of Canaan.

Spiritual Thoughts

R' **Gedaliah Schorr** used to quote R' Naftali Trop in his description of the way the saintly patriarchs traveled from place to place. The Torah tells us that when Avraham was taking Yitzchak to what he presumed was to be the latter's sacrifice to God, "they both walked *together*" (*Bereishis* 22:6). The Midrash explains this expression: Avraham, who thought he was about to lose his beloved son, and Yitzchak, who had no idea of what was in store for him, both walked *together* — that is, with the same conviction and enthusiasm. Avraham showed no hesitation whatsoever in his fulfillment of God's command, despite the fact that it was so difficult for him personally. But we may use the same textual analysis in reverse as well, R' Naftali noted. Avraham was aware of the fact that he was about to perform an awesome act of service to God, one which was to demonstrate his unwavering faith in Him and his unparalleled dedication to the fulfillment of His will. Yitzchak, on the other hand, thought that they were going for a simple "trip" to an undisclosed location. If the verse tells us that the two traveled *together,* we may derive that Yitzchak, who was "just going for a walk," shared the lofty, sublime frame of mind of his father, who was on his way to achieve the greatest imaginable spiritual heights.

Actually, the *Zohar* already informs us of the lofty levels of spirituality involved in the "simple travelings" of the patriarchs, for it draws a comparison between the verses, "And Avram *passed* through the land" (*Bereishis* 12:6) to "And Hashem *passed* before his face and called" (*Shemos* 34:6).

וָאוֹלֵךְ אוֹתוֹ בְּכָל אֶרֶץ כְּנָעַן
And I had him travel through all the land of Canaan.

Abraham's Tent

R' **Shneur Kotler** (quoting Rabbi Y. L. Fein of Slonim) noted that when the Torah delineates the location where Avraham pitched his tent when he first arrived in Canaan, it says, "He traveled from there to

> Then I took your father Avraham from beyond the river and I had him travel through all the land of Canaan. I multiplied his offspring and

the mountain east of Beis El, and he pitched his tent; Beis El was on the west and Ai on the east" (*Bereishis* 12:8). This description is somewhat strange. Beis El and Ai were major cities (as can be seen from *Yehoshua* and *Shoftim*); one would expect a barren hilltop between these two well-known landmarks to be described as "to the east of Beis El and to the west of Ai." But the Torah in fact tells us where Beis El and Ai were in relation to Avraham's tent, instead of vice versa.

The message the Torah conveys with this description is that the major population centers were indeed subordinate to Avraham's location, for Avraham's tent was the center for Torah dissemination and for the furtherance of the recognition of God's mastery over the Universe. Although we often tend to overlook the fact, this is the true purpose of the existence of mankind, and it is Avraham's tent, and not the major urban and commercial centers, that is the focus of the world. The same is true for all time and in all situations; the Torah centers of the world are the truly important locations, and all the other "major" sites of the world are in fact secondary in importance.

A similar concept is expressed elsewhere in the Torah as well. After the sin of the Golden Calf, Moshe took his tent and pitched it outside the camp. It was called the "Tent of Meeting," for "all those who sought Hashem would go out" to this tent (*Shemos* 33:7). When Moshe would arrive at the tent, "the pillar of cloud would descend and stand at the entrance of the tent, and He would speak to Moshe" (ibid., 33:9). This Tent of Meeting, though it was physically located beyond the boundaries of the camp, was nevertheless the epicenter of the people's search for spiritual growth, where even the pillar of cloud (representing the presence of the *Shechinah*) would come and rest itself.

וָאוֹלֵךְ אוֹתוֹ בְּכָל אֶרֶץ כְּנָעַן
And I had him travel through all the land of Canaan.

Why Abraham Went to Canaan

What was God's purpose in having Avraham travel to Canaan? Could he not have "called out in the Name of God" (*Bereishis* 12:8; 13:4; 21:33) and propagated the faith in the One true God just as well in his native Aram? In any event, God told him that the land of Canaan would not be given to him or his descendants for four hundred years (ibid. 15:13). (See above, p. 67), where this matter is also discussed.) Furthermore, even if we can find a reason for Avraham traveling to Canaan — and the commentators offer many such reasons — we must understand why God had him travel *through all* the land of Canaan.

R' Zalman Sorotzkin offered an answer for these questions, as follows. Eretz Yisrael is imbued with a unique degree of sanctity, and this was true even before the Land was given to the Jews or promised to the patriarchs; its innate holiness dates all the way back to Creation. Now, there is a Kabbalistic doctrine that teaches that the more sanctity an item has the more the forces of impurity are attracted to it. For

וָאֶתֵּן לוֹ אֶת יִצְחָק. וָאֶתֵּן לְיִצְחָק אֶת יַעֲקֹב וְאֶת עֵשָׂו,

instance, a dead human being imparts a much more severe level of ritual impurity than a dead animal, because a human being (in his lifetime) is obviously on a higher spiritual plane than a beast. Similarly, the body of a Jewish person has a higher degree of impurity than that of a non-Jew. Of all lands, therefore, the forces of impurity were particularly attracted to Eretz Yisrael. As Rashi (on *Bereishis* 12:6) tells us, this area was originally allocated to Noach's son Shem, while Cham's sons (Canaan among them) were given the lands of Africa. Just at the time Avraham was told to travel to Eretz Yisrael, however, the Canaanites were in the midst of their conquest of that land. The ancestor of the Canaanite nation (Canaan) was, of course, best known for his immoral, vulgar behavior with his grandfather Noach (*Bereishis* 9:20-27), for which he was roundly cursed. The Canaanites ultimately became the epitome of perversion and immorality, as the Torah says in its introduction to the laws against incest and other perverse sexual practices, "Like the actions. . . of the land of Canaan, to where I am bringing you, you shall not do, and do not follow their practices" (*Vayikra* 18:3). God therefore sent Avraham there for the purpose of "cleaning up" the land and removing this taint of corruption and impurity from it, and to this end it was imperative that Avraham travel throughout the length and breadth of the land, proclaiming the Name of God wherever he went and seeking to improve the poor spiritual condition of its inhabitants.

וָאַרְבֶּה אֶת זַרְעוֹ, וָאֶתֵּן לוֹ אֶת יִצְחָק
I multiplied his offspring and gave him Yitzchak.

The Many Children of Abraham

When the verse mentions that God "multiplied Avraham's offspring," the reference is apparently to the many sons that Avraham had besides Yitzchak (see *Bereishis* 25:1ff). The question may be asked, however: What is the relevance of all of Avraham's offspring to the context of this verse, which speaks of God's selection of the patriarchs and the people of Israel? Doesn't the Torah say that Avraham's heritage and lineage would be considered to continue through Yitzchak alone (ibid., 21:12; see *Nedarim* 31a)?

R' Gedaliah Schorr used to relate an answer to this question given by the Koznitzer Maggid. The other children of Avraham in fact did play a role in the formation of the Jewish people, for it was from their number through which Yitzchak was chosen. One cannot be "chosen" if there is no group from which to choose.

R' Schorr himself suggested a different approach to this problem. According to the Kabbalists the birth of twins to Yitzchak — and the birth of several sons to Avraham as well — was necessary to filter out all negative spiritual characteristics from their respective parents, to ensure Yaakov's and Yitzchak's absolute perfection. It is therefore entirely relevant to speak of Yitzchak's half brothers when discussing the choosing of Yitzchak to be the one to continue Avraham's tradition.

gave him Yitzchak. To Yitzchak I gave Yaakov and Esav,

וָאֶתֵּן לוֹ אֶת יִצְחָק / *And I gave him Yitzchak.*

Abraham's Desire to Serve Hashem

People sometimes ask about the *Akeidah* (when Avraham bound Yitzchak on the altar and prepared himself to sacrifice him in obedience of God's command): "How does this act show the phenomenal greatness of Avraham? Jews have sacrificed their lives and the lives of their children for the sake of God's Name for centuries!"

The answer to this question, **R' Elchanan Wasserman** explained, is that when a martyr shows willingness to give up his life for the sanctification of God's Name he is comforted by the fact that he is exchanging a fleeting physical life for a more permanent and sublime spiritual life, in the World to Come. Let us imagine a case, however, where a man is faced with giving up his life for the sake of God's glory but is told that he will also lose his share in the World to Come. This would be a true display of selfless devotion to God's will, for it would remove any trace of compensation for his actions. To give up one's life without receiving anything whatsoever in return would indeed be the ultimate test of faith.

Now, when God told Avraham, "Do not fear... I am a shield for you; your reward is very great" (*Bereishis* 15:1), the Sages explain: "I am a shield for you" refers to physical protection in this world, and "your reward is very great" alludes to spiritual reward, in the World to Come. Yet Avraham answered God, "What can you give me? For I am childless" (ibid., v. 2). In other words, Avraham was unsatisfied with the reward of a share in the World to Come that had just been promised to him; it was meaningless to him if he did not have a child. To understand the reason behind Avraham's surprising sentiments we must realize that Avraham's entire goal in life was to spread the knowledge of God in the land; reward for his actions was the furthest thing from his mind. Avraham knew that without a son to carry on his legacy, all his work would have no continuation or permanence in the world. The thought that he was probably going to die childless was therefore so troublesome to Avraham that the promise of a share in the World to Come could not make up for this deficiency.

When we consider Avraham's willingness to sacrifice his son in order to obey God's command, we must keep his set of priorities in mind. For Avraham's desire to have a son to continue his mission in the world was greater even than his desire to achieve eternal spiritual life — and yet he was willing at the *Akeidah* to give up this ultimate of goals for God's sake. In his eyes, this was even greater than giving up his share in the World to Come, as we have shown. It is therefore impossible to compare Avraham's actions to those of Jewish martyrs over the ages.

וָאֶתֵּן לְיִצְחָק אֶת יַעֲקֹב וְאֶת עֵשָׂו
To Yitzchak I gave Yaakov and Esav,

To Give Is to Benefit

The verse lists both sons of Yitzchak, but when it comes to Avraham it mentions only Yitzchak, without explicit mention of Yishmael or any of his numerous other children. **R' Zalman Sorotzkin** explained that in the end Avraham received no benefit at all from any of his sons

וָאֶתֵּן לְעֵשָׂו אֶת הַר שֵׂעִיר לָרֶשֶׁת אוֹתוֹ, וְיַעֲקֹב וּבָנָיו יָרְדוּ מִצְרָיִם.[1]

בָּרוּךְ שׁוֹמֵר הַבְטָחָתוֹ לְיִשְׂרָאֵל, בָּרוּךְ הוּא. שֶׁהַקָּדוֹשׁ בָּרוּךְ הוּא חִשַּׁב אֶת הַקֵּץ, לַעֲשׂוֹת כְּמָה שֶּׁאָמַר לְאַבְרָהָם אָבִינוּ בִּבְרִית בֵּין הַבְּתָרִים, שֶׁנֶּאֱמַר, וַיֹּאמֶר לְאַבְרָם, יָדֹעַ תֵּדַע כִּי גֵר יִהְיֶה זַרְעֲךָ בְּאֶרֶץ לֹא לָהֶם, וַעֲבָדוּם וְעִנּוּ אֹתָם, אַרְבַּע מֵאוֹת שָׁנָה. וְגַם אֶת

except Yitzchak, who carried on his tradition. The verb "to give" is appropriate only when what is given is beneficial in some way to the receiver. Yitzchak, on the other hand, benefited greatly from Esav, for the latter fed him and cared for him with great devotion (see *Bereishis* 25:28, and *Targum Onkelos* ad loc.).

וָאֶתֵּן לְעֵשָׂו אֶת הַר שֵׂעִיר / To Esav I gave Mount Seir

The Blessing of Yitzchak

Seir was the chieftain of the original inhabitants (the Horites) of Mount Seir, whom Esau and his clan supplanted. The verse quoted here uses the word "I gave" (וָאֶתֵּן), **R' Zalman Sorotzkin** noted, intimating that this territory was not conquered by Esau with great toil and hardship, but rather it was "given" to him as a gift. It was in the merit of Yitzchak's blessing to Esau ("Your dwelling place shall be on the fat of the land. . . and you will live by your sword" — *Bereishis* 27:39-40) that enabled him to overtake this land effortlessly. The reason for this was so that Esau would be removed from any stake in Eretz Yisrael, leaving this sacred Land incontestably for Yaakov and his descendants.

שֶׁהַקָּדוֹשׁ בָּרוּךְ הוּא חִשַּׁב אֶת הַקֵּץ / For the Holy One, Blessed is He, calculated the End

How Hashem Calculated "the End"

Rav Elchanan Wasserman offered an explanation as to what the Haggadah means by "the End." The Talmud (*Eruchin* 16b) discusses the extent of what may be considered "suffering." Ordering a garment from a tailor and then finding out that it does not fit properly, minor inconvenience though it may seem, is considered to be an example of undergoing suffering. Another example is asking for a cold drink and receiving a warm one instead (or vice versa). Accidentally putting on one's shirt inside out and having to remove it and don it again is also mentioned. The Talmud even goes so far as to speak of a case where someone reaches into his pocket for a certain amount of money and draws out an incorrect amount, requiring him to put his hand into the pocket an extra time. These examples are what the Talmud refers to as the "extreme limits" (תַּכְלִית, more literally *end*) of what can be considered suffering. Of course the purpose of the Talmud is to show how far the definition of "suffering" can be stretched in the direction of minor misfortune; we are well aware of how serious suffering can become towards the upper bounds of

to Esav I gave Mount Seir to inherit, but Yaakov and his children went down to Egypt."[1]

Blessed is He Who keeps His pledge to Israel; Blessed is He! For the Holy One, Blessed is He, calculated the End in order to do as He said to our father Avraham at the Bris bein Habesarim, as it says: He said to Avram, "Know with certainty that your offspring will be aliens in a land not their own, they will serve them, and they will oppress them four hundred years; but also upon the

---
1. *Yehoshua* 24:2-4.

---

its definition. The Talmud tells us that there are some forms of torture that are even more difficult than death (*Kesubos* 33b).

God decreed at the "Covenant Between the Parts" (*Bereishis* 15) that Avraham's descendants would have to undergo a period of exile and affliction (four hundred years — ibid., 15:13). But what exactly would constitute "exile" and the precise parameters that the "affliction" would entail were not defined. We know that when Israel first descended to Egypt they were treated well. Afterwards there was a period of "voluntary subjugation," until the situation deteriorated to outright enslavement. At which point was the four hundred-year countdown to deliverance to begin? Another question left open was: What exactly is the definition of "descendants [of Avraham]" (זַרְעֲךָ) in the Covenant? Perhaps this should be seen as a reference to the seventy souls who descended to Egypt; perhaps it refers to the 600,000 Jews who lived at the time of the Exodus. On the other hand, Yitzchak was a descendant as well, and perhaps we should count from the time of his birth, for even a newborn infant suffers when his parents are exiles in a land not their own.

Of all the possible interpretations that could have been assigned to the terms of the Covenant Between the Parts, God "calculated *the end,*" meaning that he chose the lowest possible *limit* that could be considered to fall within the range of the terms "exile" and "affliction" and "offspring," for He began to count the four hundred years from the birth of Yitzchak.

יָדֹעַ תֵּדַע כִּי גֵר יִהְיֶה זַרְעֲךָ בְּאֶרֶץ לֹא לָהֶם, וַעֲבָדוּם וְעִנּוּ אֹתָם, אַרְבַּע מֵאוֹת שָׁנָה
Know with certainty that your offspring will be aliens in a land not their own, and they will serve them, and they will oppress them four hundred years;

Three Stages of Exile — There are three distinct steps to the suffering foretold to Avraham for his descendants in this verse, **R' Zalman Sorotzkin** noted: (1) "Your offspring will be aliens"; (2) "in a land not their own"; (3) "they will serve them and they will oppress them." Together the three stages were to cover a four hundred-year period. The first period (of being an alien) began at Yitzchak's birth (for Avraham himself was treated well by the natives of Canaan,

[103] THE HAGGADAH OF THE ROSHEI YESHIVAH

הַגּוֹי אֲשֶׁר יַעֲבֹדוּ דָּן אָנֹכִי, וְאַחֲרֵי כֵן יֵצְאוּ בִּרְכֻשׁ
גָּדוֹל.[1]

The matzos are covered and the cups lifted as the following paragraph is proclaimed joyously. Upon its conclusion, the cups are put down and the matzos are uncovered.

וְהִיא שֶׁעָמְדָה לַאֲבוֹתֵינוּ וְלָנוּ, שֶׁלֹּא אֶחָד

and was considered an honorary resident — see *Bereishis* 23) and continued through part of Yaakov's lifetime. The second stage (being in a land not their own) began when Yaakov fled to Aram, extended to when he went down to Egypt toward the end of his life, and continued through the lifetimes of the twelve progenitors of the tribes of Israel. The third period (servitude and oppression) extended from the death of the last of Yaakov's sons down to the Exodus.

Although there was a clear time span decreed for the sum total of the three stages, God deliberately left it vague as to how long each of the individual stages would last. If Avraham's offspring would prove to be exceptionally virtuous, the first period would be drawn out and the harsher second and third periods would be cut down to the bare minimum. If they would show themselves to be wanting in certain essential qualities, the second stage and the third, most difficult stage would be extended accordingly.

As it happened, the third stage was brought on by the quarreling and animosity that existed between the sons of Yaakov's main wives and the sons of the maidservants, and between the sons of Rachel and the sons of Leah, for it was the selling of Yosef as a slave that eventually led to the entire family's relocation in Egypt.

This is what the Sages meant when they said, "A man should never treat one son differently from the others, for it was over two *selas* (a certain unit of weight) of silk (that Yaakov placed in Yosef's famous coat) that ultimately led to our fathers going into exile in Egypt" (*Shabbos* 10). *Tosafos* (ad loc.) asks how the chain of events leading to exile in Egypt can be blamed on the jealousy of Yosef's brothers. After all, wasn't the Egyptian exile explicitly foreordained by God at the Covenant Between the Parts? How could subsequent events affect that decree? According to the way we have presented the issues, we can suggest an answer to the question of *Tosafos*. It is true that four hundred years of suffering were decreed, but, as explained above, the three stages of suffering could have been divided up in many different ways over these four centuries. The fact that there was such bitter jealousy between the brothers was indeed a factor in the onset of the Egyptian exile, for it was the catalyst of the onset of the second — and ultimately the third and most difficult — stage of the decree of the Covenant Between the Parts.

וְאַחֲרֵי כֵן יֵצְאוּ בִּרְכֻשׁ גָּדוֹל
And afterwards they shall leave with great possessions.

Forging a United Nation

Although "the understanding of the Torah's words never veers from the plain meaning" (*Shabbos* 63a), and in fact the Jews did leave Egypt with great wealth (*Shemos* 12:36), it seems that there is a secondary, deeper meaning behind these words as well, **R' Zalman Sorotzkin** wrote. For what sort of consolation could a promise of material wealth be

הגדה של פסח [104]

nation which they shall serve will I execute judgment, and afterwards they shall go out with great possessions."[1]

The matzos are covered and the cups lifted as the following paragraph is proclaimed joyously. Upon its conclusion, the cups are put down and the matzos are uncovered.

And it is this that has stood by our fathers and us. For not

---

1. *Bereishis* 15:13-14.

---

for Avraham after he had been told that his descendants would be subject to four hundred years of homelessness and enslavement? Can any price be attached to the lives of innocent babies thrown into the river or the degradation and disparagement of slavery? Rather, it appears that God was telling Avraham that the four hundred years of affliction would in the end be considered worthwhile because of the great *spiritual* wealth that his descendants would acquire as a result of that experience. These centuries of hardship and adversity would purge the people of whatever negative traits lurked within them and prepare them for total dedication in servitude to God. For instance, the divisiveness and hostility that plagued the twelve progenitors of the tribes was a trait that would have interfered considerably with their ability to coalesce into a single, united nation. But by the time the Egyptian exile came to an end, the Midrash tells us, one of the most outstanding qualities of the people was that they were fiercely loyal to each other and protective of one another, which made the idea of a single, unified nation possible.

וְהִיא שֶׁעָמְדָה לַאֲבוֹתֵינוּ וְלָנוּ
And it is this that has stood by our fathers and us.

Stopping Assimilation

What does the Haggadah refer to when it speaks of "this"? *What* is it that has stood by our forefathers and us? The commentators generally assume that the reference is to the Covenant Between the Parts just mentioned. God's promise to Avraham that "upon the nation which they shall serve will I execute judgment" and "afterwards they will leave with great possessions" have "stood by" (i.e., were helpful to) not only Avraham, but all of our ancestors throughout the ages, down to our own time. The **Netziv** raises two questions about this interpretation, however: First, if this is the Haggadah's intention, how can we understand the transition to the following paragraph, "Go and learn what Lavan the Aramean attempted to do to our father Yaakov"? What does Lavan's desire to kill Yaakov have to do with our paragraph here? Is it just one example of the near extermination of the Jewish people, from which they were saved by God's miraculous intervention? What would be the point of citing this one example out of so many hundreds? Furthermore, how can it be said that the terms of the Covenant have stood by our side and protected us throughout the generations? After all, the clause that states "and afterwards they shall go out with great possessions" is certainly not intended to be applicable for all ages, but only for the case of the Egyptian Exodus; the promise that "upon the nation which they shall serve will I execute judgment" is seemingly limited to that one occasion as well.

The Netziv therefore suggests a different interpretation of the word "this."

בִּלְבָד עָמַד עָלֵינוּ לְכַלּוֹתֵנוּ. אֶלָּא שֶׁבְּכָל דּוֹר וָדוֹר עוֹמְדִים עָלֵינוּ לְכַלּוֹתֵנוּ, וְהַקָּדוֹשׁ בָּרוּךְ הוּא מַצִּילֵנוּ מִיָּדָם.

צא וּלְמַד מַה בִּקֵּשׁ לָבָן הָאֲרַמִּי לַעֲשׂוֹת לְיַעֲקֹב אָבִינוּ, שֶׁפַּרְעֹה לֹא גָזַר אֶלָּא עַל הַזְּכָרִים, וְלָבָן בִּקֵּשׁ לַעֲקֹר אֶת הַכֹּל. שֶׁנֶּאֱמַר:
אֲרַמִּי אֹבֵד אָבִי, וַיֵּרֶד מִצְרַיְמָה וַיָּגָר שָׁם בִּמְתֵי מְעָט, וַיְהִי שָׁם לְגוֹי, גָּדוֹל עָצוּם וָרָב.[1]

According to him, it refers to the *first* part of the Covenant, which declares, "Know with certainty that your offspring will be strangers in a land not their own." It is part of the Divine plan that Avraham's descendants should not intermingle with other nations, that they should remain separate and distinct, like strangers. History has taught us that it is precisely when our people seek to abrogate these terms of the Covenant by assimilating and intermingling with the other nations that the persecution against us becomes most intense. This pattern is reflected in the Midrash, which relates that after Yosef's death the Jews began to neglect circumcising their young, saying, "Let us be like the Egyptians." At that point, the Midrash continues, God turned around the hearts of the Egyptian people, who had previously been favorably disposed towards the Jews, to be vehemently hostile to them. Similarly the Talmud (*Pesachim* 118b), in a homiletic interpretation of *Tehillim* 68:31, states: "What causes the Jews to be so dispersed among the nations? Because they desire to become close [to the other nations], to settle among them and to imitate them. So what does God do? He uproots them and scatters them elsewhere."

It emerges, then, that the clause "your offspring will be strangers in a land not their own" is not a curse or a punishment, but is in fact a blessing, for it is in this manner, by retaining the status of *strangers* among others, that Avraham's offspring would be ensured God's protection. It is *this* prophecy of being "strangers in a land not their own," the Haggadah tells us, that has "stood by our forefathers and by us," throughout Jewish history. "For not only one nation has risen against us to annihilate us" — whenever we break the terms of this prophecy and seek to defy God's will that we should remain distinct and different from the other nations, they are instigated by God to rise up against us to annihilate us. However, in the end "God saves us from their hand."

This situation, of course, seems to defy reason. Logically speaking, one would expect that the more a foreigner tries to emulate and imitate the culture of his adopted homeland the more he should become accepted and beloved by them. And, in fact, this is the reaction that many individuals experience when they first pursue this path of assimilation; they are welcomed with friendly faces and words of encouragement. But eventually this outward facade is exposed for what it truly

only one has risen against us to annihilate us, but in every generation they rise against us to annihilate us. But the Holy One, Blessed is He, rescues us from their hand.

Go and learn what Lavan the Aramean attempted to do to our father Yaakov! For Pharaoh decreed only against the males, and Lavan attempted to uproot everything, as it says:

An Aramean attempted to destroy my father, and he descended to Egypt and sojourned there, with few people; and there he became a nation — great, mighty and numerous.[1]

---
1. *Devarim* 26:5.

---

is — nothing but empty, superficial gestures. To prove this point, the Haggadah cites the example of Lavan and Yaakov. To the naked eye, "Uncle Lavan" seems to be the most hospitable of hosts, harboring his nephew from his fratricidal brother. He welcomed him with a big hug and kiss (*Bereishis* 29:13); he would not allow him to help out around the house without paying him ("Because you are my brother, should you work for free?" — ibid., 29:15); he allowed him to have his daughter's hand in marriage; etc. True, he acted with treachery and deceit, but this was his nature — nothing personal. But in the end Lavan's tolerance of Yaakov for the twenty years they lived together showed its true nature when he said, "I have the power in my hands to do harm to you (עִמָּכֶם — in the plural, including Yaakov and his entire family, the entire nascent Jewish nation), except that the God of your father warned me. . ." (ibid., 31:29). Thus, it is to show the inevitably tragic results of living together in brotherhood with other peoples that the Haggadah brings in the example of Lavan, telling us to "go and learn" from this case, and apply its lessons to our own situations, throughout the generations.

אֲרַמִּי אֹבֵד אָבִי, וַיֵּרֶד מִצְרַיְמָה וַיָּגָר שָׁם
An Aramean attempted to destroy my father,
and he descended to Egypt and sojourned there,

A Permanent Sojourner

From this point on the Haggadah expounds on a passage in the Torah known as *Mikra Bikkurim*, the declaration made by farmers as they brought their first-ripening produce to the Temple to offer to the Kohen there (*Devarim* 26:5-8). Each word or phrase of this declaration is quoted and elaborated upon. Sometimes all the Haggadah does is to cite a corresponding verse in the context of the story of the Exodus that parallels a statement made in *Mikra Bikkurim*. There is always some new insight that can be learned from this parallel support-verse, wrote the **Netziv**, for otherwise what would be the point of proving the veracity of one verse by citing another?

A case in point is the Haggadah's comment on the words, "He sojourned there," from *Mikra Bikkurim*. The Haggadah explains: "This teaches that our father Yaakov did not descend to Egypt to settle, but only to sojourn there, as it says, 'They said to Pharaoh: We have come to sojourn in this land... and now, please let your servants dwell in the land of Goshen.' " What does the Haggadah gain by proving that Yaakov and his sons went to Egypt with the intention to sojourn there by citing another verse that states, "We have come to sojourn in the land"? What does this second verse show that the original verse did not?

The Netziv explains the Haggadah's comment as follows: When the Haggadah tells us that Yaakov did not go down to Egypt "to settle there" it does not mean to say that his intention was not to live there permanently. Yaakov knew the terms of the Covenant Between the Parts, and he was aware of the fact that Avraham's descendants would have to be "strangers in a land not their own." He was also told prophetically that there would be no return from Egypt until the Exodus, centuries later (*Bereishis* 46:4; see commentaries ad loc.). No, Yaakov knew that he would be staying in Egypt for the rest of his life. What the Haggadah means to tell us is that when Yaakov went to Egypt he did so with the intention of retaining the *mindset* of a sojourner and stranger — that is, avoiding, for himself and his children and grandchildren, excessive contact with the Egyptians and the danger of assimilation.

The Torah writes in *Devarim* 33:28: "Israel dwelt securely and separately, the eye of Yaakov." What is meant by the mysterious expression, "the eye of Yaakov"? The Netziv explained that these two conditions — security and separateness — were the "eye," or the foremost desire and hope of Yaakov for his family as they settled in a foreign land: *security*, that they should not become physically endangered through strife or confrontation with their enemies, and *separateness*, that they should not face spiritual decimation through assimilation and acculturation with their new hosts. Indeed, this latter threat can be even more perilous than the first, for it carries with it not only spiritual harm but physical devastation as well, as the Talmud (*Sanhedrin* 104a) tells us in a comment on the verse, "How does she dwell alone, the city that was full of people?" (*Eichah* 1:1): "I (God) had said, 'Israel shall dwell securely and separately (or, *alone*, in the positive sense), the eye of Yaakov'; now (that they have sinned) they will 'dwell alone' (in the negative sense)." Failing to keep our separate identity and to avoid excessive intermingling among the nations around us is a recipe for *physical*, as well as spiritual, disaster.

The Haggadah now seeks to prove its assertion that וַיָּגָר שָׁם ("He sojourned there") is to be interpreted in the sense that Yaakov's prime intention was to retain for himself and future generations the critical element of separateness and foreignness during their stay in Egypt. To this end it cites the supporting verse, "And they said to Pharaoh: We have come to sojourn in the land... and now, please let your servants dwell in the land of Goshen." The very first request of Yaakov and his sons from Pharaoh was not that they be granted decent living conditions or ample provisions to sustain them in the midst of a devastating famine — but only to be granted permission to settle in the land of Goshen, far away from the centers of Egyptian culture, where they would be able to set up for themselves a relatively isolated, separate community. This shows beyond a shadow of a doubt that

Yaakov's major concern at that point was to ensure a permanent status of "sojourner" for himself and his family, as the Haggadah had asserted.

אֲרַמִּי אֹבֵד אָבִי, וַיֵּרֶד מִצְרַיְמָה

*An Aramean attempted to destroy
my father, and he descended to Egypt*

Lavan's Wickedness Yaakov was confronted by Lavan as he was making his way back to Eretz Yisrael; he did not go down to Egypt until some thirty years after that episode, under completely unrelated circumstances. Why does the Torah seem to imply that there is a connection between the two events, that in some way Yaakov's experiences with Lavan led to his exile to Egypt? This question is raised by many commentators on the Haggadah and on the *Chumash*. **R' Zalman Sorotzkin** suggested the following explanation.

It should be recalled that God did not decree that Avraham's descendants should be exiled specifically to Egypt; the prophecy declared only that they would be "aliens in a land not their own." This decree could have been fulfilled in *any* land other than Eretz Yisrael. The question thus arises: Since Yaakov was compelled to flee to Aram and spend many years of his life there in any event, why did God not simply allow this "Aramean exile" to continue to the end of the ordained four hundred-year period? Why did God have to bring Yaakov and his family back to Eretz Yisrael, only to have them uproot themselves once again several years later? The answer to this question is alluded to here in the Haggadah: "An Aramean (Lavan) attempted to destroy my father (Yaakov)." Lavan wanted to go further than Pharaoh ever desired, to "uproot everything" and bring an end to the nascent Jewish nation. His goal was to eliminate Yaakov and to appropriate his immense wealth, to which he felt he was entitled, as he said, "The daughters are my daughters, the sons are my sons and the flocks are my flocks" (*Bereishis* 31:43). This is why he expressed no reservation whatsoever when Yaakov proposed his new idea for payment to him (ibid., 30:31-34). His reaction was, "Fine! Let it be as you say!" (ibid. v. 34) — in any event he would take it all back eventually! No, it would not be possible to have Avraham's descendants spend four centuries under such conditions. It was not only Lavan, but his fellow Arameans, his partners in crime — who helped him conceal his deceitful plan to switch Leah with Rachel and who aided him in his chase after Yaakov — who would have made such an exile impossible. (This is why the verse does not mention Lavan specifically by name, but refers only to "an Aramean" — for it was the Aramean people as a whole who were hostile to Yaakov.) This, then, accounts for the causal relationship implied by the verse: "An Aramean attempted to destroy my father, and hence (because of this implacable hostility, made it impossible to carry out the decree of exile in Aram), my father had to go down to Egypt (to fulfill the terms of the Covenant Between the Parts)."

R' Zalman used this idea to explain another difficult passage found in the story of Yaakov and Lavan. The night before Lavan caught up with Yaakov, God appeared to him in a dream and warned him not to speak to him "either good or bad." We can easily understand why Lavan was instructed not to speak harshly to Yaakov, for this

וַיֵּרֶד מִצְרַיְמָה – אָנוּס עַל פִּי הַדִּבּוּר.

would have led to a dangerous physical confrontation. But why was he cautioned not to speak *good* words to him? Rashi (ad loc., quoting from *Yevamos* 103) comments that "the good of the wicked is in effect evil for the righteous." But it is still unclear exactly what harm might come from Lavan's kind words. Another question we might ask is: Why did God have to issue a warning to Lavan not to speak kindly to Yaakov? After hotly pursuing him for seven days (actually, Rashi tells us that Lavan traveled the seven-day distance in one day, so infuriated was he with Yaakov's behavior) and declaring, "I have the power in my hand to do harm to you" (*Bereishis* 31:29), it does not seem that Lavan had the slightest intention of exchanging niceties with Yaakov over a friendly cup of tea!

The answer to these questions, R' Zalman explained, is that it is indeed certain that Lavan's intentions were always to "uproot everything." But to achieve that end Lavan, that master of deceit, might try a novel approach — rapprochement with Yaakov. He might decide that the best way to fulfill his evil plan was to convince Yaakov that peace could be made between them, that Lavan would see to it that his sons and kinsmen would cease their hostility toward Yaakov (which was the original impetus for Yaakov's leaving — *Bereishis* 31:1). In this manner he could persuade Yaakov to return and work for him again, adding greater and greater fortune to what would eventually become Lavan's coffers. This is why God cautioned him not to speak to Yaakov, "either good or bad." As the Talmud explains, even the "good" plan of the wicked person spells nothing but disaster for the righteous victim of his deception.

The **Chafetz Chaim** also reflected upon the possibility of fulfilling the decree of exile in Aram, with Lavan and his family, as opposed to going down to Egypt. It was after the Communist Revolution in Russia, when the new government was seeking to force Communist ideology — and its concomitant atheism — upon all the people of the land. There was a special group, called the Yevsektzia, that was comprised of Jews who had abandoned and turned against their faith in favor of the new "religion" of Communism. These people harassed the religious Jews in every imaginable way: they closed down synagogues, sealed up mikvehs, disbanded yeshivos and Talmud Torahs, imprisoned rabbis and teachers, and outlawed the keeping of Shabbos and circumcision. When the Chafetz Chaim heard about the extent of the hatred these people exhibited towards their fellow Jews, he mentioned the question posed above: Why was the decree of exile not carried out in Aram? He quoted our passage from the Haggadah, "Go and see. . . that Pharaoh decreed only against the males, while Lavan sought to uproot everything." "From here we have proof," the Chafetz Chaim noted sadly, "that it is much more dangerous to be exiled among one's family than to be exiled among total strangers!"

This also explains why Yaakov prayed to God that He save him "from the hands of my brother, from the hands of Esav" (*Bereishis* 32:12). It was perfectly clear who Esav was; why did Yaakov have to identify him as "my brother"? The Chafetz Chaim

And he descended to Egypt — compelled by Divine decree.

explained that the fact that Esav was Yaakov's brother made the extent of his hatred that much more extreme, and Yaakov had to offer an extra prayer specifically because of the factor of brotherhood that existed between them.

וַיֵּרֶד מִצְרַיְמָה – אָנוּס עַל פִּי הַדִּבּוּר
And he descended to Egypt — compelled by Divine decree.

Yaakov's descent to Egypt

Where in the words "he descended to Egypt" does the Haggadah find an allusion that Yaakov was forced against his will to go to Egypt by the command of God?

The **Netziv** explained that the Haggadah derives its inference from the fact that this verse in *Mikra Bikkurim* (*Devarim* 26:5) changes the expression that was originally used to describe Yaakov's trip to Egypt: "I will *go* (not *go down*) and see [Yosef]" (*Bereishis* 45:28). Normally travel to and from the Land of Israel vis-a-vis other places is termed "going up" and "going down," respectively. However, in this case, Yaakov did not say he was "going down" to Egypt, because his place of departure was "the valley of Chevron," a low area, from which he would have to first ascend in order to journey to Egypt. The fact that this expression is changed in *Devarim* to "went *down*" implies, the Haggadah tells us, that Yaakov's travels involved a descent, not physical, perhaps, but in Yaakov's condition — for he knew that this would be a one-way trip — the beginning of a long ordeal for him and especially for his children. His departure from Eretz Yisrael was therefore less than enthusiastic under these circumstances. As the Haggadah puts it, his journey was undertaken under pressure and duress, "by the word of God."

But where, one may ask, do we find that Yaakov was ordered by Divine command to go to Egypt in the first place? Did he not say himself, as soon as he heard that Yosef was still alive and well in Egypt, "I shall go and see him before I die" (*Bereishis* 45:28)?

The Netziv pointed out that Yaakov's words in this verse sound like a desire to pay his long lost, beloved son a short visit — to "see him" — and then return to Eretz Yisrael. He certainly did not wish to take his entire seventy-member family with him and settle there; he was concerned about the extreme negative spiritual effects that dwelling in Egypt would likely entail, as discussed above (see above, p. 107). But then, when he traveled to Be'er Sheva to offer sacrifices to God before heading for Egypt, God told him, "Do not fear going down to Egypt . . . Yosef will place his hand upon your eyes" (*Bereishis* 46:3-4). As the Netziv explained above, the "eye of Yaakov" is an allusion to his intense longing and desire that his descendants remain separate and isolated from other nations and their cultures, so as not to become influenced by them. God therefore assured him that Yosef would put his hand on his *eyes*, meaning that he would arrange it that his family would live separately, away from the major Egyptian population centers. And so it was, for Yosef was the one who initially suggested the isolated land of

וַיָּגָר שָׁם – מְלַמֵּד שֶׁלֹּא יָרַד יַעֲקֹב אָבִינוּ לְהִשְׁתַּקֵּעַ בְּמִצְרַיִם, אֶלָּא לָגוּר שָׁם. שֶׁנֶּאֱמַר, וַיֹּאמְרוּ אֶל פַּרְעֹה, לָגוּר בָּאָרֶץ בָּאנוּ, כִּי אֵין מִרְעֶה לַצֹּאן אֲשֶׁר לַעֲבָדֶיךָ, כִּי כָבֵד הָרָעָב בְּאֶרֶץ כְּנָעַן, וְעַתָּה יֵשְׁבוּ נָא עֲבָדֶיךָ בְּאֶרֶץ גֹּשֶׁן.[1]

בִּמְתֵי מְעָט – כְּמָה שֶׁנֶּאֱמַר, בְּשִׁבְעִים נֶפֶשׁ יָרְדוּ אֲבֹתֶיךָ מִצְרָיְמָה, וְעַתָּה שָׂמְךָ יהוה אֱלֹהֶיךָ כְּכוֹכְבֵי הַשָּׁמַיִם לָרֹב.[2]

Goshen as a place in which his family could settle (*Bereishis* 45:10).

Once Yaakov was reassured that traveling to Egypt — even permanently, and even with his family — would not result in adverse spiritual consequences, he changed his original plans and set out for a long-term sojourn in Egypt, not of his own motivation, but only because he was "compelled by Divine decree."

יֵשְׁבוּ נָא עֲבָדֶיךָ בְּאֶרֶץ גֹּשֶׁן
Please let your servants dwell in the land of Goshen.

The Significance of Goshen — Yaakov and his sons, **R' Zalman Sorotzkin** observed, did not want to live in the major population centers of Egypt, although there they would be in close proximity to their kinsman and patron Yosef, for they did not want to face the danger of exposure to the corrupt Egyptian culture or to risk any hint of assimilation to it. In order to obtain Pharaoh's permission to settle in Goshen, the brothers were told to present themselves as shepherds, and since men of this profession were considered an abomination in Egyptian society (*Bereishis* 46:34), Pharaoh would want them to settle far away from the Egyptian masses. The brothers were indeed shepherds at any rate, but they might have been tempted to change their profession (or at least to claim to have done so) in order to avoid the embarrassment of putting themselves in the category of "abominations" before the mighty king of Egypt. But no humiliation was too great to bear in order to secure the desired result of obtaining permission to live in the secluded area of Goshen.

The idea that the brothers should settle in Goshen was originally raised by Yosef (*Bereishis* 45:10), when he first revealed himself to them. He subsequently instructed them to put the request to Pharaoh to be settled in this particular area (ibid., 46:34), which they did (ibid., 47:4). Although we have explained the importance of securing an isolated location in which to settle, what was the significance of this *specific* territory that Yosef and his brothers took such great pains to ensure that they would be allowed to live precisely there?

R' Zalman listed several possible reasons for the preference shown to Goshen.

(1) The *Chumash* commentary *Da'as Zekeinim* notes that when Yosef traveled from Egypt proper to Goshen to be reunited with his father, the Torah writes that

He sojourned there — this teaches that our father Yaakov did not descend to Egypt to settle, but only to sojourn temporarily, as it says: They (the sons of Yaakov) said to Pharaoh: "We have come to sojourn in this land because there is no pasture for the flocks of your servants, because the famine is severe in the land of Canaan. And now, please let your servants dwell in the land of Goshen."[1]

With few people — as it is says: With seventy persons, your forefathers descended to Egypt, and now HASHEM, your God, has made you as numerous as the stars of heaven.[2]

---

1. Bereishis 47:4.   2. Devarim 10:22.

"Yosef *went up* to meet his father, to Goshen" (Bereishis 46:29). Why is the word "went up" (וַיַּעַל) used rather than the simpler "went" (וַיֵּלֶךְ)? *Da'as Zekeinim* explains that Goshen was in an elevated location, for it was near the border of Eretz Yisrael (for which the expression "going up" is always used), as suggested by *Yehoshua* 15:51. This location was thus ideal in that it was officially part of Egypt on the one hand, allowing Yosef the possibility of visiting Yaakov frequently, and yet it was adjacent to Eretz Yisrael, which would facilitate the return of Yaakov's family to that land when the famine would end, or whenever God would instruct them to head back to their homeland.

(2) *Da'as Zekeinim* also mentions the idea (found in the Midrash) that a previous Pharaoh had given the land of Goshen to Sarah as a gift when he took her to be his wife (*Bereishis* 12:15). This region thus belonged by right to Sarah's descendants, Yaakov and his children, and the Egyptians would not be able to complain — now or in the future — that the Jews were encroaching on their territorial rights.

(3) R' Zalman suggested that this area was a royal territory, and not owned by private individuals, so that the Egyptian populace could not accuse Yosef of expropriating their private property just to accommodate his brothers.

וְעַתָּה שָׂמְךָ ה' אֱלֹהֶיךָ כְּכוֹכְבֵי הַשָּׁמַיִם לָרֹב
And now Hashem, your God, has made you as numerous as the stars of heaven.

Like Stars   The fact that the Jewish people is compared metaphorically to the stars has deep significance, **R' Gedaliah Schorr** wrote. When we look at a tiny star in the sky we know that it is actually a tremendous celestial body, and appears small to us only because it so far away. Similarly, the spiritual powers hidden in the soul of every Jew are awesome and mighty, but their true potential is often distorted by the fact that we view them from a distance and their true dimensions are not appreciated by us.

R' Gedaliah explained the figure of speech in another manner as well. We are told that God "gives names to all the stars" (*Tehillim* 147:4). The giving of a name to an

וַיְהִי שָׁם לְגוֹי – מְלַמֵּד שֶׁהָיוּ יִשְׂרָאֵל מְצֻיָּנִים שָׁם.
גָּדוֹל עָצוּם – כְּמָה שֶׁנֶּאֱמַר, וּבְנֵי יִשְׂרָאֵל פָּרוּ וַיִּשְׁרְצוּ וַיִּרְבּוּ וַיַּעַצְמוּ בִּמְאֹד מְאֹד, וַתִּמָּלֵא הָאָרֶץ אֹתָם.[1]
וָרָב – כְּמָה שֶׁנֶּאֱמַר, רְבָבָה כְּצֶמַח הַשָּׂדֶה נְתַתִּיךְ, וַתִּרְבִּי וַתִּגְדְּלִי וַתָּבֹאִי בַּעֲדִי עֲדָיִים, שָׁדַיִם נָכֹנוּ וּשְׂעָרֵךְ צִמֵּחַ, וְאַתְּ עֵרֹם וְעֶרְיָה; וָאֶעֱבֹר עָלַיִךְ וָאֶרְאֵךְ מִתְבּוֹסֶסֶת בְּדָמָיִךְ, וָאֹמַר לָךְ, בְּדָמַיִךְ חֲיִי, וָאֹמַר לָךְ, בְּדָמַיִךְ חֲיִי.[2]

---

object indicates that it has a particular function or possesses certain unique characteristics. Each star, then, has some specific purpose in the scheme of Creation. So too, each Jew has a unique essence and a corresponding task to perform in life, a manner in which to bring glory to God, which cannot be accomplished by anyone else. On the other hand, there is another verse that declares, "He calls a name to them [to the heavenly bodies]" (*Yeshayahu* 40:26) — one name for all of them together. This is because just as the individual has his own unique task through which to give honor to God, so too there is a communal plane, by which the Jewish people as a unit must work to accomplish this goal. Every person must therefore strive throughout his life to achieve his unique potential both as an individual and as a member of the community at large, just as the stars are viewed by God both individually and compositely.

וּבְנֵי יִשְׂרָאֵל פָּרוּ וַיִּשְׁרְצוּ וַיִּרְבּוּ וַיַּעַצְמוּ בִּמְאֹד מְאֹד
And the Children of Israel were fruitful, increased greatly, multiplied, and became very, very mighty;

A Fruitful Nation — The Sages derive from the sixfold expression of fecundity that the Jewish women gave birth to six children at a time. **R' Zalman Sorotzkin** recalled how his father-in-law (R' Eliezer Gordon, the Rabbi and *Rosh Yeshivah* of Telz, Lithuania) was once encountered by an intellectual who found these words of the Rabbis to be unacceptably farfetched. The Rabbi countered this argument by noting some statistical details from the *Chumash* itself. The Israelite nation began in Egypt with seventy men, and 210 years after that numbered over 600,000. According to the ordinary statistical rules of population growth, the people should have increased in number to no more than several thousand. The Torah itself, then, testifies to the abnormal rate of increase in population among the Jews in Egypt.

Another indication of this can be found in the beginning of the book of *Bamidbar*, where the members of each tribe are counted in a census, including only males between the age of twenty and sixty, and the total population count (not counting Levi) is given at 603,550 (*Bamidbar* 1:46). After this another census was taken, this time to determine the number of firstborn males among the twelve tribes (again, not counting Levi). The number given for this count is 22,273 (ibid., 3:43), and this included all firstborn, even those younger than twenty years of age. Now, considering that the first census, which totaled 603,550, included only grown men (up to age sixty), we must conclude that if we would include women, children, and old men we

There he became a nation — this teaches that the Israelites were distinctive there.

Great, mighty — as it says: And the Children of Israel were fruitful, increased greatly, multiplied, and became very, very mighty; and the land was filled with them.[1]

Numerous — as it says: I made you as numerous as the plants of the field; you grew and developed, and became charming, beautiful of figure; your hair grown long; but you were naked and bare. And I passed over you and saw you downtrodden in your blood and I said to you: "Through your blood shall you live"; and I said to you: "Through your blood shall you live."[2]

---

1. *Shemos* 1:7.   2. *Yechezkel* 16:7,6.

---

would arrive at the conclusion that the Jewish people numbered at that time well over two million souls! Now, let us consider the fact that the firstborn who were counted were only the males, so that the total number of firstborn children (including girls) was approximately twice as much, or around 50,000. The ratio of firstborn to the total population was thus 50,000:2,000,000, or 1:40, meaning that out of every forty people, only one of them was a firstborn. In other words, each family had approximately forty children in it! (The number is actually higher, for we assumed that grown men under sixty make up 30 percent of the population, when the actual number is probably closer to 25 percent.) It is not possible for a woman to give birth to forty children in her lifetime unless she has an extraordinary number of multiple births. Hence, we see that the words of the Sages in the Midrash are not taken out of thin air, but have a solid basis in the Torah itself!

וָאֹמַר לָךְ, בְּדָמַיִךְ חֲיִי, וָאֹמַר לָךְ, בְּדָמַיִךְ חֲיִי
And I said to you: "Through your blood shall you live";
and I said to you: "Through your blood shall you live."

The Blood of Circumcision and the Blood of Sacrifice

This verse is taken from a passage in *Yechezkel* (Chapter 16) where the prophet describes metaphorically the liberation of the Jews from Egypt, comparing Israel to an abandoned baby, whom God pities and takes under His care. When the time for redemption arrived, God saw that the child was "naked and bare" (v. 7), meaning that the people were bereft of merits that might entitle them to be delivered from Egypt. God thereupon gave them two mitzvos with which to occupy themselves and thereby to earn their liberation — namely, the mitzvah of circumcision and that of the *pesach* sacrifice — and exclaimed, "Through your blood shall you live; through your blood shall you live." The double expression referred to the blood of circumcision and the blood of the sacrifice (see *Mechilta*, *Parashah* 5; *Rashi* on *Shemos* 12:6), by whose merit the people would merit eternal life.

Granted that the Jews needed to be supplied with a source of merit to earn their

וַיָּרֵעוּ אֹתָנוּ הַמִּצְרִים, וַיְעַנּוּנוּ, וַיִּתְּנוּ עָלֵינוּ עֲבֹדָה קָשָׁה.[1]

release, but why these two particular mitzvos, of all the commandments of the Torah?

R' Gedaliah Schorr explained the reason for this choice as follows. The Jews, during their sojourn in Egypt, had sunk to an extremely low level of immorality and corruption, having learned from the depraved Egyptian culture that had engulfed them for so many years (see *Mechilta*, ibid.).

Spiritual impurity consists of two components — sexual immorality and idolatry (see *Berachos* 12b). It was in order to counteract these two sources of impurity that God gave the Jews these two particular mitzvos at this time. As the Rambam writes in *Moreh Nevuchim*, the rationale behind the mitzvah of circumcision is to curtail one's sexual desires. The Pesach sacrifice was designed to obliterate any vestige of idolatry from the minds of the Israelites and to prepare them for service to God, as was discussed above, p. 15. It was therefore these specific two mitzvos that were given to the Jews at this point, in order to cleanse their souls of the pernicious effects of Egyptian immorality that had pervaded them so thoroughly, and to prepare them for lives of sanctity and purity.

It is interesting to note that in the First Temple period, whenever a particular righteous king purged his kingdom of idolatry there was always an exceptionally significant *pesach* sacrifice that was associated with this purification process. So it happened in the days of Chizkiyah (see *II Divrei Hayamim* 29), and so too in the reign of Yoshiyahu (*I Melachim* 23). This is due to the fact that, as explained above, the *pesach* sacrifice symbolizes the renouncing of idolatry and the acceptance of the yoke of the service of God in its place.

On another occasion, **R' Gedaliah** offered a different possible explanation as to why these two particular mitzvos were chosen by God to be the ones through which the Jews would merit their deliverance, as follows.

The Sages caution us, "Beware of the simple mitzvos just as much as the more serious ones, for you do not know the reward of the various mitzvos" (*Avos* 2:1). Nevertheless, the Rambam writes (Mishnah Commentary, ad loc.) that it is possible to ascertain the relative importance of certain mitzvos by noting the punishment prescribed by the Torah for disregarding these commandments. As examples the Rambam notes that there are only two positive commandments for which the punishment is *kares* (spiritual excision) — namely, failing to have oneself circumcised and refraining from offering the *pesach* sacrifice. With these two exceptions, the positive mitzvos generally do not carry any punishment at all for their neglect.

The Ramban (on *Vayikra* 18:29) explains that the punishment of *kares* (lit., "cutting off") consists of man's soul losing its connection with its Divine source, just as a branch loses its source of life when cut from the tree. If the abrogation of these two mitzvos causes the soul to lose its connection to the Divine source of life, then we may deduce that the proper performance of these two commandments causes an intensification of this connection to God. It is for this reason that these two particular mitzvos were chosen to be given to the Jews, who were devoid of any other merits, at this time.

The Egyptians did evil to us and afflicted us; and imposed hard labor upon us.[1]

1. *Devarim* 26:6.

וַיָּרֵעוּ אֹתָנוּ הַמִּצְרִים
The Egyptians did evil to us

The Malignment of Bnei Yisrael

This translation expresses the simple explanation of the words וַיָּרֵעוּ אֹתָנוּ according to the way it is universally understood. But there is a difficulty with this interpretation. The grammatically correct usage of the word לְהָרַע (*to mistreat*) should normally call for the preposition ל (*to*) to follow the verb, as found in many places in *Tanach* (e.g., *Bereishis* 43:6, *Shemos* 5:22, 5:23), but here it is followed by אֶת (a word used in Hebrew to denote a direct object). In fact the very same idea expressed in this verse is found elsewhere in the Torah (*Bamidbar* 20:15), and there the "correct" usage indeed appears: וַיָּרֵעוּ לָנוּ מִצְרָיִם. What, asked **R' Zalman Sorotzkin,** is the significance of the departure from ordinary grammatical form in our verse, and why is this departure not retained in the parallel phrase in *Bamidbar*?

The way the phrase stands in our verse (using אֶת instead of ל), R' Zalman noted, it actually means, if translated literally, "the Egyptians made us bad" — i.e., they maligned us and made us appear to be bad and corrupt. This, in fact, appears to be the Haggadah's understanding of the phrase. For the Haggadah cites as a proof to the words וַיָּרֵעוּ אֹתָנוּ the verse "Let us deal with them wisely lest they multiply and, if we happen to be at war, they may join our enemies and fight against us, forcing us to leave the country" (*Shemos* 1:10). According to the conventional understanding of וַיָּרֵעוּ אֹתָנוּ, "they mistreated us," this verse proves nothing. The Haggadah should rather have quoted a verse that deals with the throwing of the baby boys into the river, or one that speaks of the hardships and backbreaking labor the Egyptians imposed upon the Jews. What the cited verse does indeed prove is that the Egyptians maligned us, casting groundless aspersions on our reliability and loyalty to their country, accusing us of having designs on taking over the country and expelling the native Egyptians. The Egyptians were thus the first on an unfortunately long list of antagonists to invent and propagate anti-Semitic canards as an excuse to exploit the local Jewish population.

In *Bamidbar* 20:15, however, the context of the words וַיָּרֵעוּ לָנוּ is in a message sent by Moshe to the king of Edom, describing the travails the Jews had gone through in Egypt and explaining why they were poised to pass through Edomite territory on their way to Eretz Yisrael. There was no longer any reason for Moshe to record the fact that the Egyptians "maligned us," falsely accusing us of attempting to overrun their country, because it was quite obvious at that point that nothing of the sort had happened. What was more relevant, however, was the fact that the Egyptians had *maltreated* the Jews and that this brought about their redemption by God and their subsequent journey to the Promised Land. Therefore, the expression used in that situation was וַיָּרֵעוּ לָנוּ, not וַיָּרֵעוּ אֹתָנוּ.

וַיָּרֵעוּ אֹתָנוּ הַמִּצְרִים – כְּמָה שֶׁנֶּאֱמַר, הָבָה נִתְחַכְּמָה לוֹ, פֶּן יִרְבֶּה, וְהָיָה כִּי תִקְרֶאנָה מִלְחָמָה, וְנוֹסַף גַּם הוּא עַל שֹׂנְאֵינוּ, וְנִלְחַם בָּנוּ, וְעָלָה מִן הָאָרֶץ.[1]

וַיְעַנּוּנוּ – כְּמָה שֶׁנֶּאֱמַר, וַיָּשִׂימוּ עָלָיו שָׂרֵי מִסִּים, לְמַעַן עַנֹּתוֹ בְּסִבְלֹתָם, וַיִּבֶן עָרֵי מִסְכְּנוֹת לְפַרְעֹה, אֶת פִּתֹם וְאֶת רַעַמְסֵס.[2]

וַיִּתְּנוּ עָלֵינוּ עֲבֹדָה קָשָׁה – כְּמָה שֶׁנֶּאֱמַר, וַיַּעֲבִדוּ מִצְרַיִם אֶת בְּנֵי יִשְׂרָאֵל בְּפָרֶךְ.[3]

וַיְעַנּוּנוּ – כְּמָה שֶׁנֶּאֱמַר, וַיָּשִׂימוּ עָלָיו שָׂרֵי מִסִּים, לְמַעַן עַנֹּתוֹ
And they afflicted us — as it says: They set taskmasters over them in order to oppress them.

Malicious Enslavement — What does the Haggadah show from the supporting verse ("They set taskmasters over them... to oppress them") that was not already evident from the first quote ("and they afflicted us")? It is absurd to imagine that the Haggadah is simply trying to prove the veracity of one verse by citing another (see above, on אֲרַמִּי אֹבֵד אָבִי)!

The **Netziv** answered this question as follows. From the original verse alone we might have formed the impression that the Egyptians' concern in enslaving the Jews was primarily a monetary consideration. A large force of slave laborers, after all, can do wonders for a nation's economy! Of course, the slaves themselves do not benefit from this arrangement, and this is why the Torah writes that the Egyptians "afflicted us." But in fact this was not the case. The primary objective of the Egyptians was to break the strength and spirit of the Jews (as implied by *Shemos* 1:10); the fact that they were used as forced labor was only incidental. The Talmud (*Sotah* 11a) relates that the names of the cities that were built by Jewish slave labor, Pisom and Raamses, got their names from the fact that whatever building took place in these areas was doomed to collapse due to the particular properties of the local soil and building materials. These cities were not built for any utilitarian purpose, then, but only to keep the Jews busy and miserable. This is the point the Haggadah is trying to make with its supporting verse, "And they set taskmasters over them in order to oppress them with their burdens." This verse makes it clear that the purpose of the enslavement was simply "in order to oppress them," and not for any economic benefit.

וַיָּשִׂימוּ עָלָיו שָׂרֵי מִסִּים, לְמַעַן עַנֹּתוֹ בְּסִבְלֹתָם, וַיִּבֶן עָרֵי מִסְכְּנוֹת לְפַרְעֹה, אֶת פִּתֹם וְאֶת רַעַמְסֵס
They set taskmasters over them in order to oppress them with their burdens; and they built Pisom and Raamses as treasure cities for Pharaoh.

Unproductive Labor — The Talmud explains the reason these places were called by these names: רַעַמְסֵס (*Raamses*) because one by one the buildings would crumble (מִתְרוֹסֵס), and פִּתֹם (*Pisom*) because one by one the

הגדה של פסח [118]

The Egyptians did evil to us — as it says: Let us deal with them wisely lest they multiply and, if we happen to be at war, they may join our enemies and fight against us and then leave the country.¹

And they afflicted us — as it says: They set taskmasters over them in order to oppress them with their burdens; and they built Pisom and Raamses as treasure cities for Pharaoh.²

They imposed hard labor upon us — as it says: The Egyptians subjugated the Children of Israel with hard labor.³

---

1. *Shemos* 1:10.   2. Ibid. v. 11.   3. Ibid. v. 13.

---

buildings would be swallowed up by the earth (פִּי תְהוֹם). In other words, the Egyptians forced the Jews to build buildings in areas that were not suitable to hold secure foundations, and all their efforts ended up being applied toward useless structures that would collapse almost as soon as they were built. **R' Zalman Sorotzkin** wrote that a laborer usually has two sources of satisfaction for his hard work — (1) his salary that he earns doing the job and (2) the feeling of accomplishment upon seeing the job successfully finished. Our verse illustrates for us the extent to which the Egyptians "oppressed them with their burdens" — not only did they force them to work without pay, thus withholding from them the first source of satisfaction, but they also crushed their spirits even further by forcing them to labor at fruitless, nonproductive assignments, depriving them of the second type of satisfaction as well.

וַיַּעֲבִדוּ מִצְרַיִם אֶת בְּנֵי יִשְׂרָאֵל בְּפָרֶךְ
The Egyptians subjugated the Children of Israel with hard labor.

The Reward of Silence

Rashi on *Shemos* 2:14 tells us that Moshe used to wonder why the Jews, of all the nations of the world, were being subjected to such harsh forced labor. Then one day he discovered the answer, when he heard an Israelite man threaten to inform the Egyptian authorities that Moshe had killed an Egyptian the day before. Rashi comments:

> *And Moshe feared* (ibid.) — he feared that perhaps the Jews were really not deserving of redemption.
>
> *And he said, "Indeed the matter is known!"* — the matter over which I had wondered has become known to me. The reason the Jews are subjected to such persecution is that there are informers among them!

The **Chafetz Chaim** was puzzled by Rashi's words. We know that the Jews at that time had sunk to an extremely low level of impurity when they were in Egypt, to the point where the angels could not understand why God favored the Jews over the Egyptians (*Mechilta*, *Beshalach*). Why, then, was Moshe so bewildered by the fact that the Jews were subjected to such harsh labor? After all, they were involved in the most grievous sins!

The Chafetz Chaim answered that we know that each sin a person commits

וַנִּצְעַק אֶל יהוה אֱלֹהֵי אֲבֹתֵינוּ, וַיִּשְׁמַע יהוה אֶת קֹלֵנוּ, וַיַּרְא אֶת עָנְיֵנוּ, וְאֶת עֲמָלֵנוּ, וְאֶת לַחֲצֵנוּ.[1]

וַנִּצְעַק אֶל יהוה אֱלֹהֵי אֲבֹתֵינוּ – כְּמָה שֶׁנֶּאֱמַר, וַיְהִי בַיָּמִים הָרַבִּים הָהֵם וַיָּמָת מֶלֶךְ מִצְרַיִם, וַיֵּאָנְחוּ בְנֵי יִשְׂרָאֵל מִן הָעֲבֹדָה, וַיִּזְעָקוּ, וַתַּעַל שַׁוְעָתָם אֶל הָאֱלֹהִים מִן הָעֲבֹדָה.[2]

וַיִּשְׁמַע יהוה אֶת קֹלֵנוּ – כְּמָה שֶׁנֶּאֱמַר, וַיִּשְׁמַע אֱלֹהִים אֶת נַאֲקָתָם, וַיִּזְכֹּר אֱלֹהִים אֶת בְּרִיתוֹ אֶת אַבְרָהָם, אֶת יִצְחָק, וְאֶת יַעֲקֹב.[3]

וַיַּרְא אֶת עָנְיֵנוּ – זוֹ פְּרִישׁוּת דֶּרֶךְ אֶרֶץ, כְּמָה שֶׁנֶּאֱמַר, וַיַּרְא אֱלֹהִים אֶת בְּנֵי יִשְׂרָאֵל, וַיֵּדַע אֱלֹהִים.[4]

וְאֶת עֲמָלֵנוּ – אֵלּוּ הַבָּנִים, כְּמָה שֶׁנֶּאֱמַר, כָּל הַבֵּן הַיִּלּוֹד הַיְאֹרָה תַּשְׁלִיכֻהוּ, וְכָל הַבַּת תְּחַיּוּן.[5]

---

creates an accusing force that testifies against him on Judgment Day. Many sins create many accusers, and grievous sins create grievous accusers. But as long as a person does not sin with his speech these accusers also do not open their mouths against him. When he uses his mouth to speak ill of others — or, in this case, to inform on others — he grants the power to all the accusers that have been created by his other sins to begin their accusations. The Jews in Egypt had indeed committed many serious sins, but until Moshe saw that there were informers among them, he could not understand why his people were singled out for such harsh punishment.

Concerning the sin of informing on a fellow Jew, the **Chafetz Chaim** used to tell a story about the Vilna Gaon. One time the Gaon was traveling in a wagon when the driver carelessly allowed the horses to veer off the road into an adjacent field, which was sown with crops. The carriage became stuck and the Gaon had to alight while the driver attempted to get it back to the road. The furious owner of the field ran over to the carriage and began beating and cursing the Gaon, mistaking him for the driver. The Gaon's first thought was that he should clarify the fact that he was the passenger and the other man was the driver, but he realized that this would constitute informing on a fellow Jew. He therefore decided to remain silent, despite the severe blows that were being rained down upon him.

After this incident the Gaon remarked to his students that if he had not withstood the temptation to simply tell the farmer that he was not the driver and was therefore not to blame, all of his greatness in Torah and his righteous deeds would not have done him any good on the Day of Judgment, for the sin of informing would have prevented all these merits from being of any benefit to him!

We cried out to Hashem, the God of our fathers; and Hashem heard our cry and saw our affliction, our burden, and our oppression.[1]

We cried out to Hashem, the God of our fathers — as it says: It happened in the course of those many days that the king of Egypt died; and the Children of Israel groaned because of the servitude and cried; their cry because of the servitude rose up to God.[2]

Hashem heard our cry — as it says: God heard their groaning, and God recalled His covenant with Avraham, with Yitzchak, and with Yaakov.[3]

And saw our affliction — that is the disruption of family life, as it says: God saw the Children of Israel and God knew.[4]

Our burden — refers to the children, as it says: Every son that is born you shall cast into the river, but every daughter you shall let live.[5]

---

1. *Devarim* 26:7.   2. *Shemos* 2:23.   3. Ibid. v. 24.   4. Ibid. v. 25.   5. Ibid. 1:22.

וְכָל הַבַּת תְּחַיּוּן
but every daughter you shall let live.

Caring for the Female Babies

The word תְּחַיּוּן actually means much more than "let live"; the literal translation is "give [them] life." What is the significance of this expression?

Another question is: The first time the Torah mentions Pharaoh's decree to kill all Jewish males at birth, it says (*Shemos* 1:16), "and if it is a daughter, she may live." Why is this expression altered in our verse (ibid., v. 22), when the Torah records Pharaoh's second decree?

The **Netziv** explained that Pharaoh at first instructed the midwives simply to kill the males and to spare the females. But the midwives subsequently reported back to him that the Jewish women were giving birth without the assistance of midwives, "for they are robust" (ibid., v. 19). Pharaoh was very impressed with the physical hardiness of the Jewish women, and he reasoned that this was probably one of the major factors involved in the unnatural rate of increase in the Jewish population. He thereupon decided to use this for his own benefit, and issued instruction at this point not only to *spare* the Jewish girls, but to actually make a conscious effort to give them postnatal assistance to enhance their ability to survive and thrive (to *give them life*). Having mandated the killing of all Jewish baby males, Pharaoh knew (or expected) that the females would one day grow up and marry into the Egyptian population. He wanted to encourage this process, figuring that the physical qualities of the Jewish women would now be turned to the service of the Egyptian nation, allowing them to become numerous and powerful just as the Jews had.

וְאֶת לַחֲצֵנוּ – זוֹ הַדְּחַק, כְּמָה שֶׁנֶּאֱמַר, וְגַם רָאִיתִי אֶת הַלַּחַץ אֲשֶׁר מִצְרַיִם לֹחֲצִים אֹתָם.[1]

וַיּוֹצִאֵנוּ יהוה מִמִּצְרַיִם בְּיָד חֲזָקָה, וּבִזְרֹעַ נְטוּיָה, וּבְמֹרָא גָּדֹל, וּבְאֹתוֹת וּבְמֹפְתִים.[2]
וַיּוֹצִאֵנוּ יהוה מִמִּצְרַיִם – לֹא עַל יְדֵי מַלְאָךְ,

וְאֶת לַחֲצֵנוּ – זוֹ הַדְּחַק, כְּמָה שֶׁנֶּאֱמַר, וְגַם רָאִיתִי אֶת הַלַּחַץ
Our oppression — refers to the pressure expressed in the words:
I have also seen how the Egyptians are oppressing them.

Opression and Pressure   The question is raised by many Haggadah commentators: How does the support verse ("I have also seen...") prove the assertion made by the Haggadah — that "oppression" refers to "pressure"? The support verse itself merely uses the word "oppression," just as the original verse did!

R' Zalman Sorotzkin, quoting his father-in-law (R' Eliezer Gordon, the Rabbi and *Rosh Yeshivah* of Telz, Lithuania), explained that in this section of the *Haggadah*, which is in effect a midrashic analysis of each phrase of four verses in *Devarim* 26:5-8 (beginning with אֲרַמִּי אֹבֵד אָבִי — a passage known as *Mikra Bikkurim*), the Haggadah takes each phrase of this passage and expounds upon it in one of three ways: (1) Sometimes the Haggadah takes a vague or difficult word and gives an exact definition of it, or provides an added insight to the original. (2) In other instances the Haggadah cites a selection from the actual narrative of the Egyptian exile and Exodus in the beginning of *Shemos* to illustrate that the facts mentioned in the *Mikra Bikkurim* passage indeed took place as stated (see, however, above, p. 107. (3) In yet other cases the Haggadah presents *both* of these types of analysis.

Let us clarify this observation with a few examples. "An Aramean destroyed my father" (*Devarim* 26:5) is a vague, enigmatic statement. The Haggadah explains clearly what is meant by these words: Lavan (the Aramean) *attempted* to destroy Yaakov (my father). "And he went down to Egypt" (ibid.) is elaborated upon further with an added insight: Yaakov's descent to Egypt was not undertaken by choice, but under Divine command. "With an outstretched arm" is a vague, undefined figure of speech; the Haggadah explains: "this refers to the sword." These are examples of type (1) discussed above. Often this type of analysis is bolstered with a supporting verse as well.

The intention of "with few people" (ibid.) is clear enough, but the Haggadah introduces a supporting verse to show that this is indeed what happened: "With seventy persons your forefathers descended to Egypt." *Mikra Bikkurim* states "and they afflicted us" (*Devarim* 26:6), and the Haggadah proves that this was so with the supporting verse, "And they set taskmasters over them in order to oppress them." These are examples of type (2) of the Haggadah's analysis of *Mikra Bikkurim*.

In *Mikra Bikkurim* it states, "And He saw our affliction." "Affliction" is a vague term, and the Haggadah elaborates on its exact meaning — forced separation

הגדה של פסח   [122]

Our oppression — refers to the pressure expressed in the words: I have also seen how the Egyptians are oppressing them.[1]

HASHEM took us out of Egypt with a mighty hand and with an outstretched arm, with great fear, with signs and with wonders.[2]

HASHEM took us out of Egypt — not through an angel,

---

1. *Shemos* 3:9. 2. *Devarim* 26:8.

---

between man and wife. Then the Haggadah brings a supporting verse: "as it says, *And God saw*. . . ." This supporting verse does not prove the Haggadah's assertion that "affliction" indicates forced separation between man and wife; rather, it simply proves that there *was* such a forced separation (as the commentators explain). In this example, the Haggadah *both* elaborates on a vague term and brings a proof that this is what actually happened. This represents type (3) discussed above. Another instance of this type is when the Haggadah discusses the word "our burden" from *Mikra Bikkurim*. First it elaborates on the meaning of this word, explaining that it refers to the children, and then it brings a supporting verse — not to support the assertion that "burden" means children, but to prove that the Egyptians did indeed afflict us through killing our children.

Now, returning to our passage, it becomes clear what the Haggadah is trying to tell us. This section is an example of type (3). First the Haggadah clarifies the meaning of the vague term "oppression" and explains that it means "pressure." Then the Haggadah proves from the supporting verse not that "oppression" is to be understood as "pressure," but only that this kind of oppression indeed existed in Egypt.

וַיּוֹצִיאֵנוּ ה' מִמִּצְרַיִם – לֹא עַל יְדֵי מַלְאָךְ, וכו'
*Hashem took us out of Egypt —
not through an angel (or emissary), . . .*

Hashem Alone Directed the Exodus

The Haggadah interprets the words "Hashem took us out of Egypt" to imply that there was no intermediary or emissary involved in the Exodus from Egypt, but only Hashem Himself, with His direct action. But this assertion seems to be contradicted by another verse in the Torah: "Moshe sent messengers from Kadesh to the king of Edom: Thus says your brother Israel: You are aware of all the travails that have befallen us. Our forefathers went down to Egypt. . . and [Hashem] *sent an emissary who took us out of Egypt*" (*Bamidbar* 20:14-16).

R' Zalman Sorotzkin offered two possible solutions to this apparent contradiction: First, it is possible that when the Haggadah asserts that the Exodus was accomplished without the services of any emissary it refers specifically to the Plague of the Firstborn, which is the topic of the supporting verse cited by the Haggadah. The rest of the aspects of the Exodus, however, were indeed accomplished through intermediaries. This approach has its difficulties, however (see below, on וְהֵבֵיתִי).

R' Zalman presented the second possible answer to the contradiction by means

וְלֹא עַל יְדֵי שָׂרָף, וְלֹא עַל יְדֵי שָׁלִיחַ, אֶלָּא הַקָּדוֹשׁ בָּרוּךְ הוּא בִּכְבוֹדוֹ וּבְעַצְמוֹ. שֶׁנֶּאֱמַר, וְעָבַרְתִּי בְאֶרֶץ מִצְרַיִם בַּלַּיְלָה הַזֶּה, וְהִכֵּיתִי כָל בְּכוֹר בְּאֶרֶץ מִצְרַיִם מֵאָדָם וְעַד בְּהֵמָה, וּבְכָל אֱלֹהֵי מִצְרַיִם אֶעֱשֶׂה שְׁפָטִים, אֲנִי יהוה.¹ וְעָבַרְתִּי בְאֶרֶץ מִצְרַיִם בַּלַּיְלָה הַזֶּה — אֲנִי וְלֹא מַלְאָךְ. וְהִכֵּיתִי כָל בְּכוֹר בְּאֶרֶץ מִצְרַיִם — אֲנִי וְלֹא שָׂרָף.

---

of an anecdote. One time one of the leading rabbis of Vilna saw a Jewish farmer walking down the road with a cow tied to his wagon, which was being pulled by a horse. The rabbi informed the farmer that what he was doing was a violation of the Torah's prohibition of *kilayim* (*Devarim* 22:10). The farmer was not impressed, however, and ignored the warnings of the rabbi, whom he did not know from before. At that point the rabbi shouted to the farmer, "I am the foremost rabbi of Vilna — and one of the most well-known rabbis in the world for that matter! When we get to town I will declare a *cherem* (religious ban) against you and then you will be sorry for defying me!" This threat struck at the heart of the farmer, and he immediately obeyed the rabbi's orders and untied his cow.

Such, explained R' Zalman, was the situation with Moshe and the king of Edom. It must be remembered that when Moshe spoke of an emissary sent by Hashem to take the Jews out of Egypt, he was referring to himself (see *Rashi* ad loc.). Moshe knew that the king would not be impressed if he received a message from some unknown rabbi named "Moshe," asking for a favor. Therefore, although he was "the most modest of all men" (*Bamidbar* 12:3) he referred to himself as a מַלְאָךְ (which means *emissary*, but can also mean *angel*), in the hope that this august title might impress and intimidate the king a bit. The Exodus was, as the Haggadah tells us here, accomplished by Hashem directly, but Moshe was, of course, the leader who implemented Hashem's commands and physically led the people out of Egypt.

וּבְכָל אֱלֹהֵי מִצְרַיִם אֶעֱשֶׂה שְׁפָטִים
And upon all the gods of Egypt will I execute judgments;

Destroying False Ideologies — Once, in a discussion of current events, **R' Elchanan Wasserman** posed the question: What is the great tribute to God that He meted out judgments against the gods of Egypt? Why is it considered to be so astonishing that the all-powerful God Who created heaven and earth vanquished a number of idols made of stone and wood?

The Torah means to describe a much more far-reaching process, R' Elchanan explained. Not only did God dispose of the actual idols used by the Egyptians in their worship, but He eradicated the belief in them and in all the false religious and philosophical notions to which the Egyptians had held so firmly.

Consider our own day and age, R' Elchanan continued. Many Jews were swept up with the surging tide of Socialism when this philosophy first became prominent. After this, many of our people embraced the more extreme positions of the

not through a seraph, not through a messenger, but the Holy One, Blessed is He, in His glory, Himself, as it says: I will pass through the land of Egypt on that night; I will slay all the firstborn in the land of Egypt from man to beast; and upon all the gods of Egypt will I execute judgments; I, HASHEM.[1]

"I will pass through the land of Egypt on that night" — I and no angel; "I will slay all the first-born in the land of Egypt" — I and no seraph;

---

1. *Shemos* 12:12.

Communists and the Bolsheviks. So what did God do? He sent us Hitler, who was also a great believer in Socialism, as the name of his party proudly declares — the *Nationalsozialsten* (*Nazi*, for short). So much for Socialism! Then God sent us, as chairman of the Communist party, the murderer Stalin, who is supposed to be the embodiment of the Communist ideal. So much for Communism!

In this manner we can see in our own day and age how God metes out judgments upon today's gods just as He did then, by completely undermining the foundations upon which the justification of this form of "worship" rests.

וְהִכֵּיתִי כָל בְּכוֹר בְּאֶרֶץ מִצְרַיִם – אֲנִי וְלֹא שָׂרָף
"I will slay all the firstborn in the land of Egypt" — I and no seraph;

Only Hashem Knows — The Haggadah makes it unequivocally clear that at least the Plague of the Firstborn was administered directly by God and not by any intermediary — angel, seraph, emissary, etc. But there is a formidable difficulty with this assertion, which the commentators note: In *Shemos* 12:23 the Torah writes, "When Hashem will pass by to strike the Egyptians, He will see the blood on the lintels and the two doorposts, and Hashem will pass over that doorway, and not allow *the Destroyer* to enter your houses." There *was,* then, an intermediary — the "Destroyer" — who administered the Plague of the Firstborn!

R' Zalman Sorotzkin quoted an answer to this question in the name of the commentator *Chelkas Yoav*. According to the Talmud (*Bava Metzia* 61b) it becomes apparent that it was not only children who were firstborn to their mothers that died in the plague, but also those who were firstborn to their fathers (such as in a woman's second marriage). This is the Talmud's statement: "I [God] am the One Who differentiated between the first seed of a man and the seed which was not his first, and I will also punish those who... put *kala ilan* (an inexpensive indigo-like dye) in their tzitzis instead of the (very expensive) *techeles* (whose appearance is identical to *kala ilan*)." The Talmud is thus dealing with issues that it is not possible for any human to know about. Only God can know for sure which child is a father's first (for it is impossible for any person to know if any particular man has ever fathered a child before what appears to be his "first"), and only God knows whether a person is wearing genuine or false *techeles*. *Chelkas Yoav* therefore

וּבְכָל אֱלֹהֵי מִצְרַיִם אֶעֱשֶׂה שְׁפָטִים – אֲנִי וְלֹא הַשָּׁלִיחַ. אֲנִי יהוה – אֲנִי הוּא, וְלֹא אַחֵר.

בְּיָד חֲזָקָה – זוֹ הַדֶּבֶר, כְּמָה שֶׁנֶּאֱמַר, הִנֵּה יַד יהוה הוֹיָה בְּמִקְנְךָ אֲשֶׁר בַּשָּׂדֶה, בַּסּוּסִים בַּחֲמֹרִים בַּגְּמַלִּים בַּבָּקָר וּבַצֹּאן, דֶּבֶר כָּבֵד מְאֹד.[1]

וּבִזְרֹעַ נְטוּיָה – זוֹ הַחֶרֶב, כְּמָה שֶׁנֶּאֱמַר, וְחַרְבּוֹ שְׁלוּפָה בְּיָדוֹ, נְטוּיָה עַל יְרוּשָׁלָיִם.[2]

---

suggests that the killing of the children who were firstborn to their mothers — whose identity was well known to everyone — was given over to the Destroyer to accomplish. But the striking down of the children who were firstborn to their fathers — whose identity was known only to God — had to be carried out by Him Himself, for there is no angel who would be able to fulfill such a mission.

בְּיָד חֲזָקָה – זוֹ הַדֶּבֶר. . . , וּבִזְרֹעַ נְטוּיָה – זוֹ הַחֶרֶב. . . , וּבְמֹרָא גָּדֹל זוֹ גִּלּוּי שְׁכִינָה
With a mighty hand — refers to the pestilence. . . . With an outstretched arm — refers to the sword. . . . And with great fear — refers to the revelation of the Shechinah (God's presence).

Deterring the Wicked

It is apparent, then, remarked **R' Zalman Sorotzkin**, that the revelation of God's presence would not have made any impression upon the Egyptians and induced them to release the Jews unless they were preceded by pestilence and the sword, so insensitive were they to matters of spirituality and godliness.

We find a similar phenomenon in connection with the story of Bilaam. At one point, "Hashem opened up Bilaam's eyes and he saw the angel of Hashem standing in the road with his sword drawn in his hand" (*Bamidbar* 22:31). Apparently seeing an angel right in front of him would not have affected him one way or another; the angel had to show him the outstretched sword in order to make an impression upon him. It is only when their lives are threatened that the wicked begin to sense God's existence and recognize His presence, even when it is quite obvious and revealed for all (who are willing) to see.

בְּיָד חֲזָקָה – זוֹ הַדֶּבֶר
With a mighty hand — refers to the pestilence.

The Undeserving Jews

The "pestilence" mentioned by the Haggadah here, the **Netziv** wrote, is not to be identified with the plague by that name, for why should this verse refer specifically to this particular one of the ten plagues? Rather, he explains, it refers to the annihilation of a large sector of the Jewish population during the plague of Darkness, as related in the

הגדה של פסח [126]

"And upon all the gods of Egypt will I execute judgments" — I and no messenger; "I, HASHEM" — it is I and no other.

With a mighty hand — refers to the pestilence, as it is stated: Behold, the hand of HASHEM shall strike your cattle which are in the field, the horses, the donkeys, the camels, the herds, and the flocks — a very severe pestilence.[1]

With an outstretched arm — refers to the sword, as it says: His drawn sword in His hand, outstretched over Jerusalem.[2]

---

1. *Shemos* 9:3.   2. *I Divrei Hayamim* 21:16.

Midrashim. These people, who were comfortable in their positions in Egypt and were opposed to leaving, did not merit to experience the miracles of the Exodus and were wiped out in the space of a few days — apparently by some disease or epidemic. It is this disease that the Haggadah speaks of when it mentions "the pestilence." Although the supporting verse cited by the Haggadah speaks explicitly of the *plague* of pestilence, this verse is brought only to illustrate that the expression "God's hand" is used to allude to pestilence, and no further comparison between the two verses is intended. The term "mighty hand" in our verse is thus related to the same expression in *Yechezkel* 20:33, which speaks of God's wrath being poured out upon those who are unfaithful to Him.

וּבִזְרֹעַ נְטוּיָה – זוֹ הַחֶרֶב
With an outstretched arm — refers to the sword,

Civil War in Egypt

Which "sword" is the Haggadah referring to here? We do not find any sword whatsoever mentioned in the Torah in connection with the Exodus.

R' Zalman Sorotzkin suggested an answer based on a Midrash which expounds the verse, "[Give thanks] to the One Who struck the Egyptians by their firstborn" (*Tehillim* 136:10). The verse would have been clearer had it stated, "[Give thanks] to the One Who struck the Egyptian firstborn." Why was this cumbersome manner of speech used? The Midrash explains that when the firstborn of Egypt heard that a plague was soon to strike them down, they demanded that Pharaoh and his advisers capitulate to the Jews and release them rather than remain obstinate at their (the firstborns') expense. When Pharaoh refused to listen to their request they turned to violence and began to kill their fellow Egyptians (who were not firstborn). This, the Midrash explains, is why the verse says, "[Give thanks] to the One Who struck the Egyptians *by* their firstborn" — it was *through* the firstborn that God struck down many ordinary Egyptians on that day. It is this "sword" — the sword of one Egyptian against another — that the Haggadah is referring to here.

THE HAGGADAH OF THE ROSHEI YESHIVAH

וּבְמֹרָא גָּדֹל – זוֹ גִּלּוּי שְׁכִינָה, כְּמָה שֶׁנֶּאֱמַר, אוֹ הֲנִסָּה אֱלֹהִים לָבוֹא לָקַחַת לוֹ גוֹי מִקֶּרֶב גּוֹי, בְּמַסֹּת, בְּאֹתֹת, וּבְמוֹפְתִים, וּבְמִלְחָמָה, וּבְיָד חֲזָקָה, וּבִזְרוֹעַ נְטוּיָה, וּבְמוֹרָאִים גְּדֹלִים, כְּכֹל אֲשֶׁר עָשָׂה לָכֶם יהוה אֱלֹהֵיכֶם בְּמִצְרַיִם לְעֵינֶיךָ.[1]

וּבְאֹתוֹת – זֶה הַמַּטֶּה, כְּמָה שֶׁנֶּאֱמַר, וְאֶת הַמַּטֶּה הַזֶּה תִּקַּח בְּיָדֶךָ, אֲשֶׁר תַּעֲשֶׂה בּוֹ אֶת הָאֹתֹת.[2]

וּבְמֹרָא גָּדֹל – זוֹ גִּלּוּי שְׁכִינָה
And with great fear — alludes to the revelation of the Shechinah,

The Revelation of Hashem's Glory

The Haggadah's intention here is quite vague. To specifically which event or events of the Exodus does it refer when it speaks of "the revelation of the *Shechinah*"? Furthermore, what is the basis of the Haggadah's connection between the verse's words "great fear" and "revelation of the *Shechinah*"? Another question is: What does the Haggadah accomplish by citing the supporting verse that states yet again that God's extraction of the people of Israel from Egypt was achieved through "great wonders. . . and great fear"? What new insight does this new verse supply that was not apparent from the first verse? The commentators have offered many different interpretations, and the **Netziv** proposed his own as well.

The revelation spoken of here, he explained, does not refer to any event that took place in Egypt, but rather to events that occurred as the Israelites were wandering in the desert for forty years. On several occasions, when there was rebellion or defiance among the people, the Torah tells us that suddenly "the glory of God appeared in the Tent of Meeting" — when the people complained about lack of food (*Shemos* 16:10), during the incident of the spies (*Bamidbar* 14:10), during Korach's rebellion (ibid., 16:19), etc. (see also ibid., 17:7 and 20:6). In all these cases the sudden appearance of God's glory (the *Shechinah*) filled the people with "great fear" and brought them to the immediate, sobering realization that they had committed a grave offense.

As far as the supporting verse is concerned, the Netziv explained that having established that the term "great fear" is to be associated with the Jews' experiences in the desert, the first "great fear" that comes to mind is the fear of traversing a perilous, barren wilderness — "a great and fearsome desert, a place of snakes, fiery serpents, and scorpions, and thirst without water" (*Devarim* 8:15) — without any sort of provisions. In order to prove its assertion that the "great fear" of our verse does not refer to these types of dread, but to revelations of God's presence, it quotes the supporting verse from *Devarim* 4:34 that speaks of "great fears" in the *plural*. Now, the fear of hunger, snakes, scorpions, etc. is actually one long, continuous fear, unlike the occasions when God's glory revealed itself to the

And with great fear — alludes to the revelation of the Shechinah, as it says: Has God ever attempted to take unto Himself a nation from the midst of another nation by trials, miraculous signs, and wonders, by war and with a mighty hand and outstretched arm and by awesome revelations, as all that HASHEM your God did for you in Egypt, before your eyes?[1]

With signs — refers to the miracles performed with the staff as it says: Take this staff in your hand, that you may perform the miraculous signs with it.[2]

---

1. *Devarim* 4:34. 2. *Shemos* 4:17.

---

people, which were a series of individual incidents. The use of the plural word "fears," then, shows that the Haggadah's interpretation of the expression "great fear" in *Mikra Bikkurim* is the correct one.

וּבְאֹתוֹת – זֶה הַמַּטֶּה
With signs — refers to the miracles performed with the staff

Moshe's Staff How does this supporting verse prove the Haggadah's assertion that "signs" refers to "the staff"? Here again (see previous piece) the **Netziv** saw the Haggadah's interpretation of the word וּבְאֹתוֹת (*And with signs*) as referring not to events in Egypt, but to the period when the Jews were traveling in the desert. For it was by means of the staff that many of the miracles of that time period were accomplished, such as the war against Amalek (*Shemos* 17:9), the splitting of the Reed Sea (ibid., 14:16), and the extraction of water from a rock (ibid., 17:6, *Bamidbar* 20:8). The first association one would likely make when the words "signs and wonders" are mentioned in connection with the Exodus would be the ten plagues, which are often described by these terms (*Shemos* 7:3, 10:1, 11:10, etc.). (This association is in fact adopted by the other opinion, דָּבָר אַחֵר, which follows in the Haggadah.) But the Haggadah here interprets them instead as references to the travels of the Jews in the desert *after* the Exodus from Egypt.

In order to back up its assertion that the word "sign" can be used to refer to the staff, the Haggadah adduces a verse which speaks of the "staff with which you will perform the miraculous signs." It is not uncommon in Hebrew for an object (or person) to be called by a name that reflects the activity in which that object (or person) is constantly involved. Examples are: "Be a blessing" (and not "Be a man who gives blessings" — *Bereishis* 12:2); "I am a prayer" (and not "I fervently pray" — *Tehillim* 69:14). Here too, since the staff's main purpose was to serve as a medium through which miracles and signs were achieved, itself is referred to by the Torah as "signs," according to the Haggadah's interpretation of the word.

וּבְמוֹפְתִים – זֶה הַדָּם, כְּמָה שֶׁנֶּאֱמַר, וְנָתַתִּי מוֹפְתִים בַּשָּׁמַיִם וּבָאָרֶץ:

As each of the words דָּם, *blood*, אֵשׁ, *fire*, and עָשָׁן, *smoke*, is said, a bit of wine is removed from the cup, with the finger or by pouring.

דָּם וָאֵשׁ וְתִימְרוֹת עָשָׁן.[1]

___

זֶה הַמַּטֶּה / **This refers to the miracles performed with the staff**

An Affirmation of Moshe's Mission

God could certainly have implemented the ten plagues and the splitting of the Sea (and the miracles in the wilderness) without this staff. What, then, was the point in making the staff such a central feature of the miracles of the Exodus?

R' Zalman Sorotzkin compared this situation to a Talmudic ruling in *Yevamos* 117a. The Mishnah states there that there are certain people (for example, a sister-in-law or a rival-wife) who may not testify concerning the death of a woman's husband in order to permit her to remarry. The reason is that there is basis for concern that these people might lie just in order to cause the woman to sin by marrying another man while her first husband is in fact still alive. However, these same people *may* testify on behalf of the same woman that a *get* (divorce document) is valid, thus permitting her to remarry. What, asks the Mishnah, is the difference between the two cases? In either event the woman is being granted permission to remarry on the basis of these people's testimony! The Mishnah answers that in the latter case the fact that the person testifying is in possession of a document establishes a reasonable basis for their claim; the verbal testimony in this case is not the only factor. In the former case, however, there is no evidence in the matter whatsoever other than the testimony of these people.

R' Zalman asserted that the same psychological factor is involved here as well. If Moshe would appear before his fellow Jews or before Pharaoh with a mere verbal claim that he is the emissary of God, charged by Him with taking the Jews out of Egypt, it would have been difficult for these people to give credence to this claim, miracles and signs notwithstanding. Therefore God provided him with a physical object that was a concrete affirmation of his claim to having been sent by God.

The same concept was applied by R' Zalman to explain another issue as well. The question has been asked: In consideration of the fact that God gave the entire Torah to Moshe anyway, why was it necessary to give him the two tablets upon which were engraved the Ten Commandments? These commandments were incorporated into the written Torah in any event! Based on the idea explained above, we can now understand quite clearly the function of a tangible, concrete token that testifies as to the authenticity of Moshe's transmission of God's word to the people.

וּבְמוֹפְתִים – זֶה הַדָּם / **With wonders — alludes to the blood,**

The Sanctity of Bnei Yisrael

Most commentators understand the "blood" mentioned here as a reference to the first plague, in which all the waters of Egypt turned into blood. According to this interpretation, however, the question arises: Why did the Torah single out this particular one of the ten plagues for special mention? Because of this question, the **Netziv** offered a

> With wonders — alludes to the blood, as it says: I will show wonders in the heavens and on the earth:
>
> As each of the words דָּם, *blood*, אֵשׁ, *fire*, and עָשָׁן, *smoke*, is said, a bit of wine is removed from the cup, with the finger or by pouring.
>
> **Blood, fire, and columns of smoke.**[1]

---

1. *Yoel* 3:3.

---

different explanation of the Haggadah's comment. The blood, he wrote, refers not to the plague of Blood in Egypt, but, once again (see above, on וּבְמֹרָא גָּדֹל and וּבְאֹתוֹת), to events experienced by the Jews as they were wandering in the desert.

Rashi (on *Shemos* 10:10) quotes a Midrash relating that Pharaoh warned Moshe that he foresaw astrologically that there was a star (called רָעָה, *Evil*) that forebode "blood and killing" for the Jews if they would venture out into the desert. And so it was, for the Jews were punished swiftly and severely for every misdeed they committed while traveling in the desert. This, explained the Netziv, is the "blood" that the Haggadah refers to in its interpretation of the word "wonders." The obvious question, however, is: Why would the verse, which seeks to describe the Exodus in terms that are favorable and glorious, suddenly mention this "blood" of punishment and Divine retribution against the Jews? The Netziv answered that although it might seem somewhat paradoxical, the fact that the Jews were held to such a strict standard shows the high level of spirituality and sanctity on which they lived. Similarly, Moshe told Aharon after his two sons died suddenly as a punishment for violating the sanctity of the *Mishkan*: "This is what God has said: 'Through My holy ones I become sanctified' " (*Vayikra* 10:3). Sometimes a strict punishment is an indication of the greatness of the individual involved.

Thus, according to the Netziv the three terms מֹרָא גָּדֹל, אֹתוֹת, and מוֹפְתִים are all applied by the Haggadah not to the Exodus from Egypt itself, but to the period of wandering in the wilderness that followed it.

דָּם וָאֵשׁ וְתִימְרוֹת עָשָׁן / *Blood, fire, and columns of smoke.*

A Cup of Blessing It is customary to spill out some wine from the cup while reciting these words and the names of the ten plagues. This is an ancient custom, and is mentioned in the Rema's addenda to the *Shulchan Aruch*, quoting *Maharil*. What is the reason for this practice?

R' Zalman Sorotzkin explained the custom as follows. The four cups of the Seder are "cups of blessing," over which we recite songs and praises of God. The Talmud teaches that when a "cup of blessing" is drunk (such as at Kiddush, etc.) it is appropriate to give some of its wine to the members of one's family (especially one's wife), for partaking in this form of praising God brings blessings to all involved. The second cup of the Seder is the one over which we praise God for all the miracles He performed for us during the Exodus, but there is one place in the discussion of the Haggadah which speaks not of blessing but of misfortune and plague — namely, the passage under discussion here. When drinking the cup of wine later in the Seder we wish to partake only of the wine of the "cup of blessing," not of "wine of curses." Therefore, we remove the wine from the cup while reciting these words of misfortune, so as to retain the status of the wine as "wine of blessing."

דָּבָר אַחֵר – בְּיָד חֲזָקָה, שְׁתַּיִם. וּבִזְרֹעַ נְטוּיָה, שְׁתַּיִם. וּבְמֹרָא גָּדֹל, שְׁתַּיִם. וּבְאֹתוֹת, שְׁתַּיִם. וּבְמֹפְתִים, שְׁתַּיִם. אֵלּוּ עֶשֶׂר מַכּוֹת שֶׁהֵבִיא הַקָּדוֹשׁ בָּרוּךְ הוּא עַל הַמִּצְרִים בְּמִצְרַיִם, וְאֵלּוּ הֵן:

As each of the plagues is mentioned, a bit of wine is removed from the cup. The same is done by each word of Rabbi Yehudah's mnemonic.

דָּם. צְפַרְדֵּעַ. כִּנִּים. עָרוֹב. דֶּבֶר. שְׁחִין. בָּרָד. אַרְבֶּה. חֹשֶׁךְ. מַכַּת בְּכוֹרוֹת.

אֵלּוּ עֶשֶׂר מַכּוֹת
These are the ten plagues...

Mankind Gets a Second Chance

According to the *Zohar* the reason there were exactly ten plagues visited upon the Egyptians is that this number corresponds to the Ten Utterances (עֲשָׂרָה מַאֲמָרוֹת) through which God created the world (see *Avos* 5:1). Surely the *Zohar* means more than to simply note a numerical coincidence; what is the deeper idea that lies behind this correspondence? This matter was addressed by **R' Gedaliah Schorr**.

Let us begin by citing the Mishnah in *Avos* (ibid.) where the idea of the Ten Utterances is first introduced:

> The world was created with Ten Utterances. And why does the Torah tell us this? Could it not have been created with just one utterance? The reason is in order to [increase] the punishment of the wicked, who destroy the world that was created with Ten Utterances, and to [increase] the reward of the righteous, who uphold the world that was created with Ten Utterances.

Upon examining the words of this Mishnah the question presents itself: Why should a larger number of utterances involved in Creation lead to an increased reward for the righteous and greater punishment for the wicked? The *Sefas Emes* explained the relationship as follows. If the world had been created with one utterance, the mastery of God over the universe and the fact that it was created by Him would have been self-evident. There would be no challenge in accepting God, and there would be no intelligent human being who would ever doubt His existence and dominion. By creating the world in ten distinct steps — or utterances — however, the role of God in Creation became more and more hidden and inconspicuous, perceived only by those who are sensitive enough to spiritual matters to draw the proper conclusions. Now that the world was created with so many utterances, the realization and acceptance of God's mastery over ourselves and over the entire universe is much more of a challenge. It provides an opportunity for the stubborn hearted to miss the point, and thereby presents a situation through which the righteous can be rewarded for discovering the subtle truth. The task of man in this world is to see through all the ''veils'' that obstruct his spiritual ''vision'' to achieve an awareness of God's role in the Universe. The prophet Yeshayahu exhorts us, ''Lift your eyes on high and realize Who created these things!'' (40:26). It has been

Another explanation of the preceding verse: [Each phrase represents two plagues,] hence: mighty hand — two; outstretched arm — two; great fear — two; signs — two; wonders — two. These are the ten plagues which the Holy One, Blessed is He, brought upon the Egyptians in Egypt, namely:

<small>As each of the plagues is mentioned, a bit of wine is removed from the cup. The same is done by each word of Rabbi Yehudah's mnemonic.</small>

1. Blood 2. Frogs 3. Vermin 4. Wild Beasts
5. Pestilence 6. Boils 7. Hail 8. Locusts 9. Darkness
10. Plague of the Firstborn.

---

noted that the words for *Who* (מִי) and *these* (אֵלֶּה) are formed from exactly the same letters as God's name (אֱלֹהִים), symbolizing the fact that through contemplating the wonders of nature and the vastness of the Universe we can come to an awareness of their Creator. The Chassidic masters also point out that the numerical value of God's Name (אֱלֹהִים) is identical to that of הַטֶּבַע (*nature*), which also teaches us that pondering nature leads to a recognition of God's existence.

But there are people who, whether because of spiritual obtuseness or outright wickedness, do not reach the proper conclusions. For such people, the Chasam Sofer writes, the ten plagues provided a second opportunity to recognize the Hand of God in the world, as the Torah says concerning the plagues, "... in order that I might place these signs of Mine in their midst." In case someone missed the message of "Who created *these* things" he has a chance to learn it through "*these* signs."

We can now understand the connection between the Ten Utterances and the ten plagues posited by the *Zohar*. The Ten Utterances in effect obscured God's mastery over the Universe; the ten plagues were designed to shed light and clarity upon that mastery.

דָּם / Blood

Gratitude The Torah tells us that Moshe told Aharon to initiate the plagues of Blood and Frogs (*Shemos* 7:19, 8:1), unlike many of the other plagues that were actuated by Moshe. The Sages explain the reason for this course of action: These two plagues emerged from the Nile River, and since Moshe was protected by the river when he was a baby, it would have been improper for him to strike the very river that had saved his life. So far does the concept of gratitude extend that the Torah applies it even to inanimate objects!

A story is told about the **Chafetz Chaim** that illustrates the extent of his concern for this trait. One time he was walking down the street in Vilna with his son-in-law, R' Hersh Levinson, when a stranger, who was walking in the other direction, paused and brushed off some dirt that he had noticed on the Chafetz Chaim's coat. Before the Chafetz Chaim had a chance to thank the man for his consideration he disappeared into the crowd. The rabbi was greatly upset by the fact that he was unable to express his gratitude to the man for taking the trouble to clean off his coat, and this thought kept causing him anxiety as he walked toward the hotel where he was staying.

When he arrived at the hotel, the Chafetz Chaim was surprised to find that a ruble coin that he had had in his pocket was missing. He could not imagine where he had lost this coin, until R' Hersh presented the obvious possibility that the stranger who had stopped to brush the Chafetz Chaim's coat did so only as a ruse to distract him while he picked his pocket!

The Chafetz Chaim's eyes lit up. "If so," he declared with satisfaction, "then he has indeed received the reward for his trouble!"

צְפַרְדֵּעַ / Frogs

The Severity of Lashon Hara

The **Chafetz Chaim** contrasted this incident with another one in *Bamidbar* (21:4-9). Concerning the plague of Frogs the Torah tells us that Pharaoh asked Moshe to pray to God to remove the scourge from himself and his people (*Shemos* 8:4). Moshe agreed, and told him that the following day the frogs would depart. Moshe's prayer was answered, and God brought an immediate end to the plague.

In *Bamidbar* (ibid.) the Torah relates that as the Jews were traveling in the desert, "the people spoke against God and against Moshe, 'Why did you take us up out of Egypt. . .?'" God punished the people by sending "fiery serpents" against them, who killed many of them. The Torah then tells us that Moshe prayed on behalf of the people. In this case, however, "Hashem said to Moshe, 'Make a serpent and place it on top of a pole. . . And it shall be that whoever has been bitten will look at it and live.'"

In this case God did not directly accept Moshe's prayer and bring an end to the affliction that was ravaging the people. In order to halt the punishment God prescribed a particular procedure that had to be followed. Why was it, asked the Chafetz Chaim, that the plague that affected Pharaoh was unconditionally and immediately discontinued, while that which afflicted the Jews in the desert was only brought to a halt by means of a more complicated process?

The Chafetz Chaim answered that this distinction teaches us the severity of the sin of speaking evil against others (*lashon hara*), as the Jews did in this incident in the desert. All other sins — even those on the magnitude of Pharaoh's — may be atoned for through mere contrition and prayer, but when it comes to *lashon hara* a much higher level of repentance is required before it can be forgiven. For the Talmud (*Rosh Hashanah* 29a) explains how a graven serpent on a pole could heal people from the serpent's bite: "The people would look up to heaven and subjugate their hearts to their Father in Heaven, and thereby be healed."

כִּנִּים / Lice

Lice in Goshen

Concerning many of the plagues, the Torah states explicitly that they did not affect the Jewish area of Egypt at all, and regarding several others the Torah is not explicit on this issue, but implicitly suggests that they did not affect the Jews. When it comes to Lice, however, the Torah does not give any indication whatsoever as to whether it affected the Jews or not. The Rambam writes, in his Mishnah Commentary, that there is a tradition that the lice did indeed infest the Jewish areas of Egypt, but that it did not cause them any harm. In *Torah Sheleimah* (an immense compendium of the Sages' comments on the Torah, culled from the Talmudim, Midrashim, etc.) the author comments that it appears that the Rambam's tradition has no source in any known Midrash or Talmudic statement.

R' Zalman Sorotzkin, however, showed that this tradition, though perhaps not explicitly stated by the Sages, was certainly assumed by them, as follows. When Yaakov was about to die he commanded his sons to carry his remains to Eretz Yisrael for burial there. Why was Yaakov so adamant about not being buried in Egypt and troubling his children to bury him in this distant land? The Midrash gives several answers to this question, among them: Yaakov knew prophetically that one day the soil of Egypt would turn into lice, and in order to avoid the indignity of lying in such soil he left instructions to be buried elsewhere. Now, if the land of Goshen was not afflicted with the plague of Lice, as it was protected from the other plagues, why did Yaakov not consent to be buried there? It was, after all, the place where he had spent the last seventeen years of his life, and was the home of all of his children and grandchildren! Apparently, then, we must conclude that the plague of Lice did indeed affect the land of Goshen, and this is why Yaakov refused to be buried there.

In regard to the Rambam's tradition, the question arises: Why indeed was it that this one plague, of all ten plagues, affected the Jewish areas as well? Surely there must be some reason behind this remarkable exception.

R' Zalman suggested that the reason for this phenomenon might be based upon a Midrashic comment that states that from the time of the plague of Lice and onwards, the Jews no longer were forced to labor at making bricks. The reason for this is that as a result of the lice, soil of sufficient quality for baking bricks could not be found. Now, if the plague of Lice had not affected Goshen, this incidental benefit would not have been received by the Jews, for they would have simply been sent to Goshen (which is where their homes were anyway) to find soil for their brick-producing tasks. This is why God saw to it that this plague, which ruined the soil, affected the Jewish areas as well.

עָרוֹב / Wild Beasts

Beasts From Afar

In the warning that Moshe gave Pharaoh before this plague, he told him, "If you do not send out my people, behold, I am sending against you. . . wild beasts, and the houses of Egypt will be filled with the wild beasts, and also the land upon which they are" (*Shemos* 8:17). What is meant by the seemingly extraneous phrase, "and also the land upon which they are"?

The **Chafetz Chaim** offered an explanation for these puzzling words. If Pharaoh had been informed simply that wild beasts were to invade his country he would not have felt particularly threatened. After all, beasts that are native to Egypt would not pose much of a problem, as the people were used to them and could probably cope even with a large influx of such animals. As far as beasts from faraway lands — they do not normally leave their natural habitat and venture into new lands and climates, for they would not survive long under these new, unfamiliar conditions. For this reason Moshe warned Pharaoh that not only would swarms of beasts overrun Egypt, but God would see to it that some of their native soil ("the land upon which they are") and habitat would come along with them, so that animals from the most distant locations would be able to migrate and survive in Egypt. This was indeed a formidable threat.

רַבִּי יְהוּדָה הָיָה נוֹתֵן בָּהֶם סִמָּנִים:
דְּצַ"ךְ • עֲדַ"שׁ • בְּאַחַ"ב.

ר' יְהוּדָה הָיָה נוֹתֵן בָּהֶם סִמָּנִים
Rabbi Yehudah abbreviated them by their Hebrew initials:

Why a Mnemonic? There is a Mishnah in *Menachos* (11:4) that states: "The two breads (offered on Shavuos — *Vayikra* 23:17) were 7 (*tefachim*, handbreadths) long and 4 wide; its 'horns' (protrusions on its corners) were 4 fingerbreadths. The showbread (placed every week inside the Sanctuary of the Temple) was 10 (*tefachim*) long and 5 wide; its 'horns' were 7 fingerbreadths. R' Yehudah says: So that you do not make a mistake, [remember] זד"ד יה"ז (the Hebrew letters representing the numbers 7-4-4, 10-5-7)." The commentator R' Ovadiah of Bartenura notes: "It was R' Yehudah's custom to make such abbreviations, as in the Haggadah's דצ"ך עד"ש באח"ב." The question arises, however: In the case of *Menachos* we can understand why a mnemonic was necessary, for there are two sets of numbers for the two types of bread, and one could certainly confuse the figures for the two or reverse them without some way of remembering them accurately. But in the case of the Haggadah, what possible confusion could arise in the listing of the Ten Plagues? There are no alternate versions with which to confuse them!

R' Zalman Sorotzkin noted that the story of the ten plagues is recorded not only in the Torah, but also in *Tehillim* (Chap. 78). In that place, however, the plagues are mentioned in a different order than they are listed in the Torah. (For instance, Wild Beasts precedes Frogs, and Locusts precedes Pestilence.) R' Yehudah therefore saw fit to make a mnemonic in this case as well, to ensure that people realize that the correct chronological order of the plagues was as recorded in the Torah, while the version in *Tehillim* is rearranged into a nonchronological order. (See *Malbim* ad loc., who explains the reason for the revision of the order given in *Tehillim*.)

דְּצַ"ךְ עֲדַ"שׁ בְּאַחַ"ב
D'TZACH, ADASH, B'ACHAV.

No Excuses! R' Yehudah's abbreviation is a mnemonic device (see above), but it is also much more than that. He took care to divide the ten plagues into three distinct groups, and the commentators attach a great deal of significance to this fact, **R' Zalman Sorotzkin** wrote. The Rashbam notes that in each of the three sets of plagues the first two were preceded by warnings while the third came without advance notice. We might add to this the observation of the fact that the first plague of each set was accompanied by a warning issued early in the morning, when Pharaoh took his daily walk to the river. The warning for the second plague in each set was given in a confrontation with Pharaoh in his palace (the words of the Torah in these cases are בֹּא אֶל פַּרְעֹה — enter [the palace] of Pharaoh). In other words, the plagues were sent against Pharaoh under three different circumstances — after a private warning (the first of each set), after a public warning (the second in each set) and with no warning at all. This was done, R' Zalman explained,

Rabbi Yehudah abbreviated them by their Hebrew initials: D'TZACH, ADASH, B'ACHAV.

in order to eliminate any possible excuses that Pharaoh might have offered for his sinful obstinacy — "Your private warnings were not taken seriously"; "Your public warnings were humiliating and infuriating, and I became enraged because of them"; "You didn't warn me!"

דְּצַ"ךְ עֲדַ"שׁ בְּאַחַ"ב
D'TZACH, ADASH, B'ACHAV.

Four Stages of Freedom

As the commentators unanimously agree, R' Yehudah's abbreviation of the ten plagues in this manner is surely more than a convenient mnemonic device. Many of them see the significance of the abbreviation as lying in R' Yehudah's division of the plagues into three distinct groups (see previous comment). The **Netziv** adopted this approach as well, and offered the following analysis of the abbreviation's deeper meaning.

After each of the plagues (except for the last one, of course) Pharaoh's heart hardened and he refused to let the Israelites go. But it is interesting to note the subtle differences in wording in each of these refusals, after the words "and Pharaoh hardened his heart." After the first three plagues Pharaoh "did not listen to them" (*Shemos* 7:13, 8:11, 8:15). Following plagues #4 and #5 he "did not send out the people" (ibid., 8:28, 9:7). After plague #6 it is written again that "he did not listen to them." And finally, after plagues #7, #8, and #9 the Torah tells us that "he did not send out the Children of Israel"(ibid., 9:35, 10:20, 11:10). What is the significance of these changes in expression from one plague to the next?

As is well known, God's promise of liberation of the Jewish people consisted of the famous "four expressions of redemption": "I shall take you out from under the burdens of Egypt, and I shall rescue you from their service, and I shall redeem you with an outstretched arm and with great judgments, and I shall take you to Me for a nation" (*Shemos* 6:6-7). These four statements are not simply rephrased repetitions of the same promise, the **Netziv** explained. In fact, the liberation of the Jews from Egypt took place in four distinct steps, corresponding to these four expressions. First the people were relieved from the "*burdens* (or better, *sufferings*) of Egypt," meaning that the heavy, backbreaking labor that had been forced upon them was stopped, although they were still officially slaves and had to work for their masters. The second stage was that they were "saved from their labors," meaning that they were released from all obligations to do *any* forced work. However, they still had the legal status of slaves — property of the Egyptians, without any personal freedom, and certainly without any possibility of leaving. The final step was "redemption," or liberation from servitude, but still short of full Egyptian renunciation of claim over them. The last stage was when the people became fully liberated from Egyptian subjugation; as a people they were no longer "Pharaoh's nation," but "God's nation" ("I shall take you to me for a nation").

It is these four stages of liberation, wrote the Netziv, that are expressed in the

The cups are refilled. The wine that was removed is not used.

רַבִּי יוֹסֵי הַגְּלִילִי אוֹמֵר: מִנַּיִן אַתָּה אוֹמֵר שֶׁלָּקוּ הַמִּצְרִים בְּמִצְרַיִם עֶשֶׂר מַכּוֹת וְעַל הַיָּם לָקוּ חֲמִשִּׁים מַכּוֹת? בְּמִצְרַיִם מָה הוּא אוֹמֵר, וַיֹּאמְרוּ הַחַרְטֻמִּם אֶל פַּרְעֹה, אֶצְבַּע אֱלֹהִים הִוא.[1] וְעַל הַיָּם מָה הוּא אוֹמֵר, וַיַּרְא יִשְׂרָאֵל אֶת הַיָּד הַגְּדֹלָה אֲשֶׁר עָשָׂה יהוה בְּמִצְרַיִם, וַיִּירְאוּ הָעָם אֶת יהוה, וַיַּאֲמִינוּ בַּיהוה וּבְמֹשֶׁה עַבְדּוֹ.[2] כַּמָּה

---

changing of wording of Pharaoh's refusal to release the Jews. At first the plagues had no effect whatsoever on Pharaoh. "He did not listen to them [Moshe and Aharon]" — at all. The people's status remained exactly as it had been previously. The plagues gradually began to have an effect on Pharaoh, however, and after the plague of Wild Beasts (#4) he decided to capitulate partially. The first stage of liberation was realized, as Pharaoh released the Jews from their obligation to perform heavy-duty, backbreaking slave labor. This is why the Torah says at this point not "He did not listen to them," but "He did not send out the people." Pharaoh did indeed start to listen to them, and eased the plight of the people a bit; the only thing he refused to do was "to send out the people," i.e., to declare a complete end to their forced enslavement. The second time the Torah says "He did not send out the people" (in plague #5) indicates that Pharaoh once again lightened the burdens of the Jews, but still stopped short of "sending out the people," of releasing them from bondage. Plague #6 apparently made no further impact on Pharaoh, so the Torah says simply, "He did not listen to them" — at all.

A completely new stage was entered after plague #7. Pharaoh began to recognize the Jews and respect them as a legitimate people with their own unique identity and demands. At this point he completely released them from any obligation to perform forced labor. This is why the Torah writes from here on, "He did not send out the Children of Israel," for Pharaoh had come to recognize the people as a national, respectable unit. This was the fulfillment of the second of the four stages of deliverance.

There is support for this analysis in the Talmud, which teaches (*Rosh Hashanah* 11a) that on the Rosh Hashanah preceding the Exodus the Jews were released from servitude. According to another Talmudic teaching (*Eduyos* 2:10) the ordeal of the Egyptians, from the time Moshe first approached Pharaoh until the Exodus, lasted one year. The Sages also teach that each plague — from the initial warning until the end of the effects of the plague — lasted for one month. Thus, counting backwards from the Exodus we will come to the conclusion that Rosh Hashanah (when, according to *Rosh Hashanah* 11a, the servitude ended) was the time when the plague of Wild Beasts (#4) was beginning. This corresponds to what we established above, that it was at the time of this plague that Pharaoh abolished at least some of the slave-related duties of the people.

The cups are refilled. The wine that was removed is not used.

Rabbi Yose the Galilean said: How does one derive that the Egyptians were struck with ten plagues in Egypt, but with fifty plagues at the Sea? — Concerning the plagues in Egypt the Torah states: The magicians said to Pharaoh, "It is the finger of God."[1] However, of those at the Sea, the Torah relates: Israel saw the great "hand" which HASHEM laid upon the Egyptians, the people feared HASHEM and they believed in HASHEM and in His servant Moshe.[2] How many plagues

---

1. *Shemos* 8:15.   2. Ibid. 14:31.

At any rate, we have shown clearly that there is a definite pattern of progressive capitulation during the ten plagues, that can be divided into three stages — D'TZACH, ADASH, B'ACHAV.

וַיַּרְא יִשְׂרָאֵל אֶת הַיָּד הַגְּדֹלָה אֲשֶׁר עָשָׂה ה' בְּמִצְרַיִם
... וַיַּאֲמִינוּ בַּה' וּבְמשֶׁה עַבְדּוֹ

Israel saw the great "hand" which Hashem laid upon the Egyptians
... and they believed in Hashem and in His servant Moshe.

Complete Faith in Moshe   When Moshe was originally sent by God on his mission to Pharaoh, he first approached the Jewish people and told them that God had heard their cries and was going to deliver them from Egypt. The Torah describes their reaction to Moshe's words: "The people believed" (*Shemos* 4:31). Furthermore, the Sages tell us that when Moshe had at first protested to God that "They will not believe me!" (*Shemos* 4:1) he was severely reprimanded for making this baseless, slanderous remark (see *Rashi* ad loc.). "They are believers, sons of believers!" God admonished him. How, then, can we understand the Torah's statement in this verse cited in the Haggadah, that it was only when Israel saw God's might at the parting of the Reed Sea that they feared Him and believed in Him?

R' **Gedaliah Schorr** explained that when it comes to faith in God, there are many different degrees, and one cannot compare faith at a lower level to belief on a higher plane. That this is so can be seen by the fact that the Torah requires every Jewish man to recite the *Shema*, a declaration of our belief in the unity of God and our devotion to Him. Apparently each declaration of faith adds a certain dimension to our level of dedication to these principles, for otherwise this constant repetition would be pointless.

Korach and his coconspirators were swallowed up by the earth (*Bamidbar* 16:32) for their denial of one of the basic principles of the Jewish faith — the supremacy and uniqueness of Moshe's prophecy (see Rambam's Mishnah Commentary, *Sanhedrin*, Chapter 10). The Sages (*Bava Basra* 74a) tell us that these people, lodged in Gehinnom surrounded by fire, are heard to declare every thirty days, "Moshe is true and his Torah is true, and we are liars." The reason for this monthly pronouncement is that we find that thirty days is the amount of time that it takes a person to forget. Thus we are told that R' Chiyya reviewed the entire corpus of his Torah knowledge every thirty days (*Berachos* 38b), in order to ensure that it not be forgotten. Furthermore, the Talmud tells us that certain blessings are to be recited when a situation arises that had not occurred in thirty days, for before this amount of time the previous occurrence is still fresh in one's mind and does not make such a striking impression (see *Berachos* 58b, 59b). This is why the people of Korach's camp must remind themselves every thirty days of the lesson they had learned many thousands of years ago. Faith cannot go on indefinitely unless it is constantly reinforced and augmented.

The Rambam expresses the same sentiment in his Mishnah Commentary (ibid.), after he finishes presenting his famous thirteen principles of the Jewish faith: "Therefore, know these [principles] and review them many times and contemplate them thoroughly. And if your heart tries to persuade you to do otherwise, and you think that you have acquired an understanding of these matters after reading them once or even ten times, God knows that you are being persuaded falsely!" For superficial faith is not the same as deeply ingrained faith, and each review, each contemplation, adds a dimension to what had already been established.

As an example of how superficial faith in God can be at its lowest level, let us consider the following saying of the Sages of the Talmud (*Berachos* 63a, omitted in most texts but found in marginal note): "Even a thief, as he is about to break in, calls out to God for help." If this criminal would think about the implications of his prayers and about how absurdly they stand in contradiction to his deeds, he would certainly refrain from what he is about to do and find himself a new source of livelihood! But his faith in God has apparently not reached even this simple level of sophistication. Full faith in God, on the other hand, implies total, unquestioning obedience and allegiance.

It is true that the people believed Moshe when he first approached them and told them of their impending deliverance. However, this faith was sorely lacking in its substance. The Midrash tells us (see *Rashi* to *Shemos* 5:1) that by the time Moshe got to Pharaoh's palace to confront Pharaoh, his original entourage of seventy elders had completely dispersed until he was left with no one but Aharon to accompany him. When the Torah tells us that after the splitting of the Sea Israel "believed in Hashem and in Moshe," however, it is speaking of an unshakable faith on such a completely different plane that it constituted a new entity altogether from that which had existed before.

וַיַּרְא יִשְׂרָאֵל אֶת הַיָּד הַגְּדֹלָה אֲשֶׁר עָשָׂה ה' בְּמִצְרַיִם
. . . וַיַּאֲמִינוּ בַּה' וּבְמֹשֶׁה עַבְדּוֹ

Israel saw the great "hand" which Hashem laid upon the Egyptians
. . . and they believed in Hashem and in His servant Moshe.

Punishment With Precision

The Jews had just a short time ago witnessed the ten plagues, which demonstrated beyond a shadow of a doubt God's mastery over all the forces of nature and His willingness to override them when He sees fit. What did the Jews see now that they hadn't seen before, asked the **Chafetz Chaim**, that induced them to "believe in Hashem"?

The answer he gave is based on Rashi's comments to the Song of the Sea (*Shemos* 15), where three different metaphors are used to describe the drowning of the Egyptians in the Sea: The Egyptians are compared to "straw" (v. 7), to "lead" (v. 10), and to "stones" (v. 5). Rashi explains that each individual Egyptian was punished according to his particular level of culpability. The most wicked were thrashed about by the waters like straw; the better ones descended into the water like rocks; and the ones who were still better sank like lead, and met their end swiftly, without much suffering.

It was this fairness of punishment that so impressed the Israelites at this point. During the plagues all the Egyptians suffered more or less equally; it was only now that they realized the extent to which God punishes and rewards man exactly in accordance with his deeds, and it was this realization that induced them to "fear Hashem," and to acquire an even higher level of faith than what they had had previously.

וַיַּאֲמִינוּ בַּה' וּבְמֹשֶׁה עַבְדּוֹ
and they believed in Hashem and in His servant Moshe.

Hashem's Master Plan — Did the Israelites not already believe in God before this time (see above)? The *Sefas Emes* explains that it was at this time that the Jews first realized that not only deliverance and liberation were achieved by the hand of God, but also the suffering and trials of exile. This, he explains, is why they mentioned in their song a portrayal of Pharaoh's words as he left his palace to lead his army "in victory" against the fleeing Jews: "The enemy said, 'I shall pursue; I shall overtake; I shall distribute spoils'" (*Shemos* 15:9). Now they realized that Pharaoh's pursuit of them and the terror it had induced in them were all brought about by God, for it was through their miraculous downfall that the glory of God was revealed for all to see.

R' Gedaliah Schorr used this principle to explain a comment made by the Gemara (*Gittin* 56b). Referring to the destruction of the Temple the Sages apply the verse, "Who is like You among the mighty, Hashem?" (*Shemos* 15:11), and homiletically alter the word אֵלִים (*mighty*) to read אִלְמִים (*mute*), yielding: "Who is mute like You, Hashem, Who stands by and allows Titus to commit such blasphemy while remaining silent?" It seems odd that the Talmud should attribute such a meaning to these words, which are taken from the Song of the Sea. Why would Moshe and the Jews allude to such an idea in the middle of their song of praise over God's miraculous salvation? The answer is that, as shown above, one of the main points of this Song was to show an understanding of the fact that it is not only direct salvation but also episodes of suffering and tragedy that are orchestrated by God, and that we praise Him for the bad (or rather, what appears to be bad) as well as for the good.

A similar thought is expressed by the Beis Halevi, R' Gedaliah noted. The Midrash comments:

> The manner of the righteous is that they use the same expression with which they had sinned to rectify their sin.

לָקוּ בְאֶצְבַּע? עֶשֶׂר מַכּוֹת. אֱמוֹר מֵעַתָּה, בְּמִצְרַיִם לָקוּ עֶשֶׂר מַכּוֹת, וְעַל הַיָּם לָקוּ חֲמִשִּׁים מַכּוֹת.

רַבִּי אֱלִיעֶזֶר אוֹמֵר. מִנַּיִן שֶׁכָּל מַכָּה וּמַכָּה שֶׁהֵבִיא הַקָּדוֹשׁ בָּרוּךְ הוּא עַל הַמִּצְרִים בְּמִצְרַיִם הָיְתָה שֶׁל אַרְבַּע מַכּוֹת? שֶׁנֶּאֱמַר, יְשַׁלַּח בָּם חֲרוֹן אַפּוֹ – עֶבְרָה, וָזַעַם, וְצָרָה, מִשְׁלַחַת מַלְאֲכֵי רָעִים.[1] עֶבְרָה, אַחַת. וָזַעַם, שְׁתַּיִם. וְצָרָה, שָׁלֹשׁ. מִשְׁלַחַת מַלְאֲכֵי רָעִים, אַרְבַּע. אֱמוֹר מֵעַתָּה, בְּמִצְרַיִם לָקוּ אַרְבָּעִים מַכּוֹת, וְעַל הַיָּם לָקוּ מָאתַיִם מַכּוֹת.

Moshe said: I know that I sinned before You with the word אָז (*then*), (as it says, "Ever since [אָז] I came before Pharaoh to speak in Your Name he has only made things worse for this people" — *Shemos* 5:23). Therefore I shall praise you with אָז (as it says, "Then [אָז] Moshe and the Children of Israel sang" — *Shemos* 15:1).

In what sense does the Song of the Sea serve as a rectification of Moshe's sin of doubting God's purpose in sending him to Pharaoh? What is the relevance between these two episodes altogether?

The Beis Halevi explains that as long as the Jews were in exile in Egypt, suffering under the cruel oppression and persecution of Pharaoh's tyrannical hand, they could not — or would not — see the Hand of God guiding their destiny. But after the Exodus, culminating with the splitting of the Reed Sea and the revelation of God's power in the vanquishing of Pharaoh's mighty army, Moshe realized in retrospect that the exile — as much as the deliverance — had all been part of God's master plan.

וַיַּאֲמִינוּ בַּה' וּבְמֹשֶׁה עַבְדּוֹ
And they believed in Hashem and in His servant Moshe.

Everyone Is a Believer At this point, following the splitting of the Reed Sea and the drowning of the entire attacking Egyptian army, the people's faith in God was firmly established.

R' Elchanan Wasserman once said in the name of the Telzer *Rosh Yeshivah*, R' Eliezer Gordon: Today there are many irreligious, "secular" individuals among our people, who pride themselves on their being open-minded "nonbelievers." But in fact, they are mistaken. They are in fact great believers — but in the wrong things. They put their faith in powers and ideals that are not worthy of belief, while ignoring the One in Whom we are obligated to believe. They do not believe the words of the true prophets, but they put all their trust in the words of contemporary false prophets. The tendency to believe in something is deeply entrenched in the human psyche, but,

did they receive with the finger? Ten! Then conclude that if they suffered ten plagues in Egypt [where they were struck with a finger], they must have been made to suffer fifty plagues at the Sea [where they were struck with a whole hand].

Rabbi Eliezer said: How does one derive that every plague that the Holy One, Blessed is He, inflicted upon the Egyptians in Egypt was equal to four plagues? — as it says: He sent upon them His fierce anger: wrath, fury, and trouble, a band of emissaries of evil.[1] [Since each plague in Egypt consisted of] 1) wrath, 2) fury, 3) trouble, and 4) a band of emissaries of evil, therefore conclude that in Egypt they were struck by forty plagues and at the Sea by two hundred!

---

1. *Tehillim* 78:49.

---

like all other human traits, needs to be channeled in the proper direction.

In fact, R' Elchanan added, when a person is not guided by the view of the Torah, his belief in his own self-found principles and ideals is likely to be even more fanatical and blind than that of the religious Jew.

מִנַּיִן שֶׁכָּל מַכָּה וּמַכָּה שֶׁהֵבִיא הַקָּדוֹשׁ בָּרוּךְ הוּא
עַל הַמִּצְרִים בְּמִצְרַיִם הָיְתָה שֶׁל אַרְבַּע מַכּוֹת

How does one derive that every plague that the Holy one, Blessed is He, inflicted upon the Egyptians in Egypt was equal to four plagues?

Plagues Within Plagues — The Haggadah does not specify exactly how each plague consisted of four subplagues, but at least in the case of the first plague — Blood — a hint at this fact may be found in the Torah itself, **R' Zalman Sorotzkin** pointed out. We are told that (1) "The water changed to blood" (*Shemos* 7:20), terrifying and unnerving the Egyptians with the ghastly sight; (2) "the fish in the river died" (ibid., 7:21), decimating an important source of food and nourishment for the populace; (3) "the river stank" (ibid.), an unpleasant and annoying experience for anyone who lived anywhere near the river — namely, almost everyone in Egypt; (4) "the Egyptians were not able to drink water from the river" (ibid.), bringing about an acute water shortage, for the Nile was virtually the only source of fresh water for the country. According to R' Akiva (below), who asserts that each plague consisted of *five* parts, we might add the fact that (5) "All the Egyptians dug for water to drink all around the river" (ibid., 7:24) — the sudden need for intensive labor that was normally totally unnecessary.

These four (or five) facets are apparent only in this instance, but from this case it is possible to extend the concept to the other plagues and to apply this principle to them as well.

רַבִּי עֲקִיבָא אוֹמֵר. מִנַּיִן שֶׁכָּל מַכָּה וּמַכָּה שֶׁהֵבִיא הַקָּדוֹשׁ בָּרוּךְ הוּא עַל הַמִּצְרִים בְּמִצְרַיִם הָיְתָה שֶׁל חָמֵשׁ מַכּוֹת? שֶׁנֶּאֱמַר, יְשַׁלַּח בָּם חֲרוֹן אַפּוֹ, עֶבְרָה, וָזַעַם, וְצָרָה, מִשְׁלַחַת מַלְאֲכֵי רָעִים. חֲרוֹן אַפּוֹ, אַחַת. עֶבְרָה, שְׁתַּיִם. וָזַעַם, שָׁלֹשׁ. וְצָרָה, אַרְבַּע. מִשְׁלַחַת מַלְאֲכֵי רָעִים, חָמֵשׁ. אֱמוֹר מֵעַתָּה, בְּמִצְרַיִם לָקוּ חֲמִשִּׁים מַכּוֹת, וְעַל הַיָּם לָקוּ חֲמִשִּׁים וּמָאתַיִם מַכּוֹת.

כַּמָּה מַעֲלוֹת טוֹבוֹת לַמָּקוֹם עָלֵינוּ.

אִלּוּ הוֹצִיאָנוּ מִמִּצְרַיִם,
וְלֹא עָשָׂה בָּהֶם שְׁפָטִים, דַּיֵּנוּ.
אִלּוּ עָשָׂה בָּהֶם שְׁפָטִים,
וְלֹא עָשָׂה בֵאלֹהֵיהֶם, דַּיֵּנוּ.
אִלּוּ עָשָׂה בֵאלֹהֵיהֶם,
וְלֹא הָרַג אֶת בְּכוֹרֵיהֶם, דַּיֵּנוּ.
אִלּוּ הָרַג אֶת בְּכוֹרֵיהֶם,
וְלֹא נָתַן לָנוּ אֶת מָמוֹנָם, דַּיֵּנוּ.
אִלּוּ נָתַן לָנוּ אֶת מָמוֹנָם,
וְלֹא קָרַע לָנוּ אֶת הַיָּם, דַּיֵּנוּ.
אִלּוּ קָרַע לָנוּ אֶת הַיָּם,
וְלֹא הֶעֱבִירָנוּ בְּתוֹכוֹ בֶּחָרָבָה, דַּיֵּנוּ.
אִלּוּ הֶעֱבִירָנוּ בְּתוֹכוֹ בֶּחָרָבָה,
וְלֹא שִׁקַּע צָרֵינוּ בְּתוֹכוֹ, דַּיֵּנוּ.
אִלּוּ שִׁקַּע צָרֵינוּ בְּתוֹכוֹ,
וְלֹא סִפֵּק צָרְכֵּנוּ בַּמִּדְבָּר אַרְבָּעִים שָׁנָה, דַּיֵּנוּ.
אִלּוּ סִפֵּק צָרְכֵּנוּ בַּמִּדְבָּר אַרְבָּעִים שָׁנָה,
וְלֹא הֶאֱכִילָנוּ אֶת הַמָּן, דַּיֵּנוּ.

Rabbi Akiva said: How does one derive that each plague that the Holy One, Blessed is He, inflicted upon the Egyptians in Egypt was equal to five plagues? — as it says: He sent upon them His fierce anger, wrath, fury, trouble, and a band of emissaries of evil. [Since each plague in Egypt consisted of] 1) fierce anger, 2) wrath, 3) fury, 4) trouble, and 5) a band of emissaries of evil, therefore conclude that in Egypt they were struck by fifty plagues and at the Sea by two hundred and fifty!

>The Omnipresent has bestowed
>so many favors upon us!

Had He brought us out of Egypt,
    but not executed judgments against the Egyptians,
                it would have sufficed us.
Had He executed judgments against them,
    but not acted against their gods,
                it would have sufficed us.
Had He acted against their gods,
    but not slain their firstborn,
                it would have sufficed us.
Had He slain their firstborn,
    but not given us their wealth,
                it would have sufficed us.
Had He given us their wealth,
    but not split the Sea for us,
                it would have sufficed us.
Had He split the Sea for us,
    but not led us through it on dry land,
                it would have sufficed us.
Had He led us through it on dry land,
    but not drowned our oppressors in it,
                it would have sufficed us.
Had He drowned our oppressors in it,
    but not provided for our needs in the desert
    for forty years,   it would have sufficed us.
Had He provided for our needs in the desert
    for forty years,
    but not fed us the manna,
                it would have sufficed us.

אִלּוּ הֶאֱכִילָנוּ אֶת הַמָּן,
וְלֹא נָתַן לָנוּ אֶת הַשַּׁבָּת, דַּיֵּנוּ.
אִלּוּ נָתַן לָנוּ אֶת הַשַּׁבָּת,
וְלֹא קֵרְבָנוּ לִפְנֵי הַר סִינַי, דַּיֵּנוּ.
אִלּוּ קֵרְבָנוּ לִפְנֵי הַר סִינַי,
וְלֹא נָתַן לָנוּ אֶת הַתּוֹרָה, דַּיֵּנוּ.
אִלּוּ נָתַן לָנוּ אֶת הַתּוֹרָה,
וְלֹא הִכְנִיסָנוּ לְאֶרֶץ יִשְׂרָאֵל, דַּיֵּנוּ.

אִלּוּ נָתַן לָנוּ אֶת הַתּוֹרָה, וְלֹא הִכְנִיסָנוּ לְאֶרֶץ יִשְׂרָאֵל, דַּיֵּנוּ
Had He given us the Torah, but not brought us into the Land of Israel, it would have sufficed us.

The Contemptuous Son-In-Law

The juxtaposition of the mention of the Torah and Eretz Yisrael is no mere coincidence, as may be seen in the following anecdote concerning the **Chafetz Chaim**.

In 1918 elections were held for a local council, in which several Jewish parties ran on several different lists. One day some delegates from the "Zionist Youth" movement came to the town where the Chafetz Chaim lived at the time (because of the war, he had to relocate temporarily to Shumiach) to campaign for votes, and they stopped in to see the Chafetz Chaim and receive his blessing. The youngsters told him, "We would like to know the Rabbi's opinion on the recent resurgence in interest in settling Eretz Yisrael."

The Chafetz Chaim responded with an allegory. "A person is made up of a body and a soul. A soul can exist independently — although it will be lacking its crucial connection to its physical counterpart — but a body without a soul is simply a hunk of decomposing chemicals and minerals. The same may be said for the people of Israel. They have a soul, a spiritual component, which is the Torah; in addition to this they have a physical entity, which is Eretz Yisrael. Of course, a soul without a body — in this case, the Torah without Eretz Yisrael — is incomplete, for there are many mitzvos of the Torah that cannot be fulfilled outside of the Land of Israel. Furthermore, our situation here in exile is so miserable — we are tormented and persecuted, and it is almost impossible for many people to earn a living. Nevertheless, the Torah that we live by enables us to somehow survive despite it all. But Eretz Yisrael without the Torah, following the above analogy, is like a body without a soul; it is nothing but a meaningless heap of dirt.

On another occasion, at the *Kenesiah Gedolah* (Great Assembly) of *Agudas Yisrael* in 1923, the Chafetz Chaim used another parable to describe the situation

> Had He fed us the manna,
>   but not given us the Shabbos,
>   it would have sufficed us.
> Had He given us the Shabbos,
>   but not brought us before Mount Sinai,
>   it would have sufficed us.
> Had He brought us before Mount Sinai,
>   but not given us the Torah,
>   it would have sufficed us.
> Had He given us the Torah,
>   but not brought us into the Land of Israel,
>   it would have sufficed us.

---

in which people desired to live in Eretz Yisrael without having the slightest connection with the ways of the Torah:

Once there was a king who had an only daughter, who was beautiful and blessed with many fine attributes. One day he chose a boy who would eventually take his daughter's hand in marriage. The boy was from a common peasant family, and the king had him brought to the palace, where he hired the best tutors to teach him and to make a polished, distinguished gentleman out of him. Several years later, when the boy and girl came of age, a royal wedding was held in the palace. The groom, who had blossomed into a refined, noble young man, was promoted to the highest position in the kingdom and given great recognition and honor. An entire wing of the palace was set aside for his residence and usage.

All was well for the first few months. But gradually all the honor and luxury enjoyed by the king's son-in-law began to go to his head. He began to show insubordination towards the king and started disobeying orders. He even treated his wife, the king's daughter, poorly and caused her great aggravation and misery. The king was furious, and he had no choice but to strip his son-in-law of his powers and expel him from the palace.

The young man realized that he was in trouble now. He had no family to turn to for help, and had no independent source of income. Privation and even starvation were sure to be his lot now! What a fool he had been! He had had it so good, and now he had lost everything simply because he could not bring himself to act with respect and dignity towards the king! He resolved to change his ways. He went back to the king and begged for his forgiveness. He was a different man now, he assured the monarch, and would never repeat his previous offenses.

He managed to touch the king's heart, and he was reaccepted into the palace. But before long he returned to his old ways. Once again he defied the king and treated his daughter with contempt. The king was outraged that his son-in-law had taken advantage of his grace, and he once again banished the young man from the royal household.

אִלּוּ הִכְנִיסָנוּ לְאֶרֶץ יִשְׂרָאֵל,
וְלֹא בָנָה לָנוּ אֶת בֵּית הַבְּחִירָה, דַּיֵּנוּ.

עַל אַחַת כַּמָּה, וְכַמָּה טוֹבָה כְפוּלָה וּמְכֻפֶּלֶת לַמָּקוֹם עָלֵינוּ. שֶׁהוֹצִיאָנוּ מִמִּצְרַיִם, וְעָשָׂה בָהֶם שְׁפָטִים, וְעָשָׂה בֵאלֹהֵיהֶם, וְהָרַג אֶת בְּכוֹרֵיהֶם,

---

The young man went out into the world to fend for himself, but it did not take long for him to realize once again that his situation was hopeless. He knew no trade and had no connections. How was he to make a living? He lived in the street and begged for money, but he could barely keep himself alive. The winter would soon come and he would need a place to live. In desperation he gathered up his nerve and decided to request an audience with the king.

The king thought, "Perhaps he has come in contrition once again to ask my forgiveness. I don't know if I can trust him, but we'll give him a chance to present his case; perhaps he has completely changed his attitude."

The young man entered the king's chamber and told him, "It is true that I do not obey you. It is also true that I cannot live with your daughter. But I beg you to recall for me the kindness you showed me in my youth and to remember that I was once your beloved son-in-law."

"And what exactly is your request?" asked the king somewhat bewildered.

"Well, you know that you set aside a wing of the palace for me," the young man reminded the king. "Now, though I do not care for either you or your daughter, I would like you to take your daughter away and allow me to live in that wing by myself!"

The lesson of the parable is clear: The king represents God, the daughter is the Torah, and the wing in the palace is Eretz Yisrael. If the Jewish people have the audacity to think that they are entitled to Eretz Yisrael without expressing any loyalty toward God or the Torah, they are no better than the contemptuous prince in the parable!

אִלּוּ עָשָׂה בָהֶם שְׁפָטִים
Had He executed judgments against them,

A New Twist on Democracy

During the **Chafetz Chaim's** lifetime and shortly before it there was a noticeable trend in world politics. Nations were rebelling against their kings and deposing them, and setting up democratic republics in place of the old monarchies. The Chafetz Chaim saw in this pattern yet another sign that the Messianic redemption was soon to come.

We find that when Moshe first approached Pharaoh with his demand to allow the Israelite nation to leave his land, Pharaoh responded by intensifying the burden

> Had He brought us into the Land of Israel,
> but not built the Temple for us,
> it would have sufficed us.

Thus, how much more so should we be grateful to the Omnipresent for all the numerous favors He showered upon us: He brought us out of Egypt; executed judgments against the Egyptians; acted against their gods; slew their firstborn;

---

of work enforced on the Jews, decreeing that they would have to collect their own straw rather than have it supplied to them. Instead of bringing about liberation Moshe had caused a setback in the people's condition. There is a question that arises here — and, in fact, Moshe himself asked it of God (*Shemos* 5:22-23): Obviously God knew that Pharaoh would respond in this manner; what indeed was the purpose of Moshe going to Pharaoh in the first place?

The Midrash addresses this problem, and explains that the decree requiring the Jews to gather their own straw was actually for their benefit. By being forced to collect straw, the Midrash tells us, the Jews had to go begging for it from Egyptian householders and farmers. Even if the Egyptian had plenty of unneeded straw, instead of pitying the unfortunate, impoverished Hebrew slave at his door, he would respond with derision and animosity, and then slam the door in his face, leaving him empty-handed.

Then, a short while afterwards, the ten plagues began to wreak havoc in Egypt. The populace might have advanced an argument to protect themselves from these plagues: "We didn't do anything wrong! The enslavement of the Jews was official government policy! We don't make the laws; the king and his officers do. They are the ones who deserve to be punished, not us!"

But the behavior of the Egyptians during the incident of the collection of straw now invalidated this possible grievance, for even the lowliest Egyptian had participated in the humiliation and suffering of the Jews. They could no longer plead their innocence and demand immunity from punishment. In the end the plagues did affect even the common Egyptians, and God "executed judgments against them."

Nowadays too, the Chafetz Chaim concluded, the world order as we know it is coming to an end, and the Messianic age will soon be upon us, when all the peoples of the world will stand before God in judgment. The masses among the nations might have been able to claim, "The persecution of the Jews was not our idea! It is all the fault of the king (or kaiser, or czar)!" But now that the nations have formed republics, in which each and every citizen has a share in determining the makeup and policies of the government, this argument has been voided, for each individual is responsible when the government acts unjustly.

וְנָתַן לָנוּ אֶת מָמוֹנָם, וְקָרַע לָנוּ אֶת הַיָּם, וְהֶעֱבִירָנוּ

וְנָתַן לָנוּ אֶת מָמוֹנָם
(He) gave us their wealth;

Fair Compensation

The question is sometimes asked: Why wasn't it considered stealing when the Jews "borrowed" precious articles from the Egyptians, knowing full well that they would never be returned? How could God condone — and even encourage — such seemingly unethical behavior (*Shemos* 11:2)? Another question we may ask concerns the verse which describes the "borrowing": "Each woman will borrow from her neighbor and from the woman who lives in her building silver and gold objects" (ibid., 3:22). Why does the Torah speak of women borrowing specifically from their "neighbors and women who live in their building"? It would have been sufficient to say simply, "The Children of Israel will borrow from the Egyptians. . . ."

R' Zalman Sorotzkin addressed these issues. Concerning the first question, it must be recalled that the Talmud itself deals with this problem. In *Sanhedrin* 91a the following story is related:

> One time, during the reign of Alexander the Great, the Egyptians came before Alexander with the following claim against the Jews: "The Torah writes that the Jews 'borrowed' money from our ancestors. We demand that they now return all the stolen silver and gold."
>
> Geviha ben Pesisa. . . received permission from the Sages of Israel to represent the Jewish people in this case. He asked the Egyptians, "From where do you bring your proof against us?"
>
> "From your Torah," came the reply.
>
> "Very well," he told them. "I, too, will bring my testimony from the Torah. It is written there, 'The dwelling of the Children of Israel that they dwelt in Egypt was four hundred and thirty years.' Give us the compensation due to us for 600,000 people whom you enslaved for 430 years!"
>
> The Egyptians requested three days to think of a response, but they could not find any answer (and they withdrew their claim).

The clear implication of this story is that the amount of money plundered from the Egyptians was much less than the amount that was justifiably due the Jews for all their years of slave labor. There was therefore no question that this "borrowing" was fair and just.

וְקָרַע לָנוּ אֶת הַיָּם
(He) split the Sea for us;

Debate at the Reed Sea

The *Mechilta* (*Beshalach*) relates the following story: When the Israelites were standing before the Sea, [the tribe of] Yehudah said, "I will go into the Sea."

But [the tribe of] Binyamin said, "*I* will go first!" And Binyamin started to plunge into the Sea.

The officers of Yehudah started to pelt them with stones. . . .

This situation may be compared to a king who had two sons. He told the

gave us their wealth; split the Sea for us; led us

older one, "Wake me up tomorrow at 9 o'clock," and to the younger son he said, "Wake me up at daybreak."

The next morning at daybreak the younger son came to wake up his father. But the older son told him, "Father told me to wake him up at 9 o'clock!"

The younger son protested, "But he told *me* to wake him up now!"

As a result of their arguing with one another the king was roused from his sleep. He told them, "My sons, because both of you were trying only to carry out my request and to fulfill my desire, I will reward both of you!"

So too here; Yehudah was granted the privilege of kingship, and Binyamin was granted the privilege of having the Temple built in his territory.

The parable of the king seems to be somewhat incongruous with the story of the members of the tribes of Yehudah and Binyamin for the argument between the two tribes was that they both wanted to do the *same* thing, unlike the king's sons, who disagreed about what should be done altogether. Another question is: Why, indeed, did Binyamin not yield to their more senior brethren from Yehudah, who had taken the initiative before them?

The **Netziv** provided an interesting explanation for this Midrash. The splitting of the Sea, he explains, could have been carried out in one of two ways: either in a manner which was nearly natural, or in a way which was manifestly supernatural — all depending on the level of worthiness the Israelites would show themselves to be on. At first God "pushed the Sea with a powerful east wind all night long" (*Shemos* 14:21), which began the process of drying up the Sea through natural causes. If the Jews would not show absolute faith in God's salvation the natural process would continue until the Sea was totally dry and fit to traverse. If, on the other hand, they would demonstrate unlimited faith by plunging into the waters, God would bring about an overt miracle and split the water for them outright. The tribe of Yehudah believed that it was more in keeping with God's honor to allow Him to perform the more natural type of miracle, and not to "force His Hand" by jumping into the water and thus necessitating His instant, miraculous salvation. It would be better, they reasoned, to wait a few more hours until the natural drying process that had already begun would finish. The tribe of Binyamin on the other hand, maintained that, on the contrary, it is a greater honor for God to bring about an overt miracle, for all to see. It would be better to jump into the water immediately, they felt. As in the parable, there was a difference of opinion between the two parties. And since Yehudah was not ready to march into the Sea at this point, the tribe of Binyamin did not really usurp their older brother's position by jumping in first.

The reward granted to the two tribes, the Netziv concluded, was appropriate for their respective points of view. The tribe of Yehudah, who preferred to have God's purpose achieved through natural means, were granted kingship, for a king is the person who leads his people socially, economically, militarily, etc. — in a material and mundane manner. The tribe of Binyamin was rewarded by being granted the privilege of hosting the Temple, where miraculous events took place on a regular basis (as in *Pirkei Avos* 5:5).

בְּתוֹכוֹ בֶּחָרָבָה, וְשִׁקַּע צָרֵינוּ בְּתוֹכוֹ, וְסִפֵּק צָרְכֵּנוּ בַּמִּדְבָּר אַרְבָּעִים שָׁנָה, וְהֶאֱכִילָנוּ אֶת הַמָּן, וְנָתַן לָנוּ אֶת הַשַּׁבָּת, וְקֵרְבָנוּ לִפְנֵי הַר סִינַי, וְנָתַן לָנוּ אֶת הַתּוֹרָה,

וְהֶאֱכִילָנוּ אֶת הַמָּן, וְנָתַן לָנוּ אֶת הַשַּׁבָּת
(He) fed us the manna; gave us the Shabbos;

Uplifting the Physical — We find that there is some sort of relationship between the concept of Shabbos and the manna. The first time Shabbos was mentioned to the Jewish people — even before the giving of the Torah — it is in connection with the gathering of the manna (*Shemos* 16). Furthermore, the very first time the concept of Shabbos is introduced in the Torah, on the seventh day of creation, it is written that God "blessed and sanctified" the Sabbath day (*Bereishis* 2:3). In what way was this day *blessed* and *sanctified*? The Sages explain: It was *blessed* in that a double portion of manna was destined to fall in advance of the Sabbath, and it was *sanctified* in that no manna fell on that day itself (*Midrash*, quoted in *Rashi* ad loc.). What is the connection between these two seemingly disparate matters?

R' Gedaliah Schorr explained that when a Jew eats a meal on Shabbos it is, in a certain sense, reminiscent of the eating of the manna by his ancestors in the desert, for the Sabbath meal, although it may consist of food similar to that eaten during the week, is actually a spiritual experience.

The Sages (in *Midrash Rabbah*, 48:12) comment on the fact that the manna began to fall while the Israelites were in a place called Alush (אָלוּשׁ): "The manna was in the merit of Avraham, who told Sarah, 'Knead (לוּשִׁי, *Lushi*) and make cakes (for the angels who had visited them)' (*Bereishis* 18:6)." What is the connection between these two events, other than the superficial resemblance of words? R' Gedaliah explained that Avraham prepared ordinary, physical food for the angels, whose source of nourishment is not physical but spiritual — from the splendor of God's *Shechinah* (see *Ramban* to *Shemos* 16:6). It was thus within Avraham's ability to take physical food and convert it into a spiritual form of nourishment, and this is exactly what the manna did for the Jews — it was in fact a spiritual food ("the bread of the mighty [angels]" — *Tehillim* 78:25) that possessed a physical form.

The Sabbath meal and the eating of the manna thus have very much in common; they both represent the interface between physical, edible food and the spiritual experience of eating that food.

וְנָתַן לָנוּ אֶת הַתּוֹרָה
(He) gave us the Torah;

A Mitzvah Without Torah is No Mitzvah at All — In an article published in the Yiddish newspapers of the time, **R' Elchanan Wasserman** wrote the following: The Chafetz Chaim, in the course of an address, once uttered the following comment: "With the Torah, mitzvos are mitzvos; without the Torah, everything is just dirt and muck." Many people have

הגדה של פסח [152]

through it on dry land; drowned our oppressors in it; provided for our needs in the desert for forty years; fed us the manna; gave us the Shabbos; brought us before Mount Sinai; gave us the Torah;

---

asked me to elaborate on this cryptic statement, and it is with this in mind that I write these words.

Let me begin by pointing out that it was quite common for the Chafetz Chaim to encapsulate a deep thought with a few enigmatic words; it was only after much reflection and contemplation that those who had heard this utterance were able to realize that they were in fact based on a profound Torah idea found in the words of the Sages. In our case, too, the source of the Chafetz Chaim's statement is to be found in the *Yerushalmi* (*Challah* 1:5): " 'These are the mitzvos' (*Vayikra* 27:34) — if you do them as mitzvos, they are mitzvos; if not, they are not mitzvos at all."

It is impossible to fulfill a mitzvah without Torah knowledge. The Sages tell us (*Berachos* 61a), "The *yetzer hara* (man's urge to sin) sits between the two openings of the heart." The Chafetz Chaim explained this mysterious statement as follows:

In *Koheles* we read (10:2), "The wise man's heart is on his right, and the fool's heart is on his left." Of course, the verse is to be understood figuratively: The *yetzer hatov* (the drive to do what is good) has a function — to steer man toward the "right," the correct path. And the *yetzer hara* has the opposite function — to steer man toward the "left" path, the path to sin and self-destruction. What the Sages are telling us in *Berachos* is that although the *yetzer hatov* keeps to its assigned "right" position, the *yetzer hara* very often veers from its "left" location and moves over to the "right" — it "sits between the two openings of the heart." It often confuses us by appearing in the guise of a "good urge," a sudden impetus to do a mitzvah. If we would ask our *yetzer hara*, "Should I keep the mitzvos?" we would have expected its answer to be, "Certainly not! Do whatever you please, with no restraints whatsoever." But what the Sages teach us here is that the *yetzer hara* will often answer, "Of course! You need the Torah; you need to carry out the mitzvos with great zeal!" However, the *yetzer hara* adds one catch to its pious-sounding response: "It must be one of *my* mitzvos; it must be in accordance with *my* Torah." And once the *yetzer hara* is the driving force behind the performance of the mitzvah it ultimately becomes the biggest sin imaginable — *avodah zarah* (idolatry)!

A few examples will illustrate the point: It is certainly a mitzvah — a mitzvah of great importance — to build up and settle Eretz Yisrael. But the *yetzer hara* has discovered that it can make great capital out of this mitzvah! It has decreed that it can be accomplished through funds and organizations that promote atheism and values that uproot everything that Judaism stands for. Those who seek to become pioneers in the Promised Land must undergo a course of "*hachsharah*" (*preparation*, but also *making kosher*) —

וְהִכְנִיסָנוּ לְאֶרֶץ יִשְׂרָאֵל, וּבָנָה לָנוּ אֶת בֵּית הַבְּחִירָה, לְכַפֵּר עַל כָּל עֲוֹנוֹתֵינוּ.

רַבָּן גַּמְלִיאֵל הָיָה אוֹמֵר. כָּל שֶׁלֹּא אָמַר שְׁלֹשָׁה דְבָרִים אֵלּוּ בַּפֶּסַח, לֹא יָצָא יְדֵי חוֹבָתוֹ, וְאֵלּוּ הֵן,

---

the goal of which is not to make people more kosher, but to completely remove any ideas of religion from their heads! . . .

There is another mitzvah of "[See to it that] your brother shall live among you" (*Vayikra* 25:36), which commands us to concern ourselves with the financial and social betterment of our brethren. Here too the *yetzer hara* has staked its ground. It has decreed that in order to strengthen the Jewish economy in Eretz Yisrael it is imperative that the cows in the dairies must be milked on Shabbos — not, God forbid, by non-Jews, as has always been the practice, but only by Jews, for otherwise the holy principle of "Jewish labor" would be violated!

The Torah prescribes a mitzvah of *bikkurim* (bringing the first-ripening produce to the Temple as a gift to the Kohen). Of course, this mitzvah is inoperable without the Temple and is totally inappropriate and nonsensical nowadays, but the "Jewish national revival" requires the implementation of such moving ancient agricultural rituals, the *yetzer hara* assures us. An old man is therefore dutifully chosen to represent the *Kohen Gadol*, and instead of Kohanim and Leviim the meaningless ceremony is led by atheists and tramplers of the Torah! . . .

From these few examples we see clearly how it is possible for the *yetzer hara* to switch over to "the right side" and convince its victims to dedicate themselves to an important mitzvah — but only on its terms, converting that mitzvah, in the process, into nothing less than *avodah zarah*.

But, of course, the *yetzer hatov* also tries to persuade us to do mitzvos. How can we discern whether the driving force behind the urge to do a mitzvah is wholesome and sacred or profane?

The key to this question lies once again in the words of the Sages:

> R' Yehudah ben Pazi said in the name of Rebbi:
> Can we read these verses and not be distressed?
> When it comes to the good, it says, "all those whose hearts motivated them" (*Shemos* 35:5, concerning donations to the *Mishkan*); when it comes to the bad, "*All* the people removed their jewelry" (to donate to the Golden Calf — ibid., 32:3).
> When it comes to the good, it says, "And Moshe brought out the people toward God" (implying the use of coercion — ibid., 19:17,

brought us to the Land of Israel; and built us the Temple, to atone for all our sins.

Rabban Gamliel used to say: Whoever has not explained the following three things on Pesach has not fulfilled his duty, namely:

---

concerning the giving of the Torah); when it comes to the bad, "You all approached me" (enthusiastically — *Devarim* 1:22, concerning the Israelites' request to send the spies).

When it comes to the good, it says, "Then Moshe and the Children of Israel sang" (*Shemos* 15:1, implying that the people were led in song by Moshe); when it comes to the bad, "All the congregation raised up their voices" (spontaneously — *Bamidbar* 14:1).

R' Chiya bar Abba said: "They rose up early and acted with corruption" (*Tzefanyah* 3:7) — whenever they would act corruptly they would rise up early (with enthusiasm) to do so.

Here, then, we have an idea how to determine when a particular act is motivated by "the right side" and when by "the left": Whenever a mitzvah gains extreme popularity among the masses, and is adopted with great ardor and enthusiasm, we must unfortunately suspect that the driving force behind that mitzvah is from an impure source. Even if it appears to the people involved that their actions are sincere and virtuous, and they can see no possible trace of base motivations, they must consider the possibility that deep beneath the surface lies the influence of the *yetzer hara*.

The Sages teach: "Why is Israel compared to a deer (in *Shir Hashirim*)? Just as a deer looks behind it as it runs, so too Israel." The Dubno Maggid gave the following interpretation to the Sages' allegory. When a Jew finds himself running to do a mitzvah with great enthusiasm and fervor he must pause for a moment and look behind himself — to see who it is that is driving him on from behind, the forces of good or those of evil!

When it comes to the reaction of the masses to matters of mitzvos, it often functions as a sort of reverse barometer — the more enthusiastically a "mitzvah" is grasped, and the greater number of adherents attracted, the greater is the likelihood that there is an insincere motivation behind the act.

The Jew is obligated to be cautious not to be swept up with the winds of the times. We must be guided solely by *true* Torah values, not by fads and popular movements. After all, Avraham was called "Ivri" (Hebrew), the Sages of the Midrash tell us, because "the whole world was on one side (philosophically) and he was on the other."

A "mitzvah" that is not based on the Torah, as the Chafetz Chaim taught us, is nothing but dirt and muck.

פֶּסַח. מַצָּה. וּמָרוֹר.

פֶּסַח שֶׁהָיוּ אֲבוֹתֵינוּ אוֹכְלִים בִּזְמַן שֶׁבֵּית הַמִּקְדָּשׁ הָיָה קַיָּם, עַל שׁוּם מָה? עַל שׁוּם שֶׁפָּסַח הַקָּדוֹשׁ בָּרוּךְ הוּא עַל בָּתֵּי אֲבוֹתֵינוּ בְּמִצְרַיִם. שֶׁנֶּאֱמַר, וַאֲמַרְתֶּם, זֶבַח פֶּסַח הוּא לַיהוה, אֲשֶׁר פָּסַח עַל בָּתֵּי בְנֵי יִשְׂרָאֵל בְּמִצְרַיִם בְּנָגְפּוֹ אֶת מִצְרַיִם, וְאֶת בָּתֵּינוּ הִצִּיל, וַיִּקֹּד הָעָם וַיִּשְׁתַּחֲווּ.[1]

פֶּסַח מַצָּה וּמָרוֹר
Pesach, matzah, and maror.

The Spiritual State of the Jews in Egypt

Many commentators make the following observation: We find that matzah is always mentioned before *maror* in the Torah (*Shemos* 12:8, *Bamidbar* 9:11), as here in the Haggadah, and at the Seder the matzah is eaten before the *maror*. This order, they ask, is the opposite of what logic would seem to dictate. After all, as the Haggadah explains here, matzah represents the liberation from Egypt (the fact that "the dough of our fathers did not have time to become leavened before the King of kings... appeared to them and redeemed them"), and the *maror* represents the fact that "the Egyptians embittered the lives of our fathers in Egypt." Shouldn't we eat the food that commemorates the bitterness of bondage first and only then eat the matzah, which represents the deliverance from that bondage?

R' Yisrael Salanter provided an answer for this question, and the **Chafetz Chaim** illustrated his point with a story that had happened to him personally.

During World War I the plight of the Jews in Eastern Europe was disastrous. People had to leave their homes and flee inland or to the big cities with very few possessions, abandoning their businesses or other sources of income. Shortly afterwards the situation deteriorated as the country descended into lawless chaos as a result of the czar's deposition and the Communist revolution in Russia. Finally, when the situation stabilized, the refugees began to trickle back to their hometowns and business began to return to normal. At that time a successful wheat merchant came to the Chafetz Chaim and asked for his blessing for continued success in business.

"If you managed to make money during the bad times," the Chafetz Chaim exclaimed, "you should certainly have no problem now, when the economy is back on its feet again!"

"On the contrary!" declared the businessman. "Grain merchants are at an advantage during times of famine and distress! People are willing to pay any price for our wares, and are not meticulous about the quality of the merchandise. It is now, when food is plentiful and people can afford to be choosy, that business becomes difficult for us!"

The Chafetz Chaim immediately derived a lesson from the businessman's

PESACH — the pesach offering; MATZAH — the unleavened bread; MAROR — the bitter herbs.

Pesach — Why did our fathers eat a pesach offering during the period when the Temple stood? Because the Holy One, Blessed is He, passed over the houses of our fathers in Egypt, as it says: You shall say: "It is a pesach offering for HASHEM, Who passed over the houses of the Children of Israel in Egypt when He struck the Egyptians and spared our houses"; and the people bowed down and prostrated themselves.[1]

---

1. *Shemos* 12:27.

---

explanation. In past generations, when Jews of all walks of life and of every stratum in society were Torah observant, and when the *batei midrash* were filled to capacity with people who dedicated every spare moment to the study of Torah — when "the merchandise" was plentiful — the Heavenly Tribunal could afford to be choosy, rewarding those whose deeds and study were of the highest caliber and rejecting those of lesser quality. But nowadays, when observance and Torah study has declined to such alarmingly low levels — when there is a spiritual "famine" in progress — they are not so selective, and give credit to any virtuous act and any form of Torah study whatsoever. This is the time to "make a fortune," in the spiritual sense — to "cash in" on the exceptional opportunity to be granted immense reward for actions that would have gone unnoticed in the past.

This idea is the basis for R' Yisrael Salanter's answer to the question posed above: Why does *maror*, which represents bondage, *follow* matzah, which represents freedom? The Sages tell us that when the time came for the Jews in Egypt to be redeemed, God found them so lacking in spiritual stature that there was no source of merit to justify their liberation. Therefore God gave the people two mitzvos to perform — the *pesach* sacrifice and circumcision (which had been neglected by the masses) — to serve as a basis for their deliverance. We might ask: How can just two mitzvos have the ability to counteract the appalling spiritual state that the Jews were in at that time? We are told that they had reached the forty-ninth — the next to the last — level of impurity in Egypt, and that they engaged in idolatry no less than their Egyptian neighbors!

The answer is that it was precisely *because* Israel was in such a deplorable spiritual state, with no sources of merit, that these two simple mitzvos were invested with such great significance. It was a time of spiritual "famine," and any "merchandise," even if lacking in quantity and quality, was gladly accepted. Thus, the bitterness of bondage and the miserable spiritual state of our ancestors that was brought on by that bondage, was in effect the very cause for our redemption from Egypt, for it was out of that bitter taste that redemption was born. The *maror*, a symbol of the harshness of slavery, is at the same time a symbol of redemption as well.

The middle matzah is lifted and displayed while the following paragraph is recited.

מַצָּה זוּ שֶׁאָנוּ אוֹכְלִים, עַל שׁוּם מָה? עַל שׁוּם שֶׁלֹּא הִסְפִּיק בְּצֵקָם שֶׁל אֲבוֹתֵינוּ לְהַחֲמִיץ, עַד שֶׁנִּגְלָה עֲלֵיהֶם מֶלֶךְ מַלְכֵי הַמְּלָכִים הַקָּדוֹשׁ בָּרוּךְ הוּא וּגְאָלָם. שֶׁנֶּאֱמַר, וַיֹּאפוּ אֶת הַבָּצֵק אֲשֶׁר הוֹצִיאוּ מִמִּצְרַיִם עֻגֹת מַצּוֹת כִּי לֹא חָמֵץ, כִּי גֹרְשׁוּ מִמִּצְרַיִם, וְלֹא יָכְלוּ לְהִתְמַהְמֵהַּ, וְגַם צֵדָה לֹא עָשׂוּ לָהֶם.[1]

שֶׁלֹּא הִסְפִּיק בְּצֵקָם שֶׁל אֲבוֹתֵינוּ לְהַחֲמִיץ
Because the dough of our fathers did not have time to become leavened

Without Interruption — As this paragraph states, we eat matzah on Pesach to commemorate the haste of the deliverance from Egypt and the consequent fact that our forefathers did not have enough time to leaven their dough.

The Torah exhorts us, "You shall guard the matzos [from becoming leavened]" (*Shemos* 12:17). The Sages interpret this verse homiletically by reading the word מַצּוֹת as מִצְוֹת, yielding the message, "You shall guard the *mitzvos* from becoming leavened" — that is, "When a mitzvah comes your way, do not allow it to 'leaven,' but perform it immediately" (*Mechilta,* cited by *Rashi* ad loc.). The comparison between matzah and mitzvos in general, is difficult, however, as **R' Shneur Kotler** noted. If one allows his matzah to become leavened, this strikes at the very identity of the matzah, disqualifying it completely. But if one delays the performance of another mitzvah he has not affected the end result of that mitzvah at all. Hesitation in performing a mitzvah might be considered reprehensible, being regarded as a disparagement of that mitzvah, but it does not seem appropriate to designate it as "leavening" (ruining) the mitzvah.

R' Shneur explained that, in fact, through this comparison the Sages are teaching us an important lesson in our attitude towards mitzvos. When someone allows dough to sit passively, external forces (yeast cells, etc.) go into action on the dough and cause it to ferment. The same is true with mitzvos in general. Once a person puts a mitzvah off in order to attend to other, mundane matters, these external forces detract from the fervor and enthusiasm which are essential to following God's commandments, to the extent that the mitzvah performed in the end is in fact altered in its essence.

In a similar vein, R' Shneur explained a verse found elsewhere in the Torah. We are told that we must remember what Amalek did to us "on the way, when we were going out of Egypt" (*Devarim* 25:17). The words "on the way" seem to be extraneous. R' Shneur explained that the Exodus was not an end in itself, but was the beginning of a process that culminated in the giving of the Torah at Mount Sinai fifty days afterwards. All the tremendous, sensational miracles that the Jews experienced during this time were merely intended to prepare them for this awesome climactic event. But then, in the middle of this preparatory process — "*on the way*

The middle matzah is lifted and displayed while the following paragraph is recited.

Matzah — Why do we eat this unleavened bread? Because the dough of our fathers did not have time to become leavened before the King of kings, the Holy One, Blessed is He, revealed Himself to them and redeemed them, as it says: They baked the dough which they had brought out of Egypt into unleavened bread, for it had not fermented, because they were driven out of Egypt and could not delay, nor had they prepared any provisions for the way.[1]

---

1. *Shemos* 12:39.

---

out of Egypt" — Amalek attacked the Israelites, weakening their impressions of God's omnipotence and glory and curtailing their sublime spiritual progress. Although it was only a temporary interruption, and the Israelites returned to their process of spiritual preparation afterwards, it nevertheless affected the final spiritual condition of the Israelites for all time. The slightest disruption or delay in a spiritual process is bound to influence the final outcome of that process.

Similarly, the Sages teach that "Whoever interrupts his Torah learning to admire a beautiful tree or a beautiful field it is as if he has forfeited his life" (*Avos* 3:7). The *Chazon Ish* (*Igros*, #3) explains this as follows. Interrupting one's learning is more than simply causing a lack of continuity in his thought process. To learn and then stop, he writes, may be compared to sowing seeds and then washing them away with water. The interruption in study actually *destroys* the learning that preceded it, and when the learning is resumed it must begin anew from the start.

וְלֹא יָכְלוּ לְהִתְמַהְמֵהַּ / *and (they) could not delay*

Only Torah Preserves Jewish Identity

Why could the Jews not delay a few moments while their dough rose? There is a Kabbalistic teaching that tells us that since the Jews had reached the forty-ninth level of spiritual impurity there was an imminent danger that they might sink yet further, into the fiftieth level, from which there is no possible redemption.

R' Zalman Sorotzkin made the following observation concerning this concept. The Sages teach that the whole time the Jews were in Egypt they preserved their unique ethnic manner of dress and speech and gave their young only Jewish names — quite an accomplishment for a people that had lived for over two centuries, under the harshest conditions, among a host nation. Yet, when it came to more concrete issues of spirituality the Jews had lapsed almost to the point of no return. Despite all the trappings of ethnic identity, such as a distinctive language and style of dress, their continued existence as a nation was endangered after a mere 210 years. Once the Torah was given on Mount Sinai, however, the Jewish nation is alive and thriving after some 3500 years! As important as it is, the will to exist as an independent nationality is insufficient for our existence as a people without the requisite spiritual content. Nationalism and patriotism are no substitute for the Torah!

The *maror* is lifted and displayed while the following paragraph is recited.

מָרוֹר זֶה שֶׁאָנוּ אוֹכְלִים, עַל שׁוּם מָה? עַל שׁוּם שֶׁמֵּרְרוּ הַמִּצְרִים אֶת חַיֵּי אֲבוֹתֵינוּ בְּמִצְרָיִם.

וְלֹא יָכְלוּ לְהִתְמַהְמֵהַּ / *and (they) could not delay.*

The Hastening of Mashiach

The Talmud states (*Sanhedrin* 98b), "The *Mashiach* will not come [during a time when the Jews are on an average level of righteousness], but in a generation which is either totally virtuous or totally corrupt." Why, wondered **R' Elchanan Wasserman,** is a generation that is totally corrupt more likely to experience the coming of the *Mashiach* than a generation that is only somewhat corrupt?

R' Elchanan explained that the arrival of the Messianic redemption has two possible scenarios, as the Sages (*Sanhedrin* 98a) derive from the verse, "I am Hashem; I will hasten it in its time" (*Yeshayahu* 60:22). There is the approach of "in its time," if the *Mashiach* will come at the moment that was preordained for his advent long ago, and there is the alternative of "I will hasten it," if, for some reason, the *Mashiach* will appear before this preordained time. This latter scenario will come about for one of two reasons: Either the Jewish people will achieve such a high level of spirituality that they will be found deserving of redemption before the preordained time for the Messianic age, or they will be so dreadfully lacking in merit that they would not be able to survive as a nation any longer without the help of the Messianic salvation. This, explained R' Elchanan, is why the Talmud says that the *Mashiach* will come only in a generation that is either totally virtuous or totally corrupt. This, of course, applies only if the *Mashiach* comes within the framework of "I will hasten it." If the preordained time for him arrives he will certainly come immediately, regardless of the situation of the generation living at that time.

Such were the circumstances of the deliverance from Egypt. The people were actually supposed to undergo enslavement for four hundred years, as prophesied at the Covenant Between the Parts (*Bereishis* 15:13). In fact, however, they were in Egypt only 210 years, and even that time was not totally spent in servitude. The reason for their early deliverance was that, as the Midrash teaches, the people had sunk so low in their spirituality that they had almost reached the fiftieth, unredeemable level of impurity; if they had stayed any longer they would have been corrupted beyond repair. This is what the Torah means when it says, "they could not delay."

מָרוֹר זֶה שֶׁאָנוּ אוֹכְלִים, עַל שׁוּם מָה?
עַל שׁוּם שֶׁמֵּרְרוּ הַמִּצְרִים אֶת חַיֵּי אֲבוֹתֵינוּ בְּמִצְרָיִם
Why do we eat this bitter herb? Because the Egyptians embittered the lives of our fathers in Egypt.

A Nation Alone

The question has been asked: Is it not somewhat inappropriate that *maror*, which is a reminder of the bitterness of slavery, is eaten at the Seder, which is a celebration of our liberty and delivery from slavery? **R' Gedaliah Schorr** quoted the *Sefas Emes* as noting that what the *maror* teaches us is that the intensity of our bitter enslavement to the Egyptians was in fact one of the

The maror is lifted and displayed while the following paragraph is recited.

Maror — Why do we eat this bitter herb? Because the Egyptians embittered the lives of our fathers in Egypt,

causes of our ultimate redemption from them. This is because the difficulties and adversity they faced during their oppression by the Egyptians helped to preserve their identity as a separate nation and to prevent assimilation. History has taught us that in fact anti-Semitism is often the greatest catalyst of preserving Jewish identity.

This fact is alluded to in the Torah itself. When Yaakov struggled with Esav's angel (*Bereishis* 32:25ff), he was victorious because "Yaakov remained alone" (ibid.) — isolated and separate from Lavan and Esav and all others whose spirituality was inferior. Bilaam noted this secret of Israel's survival when he said, "Behold, a people that dwells alone, and is not counted among the nations" (*Bamidbar* 23:9). Moshe, too, pronounced, "And Israel lived securely — alone" (*Devarim* 33:28).

The verse, "Behold a people that dwells alone, and is not counted among the nations," is rendered by *Targum Yonasan* as follows: "Behold, a people who alone are destined to inherit the World (to Come), because they do not follow the customs of the nations." The future redemption from the exile and from subservience to the other nations is dependent upon the Jews' resistance to imitating the ways of those nations. We find that the Sages long ago instituted many laws designed to prevent excessive intermingling between Jews and non-Jews — such as the prohibition to eat bread baked by a non-Jew or to drink his wine (*Avodah Zarah* 36b).

Along similar lines, there is a homiletical interpretation provided for the verse, "And Yaakov said... Save me, please, from my brother, from Esav" (*Bereishis* 32:12). Yaakov's prayer to God was that he be saved from the temptation to befriend Esav and live together with him as a *brother*.

But if the Jewish people does not live by the standard of "aloneness," God sees to it that this situation is forced upon them, violently if necessary: "That which you plan in your minds — it shall not be, that which you say, 'We will be like all the nations.' As I live... I shall rule over you with a strong hand and an outstretched arm and with poured out wrath" (*Yechezkel* 20:32-33). This is what Yirmiyahu alluded to when he opened the book of *Eichah* with the question, "How does the city of the multitude of people sit in solitude?" He did not say, "*Woe* to the city... that sits in solitude," but asked, "*How* does the city... sit in solitude?" It is a given that Jerusalem must sit in solitude, but under favorable conditions this isolation is achieved through the sanctity and voluntary aloofness of its people, who shun the other nations in order to attain the highest levels of holiness. But what happened in fact was that Jerusalem did not live up to these expectations, and therefore was forced to become isolated in a completely different manner — through desolation and the exile of its inhabitants. Yirmiyahu does not bemoan the fact that Jerusalem dwells alone per se, but *how* she dwells alone.

We have established clearly, then, that the key to Jewish survival and redemption is the maintenance of strict separation between themselves and the other nations, a detachment which is actually aided by the bitterness of oppression. It is thus entirely appropriate that *maror* is eaten as part of the commemoration of our deliverance.

שֶׁנֶּאֱמַר, וַיְמָרְרוּ אֶת חַיֵּיהֶם, בַּעֲבֹדָה קָשָׁה, בְּחֹמֶר וּבִלְבֵנִים, וּבְכָל עֲבֹדָה בַּשָּׂדֶה, אֵת כָּל עֲבֹדָתָם אֲשֶׁר עָבְדוּ בָהֶם בְּפָרֶךְ.[1]

בְּכָל דּוֹר וָדוֹר חַיָּב אָדָם לִרְאוֹת אֶת עַצְמוֹ כְּאִלּוּ הוּא יָצָא מִמִּצְרַיִם. שֶׁנֶּאֱמַר, וְהִגַּדְתָּ לְבִנְךָ בַּיּוֹם הַהוּא לֵאמֹר, בַּעֲבוּר זֶה עָשָׂה יהוה לִי, בְּצֵאתִי מִמִּצְרָיִם.[2] לֹא אֶת אֲבוֹתֵינוּ בִּלְבָד גָּאַל הַקָּדוֹשׁ בָּרוּךְ הוּא, אֶלָּא אַף אוֹתָנוּ גָּאַל עִמָּהֶם. שֶׁנֶּאֱמַר, וְאוֹתָנוּ הוֹצִיא מִשָּׁם, לְמַעַן הָבִיא אֹתָנוּ לָתֶת לָנוּ אֶת הָאָרֶץ אֲשֶׁר נִשְׁבַּע לַאֲבֹתֵינוּ.[3]

בְּכָל דּוֹר וָדוֹר חַיָּב אָדָם לִרְאוֹת אֶת עַצְמוֹ כְּאִלּוּ הוּא יָצָא מִמִּצְרַיִם. שֶׁנֶּאֱמַר, וְהִגַּדְתָּ לְבִנְךָ. . .

In every generation it is one's duty to regard himself as though he personally had gone out of Egypt, as it says: You shall tell your son. . .

Continuing the Tradition — In order to effectively impart the message of the Exodus to one's children, he himself must consider the events so real that they affect him personally.

To illustrate the importance of this concept the **Chafetz Chaim** made an analogy to the halachic concept of cooking (בִּשּׁוּל). When a very hot liquid is still in the pot in which it was heated, it is called a כְּלִי רִאשׁוֹן, a *primary vessel*. When this liquid is poured into another receptacle it is called a secondary vessel, then a tertiary vessel, and so on. The halachah states that a hot liquid in a primary vessel "cooks" whatever comes into contact with it. A secondary vessel can "cook" only certain foods, those which become edible with a minimal amount of heat. A tertiary vessel does not have the capability of "cooking" at all. (This last fact is subject to controversy — ed.)

So it is with education as well, the Chafetz Chaim declared. It is all too likely that a grandfather will be in the position of a "primary vessel," who can have an effect on all those who come into contact with him. His son, a bit more removed from the source of knowledge, is comparable to the secondary vessel, which has much less of an effect on others. The grandson will already be in the position of a tertiary vessel — and from that point on there is nothing left of the original message at all.

How can this phenomenon, which is, after all, quite natural, be combated? Only if the son sees to it that instead of descending to the level of secondary vessel he somehow retains the status of primary vessel. He himself must take the same interest that *his* father did and internalize the ideas and concepts taught to him until he himself becomes a primary source of information. This is the idea behind the Haggadah's assertion that in order to effectively fulfill "You shall tell your son on that day. . ." one must first regard himself as a primary participant in

as it says: They embittered their lives with hard labor, with mortar and bricks, and with all manner of labor in the field: Whatever service they made them perform was with hard labor.[1]

In every generation it is one's duty to regard himself as though he personally had gone out of Egypt, as it says: You shall tell your son on that day: "It was because of this that HASHEM did for 'me' when I went out of Egypt."[2] It was not only our fathers whom the Holy One, Blessed is He, redeemed from slavery; we, too, were redeemed with them, as it says: He brought "us" out from there so that He might take us to the land which He had promised to our fathers.[3]

---

1. *Shemos* 1:14. 2. Ibid., 13:8. 3. *Devarim* 6:23.

---

those events. The same goes for the teacher-student relationship as well.

The Chafetz Chaim elucidated the point further by means of a story that had actually occurred to him. During the famously harsh Russian winters it was common that the water in the mikvehs used to become unbearably cold, and even sometimes reach the freezing point. To solve this problem, a pot of water was kept over a fire next to the mikveh throughout the winter, and when the need arose it was poured into the mikveh to warm it up a bit. One day, the Chafetz Chaim related, he went to immerse himself in the mikveh, and asked the attendant how the water temperature was.

"The water is warm, Rebbe," the man responded. "You can go right in."

The Chafetz Chaim put the edge of his foot into the mikveh and immediately recoiled from the freezing water. "Why did you tell me the water is warm?" he asked the attendant. "It is practically ice!"

"But that's not possible!" the attendant protested. "I just poured half of the pot of water into the mikveh a few minutes ago!"

The Chafetz Chaim was puzzled. He didn't think the attendant would lie to him. But, on the other hand, the water was in fact ice cold. He went over to the pot of water and looked at it. It didn't appear to be too hot, and he dipped his finger into it. The water was only lukewarm!

"It was then that I understood everything," the Chafetz Chaim concluded. "If the pot is hot it can remove the chill from the mikveh. If it is only lukewarm its effect is negligible!"

In a further illustration of the point, the Chafetz Chaim said on another occasion: A father is like the engine of a locomotive pulling many cars behind it. If the stoker puts enough coal into the furnace and the heat is high enough to raise the pressure sufficiently, the train will be able to ascend the most difficult hills. But if the fire becomes weak and the steam pressure dies down, the weight of all the cars will cause them to simply roll back down the hill — pulling the engine down with them.

The matzos are covered and the cup is lifted and held until it is to be drunk. According to some customs, however, the cup is put down after the following paragraph, in which case the matzos should once more be uncovered.

לְפִיכָךְ אֲנַחְנוּ חַיָּבִים לְהוֹדוֹת, לְהַלֵּל, לְשַׁבֵּחַ, לְפָאֵר, לְרוֹמֵם, לְהַדֵּר, לְבָרֵךְ, לְעַלֵּה, וּלְקַלֵּס, לְמִי שֶׁעָשָׂה לַאֲבוֹתֵינוּ וְלָנוּ אֶת כָּל הַנִּסִּים הָאֵלּוּ, הוֹצִיאָנוּ מֵעַבְדוּת לְחֵרוּת, מִיָּגוֹן לְשִׂמְחָה, וּמֵאֵבֶל לְיוֹם טוֹב, וּמֵאֲפֵלָה לְאוֹר גָּדוֹל, וּמִשִּׁעְבּוּד לִגְאֻלָּה, וְנֹאמַר לְפָנָיו שִׁירָה חֲדָשָׁה, הַלְלוּיָהּ.

לְפִיכָךְ אֲנַחְנוּ חַיָּבִים לְהוֹדוֹת
Therefore it is our duty to thank,

To Thank Is to Admit

The word לְהוֹדוֹת in Hebrew means both "to thank" and "to admit." This is no mere coincidence, **R' Gedaliah Schorr** noted, as may be seen in the following Midrash (*Bereishis Rabbah* 71:5):

> And [Leah] said, "This time I will give thanks to Hashem" (*Bereishis* 29:35). Leah adopted the art of thankfulness (הוֹדָיָה); therefore there descended from her people who exhibited the trait of הוֹדָיָה — Yehudah, of whom it is said, "And he recognized them and said, 'She is more righteous than I' " (*ibid.*, 38:26), and David, who said, "Give thanks to Hashem, for He is good" (*Tehillim* 118:1).

The Midrash attributes Yehudah's and David's trait of הוֹדָיָה to that of their ancestress Leah. We can readily understand the connection between Leah and David, for they both excelled at giving thanks. But how does Yehudah fit in to this comparison? We do not find any indication that Yehudah exhibited the attribute of thankfulness. The verse cited in the Mishnah shows only that Yehudah was quick to *admit* his guilt, but not that he gave thanks to anybody. It is obvious, then, that the Midrash connects the two meanings of הוֹדָיָה — *thankfulness* and *admission* — and considers them to be one and the same.

The cause for Leah's joy, the Midrash tells us, is that, having borne a fourth son to Yaakov, she realized that she had received more than her share of the twelve tribes destined to issue from the patriarch (for Yaakov had four wives, and by right each should have become the mother to three of the tribes). It was this realization that she had received something beyond what she felt was her due — in effect, an *admission* of indebtedness — that prompted her to express her thankfulness to God. David, too, often expressed the sentiment that he was unworthy of all the glory and power that had become his lot as king of Israel (see, e.g., *II Shmuel* 7:18), and it was this feeling of indebtedness for having received more than he deserved that was the cause of his many psalms of praise to God.

Hence, when we recite the Haggadah's words, "Therefore we are obligated to thank. . .," we must bear in mind the true implications of the word לְהוֹדוֹת: We must realize our unworthiness of all the many favors and kindnesses that God has done

The matzos are covered and the cup is lifted and held until it is to be drunk. According to some customs, however, the cup is put down after the following paragraph, in which case the matzos should once more be uncovered.

Therefore it is our duty to thank, praise, pay tribute, glorify, exalt, honor, bless, extol, and acclaim the One Who performed all these miracles for our fathers and for us. He brought us forth from slavery to freedom, from grief to joy, from mourning to festivity, from darkness to great light, and from servitude to redemption. Let us, therefore, recite a new song before Him! Halleluyah!

for us, ever since the Exodus from Egypt, which, as we have noted many times, was brought about despite the people's woefully poor spiritual state at the time. We give thanks because we realize we have received beyond what is due us.

וְנֹאמַר לְפָנָיו שִׁירָה חֲדָשָׁה
Let us, therefore, recite a new song before Him!

The New Song   This sentence serves as an introduction to *Hallel* and leads directly into it. An interesting question was put forth by the **Netziv**: Why is *Hallel* referred to here as "a new song"? It is actually quite an ancient song; according to some opinions in the Talmud (*Pesachim* 117a) it was first recited by the Israelites at the Reed Sea, and at any rate it is certainly at least as old as David!

Actually, a similar question may be posed in connection with the morning prayers, where the Song at the Reed Sea is referred to as a "new song": "The redeemed ones praised Your name with a *new song* at the seashore. Together they all. . . said, 'Hashem shall reign forever!'" It is true that at that time the Song of the Sea was a new song, but so is every song the first time it is sung. What is so special about this song's newness that merits mention?

The Netziv, to answer these questions, cited the *Mechilta* (*Beshalach*): "R' Yosi Haglili said: If the Israelites had said (in the Song of the Sea), 'Hashem *reigns* forever,' (in the present tense) no nation would ever have been able to subjugate them." By saying "Hashem *shall* reign forever," however, they implied, "The time will come when He will reign," resembling our prayers on Rosh Hashanah (*Malchuyos*) that Hashem establish His reign over all mankind.

It was because the Song of the Sea included this prayer concerning future times, the Netziv explained, that it is called a "new song," "new" connoting that the time for its fulfillment had not arrived as yet.

The same may be said for *Hallel*. The Talmud (*Pesachim* 118a) tells us that *Hallel* incorporates the following five themes: The Exodus from Egypt, the splitting of the Reed Sea, the giving of the Torah, the resurrection of the dead, and the pains of the coming of the *Mashiach*. Since it involves some topics that are to come about only in the distant future, it is appropriate to refer to *Hallel* as a "new song."

הַלְלוּיָהּ הַלְלוּ עַבְדֵי יהוה, הַלְלוּ אֶת שֵׁם יהוה.
יְהִי שֵׁם יהוה מְבֹרָךְ, מֵעַתָּה וְעַד עוֹלָם.
מִמִּזְרַח שֶׁמֶשׁ עַד מְבוֹאוֹ, מְהֻלָּל שֵׁם יהוה. רָם עַל
כָּל גּוֹיִם יהוה, עַל הַשָּׁמַיִם כְּבוֹדוֹ. מִי כַּיהוה אֱלֹהֵינוּ,
הַמַּגְבִּיהִי לָשָׁבֶת. הַמַּשְׁפִּילִי לִרְאוֹת, בַּשָּׁמַיִם
וּבָאָרֶץ. מְקִימִי מֵעָפָר דָּל, מֵאַשְׁפֹּת יָרִים אֶבְיוֹן.

הַלְלוּיָהּ הַלְלוּ עַבְדֵי ה׳
Halleluyah! Praise, you servants of Hashem,

Making the Best of It — The Midrash applies to Eliezer, Avraham's servant, the title of "the intelligent servant" (*Mishlei* 17:2). And in what way did Eliezer's extraordinary "intelligence" express itself? The Midrash explains: Eliezer said to himself, "I am already subject to Noah's curse (of my ancestors Cham and Canaan) that I must be a slave to others. Perhaps an African or a Barbarian might come and take me to be his slave! It is better for me to be a slave in this house (of Avraham) rather than in someone else's house!" In other words, **R' Gedaliah Schorr** summed up, Eliezer's wisdom was expressed in the fact that he accepted his limitations and immediately set about to make the best of his situation, choosing to become a servant to the righteous Avraham.

This lesson applies just as well to all people, in all walks of life. We must all recognize that we are blessed with certain talents, and that our potential is limited by certain restrictions which cannot be altered. We should not waste our time brooding over the perceived lack of fairness in our lot, but should concentrate our energies on serving God in whatever capacities are available to us.

In a sense we are all in Eliezer's predicament. Every one of us is subject to the curse of Adam (*Bereishis* 3:19), to one degree or another, condemned to constant sweat and labor throughout life. "Man was born to toil" (*Iyov* 5:7). We cannot escape this curse, but we can at least choose the form of toil that will preoccupy our lives. Fortunate are those who can choose the path of Torah and, like Eliezer, declare, "It is better for me to be enslaved in this house," for this situation is infinitely better than becoming "enslaved" to primitive "Africans and Barbarians" — i.e., to physical labor and the relentless pursuit of monetary wealth.

הַמַּגְבִּיהִי לָשָׁבֶת. הַמַּשְׁפִּילִי לִרְאוֹת, בַּשָּׁמַיִם וּבָאָרֶץ. מְקִימִי מֵעָפָר דָּל וכו׳
Who is enthroned on high, yet lowers Himself to look upon the heaven and the earth. He raises the destitute from the dust, etc.

Caring for the Poor — Many commentators have endeavored to explain the connection between these two verses. What does Hashem's great loftiness have to do with His raising up the poor? The **Chafetz Chaim** offered the following explanation. God is so lofty that even to look upon the heavens involves His "lowering Himself" — and it goes without saying that by looking at what occurs on earth He is considered to be lowering Himself. And yet God *does*

Halleluyah! Praise, you servants of HASHEM, praise the Name of HASHEM. Blessed is the Name of HASHEM from now and forever. From the rising of the sun to its setting, HASHEM's Name is praised. High above all nations is HASHEM, above the heavens is His glory. Who is like HASHEM, our God, Who is enthroned on high, yet lowers Himself to look upon the heaven and the earth. He raises the destitute from the dust; from the trash heaps He lifts the needy —

indeed deign to look at what happens on earth, out of His great mercy and care for His creations. This being the case, He will certainly see the difficulties of the poor and downtrodden and alleviate their plight.

הַמַּשְׁפִּילִי לִרְאוֹת, בַּשָּׁמַיִם וּבָאָרֶץ
Yet lowers Himself to look upon the heaven and the earth.

Hashem Is Looking

The **Chafetz Chaim** used to endeavor to learn a lesson about spirituality from every novel thing that he heard about. When he heard of the invention of the telescope, he said, "With this instrument man is capable of viewing the heavens and studying the planets and stars and their motions in great detail. Now that people on earth can view the heavens so clearly, it is that much easier for man to conceptualize the fact that their deeds on earth are carefully scrutinized from Heaven!"

Along similar lines, a famous story is told about the Chafetz Chaim and his wagon driver. One time, while traveling down a country road, the driver noticed an apple orchard with big, beautiful, ripe apples glistening in the sun, beckoning at him, as it were, to help himself. He pulled the carriage over to the side, walked toward the field and began to pick some apples for himself.

Suddenly the Chafetz Chaim called out from the carriage, "You've been seen! You've been seen!"

The driver ran back toward the wagon and jumped on, grabbed the reigns and began to drive off as fast as he could, afraid he might be apprehended or shot by the owner of the field. From a safe distance, he turned around and looked in all directions, but didn't see a soul. "I thought you said I had been seen," said the driver to the Chafetz Chaim, somewhat puzzled.

"Of course you were seen!" answered the Chafetz Chaim. "The One Above was watching! As the Sages teach, 'Know what is above you: an eye that sees and an ear that hears; and everything you do is recorded in a book (*Avos* 2:1).' "

מְקִימִי מֵעָפָר דָּל, מֵאַשְׁפֹּת יָרִים אֶבְיוֹן
He raises the destitute from the dust;
from the trash heaps He lifts the needy.

The Poor Man's Connections

One time a businessman who had been quite wealthy, but had subsequently run into financial difficulty and lost all his fortune, came to the **Chafetz Chaim** to tell him of his

לְהוֹשִׁיבִי עִם נְדִיבִים, עִם נְדִיבֵי עַמּוֹ. מוֹשִׁיבִי עֲקֶרֶת הַבַּיִת, אֵם הַבָּנִים שְׂמֵחָה, הַלְלוּיָהּ.[1]

בְּצֵאת יִשְׂרָאֵל מִמִּצְרָיִם, בֵּית יַעֲקֹב מֵעַם לֹעֵז. הָיְתָה יְהוּדָה לְקָדְשׁוֹ, יִשְׂרָאֵל מַמְשְׁלוֹתָיו. הַיָּם רָאָה וַיָּנֹס, הַיַּרְדֵּן יִסֹּב לְאָחוֹר. הֶהָרִים רָקְדוּ כְאֵילִים, גְּבָעוֹת כִּבְנֵי צֹאן. מַה לְּךָ הַיָּם כִּי תָנוּס, הַיַּרְדֵּן תִּסֹּב לְאָחוֹר. הֶהָרִים תִּרְקְדוּ כְאֵילִים, גְּבָעוֹת כִּבְנֵי צֹאן. מִלִּפְנֵי אָדוֹן חוּלִי אָרֶץ, מִלִּפְנֵי אֱלוֹהַּ יַעֲקֹב. הַהֹפְכִי הַצּוּר אֲגַם מָיִם, חַלָּמִישׁ לְמַעְיְנוֹ מָיִם.[2]

---

troubles. The Chafetz Chaim — who taught (in *Ahavas Chesed* II, 8) that simply providing words of comfort to others in their time of sorrow is considered to be a fulfillment of the great mitzvah of acting kindly toward others (גְּמִילוּת חֲסָדִים) — consoled the man by telling him the following parable:

In a certain town there were two wealthy merchants, who ran a prosperous — but highly illegal — smuggling operation. The junior partner amassed a fortune of twenty thousand rubles, while the senior partner was even more wealthy, having put away fifty thousand rubles into safekeeping. One day the men were finally caught by the authorities, and they were both promptly thrown into jail to await trial.

The families of the two men tried all sorts of maneuvers to have them released, but to no avail. They spent a great deal of their savings on legal counsel and on day-to-day living expenses, until the senior partner's family was left with "only" twenty thousand rubles, while the family of the junior partner, which had started with twenty thousand rubles, was now down to its last thousand rubles. The junior partner had one advantage over his friend however; an important government minister had taken an interest in his case and was planning to testify on his behalf.

The night before the trial the two men compared their respective situations. "Although we are both in big trouble," said the junior partner to his more wealthy companion, "you are in much better shape than I am! When you finally get out of jail you will have enough money to start life over again and invest in a new business venture. I, however, am completely broke, and will have to struggle just to get by."

"You are mistaken to be jealous of me, my friend!" argued his companion. "You have an influential government minister on your side, and you will almost certainly be acquitted tomorrow. I, on the other hand, am certain to be sentenced to many years in prison. What good will my money do me while I languish away here in my cell!"

The lesson of the parable is that the poor man has the most influential "Advocate" imaginable in heaven working on his behalf, as we read in *Tehillim* (109:31): "For He stands by the right side of the poor man, to save him from those who

to seat them with nobles, with nobles of His people. He transforms the barren wife into a glad mother of children. Halleluyah![1]

When Israel went forth from Egypt, Yaakov's household from a people of alien tongue, Yehudah became His sanctuary, Israel His dominion. The Sea saw and fled; the Jordan turned backward. The mountains skipped like rams, and the hills like young lambs. What ails you, O Sea, that you flee? O Jordan, that you turn backward? O mountains, that you skip like rams? O hills, like young lambs? Before HASHEM's presence — tremble, O earth, before the presence of the God of Yaakov, Who turns the rock into a pond of water, the flint into a flowing fountain.[2]

---
1. *Tehillim* 113. 2. Ibid., 114.

---

condemn his soul." Other people might be better off financially in this world, but in the World of Truth all their fortune is worth nothing: "When a man departs this world, neither silver nor gold nor precious stones accompany him, but only his Torah and good deeds" (*Avos* 6:10).

"The poor man may have less money in the bank," the Chafetz Chaim told the man who had come to speak to him, "but he can count on his 'connections' to insure that when the moment of truth comes he will not be let down!"

הַהֹפְכִי הַצּוּר אֲגַם מָיִם, חַלָּמִישׁ לְמַעְיְנוֹ מָיִם
**Who turns the rock into a pond of water,
the flint into a flowing fountain.**

A Spiritual Feast At this point *Hallel* is interrupted and is not resumed until after the meal, in accordance with the instructions of the Mishnah (*Pesachim* 116b). This is highly irregular, as ordinarily it is forbidden to interrupt the recitation of *Hallel* for any reason. Why did the Sages institute this splitting of the *Hallel* for the Seder?

According to the **Netziv,** this is done to indicate that on this night the act of eating the *pesach* meat, matzah, and *maror* (and, incidentally, the rest of the meal) is elevated above the ordinary, materialistic act of eating as practiced the rest of the year. The Seder meal is deemed to be a spiritual, not physical experience; it is considered as if it is being eaten in the presence of God Himself. Hence, the meal itself is considered to be a *part* of the *Hallel,* not an *interruption* of it, for it constitutes an act of thanksgiving to God for having, through the Exodus from Egypt, elevated us spiritually to the point where even our eating of food can be regarded as a sacred act.

<small>According to all customs the cup is lifted and the matzos covered during the recitation of this blessing.</small>

בָּרוּךְ אַתָּה יהוה אֱלֹהֵינוּ מֶלֶךְ הָעוֹלָם, אֲשֶׁר גְּאָלָנוּ וְגָאַל אֶת אֲבוֹתֵינוּ מִמִּצְרַיִם, וְהִגִּיעָנוּ הַלַּיְלָה הַזֶּה לֶאֱכָל בּוֹ מַצָּה וּמָרוֹר. כֵּן יהוה אֱלֹהֵינוּ וֵאלֹהֵי אֲבוֹתֵינוּ, יַגִּיעֵנוּ לְמוֹעֲדִים וְלִרְגָלִים אֲחֵרִים הַבָּאִים לִקְרָאתֵנוּ לְשָׁלוֹם, שְׂמֵחִים בְּבִנְיַן עִירֶךָ וְשָׂשִׂים בַּעֲבוֹדָתֶךָ,

---

חַלָּמִישׁ לְמַעְיְנוֹ מָיִם / *the flint into a flowing fountain.*

The Proper Time for Hallel — As mentioned above (previous piece) the *Hallel* is interrupted in the middle with the Seder meal. There is a controversy in the Mishnah (*Pesachim* 116b) concerning the point in *Hallel* at which the interruption should be made. The school of *Beis Shammai* maintains that the break should occur after the first paragraph, at אֵם הַבָּנִים שְׂמֵחָה הַלְלוּיָהּ. *Beis Hillel*, the accepted opinion, holds that the interruption is made after the second paragraph, at חַלָּמִישׁ לְמַעְיְנוֹ מָיִם. What is the issue about which this disagreement revolves? The **Netziv** provided the following analysis of the matter, based on a *baraisa* (see *Tosefta, Pesachim* 10:6) cited in the *Talmud Yerushalmi* (*Pesachim* 10:5). The *baraisa* reads as follows:

> *Beis Shammai* said to [*Beis Hillel*]: Have the Jews left Egypt already, that he should mention the Exodus from Egypt?
>
> *Beis Hillel* responded: Even if he would wait until daybreak, they still would not have reached even half their deliverance. How can one mention deliverance before they were delivered? They did not go out until the middle of the day, as it says, "And it was in the middle of that day that Hashem took out the Children of Israel from the land of Egypt" (*Shemos* 12:51). Rather, when one has begun a mitzvah, we tell him, "Finish it."

Both sides of the argument, as presented in the *baraisa,* seem to be shrouded in mystery. The Netziv explained *Beis Shammai's* words as follows. The second paragraph of the *Hallel* speaks of the Exodus from Egypt ("When Israel went out of Egypt. . ."). The eating of the matzah, argues *Beis Shammai*, represents the deliverance from Egypt, as the Haggadah has explained above. It is therefore inappropriate to praise God for our liberation from Egypt before engaging in the act which represents that liberation. The second paragraph should thus be left until after the meal. The first paragraph, on the other hand, speaks of general deliverance, and this is appropriate even before eating the matzah. Although complete deliverance was not accomplished until the splitting of the Sea (for until that point the Jews were under constant threat of recapture and reenslavement by the Egyptians), at least Pharaoh himself had officially emancipated the people when he said, "Arise, go out from the midst of my nation!" (*Shemos* 12:31). This was the fulfillment of God's prophecy to Moshe that "when [Pharaoh] sends them out he will totally and

> According to all customs the cup is lifted and the matzos covered during the recitation of this blessing.
>
> Blessed are You, HASHEM, our God, King of the universe, Who redeemed us and redeemed our ancestors from Egypt and enabled us to reach this night that we may eat on it matzah and maror. So, HASHEM, our God and God of our fathers, bring us also to future holidays and festivals in peace, gladdened in the building of Your city and joyful at Your service.

completely drive them out from here" (ibid., 11:1), and constituted an absolute, irreversible declaration of freedom for the Jews. As the *Talmud Yerushalmi* elsewhere (*Pesachim* 5:5) puts it:

> Pharaoh said to the people, "Previously you were servants of Pharaoh; now you are servants of Hashem!" Thereupon the people began to sing, "Praise, you servants *of Hashem*" (the opening phrase of the first paragraph of *Hallel*) — implying, "but no longer the servants *of Pharaoh*."

This theme is entirely appropriate before the eating of matzah, for this event preceded the Jews' actual leaving of Egypt, which the matzah represents.

Beis Hillel, however, counters with the argument that Pharaoh's official granting of emancipation can not really be considered "liberation." It is only when the Jews actually set foot out of the country that they could really be considered "liberated." After all, as long as they were in the country, there was always the danger that Pharaoh and the Egyptians might change their minds (as they in fact did *after* the Jews left — *Shemos* 14:5). Thus, according to *Beis Shammai's* reasoning, it would have been inappropriate to recite even the *first* paragraph before eating matzah!

Beis Hillel then raises a second objection. *Beis Shammai* had favored the postponement of the second paragraph ("When Israel went out of Egypt. . .") until after eating the matzah. According to this line of reasoning, *Beis Hillel* argues, the recitation of this paragraph should be postponed until noon of the next day, for that is the actual time when "Israel went out of Egypt"! Rather, *Beis Hillel* concludes, we should not concern ourselves with the fact that the Exodus from Egypt is mentioned before the eating of the matzah. Since the recital of *Hallel* was already begun, we should allow it to continue, on the basis of the saying, "When one has begun a mitzvah, we tell him, 'Finish it.' "

יַגִּיעֵנוּ לְמוֹעֲדִים וְלִרְגָלִים אֲחֵרִים . . . שְׂמֵחִים בְּבִנְיַן עִירֶךָ וְשָׂשִׂים בַּעֲבוֹדָתֶךָ
bring us also to future holidays and festivals . . . gladdened in the building of Your city and joyful at Your service.

Holidays and Festivals, Gladness and Joy

Several questions arise upon contemplating this passage. Concerning the first phrase cited here: What is the difference between "holidays" and "festivals," and why are they mentioned in this order? What is their relevance to the Seder that they should be mentioned in the Haggadah altogether? Concerning the second phrase:

(On *Motzaei Shabbos* the phrase in parentheses substitutes for the preceding phrase.)

וְנֹאכַל שָׁם מִן הַזְּבָחִים וּמִן הַפְּסָחִים [מִן הַפְּסָחִים וּמִן הַזְּבָחִים] אֲשֶׁר יַגִּיעַ דָּמָם עַל קִיר מִזְבַּחֲךָ לְרָצוֹן. וְנוֹדֶה לְךָ שִׁיר חָדָשׁ עַל גְּאֻלָּתֵנוּ וְעַל פְּדוּת נַפְשֵׁנוּ. בָּרוּךְ אַתָּה יהוה, גָּאַל יִשְׂרָאֵל.

What is the difference between being "gladdened" (שָׂמֵחַ) and "joyful" (שָׂשׂ)? (Note: The English equivalents of the Hebrew words are approximate - ed.) The **Netziv** addressed these problems and gave the following explanations.

מוֹעֲדִים (holidays), asserted the Netziv, is not a reference to the other holidays of the year, but rather to the fourteenth of Nisan, the day that is called "Pesach" in the Torah, but is now known as *"Erev Pesach."* When the Torah enumerates all the holidays ("מוֹעֲדֵי ה'") of the year (in *Vayikra* 23:14-19), this day is the first holiday mentioned on that list (v. 15). רְגָלִים (*festivals*) refers specifically to the seven-day Passover festival (originally "Festival of Matzos," now known as "Pesach"). It is now clear what relevance these two terms have to the Haggadah, and why מוֹעֲדִים is mentioned before רְגָלִים.

As far as the second phrase is concerned, the Netziv explained that the difference between the two terms is that "gladness" (שִׂמְחָה) refers to a physical or emotional sense of joy, while שָׂשׂוֹן (*joyfulness*) describes a state of spiritual bliss. That this is so may be seen in *Tehillim* 51:14: "Return to me the joy (שְׂשׂוֹן) of Your salvation," which, according to the Talmud (*Yoma* 23a), is an appeal by David for the restoration of his Divine Inspiration, which had been removed from him temporarily. Through witnessing and experiencing the sacrificial service in the Temple a person can achieve a state of spiritual elevation and ecstasy. It is to this opportunity to experience this sort of elation that we refer when we pray to "be joyful at Your service."

וְשָׂשִׂים בַּעֲבוֹדָתֶךָ
and joyful at Your service.

Joy in Serving — The **Chafetz Chaim** once said to a wagon driver who traveled often from town to town, "You probably have occasion to pass through Eishishok once in a while! Would you please stop in at the rabbi's house there and ask him for a blessing for me?"

Some time later the Chafetz Chaim met the wagon driver and asked him, "Did you ever get to Eishishok since I spoke to you?"

"Yes, Rebbe!" answered the driver.

"And what did he say when you asked him for a blessing?" inquired the Chafetz Chaim.

The driver became very uncomfortable. "Forgive me, Rebbe," he apologized, "but I just cannot relay the message!"

(On *Motzaei Shabbos* the phrase in parentheses substitutes for the preceding phrase.)
There we shall eat of the offerings and pesach sacrifices (of the pesach sacrifices and offerings) whose blood will reach the wall of Your Altar for gracious acceptance. We shall then sing a new song of praise to You for our redemption and for the liberation of our souls. Blessed are You, HASHEM, Who has redeemed Israel.

"No please," insisted the Rabbi. "I really want to hear what he told you, no matter what it was."

"Well," responded the driver hesitatingly, "if you insist... He said that he wishes you that you should soon run around barefoot, with your shirt hanging out, carrying stones! I didn't want to tell you, but you persisted..." This was a perfect description of forced laborers of those days who were sentenced to haul stones from place to place.

The Chafetz Chaim laughed and said, "What a blessing! I would be satisfied if just the first part of it came true!"

The driver was more confused than ever upon hearing the Chafetz Chaim's reaction. But the Sage explained everything. "The Rav of Eishishok knows that I am a Kohen, and he gave me the blessing that I might soon have the merit of serving in the Temple, where the Kohanim go barefoot and wear long shirts. He even blessed me that I should merit to be chosen as the *Kohen Gadol,* who carries the twelve precious stones of the *Choshen* (breastplate) on his heart! As I said, I would be satisfied with the first half of the blessing. It would be enough for me to be a plain Kohen in the Temple, without being the *Kohen Gadol*!"

וְנֹאכַל שָׁם מִן הַזְּבָחִים וּמִן הַפְּסָחִים
There we shall eat of the offerings and pesach sacrifices.

Rejoicing Before Hashem

It seems odd that in this prayer, where we beseech God to rebuild the Temple, we stress the hope that we will then be able to partake of the meat of the sacrifices. Is this why we so crave the rebuilding of the Temple and the restoration of the sacrificial service — to have more meat to eat?!

An answer to this question may be suggested based on an idea once formulated by **R' Shneur Kotler**. He noted an apparent contradiction in the words of the Rambam: In one place (*Hil. Chagigah* 1:4) he writes, "The 'joy' spoken of by the Torah ('and you shall rejoice on your festival' — *Devarim* 16:14) consists of the sacrificing of peace offerings ... which are called 'peace offerings of joy.'" But elsewhere (*Sefer Hamitzvos*, Positive #54), he writes, "We are enjoined to rejoice on the festivals. The primary manner to fulfill this commandment is by sacrificing peace offerings.... Included in this commandment is what the Sages explain, to

Some recite the following before the second cup:

הֲרֵינִי מוּכָן וּמְזוּמָּן לְקַיֵּם מִצְוַת כּוֹס שֵׁנִי מֵאַרְבַּע כּוֹסוֹת. לְשֵׁם יִחוּד קֻדְשָׁא בְּרִיךְ הוּא וּשְׁכִינְתֵּיהּ, עַל יְדֵי הַהוּא טָמִיר וְנֶעְלָם, בְּשֵׁם כָּל יִשְׂרָאֵל. וִיהִי נֹעַם אֲדֹנָי אֱלֹהֵינוּ עָלֵינוּ, וּמַעֲשֵׂה יָדֵינוּ כּוֹנְנָה עָלֵינוּ, וּמַעֲשֵׂה יָדֵינוּ כּוֹנְנֵהוּ:

בָּרוּךְ אַתָּה יהוה אֱלֹהֵינוּ מֶלֶךְ הָעוֹלָם, בּוֹרֵא פְּרִי הַגָּפֶן.

The second cup is drunk while leaning on the left side
— preferably the entire cup, but at least most of it.

---

rejoice with all sorts of joy, such as eating meat, drinking wine, wearing new clothing, giving out candy to children, etc." In the first quote the Rambam implies that by definition the only way to fulfill the Torah's command is by bringing peace offerings, whereas in the second passage he writes that this is only the primary manner of fulfillment among many others.

A similar question may be asked in regard to the words of the Sages of the Talmud themselves. The Talmud states (*Pesachim* 109a): "When the Temple was standing, the 'joy' (that is mandated for the festivals) could be accomplished only through eating (sacrificial) meat, as it says (*Devarim* 27:7), 'You shall sacrifice peace offerings and eat there and rejoice.' Nowadays, however, rejoicing is accomplished only through drinking wine, as it says (*Tehillim* 104:15), 'wine brings joy to man's heart.' " The difficulty is as follows: If, as the Talmud asserts, the definition of the Torah's mitzvah of rejoicing on the festivals was originally said to be *only* through the eating of sacrificial meat, how could that definition change just because the Temple no longer stands and sacrifices are no longer offered? We should simply conclude that nowadays, without sacrifices, there is no longer any possibility of fulfilling this mitzvah, rather than to revise the definition of the mitzvah to fit the new situation!

Another question is raised concerning this passage from the Talmud as well (see *Kesef Mishneh, Hil. Chagigah* loc. cit.). The verse cited by the Talmud to prove that the only way to fulfill the mitzvah of joy on the festivals is through peace offerings comes from *Devarim* 27:7: "You shall sacrifice peace offerings and eat there and rejoice." The problem is that this verse is not speaking of the festivals at all, but is taken from a completely different context — the sacrifices that were to be offered

Some recite the following before the second cup:
Behold, I am prepared and ready to fulfill the mitzvah of the second of the Four Cups. For the sake of the unification of the Holy One, Blessed is He, and His Presence, through Him Who is hidden and inscrutable — [I pray] in the name of all Israel. May the pleasantness of my Lord, our God, be upon us — may He establish our handiwork for us; our handiwork may He establish.

Blessed are You, HASHEM, our God, King of the universe, Who creates the fruit of the vine.

The second cup is drunk while leaning on the left side — preferably the entire cup, but at least most of it.

---

on Mount Eval immediately after the Jews' entrance into Eretz Yisrael under Yehoshua.

R' Shneur dealt with all these questions by explaining that there are in fact two distinct forms of rejoicing. When the Torah commands us to rejoice on the festivals it refers to *any* action that brings a person joy. However, as was explained more fully above (p. 4), the highest, most sublime form of joy comes from the feeling of closeness to God. This is borne out by many verses in the Torah, such as, "You shall eat there *before Hashem* and rejoice" (*Devarim* 14:26); "You shall rejoice *before Hashem* your God" (ibid., 16:11); "You shall rejoice *before Hashem* (ibid., 12:12). Hence, although it is possible to achieve joy through the drinking of wine, etc., such joy is lacking a crucial element — the cultivation of the sensation of nearness to God, which, as is proven from *Devarim* 14:26 (although this verse does not deal specifically with festivals), is accomplished through the partaking of sacrificial meat. Thus, when the Temple was still standing it was obligatory to fulfill the mitzvah of rejoicing on the festivals in the most preferable manner, through achieving closeness to God — i.e., through partaking of the meat of peace offerings. Now that this option is no longer viable, with the Temple no longer standing, we have no choice but to fulfill the mitzvah in its secondary, less desirable format, through other forms of rejoicing.

In light of this explanation, we can gain an understanding of the words of our prayer in the Haggadah. We pray to Hashem to allow us to partake of the meat of the sacrifices not because of a hedonistic desire to consume meat, but because we wish to fulfill the Torah's mitzvah of rejoicing on the festivals in its fullest sense, by "rejoicing *before Hashem,*" rather than in its secondary meaning.

רָחְצָה – Rachtzah
מוֹצִיא – Motzi
מַצָּה – Matzah

Laws of Matzah

1. A piece should be broken off together from both of the top two matzos and eaten together. Each piece should be a *k'zayis* (*Orach Chayim* 475:1, *Mishnah Berurah* §3). (Those who do not have three matzos of their own take the required amount from other matzos. Many maintain that they need to eat only one *kezayis*.)

2. Although both *k'zeisim* should be put into the mouth and chewed at one time, they do not have to be swallowed at one time (ibid., *Mishnah Berurah* §9).

3. One must eat this amount of matzah with a period of *kedei achilas pras* (about 2-9 minutes) (ibid.).

4. If it is too hard for someone to eat both *k'zeisim* at one time, he should eat the *k'zayis* from the whole matzah first, and then the second from the broken matzah.

5. If for some reason two *k'zeisim* were not eaten, but only one (from either matzah or from both together), the mitzvah has nevertheless been fulfilled (*Mishnah Berurah* §11).

6. If the matzah was eaten without reclining, one *k'zayis* must be eaten again while reclining (472:7; *Be'ur Halachah* ad loc.).

7. One must be sure to eat the matzah before halachic midnight. (If one did not do so, it is doubtful whether he can still fulfill the mitzvah, and he should eat the matzah without the *berachah* of אֲשֶׁר קִדְּשָׁנוּ בְּמִצְוֹתָיו (477:1, *Mishnah Berurah* §6).

   If, for some reason, the beginning of the Seder was delayed until just before midnight, one should eat the matzah and *maror* immediately following *Kiddush*, and afterwards go back and recite the Haggadah and finish his meal (*Mishnah Berurah* ibid.).

8. It is customary not to dip the matzah in salt after *Hamotzi* at the Seder (475:1).

רחצה

The hands are washed for matzah and the following blessing is recited. It is preferable to bring water and a basin to the head of the household at the Seder table.

בָּרוּךְ אַתָּה יהוה אֱלֹהֵינוּ מֶלֶךְ הָעוֹלָם, אֲשֶׁר קִדְּשָׁנוּ בְּמִצְוֹתָיו, וְצִוָּנוּ עַל נְטִילַת יָדָיִם.

מוציא

Some recite the following before the blessing *hamotzi:*

הִנְנִי מוּכָן וּמְזֻמָּן לְקַיֵּם מִצְוַת אֲכִילַת מַצָּה. לְשֵׁם יִחוּד קֻדְשָׁא בְּרִיךְ הוּא וּשְׁכִינְתֵּיהּ, עַל יְדֵי הַהוּא טָמִיר וְנֶעְלָם, בְּשֵׁם כָּל יִשְׂרָאֵל. וִיהִי נֹעַם אֲדֹנָי אֱלֹהֵינוּ עָלֵינוּ, וּמַעֲשֵׂה יָדֵינוּ כּוֹנְנָה עָלֵינוּ, וּמַעֲשֵׂה יָדֵינוּ כּוֹנְנֵהוּ:

The following two blessings are recited over matzah; the first is recited over matzah as food, and the second for the special mitzvah of eating matzah on the night of Pesach. [The latter blessing is to be made with the intention that it also apply to the "sandwich" and the *afikoman.*]

The head of the household raises all the matzos on the Seder plate and recites the following blessing:

בָּרוּךְ אַתָּה יהוה אֱלֹהֵינוּ מֶלֶךְ הָעוֹלָם, הַמּוֹצִיא לֶחֶם מִן הָאָרֶץ.

The bottom matzah is put down and the following blessing is recited while the top (whole) matzah and the middle (broken) piece are still raised.

מצה

בָּרוּךְ אַתָּה יהוה אֱלֹהֵינוּ מֶלֶךְ הָעוֹלָם, אֲשֶׁר קִדְּשָׁנוּ בְּמִצְוֹתָיו, וְצִוָּנוּ עַל אֲכִילַת מַצָּה.

Each participant is required to eat an amount of matzah equal in volume to an egg. Since it is usually impossible to provide a sufficient amount of matzah from the two matzos for all members of the household, the other matzos should be available at the head of the table from which to complete the required amounts. However, each participant should receive a piece from each of the top two matzos. The matzos are to be eaten while reclining on the left side and without delay; they need not be dipped in salt.

מוֹצִיא מַצָּה
Motzi, Matzah

Bundling Mitzvos — As the *Shulchan Aruch* records, the *Hamotzi* blessing is recited over one of the three (or two) matzos of the Seder plate, while the blessing for the mitzvah of eating matzah is recited over another matzah. *Tosafos* (*Berachos* 39b), the **Netziv** noted, explains the reason for this practice: Since "mitzvos may not be performed in bundles" (*Berachos* 49a, *Sukkah* 8a), it is impossible to recite both of these blessings over the same object. This explanation is found in the *piyut* for *Shabbos Hagadol* as well.

RACHTZAH

The hands are washed for matzah and the following blessing is recited. It is preferable to bring water and a basin to the head of the household at the Seder table.

Blessed are You, HASHEM, our God, King of the universe, Who has sanctified us with His commandments, and has commanded us concerning the washing of the hands.

MOTZI

Some recite the following before the blessing hamotzi:

Behold, I am prepared and ready to fulfill the mitzvah of eating matzah. For the sake of the unification of the Holy One, Blessed is He, and His Presence, through Him who is hidden and inscrutable — [I pray] in the name of all Israel. May the pleasantness of my Lord, our God, be upon us — may He establish our handiwork for us; our handiwork may He establish.

The following two blessings are recited over matzah; the first is recited over matzah as food, and the second for the special mitzvah of eating matzah on the night of Pesach. [The latter blessing is to be made with the intention that it also apply to the "sandwich" and the afikoman.]

The head of the household raises all the matzos on the Seder plate and recites the following blessing:

Blessed are You, HASHEM, our God, King of the universe, Who brings forth bread from the earth.

The bottom matzah is put down and the following blessing is recited while the top (whole) matzah and the middle (broken) piece are still raised.

MATZAH

Blessed are You, HASHEM, our God, King of the universe, Who has sanctified us with His commandments, and has commanded us concerning the eating of the matzah.

Each participant is required to eat an amount of matzah equal in volume to an egg. Since it is usually impossible to provide a sufficient amount of matzah from the two matzos for all members of the household, the other matzos should be available at the head of the table from which to complete the required amounts. However, each participant should receive a piece from each of the top two matzos. The matzos are to be eaten while reclining on the left side and without delay; they need not be dipped in salt.

A similar reason is given for the eating of "*karpas*" (a vegetable) early in the Seder: Without this eating of the vegetable, when the time for eating *maror* would come we would have to recite two blessings over the *maror* (בּוֹרֵא פְּרִי הָאֲדָמָה for the vegetable itself, and עַל אֲכִילַת מָרוֹר for the mitzvah of eating *maror*), and this, as explained above, is unacceptable. It is in order to separate the two blessings that the eating of *karpas* was instituted.

This explanation for the eating of *karpas*, however, seems to contradict the Talmud (*Pesachim* 114b), which gives an entirely different reason for the practice —

namely, that it is in order to arouse the curiosity of the children. It seems to be unnecessary to contrive a new reason for an act that already has an adequate explanation.

The Netziv explained that in fact there is a need for both of these reasons; either one by itself is insufficient. If the only reason for the institution of *karpas* had been to pique the children's curiosity this could have been accomplished through the dipping of any food. Why did the Sages establish the practice of dipping a vegetable specifically? The answer to this question is supplied by *Tosafos*: It is in order to avoid the necessity to make two blessings over the *maror*. On the other hand, the reason given by *Tosafos* is by itself insufficient to explain the practice of *karpas*, for the double-blessing problem could have been avoided by instituting the taking of two pieces of *maror*, one for the הָאֲדָמָה blessing and the other for the mitzvah blessing, in the same manner the problem is addressed for the matzah, by the use of three (or two) separate matzos. Why did the Sages have to distance the two blessings from each other to such an extent? The answer is that by placing the eating of the first vegetable so early in the Seder they accomplished a secondary goal of arousing the children's attention.

It should be noted that many authorities disagree with *Tosafos'* theory altogether. The Rosh, for instance, writes that the issue of the double blessing does not arise at all in connection with *maror*, for the herb is considered to be a basic part of the Seder meal, and as such does not require an independent הָאֲדָמָה blessing. *Tosafos* himself raises the following objection against the proponents of the theory: At *Kiddush* and *Havdalah* and numerous other occasions we find that the food blessing (בּוֹרֵא פְּרִי הַגָּפֶן) and the mitzvah blessing are both recited over one cup of wine. Obviously, then, such an arrangement is not considered to be a case of "performing mitzvos in bundles." This is indeed a strong question, and *Tosafos* leaves it unanswered. The Netziv, however, offered the following defense for the adherents of *Tosafos'* theory.

The blessing recited over wine as a food (בּוֹרֵא פְּרִי הַגָּפֶן), wrote the Netziv, is different from other such blessings. It is not only a blessing over food, but it also plays a role as a praise of God for having created wine, which serves as a medium through which songs and praises of God are sung, and through which He is blessed (see *Berachos* 41b-42a and *Rashi* and *Tosafos* ad loc.). Hence, it is not considered to be a combination ("bundle") of two disparate mitzvos, for both blessings are united in their theme of praise for the greatness of God. According to this approach, the Netziv pointed out, when Kiddush is made over bread (such as when wine is not available), indeed one loaf should be used for the *Hamotzi* blessing and the other for the *Kiddush*.

מַצָּה / Matzah

The Five Grains

In 1880 a young man from Radin — the local baker's son — came home from a long stint in the Russian army. He had been stationed in a remote area of the Caucusus mountains, and the **Chafetz Chaim** was curious to find out about the conditions of the Jewish soldiers there.

"What can I tell you, Rebbe?" said the soldier plaintively. "We were completely cut off from civilization. There was not even any wheat that grew in that area! People there eat rye and oats instead. We were even unable to make matzah on Pesach!"

"So what *did* you eat on Pesach?" asked the Chafetz Chaim.

"We had no choice but to violate the custom of refraining from eating *kitniyos* (vegetables in which the seed is the main food)," confessed the soldier. "We made a bread out of rye and ate it the whole Pesach."

"Oh no!" exclaimed the Chafetz Chaim. "Don't you know? Rye is one of the five species of grain that can be used for making matzah! And furthermore, it is considered 100 percent chametz when it is cooked or baked into bread! You did not merely violate the custom of refraining from *kitniyos,* but a major Torah prohibition!"

"We had no idea!" said the soldier, ashamed of his gross error. "We thought the laws of matzah and *chametz* pertained only to wheat products!"

"It is quite explicit in the *Shulchan Aruch*!" argued the Chafetz Chaim. But, of course, as the soldier reminded him, there are no *Shulchan Aruchs* on a Russian army base!

Because of this incident the Chafetz Chaim undertook to compose a concise halachah book for the Jewish soldier, providing him with the basic rudiments of observing Jewish law under the most adverse conditions. This is how the book מַחֲנֶה יִשְׂרָאֵל ("The Camp of Israel"), which was subsequently published and used by thousands of Jewish soldiers, came to be written.

מָרוֹר – Maror

כּוֹרֵךְ – Korech

Laws of Korech

1. A *k'zayis* of matzah is broken off from the bottom matzah, and a *k'zayis* of *maror* is sandwiched together with the matzah. It should be dipped into the *charoses*, and then the *charoses* should be shaken off. Some people have the custom not to dip the sandwich into *charoses*. Although the first opinion is preferable, if someone by tradition has the second custom, he may follow it (475:1, *Mishnah Berurah* §19).

2. The entire mixture of matzah and *maror* should be eaten at one time. (That is, it should be put in the mouth and chewed together, but not necessarily swallowed at once.) (*Mishnah Berurah* §22.)

3. The *korech* sandwich should be eaten while reclining. If one forgot to recline, it would appear from the *Be'ur Halachah*'s words that he need not eat it again (475:1, *Be'ur Halachah* 472 s.v. לא).

4. One should not speak at all between the *berachah* of *Hamotzi* and the *korech* sandwich, but if he did speak he need not make another *berachah* (*Mishnah Berurah* 475:24).

מָרוֹר

The head of the household takes a half-egg volume of maror, dips it into charoses, and gives each participant a like amount.

Some recite the following before maror:

הִנְנִי מוּכָן וּמְזוּמָן לְקַיֵּם מִצְוַת אֲכִילַת מָרוֹר. לְשֵׁם יִחוּד קֻדְשָׁא בְּרִיךְ הוּא וּשְׁכִינְתֵּיהּ, עַל יְדֵי הַהוּא טָמִיר וְנֶעְלָם, בְּשֵׁם כָּל יִשְׂרָאֵל. וִיהִי נֹעַם אֲדֹנָי אֱלֹהֵינוּ עָלֵינוּ, וּמַעֲשֵׂה יָדֵינוּ כּוֹנְנָה עָלֵינוּ, וּמַעֲשֵׂה יָדֵינוּ כּוֹנְנֵהוּ:

The following blessing is recited with the intention that it also apply to the maror of the "sandwich." The maror is eaten without reclining, and without delay.

בָּרוּךְ אַתָּה יהוה אֱלֹהֵינוּ מֶלֶךְ הָעוֹלָם, אֲשֶׁר קִדְּשָׁנוּ בְּמִצְוֹתָיו, וְצִוָּנוּ עַל אֲכִילַת מָרוֹר.

כּוֹרֵךְ

The bottom (thus far unbroken) matzah is now taken. From it, with the addition of other matzos, each participant receives a half-egg volume of matzah with an equal volume portion of maror (dipped into charoses which is shaken off). The following paragraph is recited and the "sandwich" is eaten while reclining.

זֵכֶר לְמִקְדָּשׁ כְּהִלֵּל. כֵּן עָשָׂה הִלֵּל בִּזְמַן שֶׁבֵּית הַמִּקְדָּשׁ הָיָה קַיָּם. הָיָה כּוֹרֵךְ (פֶּסַח) מַצָּה וּמָרוֹר וְאוֹכֵל בְּיַחַד. לְקַיֵּם מַה שֶּׁנֶּאֱמַר, עַל מַצּוֹת וּמְרֹרִים יֹאכְלֻהוּ.[1]

כּוֹרֵךְ / **Combining the matzah and maror**

No Atheist in a Foxhole — The seeming inappropriateness of eating the bitter *maror* at the Seder, which celebrates the joy of deliverance, was discussed above. **R' Gedaliah Schorr** provided yet another insight into this matter, which sheds light on the practice of eating the matzah and *maror* at one time.

When a person is well off he tends to become self-indulgent and overly materialistic. For such people, appreciation of a spiritual experience can be quite difficult. A seemingly miraculous event, which might fill the hearts of most observers with inspiration and fear of God, will most likely leave the materialist unmoved. But when a person has troubles, be they financial, emotional, health related, or personal, he is much more likely to respond positively to a religious experience,

MAROR

The head of the household takes a half-egg volume of maror, dips it into charoses, and gives each participant a like amount.

Some recite the following before maror:

Behold, I am prepared and ready to fulfill the mitzvah of eating maror. For the sake of unification of the Holy One, Blessed is He, and His Presence, through Him Who is hidden and inscrutable — [I pray] in the name of all Israel. May the pleasantness of my Lord, our God, be upon us — may He establish our handiwork for us; our handiwork may He establish.

The following blessing is recited with the intention that it also apply to the maror of the "sandwich." The maror is eaten without reclining, and without delay.

Blessed are You, HASHEM, our God, King of the universe, Who has sanctified us with His commandments, and has commanded us concerning the eating of maror.

KORECH

The bottom (thus far unbroken) matzah is now taken. From it, with the addition of other matzos, each participant receives a half-egg volume of matzah with an equal volume portion of maror (dipped into charoses which is shaken off). The following paragraph is recited and the "sandwich" is eaten while reclining.

In remembrance of the Temple we do as Hillel did in Temple times: He would combine (the pesach offering,) matzah, and maror in a sandwich and eat them together, to fulfill what it says: They shall eat it with matzos and bitter herbs.[1]

---

1. *Bamidbar* 9:11.

---

becoming moved to the point of changing his entire outlook on life. He might show himself to be capable of complete spiritual rehabilitation, finding the strength to raise himself up even from the forty-ninth level (out of fifty) of impurity. Thus, the Sages tell us (*Berachos* 5a) that "suffering cleanses man of all his sins" — for they make him more receptive to spiritual stimuli and predispose him to improve himself and repent of his sins.

Thus, it was the bitterness of exile and oppression that our ancestors faced in Egypt, as symbolized by the *maror*, that in effect enabled them to reach the spiritual heights of the Exodus with such suddenness and swiftness, as symbolized by the matzah. This, R' Gedaliah explained, is the symbolic reason why *maror* and matzah are eaten together — for it is only through the bitterness of the *maror* that we can gain the sensitivity to achieve the spiritual growth represented by the matzah.

שֻׁלְחָן עוֹרֵךְ – Shulchan Oreich
צָפוּן – Tzafun

Laws of the Seder Meal and the Afikoman

1. A person should not eat so much during the meal that he has no appetite whatsoever for the *afikoman*. If a person is so full that he actually has to force himself to eat the *afikoman* (אֲכִילָה גַסָּה), it is considered as if he has not eaten the *afikoman* at all (476:1, *Mishnah Berurah* §6).
2. It is preferable to recline while eating the entire meal (472:6).
3. Concerning the custom of eating eggs at the Seder meal, see above: p. 37.
4. It is the custom to refrain from eating any roasted meat or poultry on the Seder night, even a pot roast cooked in its own juices (without water). Roasted meat which was subsequently boiled is permitted (but not vice versa) (476:1, *Mishnah Berurah* ad loc.).
5. It is preferable to finish the meal in time to recite the entire *Hallel* before midnight. At the very least, the eating of the *afikoman* must not be delayed until after midnight (477:1).
6. The *afikoman* should be eaten while reclining. If someone forgot to recline while eating it, he should eat another piece of matzah for *afikoman* while reclining. If this is difficult, it may be forgone (*Mishnah Berurah* 477:4).
7. If someone forgot to eat the *afikoman* altogether and remembered only after having recited *Bircas HaMazon*, he must wash and recite *Hamotzi* and eat the *afikoman*, and then *bentch* again. (The second *Bircas HaMazon* should not be said over a cup of wine, as this would constitute an addition to the requisite number of four cups. If the fourth cup of wine has not yet been drunk, however, he may say *Bircas HaMazon* over a cup of wine but not drink it until after *Hallel*.) If he remembered before *Bircas HaMazon*, but after having washed his hands for מַיִם אַחֲרוֹנִים, he should eat the *afikoman* at that point (without a *berachah*) (477:2).
8. A person should not eat the matzah of *afikoman* in two different places. Even two different tables in the same room is considered two different "places" (478:1, *Mishnah Berurah* §4).
9. It is forbidden to eat anything after the *afikoman*. If one did eat something, he should eat another *k'zayis* of matzah afterwards, which then becomes his *afikoman*. One should also not drink wine (except for the third and fourth cups of the Seder). Water, however, is permitted. Concerning other soft drinks — such as fruit juice, tea, etc. — strong-tasting drinks should be avoided, but those with a light taste may be drunk. In cases of need, the opinion of the *Gra*, which holds that only intoxicating beverages are forbidden, may be relied upon, especially at the second Seder (478:1, *Mishnah Berurah* 481:1).

שוּלְחָן עוֹרֵךְ

The meal should be eaten in a combination of joy and solemnity, for the meal, too, is a part of the Seder service. While it is desirable that *zemiros* and discussion of the laws and events of Pesach be part of the meal, extraneous conversation should be avoided. It should be remembered that the *afikoman* must be eaten while there is still some appetite for it. In fact, if one is so sated that he must literally force himself to eat it, he is not credited with the performance of the mitzvah of *afikoman*. Therefore, it is unwise to eat more than a moderate amount during the meal.

צָפוּן

From the *afikoman* matzah (and from additional matzos to make up the required amount) a half-egg volume portion — according to some, a full egg's volume portion — is given to each participant. It should be eaten before midnight, while reclining, without delay, and uninterruptedly. Nothing may be eaten or drunk after the *afikoman* (with the exception of water and the like) except for the last two Seder cups of wine.

Some recite the following before eating the *afikoman*:

הִנְנִי מוּכָן וּמְזוּמָּן לְקַיֵּם מִצְוַת אֲכִילַת אֲפִיקוֹמָן. לְשֵׁם יִחוּד קֻדְשָׁא בְּרִיךְ הוּא וּשְׁכִינְתֵּיהּ, עַל יְדֵי הַהוּא טָמִיר וְנֶעְלָם, בְּשֵׁם כָּל יִשְׂרָאֵל. וִיהִי נֹעַם אֲדֹנָי אֱלֹהֵינוּ עָלֵינוּ, וּמַעֲשֵׂה יָדֵינוּ כּוֹנְנָה עָלֵינוּ, וּמַעֲשֵׂה יָדֵינוּ כּוֹנְנֵהוּ:

SHULCHAN OREICH

The meal should be eaten in a combination of joy and solemnity, for the meal, too, is a part of the Seder service. While it is desirable that *zemiros* and discussion of the laws and events of Pesach be part of the meal, extraneous conversation should be avoided. It should be remembered that the *afikoman* must be eaten while there is still some appetite for it. In fact, if one is so sated that he must literally force himself to eat it, he is not credited with the performance of the mitzvah of *afikoman*. Therefore, it is unwise to eat more than a moderate amount during the meal.

TZAFUN

From the *afikoman* matzah (and from additional matzos to make up the required amount) a half-egg volume portion — according to some, a full egg's volume portion — is given to each participant. It should be eaten before midnight, while reclining, without delay, and uninterruptedly. Nothing may be eaten or drunk after the *afikoman* (with the exception of water and the like) except for the last two Seder cups of wine.

Some recite the following before eating the *afikoman:*

Behold, I am prepared and ready to fulfill the mitzvah of eating the afikoman. For the sake of the unification of the Holy One, Blessed is He, and his Presence, through Him who is hidden and inscrutable — [I pray] in the name of all Israel. May the pleasantness of my Lord, our God, be upon us — may He establish our handiwork for us; our handiwork may He establish.

בָּרֵךְ — Barech

בָּרֵךְ

The third cup is poured and Bircas Hamazon *(Grace After Meals) is recited. According to some customs, the Cup of Eliyahu is poured at this point.*

שִׁיר הַמַּעֲלוֹת, בְּשׁוּב יהוה אֶת שִׁיבַת צִיּוֹן, הָיִינוּ כְּחֹלְמִים. אָז יִמָּלֵא שְׂחוֹק פִּינוּ וּלְשׁוֹנֵנוּ רִנָּה, אָז יֹאמְרוּ בַגּוֹיִם, הִגְדִּיל יהוה לַעֲשׂוֹת עִם אֵלֶּה. הִגְדִּיל יהוה לַעֲשׂוֹת עִמָּנוּ, הָיִינוּ שְׂמֵחִים. שׁוּבָה יהוה אֶת שְׁבִיתֵנוּ, כַּאֲפִיקִים בַּנֶּגֶב. הַזֹּרְעִים בְּדִמְעָה בְּרִנָּה יִקְצְרוּ. הָלוֹךְ יֵלֵךְ וּבָכֹה נֹשֵׂא מֶשֶׁךְ הַזָּרַע, בֹּא יָבֹא בְרִנָּה, נֹשֵׂא אֲלֻמֹּתָיו.[1]

בְּשׁוּב ה' אֶת שִׁיבַת צִיּוֹן, הָיִינוּ כְּחֹלְמִים. . . הָלוֹךְ יֵלֵךְ וּבָכֹה נֹשֵׂא מֶשֶׁךְ הַזָּרַע, בֹּא יָבֹא בְרִנָּה, נֹשֵׂא אֲלֻמוֹתָיו
When Hashem brings back the exiles to Tziyon, we will have been like dreamers. . . . Though the farmer bears the measure of seed to the field in tears, he shall come home with joy, bearing his sheaves.

The Seeds of Redemption   The Sages of the Talmud (*Pesachim* 87b) tell us that the exile is comparable to sowing seeds, as it says, "And I shall sow her for Myself in the land" (*Hoshea* 2:25). What message does the Talmud mean to impart with this comparison? When seeds are sown they first decompose slightly, and then reach the stage in which they begin to sprout. So too, **R' Gedaliah Schorr** explained, while we are in exile we face many hardships and setbacks, but eventually our salvation will begin to sprout.

There is another similarity between the two situations as well. If the seed is allowed to rot too much it will no longer be capable of producing anything at all. In exile too, despite the many trials and tribulations, we are guaranteed that the "Jewish spark" will never be totally extinguished from the members of our people, just as the farmer never allows his seeds to decompose.

There is a Midrash in the beginning of the book of *Shemos* that expresses this thought as well, commenting on the verse, "These are the names of the Children of Israel who came to Egypt . . . Reuven, Shimon, etc." (*Shemos* 1:1). The Midrash states: "This verse is an allusion to the redemption from Egypt that occurred many years later. *Reuven* (רְאוּבֵן) stands for "I have surely seen (רָאֹה רָאִיתִי) the affliction of My people" (Ibid., 3:7). *Shimon* (שִׁמְעוֹן) stands for 'And God heard (וַיִּשְׁמַע) their cries' (ibid., 2:24)." What the Midrash means to teach us with this comment is that even as the Torah describes the beginnings of the Egyptian exile, this narrative bears within it an allusion to the seeds of redemption from that exile.

BARECH

The third cup is poured and Bircas Hamazon *(Grace After Meals) is recited. According to some customs, the Cup of Eliyahu is poured at this point.*

A song of Ascents. When HASHEM brings back the exiles to Tziyon, we will have been like dreamers. Then our mouth will be filled with laughter, and our tongue with glad song. Then will it be said among the nations: HASHEM has done great things for these, HASHEM has done great things for us, and we rejoiced. Restore our captives, HASHEM, like streams in the dry land. Those who sow in tears shall reap in joy. Though the farmer bears the measure of seed to the field in tears, he shall come home with joy, bearing his sheaves.[1]

---

1. *Tehillim* 126.

הַזֹּרְעִים בְּדִמְעָה בְּרִנָּה יִקְצֹרוּ
Those who sow in tears shall reap in joy.

Using Every Moment

We often find in *Tanach*, the **Chafetz Chaim** noted, that a man's deeds in life are compared to the sowing of crops: "Sow for yourselves righteousness and you will reap according to benevolence" (*Hoshea* 10:12); "Plow your field first, and do not sow into thornbushes" (*Yirmiyahu* 4:3). Our verse alludes to this metaphor as well. If we "sow our crops" (act properly) in this world we will "reap" the reward in the World to Come.

Contemplating this concept, the Chafetz Chaim made the following observation. Imagine passing by a huge, fertile field and seeing a farmer strolling through, every few minutes tossing some seeds haphazardly here and there onto the ground. "What a fool!" we would say to ourselves. "What a waste of a precious resource! If only he would get his act together he could produce a yield ten times as much as he will grow this way!" The farmer himself will realize his foolishness when harvest time comes and he sees a lone ear of wheat here and a stalk of barley there, with the rest of the field full of thorns and weeds.

Everyone can of course picture this imaginary scenario in his mind. But the same drama is played out every day in our own lives. How much time is wasted on foolish pursuits! How much energy we expend on unimportant ventures! We of course pay no attention to the colossal waste of the tremendous resources that God has granted us in life, but when "harvest time" comes we will realize how unwise we had been, when we see the yield that we have produced because we did not exploit these gifts. We must therefore strive to realize the preciousness of every moment of life, so that we will not be embarrassed when we see the end result.

Some recite the following before Bircas Hamazon:

הִנְנִי מוּכָן וּמְזוּמָּן לְקַיֵּם מִצְוַת עֲשֵׂה שֶׁל בִּרְכַּת הַמָּזוֹן, כַּכָּתוּב, וְאָכַלְתָּ וְשָׂבֵעְתָּ וּבֵרַכְתָּ אֶת יהוה אֱלֹהֶיךָ עַל הָאָרֶץ הַטֹּבָה אֲשֶׁר נָתַן לָךְ:

If three or more males, aged thirteen or older, participated in the meal, the leader is required to formally invite the others to join him in the recitation of Grace After Meals. Following is the *"zimun,"* or formal invitation.

The leader begins:

רַבּוֹתַי נְבָרֵךְ.

The group responds:

יְהִי שֵׁם יהוה מְבֹרָךְ מֵעַתָּה וְעַד עוֹלָם.[1]

The leader continues:

יְהִי שֵׁם יהוה מְבֹרָךְ מֵעַתָּה וְעַד עוֹלָם.[1]

If ten men join in the *zimun,* the words (in parentheses) are included.

בִּרְשׁוּת מָרָנָן וְרַבָּנָן וְרַבּוֹתַי, נְבָרֵךְ (אֱלֹהֵינוּ) שֶׁאָכַלְנוּ מִשֶּׁלּוֹ.

The group responds:

בָּרוּךְ (אֱלֹהֵינוּ) שֶׁאָכַלְנוּ מִשֶּׁלּוֹ וּבְטוּבוֹ חָיִינוּ.

The leader continues:

בָּרוּךְ (אֱלֹהֵינוּ) שֶׁאָכַלְנוּ מִשֶּׁלּוֹ וּבְטוּבוֹ חָיִינוּ.

The following line is recited if ten men join in the zimun.

בָּרוּךְ הוּא וּבָרוּךְ שְׁמוֹ.

נְבָרֵךְ (אֱלֹהֵינוּ) שֶׁאָכַלְנוּ מִשֶּׁלּוֹ
Let us bless [our God] for we have eaten from what is His.

Inviting Hashem — This introductory invitation to Grace is recited when there are three or more males present at the meal; the word אֱלֹהֵינוּ (*our God*) is added when ten or more males (i.e., a minyan) are participating. There is an opinion in the Mishnah (*Berachos* 49b), **R' Zalman Sorotzkin** noted, that introduces several more gradations of progressively august designations for God's presence: "If there are a hundred men, the leader says, 'Bless Hashem our God. . .'; if there are a thousand men he says, 'Bless Hashem our God, the God of Israel'; if there are ten thousand he says, 'Bless Hashem our God, the God of Israel, the God of Hosts. . . .' " This opinion is rejected by R' Akiva (and the halachah), however, because of the following argument: "What do we find in the synagogue? Whether there are many or few the leader says, 'Bless Hashem. . . Who is blessed.' " In other words, R' Akiva maintains that it is unnecessary to add on to God's praises just because the number of those assembled is unusually large.

As Rashi (ad loc.) implies, R' Akiva's argument for uniformity of the prayer formula is only when there are ten or more people present; he agrees that when there are *fewer* than ten the text of the Grace can indeed change, dependent upon whether there are more or less than three people participating. This requires explanation — if R' Akiva seeks uniformity in prayer for Grace After Meals just as it exists

הגדה של פסח   [194]

Some recite the following before Bircas Hamazon:

Behold, I am prepared and ready to fulfill the mitzvah of Grace After Meals, as it is written; "And you shall eat and you shall be satisfied and you shall bless Hashem, your God, for the good land which He gave you."

If three or more males, aged thirteen or older, participated in the meal, the leader is required to formally invite the others to join him in the recitation of Grace After Meals. Following is the "zimun," or formal invitation.

The leader begins:
Gentlemen, let us bless.

The group responds:
Blessed is the Name of HASHEM from this moment and forever![1]

The leader continues:
Blessed is the Name of HASHEM from this moment and forever![1]

If ten men join in the zimun, the words (in parentheses) are included.
With the permission of the distinguished people present, let us bless [our God] for we have eaten from what is His.

The group responds:
Blessed is He [our God] of Whose we have eaten and through Whose goodness we live.

The leader continues:
Blessed is He [our God] of Whose we have eaten and through Whose goodness we live.

The following line is recited if ten men join in the zimun.
Blessed is He and Blessed is His Name.

---

1. *Tehillim* 113:2.

---

in the synagogue, why does he agree that there is a distinction between fewer and more than three participants, a distinction that does not exist in the synagogue?

The answer to this question, R' Zalman wrote, may be found in another Talmudic discussion. The Mishnah (*Megillah* 23b) teaches: "We do not include God's Name in the invitation [for *Bircas Hamazon*] when there are fewer than ten [men] present." The Gemara (ibid.) explains the reason for the Mishnah's rule. The exact quote is:

> "We do not include God's Name in the invitation [for Grace After Meals] when there are fewer than ten [men] present." — Because he has to say, "Let us bless our God," it is not proper to do so with fewer than ten participants.

This Talmudic selection explains why there is a difference between the invitation recited when there are three people and when there are ten people — it is improper to mention God's Name unless there are a large number of people present. But this principle itself poses several other difficulties: (1) How can the assertion be made that it is not proper to mention God's Name without a *minyan*? God's Name appears innumerable times in the prayers and blessings that we say throughout the course of the day, and no one ever entertained the thought that these may only be said with a *minyan*! (2) The verse from which the Sages derived the concept of reciting an invitation to Grace when there are three people present is, "Praise (גַּדְּלוּ — in the plural) God with me, and we will exalt His Name together" (*Tehillim* 34:4).

בָּרוּךְ אַתָּה יהוה אֱלֹהֵינוּ מֶלֶךְ הָעוֹלָם, הַזָּן אֶת הָעוֹלָם כֻּלּוֹ, בְּטוּבוֹ, בְּחֵן בְּחֶסֶד וּבְרַחֲמִים,

The person speaking is one, and the people being addressed are two (because the plural is used) — making a total of three (*Berachos* 45a). Now here, in the very verse which is used for the source of the invitation for Grace in the presence of three people, the Name of God is used (גַּדְּלוּ לַה׳ — *Praise God*). How, then, can the Gemara assert that it is improper to mention God's Name when there are only three people? (3) To these questions we may add another, stylistic difficulty in the Gemara's discussion: After quoting the language of the Mishnah, "We do not include God's Name... when there are fewer than ten present," the Gemara provides the explanation, "Because he has to say, 'Let us bless our God,' it is improper...." Why does the Gemara alter the language used by the Mishnah in its formulation of the explanation for that Mishnah? It should have said, "It is improper to include God's Name... when there are fewer than ten present."

To answer these questions R' Zalman began by citing another passage from the Talmud (*Berachos* 6a, paralleled closely in *Avos* 3:6): "How do we know that when ten people pray together, the *Shechinah* (God's presence) is with them? ... How do we know that when three people gather together to pass judgment the *Shechinah* is with them? ... How do we know that when two people sit together and engage in Torah study the *Shechinah* is with them? ... How do we know that even if only one person sits and engages in Torah study the *Shechinah* is with him? ..." The Talmud then asks the obvious question: If the *Shechinah* comes even when only three people are gathered together, why is it necessary to state that it comes when there are ten? If there are ten people present the *Shechinah* has already come on account of the first three! The answer given is that when there are ten people the *Shechinah* arrives in advance, in anticipation of the arrival of the group, while when there are only three people present it comes only after the group has gathered. (A scriptural basis is provided for this assertion.) We may summarize as follows: Once a person — even a single individual — begins to pray or study the Torah the *Shechinah* is certainly present to hear the praises being offered to God. But for the *Shechinah* to be present even before the praises begin to be uttered there must be a minyan. The invitation to Grace is recited, by definition, before the beginning of the Grace itself. It is for this reason that the Talmud tells us that it is improper to issue an invitation to Grace — before the Grace — using God's Name when there is no *minyan*.

Now we are in the position to answer all the questions posed above. (1) How can the Gemara assert that it is improper to mention God's Name without a *minyan*, being that an individual mentions God's Name so many times in his daily prayers and blessings? The answer is that of course the *Shechinah* is present *while* we are praying to Him; the Gemara was speaking only of the situation *before* the actual prayer begins. (2) The source verse from which the invitation to Grace (for three people) is derived itself contains the Name of God. This is true, but despite

> Blessed are You, HASHEM, our God, King of the universe, Who nourishes the entire world, in His goodness — with grace, with kindness, and with mercy.

the invitation to others to praise God, He Himself is not present until the praising actually begins. (3) Why does the Gemara veer from the language of the Mishnah (from *We do not include God's Name...* to *He has to say, "Let us bless our God"*) when formulating its explanation for the Mishnah's words? The answer is now clear: The point of the Gemara is that since we are dealing with an invitation in *anticipation* of the actual Grace, this is why it is improper to mention God's Name. Therefore it stresses that the problem with mentioning God's Name (with fewer than ten participants) arises because the leader says, "Let us bless our God" — an expression of preparing oneself to bless God, in advance of the blessing itself.

הַזָּן אֶת הָעוֹלָם כֻּלוֹ
Who nourishes the entire world,

An Economic History of the Jews

The Talmud (*Berachos* 48b) teaches that the *Birkas Hamazon*, which consists of four blessings, was authored by several different people, over a long period of time. The first blessing, thanking God for supplying all living things with sustenance, was authored by Moshe, when the manna began to fall. The second blessing, which thanks God for having given us the Land of Israel, was composed by Yehoshua, when he led the Jewish people into the Promised Land. The third blessing, about Jerusalem and the Davidic dynasty, was written by David and Solomon, the founders of Jerusalem. The fourth blessing was instituted upon the occasion of the fall of Betar, after the destruction of the Second Temple, when the Roman government permitted, after a longstanding refusal, that the dead of that city might be given a decent burial.

R' Zalman Sorotzkin expounded on this Talmudic passage. There are two basic ways by which the populace of a given country earn their livelihoods, he writes — either by taking advantage of the country's natural resources (such as through mining various marketable commodities from the ground, or through agriculture), or by some other system of economy which is instituted and supervised by a sufficiently organized and centralized government. For without a strong government, roads are unsafe, border areas are vulnerable to attack, monetary laws are unenforced, and it is impossible to have any sort of vibrant economy under these circumstances. Furthermore, the government directly provides an income to a substantial portion of the population, who are employed to administer the bureaucracy, collect taxes, etc. The government might even subjugate other countries and bring further economic benefits to the populace.

When the Jews entered Eretz Yisrael under Yehoshua, the people were engaged almost exclusively in agriculture. This is why Yehoshua authored the blessing thanking God for supplying food — through the Land, representing the first type of livelihood discussed above. "In those days there was no king in Israel; each man did what was proper in his own eyes" (*Shoftim* 17:6, 21:25).

At a later time, a strongly centralized government finally took hold in Israel, under David and Solomon, affording the Jewish people vast new opportunities to earn money and support themselves. In those days David and Solomon conquered many new territories, many of which became vassal states to Israel, paying taxes and tributes to Jerusalem. Especially in the days of Solomon, prosperity grew to the point where "silver was not considered of any worth at all in the days of Solomon" (*I Melachim* 10:21), for "the king made silver in Jerusalem like ordinary stones" (ibid., 10:27). At that time these two kings composed a blessing praising God for "the kingdom of the House of David," for Jerusalem, and so forth.

(People often wonder why a prayer for sustenance and livelihood is inserted in the middle of this blessing of the Grace After Meals — אֱלֹהֵינוּ אָבִינוּ, רְעֵנוּ זוּנֵנוּ פַּרְנְסֵנוּ וכו׳ וְנָא אַל תַּצְרִיכֵנוּ וכו׳ לֹא לִידֵי מַתְּנַת בָּשָׂר, וָדָם וְלֹא לִידֵי הַלְוָאָתָם, *Our God. . . tend us, nourish us, sustain us. . . and please, make us not needful of the gifts of human hands nor of their loans. . . .* What, they ask, is the relevance of this petition to its surrounding context in this blessing? It seems to be totally out of place! According to the way we have presented the underlying theme of these blessings, the answer to this question becomes clear. It is true that the topic of this blessing is the kingdom of the house of David and the rebuilding of Jerusalem, but the basic theme that lies beneath this main topic and makes it relevant to the Grace After Meals in the first place is that the Kingdom of David and Jerusalem are symbols of prosperity and sustenance. Furthermore, the inclusion of this prayer at this point alludes to the fact that ever since the destruction of the Temple and Jerusalem, and our forced exile among hostile nations, our ability to earn a livelihood has become severely impaired.)

Besides these two sources of livelihood, which are common to all peoples, R' Zalman continued to explain, there are another two sources that are unique to Israel. The first is the manna, bread from heaven, neither harvested from the ground nor bought with earned money. It was this source of sustenance that prompted Moses to author the first blessing of the Grace, which thanks God for providing us with food, without any mention of the ground from which it grows.

The second unique source of income to Israel is the seemingly supernatural manner by which the Jewish people manages to survive — and even prosper — momentarily, despite constant, unrelenting discrimination and persecutions. This type of supernatural sustenance began to operate after the Jewish commonwealth came to an end and the people were exiled from their land — as epitomized by the fall of Betar. At that point the Sages of the day instituted the fourth blessing of the Grace, dealing with the interminable beneficence of God, describing how He "did good, does good, and will do good for us. . . with grace and with kindness and with mercy. . . consolation, sustenance, and support."

R' Zalman suggested that these four types of sustenance available to the Jewish people at various times in their history are alluded to in Yitzchak's blessing to his son Yaakov (*Bereishis* 27:28-29): "(1) May God give you of the dew of the heavens (a reference to the manna, according to the Midrash), (2) and of the fat of the land

and an abundance of grain and wine. (3) Nations shall serve you and nationalities shall bow down to you. . . (4) Those who curse you shall be cursed, and those who bless you shall be blessed" (an allusion to the days of the exile, when the welfare of the Jews is dependent on the kindness or cruelty of their host nations.)

הַזָּן אֶת הָעוֹלָם כֻּלּוֹ, בְּטוּבוֹ
Who nourishes the entire world, in His goodness —

Two Spouts in the Wine Barrel

The **Chafetz Chaim** often tried to impress on people the importance of setting aside time for Torah study, even at the expense of cutting down on one's earnings. One time two brothers came to the Chafetz Chaim to seek his advice and blessing about a business venture. They were in the lumber business, and they had earned a small fortune on a forest they had leased. A second forest was now being offered to them at an attractive price, and they were planning on leasing this one as well.

"How can I give you advice on such a deal?" asked the Chafetz Chaim. "I don't know a thing about the lumber business! But let me tell you a story, and you can then act according to how you see fit.

"A man once bought a large barrel of wine at the market. He loaded it onto his wagon and took it home. It was too large for him to move by himself, so he asked his neighbor to give him a hand in unloading it and transporting it to the cellar.

"When the job was done, the owner of the barrel opened up the tap and poured his neighbor a cup of wine, in appreciation for his help. The exhausted neighbor eagerly drank the wine to the last drop, and commented, 'This wine is unbelievable! I have never experienced such quality in a wine! What a shame that the barrel doesn't have two spouts instead of one!'

"The owner of the barrel laughed at the neighbor's preposterous idea. 'What good would two spouts do?' he scoffed. 'Would I then be able to take out more wine from the barrel? If you want to give me ideas, why don't you try to think of a way that I could increase the amount of wine in the barrel!'

"The lesson of this story," the Chafetz Chaim told the brothers, "is that man's livelihood is fixed in advance. It may appear to him that he can alter his predetermined allotment according to his toil and efforts, but this is only an illusion. What good will it do you to 'put an extra spout on the barrel'? Will you then be able to draw more 'wine' from it? What you should do instead is try to figure out how to add onto your portion! If you devote more time to studying Torah, this will provide a blessing to all your pursuits and truly enlarge your portion in life!"

In the end the brothers took the Chafetz Chaim's advice and refrained from leasing the second forest. A wealthy Polish merchant took the offer in their stead and hired a large team of workers to cut down thousands of trees. But before the trees could be hauled down to the river for transport to market, a huge downpour turned the whole area into marshland, and the lumber could not be budged from its place until it had all become rotten and ruined. The Polish lumber dealer lost all his money, while the two brothers were saved this tremendous loss by heeding the Chafetz Chaim's counsel!

הוּא נָתַן לֶחֶם לְכָל בָּשָׂר, כִּי לְעוֹלָם חַסְדּוֹ.¹ וּבְטוּבוֹ הַגָּדוֹל, תָּמִיד לֹא חָסַר לָנוּ, וְאַל יֶחְסַר לָנוּ מָזוֹן לְעוֹלָם וָעֶד. בַּעֲבוּר שְׁמוֹ הַגָּדוֹל, כִּי הוּא אֵל זָן וּמְפַרְנֵס לַכֹּל, וּמֵטִיב לַכֹּל, וּמֵכִין מָזוֹן לְכָל בְּרִיּוֹתָיו אֲשֶׁר בָּרָא. בָּרוּךְ אַתָּה יהוה, הַזָּן אֶת הַכֹּל.

נוֹדֶה לְךָ יהוה אֱלֹהֵינוּ, עַל שֶׁהִנְחַלְתָּ לַאֲבוֹתֵינוּ אֶרֶץ חֶמְדָּה טוֹבָה וּרְחָבָה. וְעַל שֶׁהוֹצֵאתָנוּ יהוה אֱלֹהֵינוּ מֵאֶרֶץ מִצְרַיִם, וּפְדִיתָנוּ מִבֵּית עֲבָדִים,

---

נוֹדֶה לְךָ . . . עַל תּוֹרָתְךָ שֶׁלִּמַּדְתָּנוּ
We thank You . . . for Your Torah which You taught us

How Absurd! Every time we recite *Birkas Hamazon* — as well as during the course of the morning and evening prayers — we thank God for having given us His precious gift of the Torah. Often people do not reflect upon the meaning of the words they are reciting, the **Chafetz Chaim** cautioned, and he illustrated his point with the following parable:

Once there was a destitute homeless man, who lived in the capital city. One day, as he was rummaging through a garbage heap for some scraps of edible food or some salvageable clothing, he heard the sound of an approaching chariot. He lifted up his eyes and saw a splendid, magnificent carriage coming down the street. The king himself was about to pass by! The poor man jumped up from the garbage heap and ran towards the chariot, throwing himself in the path of the horses. The driver managed to stop the horses in enough time to avoid a tragedy, and the carriage jolted to a sudden stop. The door of the carriage opened, and the king peered out to see what had happened.

"Have you lost your mind?" he asked when he saw the homeless man sprawled out in the middle of the street. "Are you trying to kill yourself?!"

"And why not?" responded the poor man, shivering from the cold. "I have no home, no proper clothing to wear, and no food to eat. Death would be preferable to my present state!"

The king was moved by the man's plight, and, carried away by his compassion, he made the poor man an offer. "I am traveling to the palace now. Come later today and present yourself to the guard. I will instruct my staff to take care of you! You will be brought inside, given a bath and a haircut, and fitted with decent, warm clothing. You will be assigned quarters in one of the guest rooms of the palace, and will be given a job as one of the royal chamberlains. You will be able to eat your fill at the palace along with the other employees, and will receive a handsome wage as well."

He gives nourishment to all flesh, for His kindness is eternal.[1] And through His great goodness, we have never lacked, and may we never lack, nourishment, for all eternity. For the sake of His Great Name, because He is God Who nourishes and sustains all, and benefits all, and He prepares food for all of His creatures which He has created. Blessed are You, HASHEM, Who nourishes all.

We thank You, HASHEM, our God, because You have given to our forefathers as a heritage a desirable, good, and spacious land; because You removed us, HASHEM, our God, from the land of Egypt and You redeemed us from the house of bondage;

---

1. *Tehillim* 136:25.

The poor man was beside himself with joy. He could not believe his sudden reversal in fortune. He bowed down in obeisance to the king and thanked him profusely for his kindness.

The next day, as the king was leaving the palace, he asked the guard, "Did that beggar show up yesterday?"

"No, your highness!" he answered. "No one came to the palace yesterday."

The king shrugged, and he climbed into his carriage. As he was traveling down the street he saw a familiar figure jump out from the garbage heap and run towards the carriage, waving his hand in greeting. "Your lordship, thank you so much for your most gracious gift!" he exclaimed gleefully.

On the way back to the palace toward evening the king saw the same strange sight once again. The homeless man, still dressed in rags, ran alongside the carriage shouting, "Thank you for your generosity! Thank you for your kind treatment of me!"

The absurd routine continued every day thereafter, morning and evening; the poor man would run to greet the king's carriage and shout out his feelings of gratitude for the kindness he had extended him.

Can there be any doubt about the psychological condition of that poor beggar? No normal person would have reacted in such a manner!

Yet, are we ourselves not in a similar situation to that beggar? Every day, numerous times a day, we thank God for His kindness in having given us the Torah — but when opportunities present themselves for us to take advantage of that kindness, we do not bother to avail ourselves of them. We simply exclaim over and over again how appreciative we are of God's graciousness towards us, without showing by our actions that these feelings are genuine.

וְעַל בְּרִיתְךָ שֶׁחָתַמְתָּ בִּבְשָׂרֵנוּ, וְעַל תּוֹרָתְךָ שֶׁלִּמַּדְתָּנוּ, וְעַל חֻקֶּיךָ שֶׁהוֹדַעְתָּנוּ, וְעַל חַיִּים חֵן וָחֶסֶד שֶׁחוֹנַנְתָּנוּ, וְעַל אֲכִילַת מָזוֹן שָׁאַתָּה זָן וּמְפַרְנֵס אוֹתָנוּ תָּמִיד, בְּכָל יוֹם וּבְכָל עֵת וּבְכָל שָׁעָה.

וְעַל הַכֹּל יהוה אֱלֹהֵינוּ אֲנַחְנוּ מוֹדִים לָךְ, וּמְבָרְכִים אוֹתָךְ, יִתְבָּרַךְ שִׁמְךָ בְּפִי כָּל חַי תָּמִיד לְעוֹלָם וָעֶד. כַּכָּתוּב, וְאָכַלְתָּ וְשָׂבָעְתָּ, וּבֵרַכְתָּ אֶת יהוה אֱלֹהֶיךָ, עַל הָאָרֶץ הַטּוֹבָה אֲשֶׁר נָתַן לָךְ.[1] בָּרוּךְ אַתָּה יהוה, עַל הָאָרֶץ וְעַל הַמָּזוֹן.

רַחֵם יהוה אֱלֹהֵינוּ עַל יִשְׂרָאֵל עַמֶּךָ, וְעַל יְרוּשָׁלַיִם עִירֶךָ, וְעַל צִיּוֹן מִשְׁכַּן כְּבוֹדֶךָ, וְעַל מַלְכוּת בֵּית דָּוִד מְשִׁיחֶךָ, וְעַל הַבַּיִת הַגָּדוֹל וְהַקָּדוֹשׁ שֶׁנִּקְרָא שִׁמְךָ עָלָיו. אֱלֹהֵינוּ אָבִינוּ רְעֵנוּ זוּנֵנוּ פַּרְנְסֵנוּ וְכַלְכְּלֵנוּ וְהַרְוִיחֵנוּ, וְהַרְוַח לָנוּ יהוה אֱלֹהֵינוּ מְהֵרָה מִכָּל צָרוֹתֵינוּ. וְנָא אַל תַּצְרִיכֵנוּ יהוה אֱלֹהֵינוּ, לֹא לִידֵי

וְאָכַלְתָּ וְשָׂבָעְתָּ וּבֵרַכְתָּ אֶת ה'
And you shall eat and you shall be satisfied, and you shall bless Hashem.

The Moment of Greatest Pleasure — The requirement to bless God after eating (bread) is a Torah commandment, as this verse states clearly. The blessings we say before eating, however, are not of Biblical origin, but were instituted by the Rabbis. The Talmud (*Berachos* 21a.) teaches that there is one other blessing, besides the Grace After Meals, that is a biblical requirement, and that is the blessing over Torah learning. (The commentators disagree as to whether this opinion is accepted by the halachah). In this instance, however, the opposite is the case — the blessing *beforehand* is a Torah requirement, while the blessing recited *after* reading from the Torah is only rabbinically required. What is the reason behind this contrast between the two cases?

R' Zalman Sorotzkin explained this phenomenon as follows. The halachah requires that when there are two pieces of food before a person he should choose the larger or finer or more important of the two pieces to recite the blessing over, for it is this piece that provides him with the greatest pleasure, and the feeling thus generated contributes to his ability to thank God in a more heartfelt manner. Now,

for Your covenant which You sealed in our flesh; for Your Torah which You taught us and for Your statutes which You made known to us; for life, grace, and kindness which You granted us; and for the provision of food with which You nourish and sustain us constantly, in every day, in every season, and in every hour.

For everything, HASHEM, our God, we thank You and bless You. May Your Name be blessed by the mouth of all the living, continuously for all eternity. As it is written: "And you shall eat and you shall be satisfied, and you shall bless HASHEM, your God, for the good land which He gave you."[1] Blessed are You, HASHEM, for the land and for the nourishment.

Have mercy HASHEM, our God, on Israel Your people; on Yerushalayim, Your city, on Tziyon, the resting place of Your Glory; on the monarchy of the house of David, Your anointed; and on the great and holy House upon which Your Name is called. Our God, our Father — tend us, nourish us, sustain us, support us, relieve us; HASHEM, our God, grant us speedy relief from all our troubles. Please, make us not needful — HASHEM, our God — of the

---

1. *Devarim* 8:10.

---

let us consider when it is more appropriate for a person to praise God for providing him with food — before or after partaking of that food? The answer is that it is better done afterwards, for that is when the person actually feels the benefit he has acquired from the food. Furthermore, from a spiritual point of view, it is the end of one's meal that is more beneficial to the soul than the beginning, for, as the Sages say, "Rather than pray that the words of the Torah should enter his body, a person (who wishes to acquire Torah knowledge) should pray that delicacies should *not* enter his body." A person must eat in order to sustain his body, but the eating *per se* is not considered a virtuous act; the goal is rather the arriving at a state of satiation and nourishment. When it comes to the learning of Torah, however, it is at the beginning of this activity that the person experiences the greatest pleasure, when he turns his mind away from his mundane activities and pressures and focuses on his spiritual "nourishment." Upon finishing his learning, on the other hand, he is disheartened that he must stop this most rewarding activity and return to the bothersome pressures of the "real" world. Therefore it is more appropriate to recite the blessing before engaging in Torah study rather than afterwards.

מַתְּנַת בָּשָׂר וָדָם, וְלֹא לִידֵי הַלְוָאָתָם, כִּי אִם לְיָדְךָ הַמְּלֵאָה הַפְּתוּחָה הַקְּדוֹשָׁה וְהָרְחָבָה, שֶׁלֹּא נֵבוֹשׁ וְלֹא נִכָּלֵם לְעוֹלָם וָעֶד.

On Shabbos add the following paragraph.

רְצֵה וְהַחֲלִיצֵנוּ יהוה אֱלֹהֵינוּ בְּמִצְוֹתֶיךָ, וּבְמִצְוַת יוֹם הַשְּׁבִיעִי הַשַּׁבָּת הַגָּדוֹל וְהַקָּדוֹשׁ הַזֶּה, כִּי יוֹם זֶה גָּדוֹל וְקָדוֹשׁ הוּא לְפָנֶיךָ, לִשְׁבָּת בּוֹ וְלָנוּחַ בּוֹ בְּאַהֲבָה כְּמִצְוַת רְצוֹנֶךָ,

---

שֶׁלֹּא נֵבוֹשׁ וְלֹא נִכָּלֵם לְעוֹלָם וָעֶד
that we not feel inner shame nor be humiliated for all eternity.

Don't Turn Life into Glass Chips

One time after reciting the Grace After Meals the **Chafetz Chaim** told those who were assembled around his table: "Let me tell you what went through my mind when I said the words, 'That we not feel inner shame nor be humiliated for all eternity.'

"I was thinking about a certain poverty-stricken man who heard about the diamond mines in South Africa. He convinced his wife to manage with the difficulties of supporting the family by herself for a year or two while he would go to seek his fortune in Africa. He borrowed money for the trip and set off on the long voyage that he hoped would bring him financial success at last. His dream of wealth and comfort enabled him to endure the unpleasantries of traveling the seas and trekking through the dangerous uncharted territories of deepest Africa.

"Finally the man arrived at his destination, and he immediately set out to work. There are no words to describe the hardships he endured, digging day and night at the mines, following every lead as to where new finds were sighted, etc. But all the work seemed worthwhile to him as he saw his pouch begin to bulge more and more with precious stones as each week went by.

"While working the mines he befriended another Jew from Europe who had also come to find his fortune. The two would share their dreams and aspirations with each other, and take comfort in each other's companionship. They would also compare notes in their work and exchange diamonds with one another.

"Eventually the time came when the man decided that he had put together enough riches to head home. His friend also decided to go back, and they traveled together all the way back to Europe, where, at the port city, they parted, each traveling off to his hometown.

"When the man came home he was shocked to see the dire state of poverty that his family was living in. The squalor, the broken-down condition of the house, the rags they wore for clothing — he had already forgotten how bad things were back home. 'Well, our troubles are over!' he announced triumphantly. 'I met with tremendous success in Africa, and now we will reap the fruits of my years of hard labor!'

"Off they went to the nearby city, where there was a jeweler to whom they

gifts of human hands nor of their loans, but only of Your Hand that is full, open, holy, and generous, that we not feel inner shame nor be humiliated for all eternity.

> On Shabbos add the following paragraph.
>
> May it please You, HASHEM, our God — give us rest through Your commandments and through the commandment of the seventh day, this great and holy Shabbos. For this day is great and holy before You to rest on it and be content on it in love, as ordained by Your will.

---

intended to sell their precious stones. The man proudly opened up his satchel and spilled out all the gems onto the jeweler's table for inspection. The jeweler took out his pincers and magnifying glass and began examining the stones one by one. After a while he announced his impression of the collection — they were all fakes, mere chips of glass!

"The man suddenly realized what must have happened. His 'friend' had apparently only been pretending to be a faithful companion; what he really sought from his 'friendship' was the opportunity to take advantage of his coworker's trust and swindle him out of every precious stone he had found — and he was remarkably successful at that!

"The man's heart sank. All the months of leaving the family in abject poverty and hardship were in vain; all the exhausting, backbreaking labor at the mines was for naught. And all those debts he had incurred were now waiting to be repaid! All his dreams and hopes had vanished in an instant. And, to add to all that anguish — what an idiotic fool he felt like in front of the jeweler and his wife!

"This story is a parable for man's life on earth. The soul travels a great distance from its sublime place of origin to its destination in this world of hardship and suffering. All it can hope to get out of its 'trip' is a handful of Torah and good deeds that it can accomplish while in this 'distant land.' But his 'companion,' the *yetzer hara* (man's inclination to sin), portrays himself as a friend, all the while desiring nothing from the 'partnership' but to dupe the soul out of whatever profit it manages to garner together. It seeks to minimize the importance of Torah study, mitzvos, and prayer, and to accomplish its mission without being detected by the person within whom it dwells. The individual goes through life believing that he has done a decent job of fulfilling his responsibilities toward God and his fellow man. But when the time comes for him to display his 'goods' before the Heavenly tribunal for assessment, he is likely to be shocked with the realization that what he had considered to be great sources of merit are in reality worthless deeds.

This is the situation that we pray to God that we may avoid: 'That we not feel inner shame nor be humiliated for all eternity' — that we might lead our lives in such a way that we may be proud of our accomplishments in the World to Come, the world of *eternity*."

וּבִרְצוֹנְךָ הָנִיחַ לָנוּ יהוה אֱלֹהֵינוּ, שֶׁלֹּא תְהֵא צָרָה וְיָגוֹן וַאֲנָחָה בְּיוֹם מְנוּחָתֵנוּ, וְהַרְאֵנוּ יהוה אֱלֹהֵינוּ בְּנֶחָמַת צִיּוֹן עִירֶךָ, וּבְבִנְיַן יְרוּשָׁלַיִם עִיר קָדְשֶׁךָ, כִּי אַתָּה הוּא בַּעַל הַיְשׁוּעוֹת וּבַעַל הַנֶּחָמוֹת.

אֱלֹהֵינוּ וֵאלֹהֵי אֲבוֹתֵינוּ, יַעֲלֶה, וְיָבֹא, וְיַגִּיעַ, וְיֵרָאֶה, וְיֵרָצֶה, וְיִשָּׁמַע, וְיִפָּקֵד, וְיִזָּכֵר זִכְרוֹנֵנוּ וּפִקְדוֹנֵנוּ, וְזִכְרוֹן אֲבוֹתֵינוּ, וְזִכְרוֹן מָשִׁיחַ בֶּן דָּוִד עַבְדֶּךָ, וְזִכְרוֹן יְרוּשָׁלַיִם עִיר קָדְשֶׁךָ, וְזִכְרוֹן

וְהַרְאֵנוּ... בְּנֶחָמַת צִיּוֹן עִירֶךָ, וּבְבִנְיַן יְרוּשָׁלַיִם עִיר קָדְשֶׁךָ
And show us ... the consolation of Tziyon, Your city, and the rebuilding of Yerushalayim, city of Your holiness.

Keeping the Sabbath Day   At first glance this petition for the rebuilding of Yerushayim seems to be totally irrelevant to the theme of Sabbath rest, which is the subject of this entire paragraph. The **Chafetz Chaim,** however, explained that in fact one of the greatest factors that will supply us with the merit to experience the future salvation of God is the observance of the Shabbos. This idea, he noted, is borne out in the prophecy of *Yirmiyahu* (17:24-25): "If you truly listen to Me. . . not to bring any burden into the gates of this city on the Sabbath day, and to sanctify the Sabbath day, not to do any manner of work on it, then there will always come through the gates of this city kings and princes who sit upon the throne of David. . . and this city will be inhabited forever."

כִּי אַתָּה הוּא בַּעַל הַיְשׁוּעוֹת וּבַעַל הַנֶּחָמוֹת
For You are the Master of salvations and Master of consolations.

A Second Look at Jewish History   This attribute that we ascribe to God seems to be somewhat strange. What is our intention when we praise God for being the "Master of consolations"? **R' Gedaliah Schorr,** citing the *Sefas Emes,* explained that in general when a person consoles his friend after he has experienced a loss, his main objective is to cause the friend to forget or become distracted from his sorrow. But when God grants us salvation from our misfortunes, He does much more than this; He shows us that what we had considered to be a tragedy was in fact a step toward an ultimate goal of redemption, and was thus beneficial to the person involved rather than harmful as previously perceived. In this sense He is the "Master of consolations," for He alone is capable of providing the ultimate comfort — the realization that the source of our suffering was in fact an illusion. Thus the prophet tells us that "I will return

> May it be Your will, HASHEM, our God, that there be no distress, grief, or lament on this day of our contentment. And show us, HASHEM, our God, the consolation of Tziyon, Your city, and the rebuilding of Yerushalayim, city of Your holiness, for You are the Master of salvations and Master of consolations.

Our God and God of our forefathers, may there rise, come, reach, be noted, be favored, be heard, be considered, and be remembered — the remembrance and consideration of ourselves; the remembrance of our forefathers; the remembrance of Mashiach, son of David, Your servant; the remembrance of Yerushalayim, the City of Your Holiness; the remembrance of

---

them [to their land], for I will have mercy upon them, and it will seem as if I had never rejected them" (*Zechariah* 10:6). When the Messianic deliverance occurs, the Jewish people will realize that all the suffering they had experienced all along was merely a part of a long, complicated process of redemption. They will come to understand that in fact God had never rejected them in the first place.

R' Schorr also shed light upon a difficult comment of the Midrash by applying this concept. The Midrash states the following:

> God took the casual statement of the patriarchs and turned it into the key for the redemption of their descendants. He said [to Yaakov]: "You said, 'And Hashem *shall be* (וְהָיָה) for me for a God' (*Bereishis* 28:21). By your life [I swear] that all the beneficence and blessings and comforts that I will bestow upon your descendants will be given only through this expression of וְהָיָה (*it shall be*): 'And it shall be (וְהָיָה) on that day that running water shall go forth from Jerusalem' (*Zechariah* 14:8); 'And it shall be (וְהָיָה) on that day that a great shofar will be sounded' (*Yeshayahu* 27:13)."

What is so significant about the word וְהָיָה that God saw fit to make it the cornerstone of the future redemption? Surely there is more here than a play on words!

The word וְהָיָה actually consists of the word הָיָה (*it was*), with the addition of the prefix וְ, known as the וי"ו ההיפוך, the "reversing *vav*," which transforms words from past tense to future (and vice versa). When the Messianic age dawns we will be able to look back on our past history and realize that all the numerous tragedies that had befallen us were in reality acts of beneficence, for they all played a role in the unfolding of the ultimate redemption. The events of the past (הָיָה), when perceived with the hindsight of the future, will be transformed into steps leading into a clear ultimate goal (וְהָיָה). This reversal of our perception of history is indeed the essence of the future redemption.

כָּל עַמְּךָ בֵּית יִשְׂרָאֵל לְפָנֶיךָ, לִפְלֵיטָה לְטוֹבָה לְחֵן וּלְחֶסֶד וּלְרַחֲמִים, לְחַיִּים וּלְשָׁלוֹם בְּיוֹם חַג הַמַּצּוֹת הַזֶּה. זָכְרֵנוּ יהוה אֱלֹהֵינוּ בּוֹ לְטוֹבָה, וּפָקְדֵנוּ בוֹ לִבְרָכָה, וְהוֹשִׁיעֵנוּ בוֹ לְחַיִּים. וּבִדְבַר יְשׁוּעָה וְרַחֲמִים, חוּס וְחָנֵּנוּ וְרַחֵם עָלֵינוּ וְהוֹשִׁיעֵנוּ, כִּי אֵלֶיךָ עֵינֵינוּ, כִּי אֵל חַנּוּן וְרַחוּם אָתָּה.[1]

וּבְנֵה יְרוּשָׁלַיִם עִיר הַקֹּדֶשׁ בִּמְהֵרָה בְיָמֵינוּ. בָּרוּךְ אַתָּה יהוה, בּוֹנֶה (בְרַחֲמָיו) יְרוּשָׁלָיִם. אָמֵן.

בָּרוּךְ אַתָּה יהוה אֱלֹהֵינוּ מֶלֶךְ הָעוֹלָם, הָאֵל אָבִינוּ מַלְכֵּנוּ אַדִּירֵנוּ בּוֹרְאֵנוּ גֹּאֲלֵנוּ יוֹצְרֵנוּ קְדוֹשֵׁנוּ קְדוֹשׁ יַעֲקֹב, רוֹעֵנוּ רוֹעֵה יִשְׂרָאֵל, הַמֶּלֶךְ הַטּוֹב וְהַמֵּטִיב לַכֹּל, שֶׁבְּכָל יוֹם וָיוֹם הוּא הֵטִיב, הוּא מֵטִיב, הוּא יֵיטִיב לָנוּ. הוּא גְמָלָנוּ הוּא גוֹמְלֵנוּ הוּא יִגְמְלֵנוּ לָעַד, לְחֵן וּלְחֶסֶד וּלְרַחֲמִים וּלְרֶוַח הַצָּלָה וְהַצְלָחָה, בְּרָכָה וִישׁוּעָה נֶחָמָה פַּרְנָסָה וְכַלְכָּלָה וְרַחֲמִים וְחַיִּים וְשָׁלוֹם וְכָל טוֹב, וּמִכָּל טוּב לְעוֹלָם אַל יְחַסְּרֵנוּ.

הָרַחֲמָן הוּא יִמְלֹךְ עָלֵינוּ לְעוֹלָם וָעֶד. הָרַחֲמָן הוּא יִתְבָּרַךְ בַּשָּׁמַיִם וּבָאָרֶץ. הָרַחֲמָן הוּא יִשְׁתַּבַּח לְדוֹר דּוֹרִים, וְיִתְפָּאַר בָּנוּ לָעַד וּלְנֵצַח נְצָחִים, וְיִתְהַדַּר בָּנוּ לָעַד וּלְעוֹלְמֵי עוֹלָמִים. הָרַחֲמָן הוּא יְפַרְנְסֵנוּ בְּכָבוֹד. הָרַחֲמָן הוּא יִשְׁבּוֹר עֻלֵּנוּ מֵעַל צַוָּארֵנוּ, וְהוּא יוֹלִיכֵנוּ קוֹמְמִיּוּת לְאַרְצֵנוּ. הָרַחֲמָן הוּא יִשְׁלַח לָנוּ בְּרָכָה מְרֻבָּה בַּבַּיִת הַזֶּה, וְעַל שֻׁלְחָן זֶה שֶׁאָכַלְנוּ עָלָיו.

הָרַחֲמָן הוּא יִשְׁלַח לָנוּ בְּרָכָה מְרֻבָּה בַּבַּיִת הַזֶּה
The compassionate One! May He send us abundant blessing to this house

Too Much Candy — What is meant by "abundant blessing"? The **Chafetz Chaim** explained that this expression denotes not only the negation of too little goodness, but also too *much* of a good thing. Rain, for instance, is an important phenomenon, one without which life would be impossible.

Your entire people the Family of Israel — before You for deliverance, for goodness, for grace, for kindness, and for compassion, for life, and for peace on this day of the Festival of Matzos. Remember us on it, Hashem, our God, for goodness; consider us on it for blessing; and help us on it for life. In the matter of salvation and compassion, pity, be gracious and compassionate with us and help us, for our eyes are turned to You, because You are God, the gracious, and compassionate.[1]

Rebuild Yerushalayim, the Holy City, soon in our days. Blessed are You, Hashem, Who rebuilds Yerushalyim (in His mercy). Amen.

Blessed are You, Hashem, our God, King of the universe, the Almighty, our Father, our King, our Sovereign, our Creator, our Redeemer, our Maker, our Holy One, Holy One of Yaakov, our Shepherd, the Shepherd of Israel, the King Who is good and Who does good for all. For every single day He did good, He does good, and He will do good to us. He was bountiful with us, He is bountiful with us, and He will forever be bountiful with us — with grace and with kindness and with mercy, with relief, salvation, success, blessing, help, consolation, sustenance, support, mercy, life, peace, and all good; and of all good things may He never deprive us.

The compassionate One! May He reign over us forever. The compassionate One! May He be blessed in heaven and on earth. The compassionate One! May He be praised throughout all generations, may He be glorified through us forever to the ultimate ends, and be honored through us forever and for all eternity. The compassionate One! May He sustain us in honor. The compassionate One! May He break the yoke of oppression from our necks and guide us erect to our Land. The compassionate One! May He send us abundant blessing to this house and upon this table at which we have eaten.

---
1. *Nechemiah* 9:31.

An overabundance of rain, however, is not beneficial but detrimental (see *Ta'anis* 19a). The same concept applies to all the good things in life.

הָרַחֲמָן הוּא יִשְׁלַח לָנוּ אֶת אֵלִיָּהוּ הַנָּבִיא זָכוּר לַטּוֹב, וִיבַשֶּׂר לָנוּ בְּשׂוֹרוֹת טוֹבוֹת יְשׁוּעוֹת וְנֶחָמוֹת. הָרַחֲמָן הוּא יְבָרֵךְ

Guests recite the following.
Children at their parents' table add words in parentheses.

אֶת (אָבִי מוֹרִי) בַּעַל הַבַּיִת הַזֶּה,
וְאֶת (אִמִּי מוֹרָתִי) בַּעֲלַת הַבַּיִת הַזֶּה,

The Chafetz Chaim illustrated this point by means of a parable. There was once a man who had a young son who would walk to school every day. The man asked a shopkeeper whose store was situated along the child's daily route to give the boy a candy when he would pass by each day, and he — the father — would pay the shopkeeper back. The store owner was of course happy to have a guaranteed steady customer, so he eagerly consented to the deal. Each day when he saw the boy coming down the street the storekeeper would run out with a generous helping of sweets and pour it into the delighted boy's open hands. Throughout most of the day the child was able to suck on the candies, chew the gum and taffy and munch on the chocolate bars. Of course, after several weeks the child's teeth began to decay severely, and his parents had to take him to a doctor for extensive — and expensive — dental care. One day, as the boy's father was reflecting upon the situation and brooding in his misery and aggravation over the lad's unfortunate condition, the storekeeper happened to stop in to present the bill for the sweets he had supplied over the weeks and months.

The father turned to the store owner and said, "Fool! It is true that I told you to give the boy some candy, but you acted totally irresponsibly by giving him far beyond the normal amount. You certainly knew that so much candy would cause him harm! And you expect to be paid for your indiscretion?!"

The storekeeper, on the other hand, argued that the father had not specified any particular amount, and that he had only done as he had been told.

"Who do you think would win the case in *Beis Din*?" asked the Chafetz Chaim of his students. "Of course, the father! The storeowner, as a rational human being, was responsible for interpreting the father's request in a normal, judicious manner. He should have realized that by providing the child with an unlimited supply of sweets he would be damaging the boy's health."

This idea may be applied to all of life's pleasures. People often think that they would be so happy if only they had unlimited funds and opportunities to indulge themselves. But this is not the case, for "there is wealth that is stored up for its owner, for his misfortune" (*Koheles* 5:12). What exactly is the point of prosperity beyond which it becomes detrimental? This of course depends on the individual. But it is impossible for any person to know the answer to this question in regard

> The compassionate One! May He send us Eliyahu Hanavi — he is remembered for good— to proclaim to us good tidings, salvations, and consolations.
>
> The compassionate One! May He bless
> *Guests recite the following.*
> *Children at their parents' table add words in parentheses.*
> (my father, my teacher) the master of this house, and (my mother, my teacher) lady of this house,

to his own particular case. He should therefore pray to God that he be granted whatever is fitting for his specific situation — no more and no less. This is what we mean when we pray for "abundant blessing."

הָרַחֲמָן הוּא יִשְׁלַח לָנוּ אֶת אֵלִיָּהוּ הַנָּבִיא
The compassionate One! May He send us Eliyahu Hanavi

Yaakov's Security Deposit

There are several times in *Tanach* where Eliyahu's name (usually written as *Eliyahu*) is spelled without a ו — אֵלִיָּה (*Eliyah*). Rashi on *Vayikra* 26:42 offers an explanation for this anomaly: "There are five places where Yaakov's name is spelled with an extra ו and five places where Eliyahu's name is spelled with a missing ו. Yaakov took a letter from Eliyahu's name as a security that he (Eliyahu) would eventually come and proclaim the Messianic redemption for his (Yaakov's) descendants." Of course this explanation is a metaphor, but what exactly does the removing of the letter ו from Eliyahu's name by Yaakov represent?

R' Shneur Kotler explained Rashi's comment as follows. We find in the Talmud that the deletion of the letter ו from someone's name indicates that that person was found to be incomplete or wanting in some respect. Efron, we are told (*Bava Metzia* 87a), had the ו removed from his name (*Bereishis* 23:16) because he had offered to give the field of Machpelah to Avraham for free, but in the end he took an exorbitant price.

Eliyahu was known to be a fierce zealot, who would always take upon himself the responsibility of chastising God's people for not serving Him adequately. In his own words: "I have acted extremely zealously for Hashem, God of Legions; for the Children of Israel have forsaken Your covenant, razed Your altars, and killed Your prophets by the sword . . ." (*I Melachim* 19:10). Yaakov's removal of the ו from Eliyahu's name symbolizes that Eliyahu's task as prophet and chastiser of Israel would be incomplete as long as they were still on an inferior spiritual plane. It would only be when Eliyahu would come in Messianic times and "turn back [to God] the hearts of fathers with their sons and the hearts of sons with their fathers" (*Malachi* 3:24) that his task would be complete, and he would be able to reclaim the ו that had been taken as "security" from him.

Those eating at their own table recite the following, adding the appropriate parenthesized phrases:

אוֹתִי (וְאֶת אִשְׁתִּי/בַּעֲלִי. וְאֶת זַרְעִי) וְאֶת כָּל אֲשֶׁר לִי.

All guests recite the following:

אוֹתָם וְאֶת בֵּיתָם וְאֶת זַרְעָם וְאֶת כָּל אֲשֶׁר לָהֶם.

All continue here:

אוֹתָנוּ וְאֶת כָּל אֲשֶׁר לָנוּ, כְּמוֹ שֶׁנִּתְבָּרְכוּ אֲבוֹתֵינוּ אַבְרָהָם יִצְחָק וְיַעֲקֹב בַּכֹּל מִכֹּל כֹּל, כֵּן יְבָרֵךְ אוֹתָנוּ כֻּלָּנוּ יַחַד בִּבְרָכָה שְׁלֵמָה, וְנֹאמַר, אָמֵן.

בַּמָּרוֹם יְלַמְּדוּ עֲלֵיהֶם וְעָלֵינוּ זְכוּת, שֶׁתְּהֵא לְמִשְׁמֶרֶת שָׁלוֹם. וְנִשָּׂא בְרָכָה מֵאֵת יהוה, וּצְדָקָה מֵאֱלֹהֵי יִשְׁעֵנוּ, וְנִמְצָא חֵן וְשֵׂכֶל טוֹב בְּעֵינֵי אֱלֹהִים וְאָדָם.[1]

On Shabbos add the following sentence:

הָרַחֲמָן הוּא יַנְחִילֵנוּ יוֹם שֶׁכֻּלּוֹ שַׁבָּת וּמְנוּחָה לְחַיֵּי הָעוֹלָמִים.

The words in parentheses are added on the two Seder nights in some communities.

הָרַחֲמָן הוּא יַנְחִילֵנוּ יוֹם שֶׁכֻּלּוֹ טוֹב. (יוֹם שֶׁכֻּלּוֹ אָרוּךְ. יוֹם שֶׁצַּדִּיקִים יוֹשְׁבִים וְעַטְרוֹתֵיהֶם בְּרָאשֵׁיהֶם וְנֶהֱנִים מִזִּיו הַשְּׁכִינָה וִיהִי חֶלְקֵנוּ עִמָּהֶם.)

כֻּלָּנוּ יַחַד בִּבְרָכָה שְׁלֵמָה
all of us together, with a perfect blessing.

Brotherly Love — The **Chafetz Chaim** explained that the ultimate, "perfect" blessing comes only when we are "all of us together." He illustrated his point with a parable:

Once there was a very wealthy man who had three sons. He set aside a considerable sum of money for each son and bade them to invest the capital wisely. Each of the sons went and bought merchandise with the funds they had at their disposal. It was not long before each son began to consider it a challenge to show that he could do better than his brothers. The spirit of competition grew among them, and it soon turned into jealous rivalry and enmity. Their father looked on with pain in his heart as his sons' brotherly love became brotherly strife.

Those eating at their own table recite the following,
adding the appropriate parenthesized phrases:

me (my wife/husband and family) and all that is mine,

All guests recite the following:

**them, their house, their family,
and all that is theirs,**

All continue here:

ours and all that is ours — just as our forefathers Avraham, Yitzchak, and Yaakov were blessed with everything, from everything, with everything. So may He bless all of us together, with a perfect blessing. And let us say: Amen!

On high, may merit be pleaded upon them and upon us, for a safeguard of peace. May we receive a blessing from HASHEM and just kindness from the God of our salvation, and find favor and good understanding in the eyes of God and man.[1]

On Shabbos add the following sentence:

The compassionate One! May He cause us to inherit the day which will be completely a Shabbos and rest day for eternal life.

The words in parentheses are added on the two Seder nights in some communities.

The compassionate One! May He cause us to inherit that day which is altogether good (that everlasting day, the day when the just will sit with crowns on their heads, enjoying the reflection of God's majesty — and may our portion be with them!).

---

1. *Mishlei* 3:4.

A wise man saw what was happening and he approached the brothers with a suggestion. "Why don't you pool your efforts instead of competing with each other?" he asked them. "If you put your capital and skills together into a joint endeavor, you will make much more money, your relationship with each other will once again reflect love and mutual respect, and your father will be spared the heartache of seeing his family break up. He will undoubtedly respond to the new developments positively and increase even further his generous allowance to you. Everyone will be happier and better off!"

So it is with us today. It is only through unity and mutual cooperation that we can take the fullest advantage of God's bountiful blessings which He constantly showers upon us.

הָרַחֲמָן הוּא יְזַכֵּנוּ לִימוֹת הַמָּשִׁיחַ וּלְחַיֵּי הָעוֹלָם הַבָּא.

הָרַחֲמָן הוּא יְזַכֵּנוּ לִימוֹת הַמָּשִׁיחַ וּלְחַיֵּי הָעוֹלָם הַבָּא
The compassionate One! May He make us worthy of the days of Mashiach and the life of the World to Come.

Getting Paid for Unfinished Work

This request seems to be somewhat inappropriate. If we are, by virtue of our good deeds, entitled to a share in the World to Come, we will certainly be granted our rightful portion without having to ask for it. And if we are not deserving of such reward, how can a request change this state of affairs? After all, as the **Chafetz Chaim** used to say, God uses His attribute of Divine Mercy to grant people reprieve only in This World; in the World to Come everything is determined precisely on the basis of merit, with the Attribute of Strict Justice in full command. How, then, can we expect a prayer for granting life in the World to Come to have any effect?

A similar question is often asked concerning the verse, "Mercy is Yours, my Lord, for You repay each person according to his deeds" (*Tehillim* 62:13). Why is it considered a sign of mercy that God grants each person what he has earned through his deeds? This should be called "fairness" or "justice," not "mercy"!

The Chafetz Chaim explained the idea behind these passages through a parable:

A king was in the process of having a grand, magnificent new palace built for himself. One day he heard that a dear friend of his had taken ill and was near death. He rushed to his bedside to see him and ask if there was anything he could do for him, for they were very close friends. The man responded that he did have one small request of the king.

"If it would please the king," he murmured with his last ounce of strength, "please see to it that my son is taken care of after my death. He is young, and I fear he will have great hardships in life without my guidance and assistance."

The king gladly acceded to this request. It was a small favor to do for such a dear friend! The sick man was quite relieved to hear the king's assurance, and a smile spread across his face as his soul departed from him.

The king summoned the young man to the palace, in order to meet him and plan for his future. It seems that the youth had an interest in landscaping and gardening, and was physically and mentally suited for this avocation as well. The king arranged that he should study as an apprentice under the most prestigious landscaper in the kingdom for two years — with all expenses paid by the royal treasury.

Just as the young man finished his training, the construction on the new palace was reaching its conclusion. A huge celebration was planned for its inauguration, with all the noblemen of the kingdom and several kings from neighboring kingdoms in attendance.

The king called over his friend's son and told him, "Son, there is to be a great celebration at the palace in a month's time. It is imperative that all the gardening and landscaping be taken care of by then. I would like you to be in charge of seeing to it that the palace grounds are suitably groomed as befits a royal residence! Tell the treasurer which tools and materials you need and how much manpower you

> **The compassionate One! May He make us worthy of the days of Mashiach and the life of the World to Come.**

require, and all necessary funds will be supplied to you to procure them. Moreover, you will be paid 3000 gold coins as your wages. What do you think, young man? Can you do it?"

The young man scanned the vast grounds that surrounded the palace on all sides. It was a daunting assignment, but it could be done, especially in view of the king's offer of unlimited manpower and assistance. Furthermore, this was an excellent opportunity for him to build his reputation throughout the land as a master landscaper — he would be known as the designer and executor of the king's gardens! And 3000 gold coins was nothing to sneeze at! With that money he could open up a very lucrative gardening and tree-nursery business of his own. He accepted the job.

That very day the youth went and ordered large amounts of the finest and most expensive gardening tools, at the king's expense. He hired hundreds of workers and ordered thousands of tree saplings, bushes, flowers, etc. He arrived at the palace grounds first thing in the morning and began to dig and hoe the ground. But after an hour or two he grew weary, and decided that he needed a rest. He lay down and began daydreaming about his new business that he would soon be operating. "Where will I open my business?" he mused. "How will I set it up, and what will it look like?" These thoughts made him rather agitated, and he jumped up, mounted his horse, and drove off to town to inspect different possible sites that might be suitable for his new enterprise. "The king's gardens can wait," he thought. "There are another 29 days to go!" Before he knew it, night had fallen.

The next day he again set out for the palace grounds and once again took up his spade and began working in earnest. But he soon tired once again, and stopped for a break. And once again he began to daydream about his promising future, until the minutes turned into hours and the day came to an end. Day after day the same pattern followed, until the month had gone by and been totally wasted.

The day for the festivities arrived, and the king went out to the new palace to inspect it and to see if all preparations had been carried out properly. As soon as he approached the palace grounds and he saw the acres and acres of neglected, half-dug earth, his heart fell. He was infuriated! What an embarrassment this was for him! But it was too late to do anything about it. The guests began arriving and the king tried to make up one excuse and then another to explain the sorry state of the palace grounds.

The day after the embarrassing affair, the king heard that the young gardener was requesting an audience with him. "The idiot has come to beg forgiveness!" he said to his courtiers. "I am inclined to punish him severely, but perhaps he has some excuse to offer. We will see what he says. Very well, let him in!"

The youth presented himself before the king, without showing the slightest trace of remorse or regret. "If it would please the king," he began, "I would like to know when I can expect to receive my wages."

"Wages?!" the king blurted out in disbelief. "Wages for what?"

"You told me that I would be paid 3000 gold coins for a month's work. That comes out to ten gold coins a day, or one coin an hour. Now, I worked for an hour and a half every day, so I am entitled to 450 gold coins!"

"Entitled?!" shouted the king, beside himself with rage. "Do you know what you are entitled to? A lengthy prison term! You studied at my expense, and bought tools and materials with my money. I put unlimited monetary resources at your disposal and offered you all the laborers you might need. I wanted to give you a break, to allow you to build yourself a reputation and to earn enough to start off in business on your own — but you betrayed my trust! You ruined the celebration, made a mockery of me in front of all the distinguished guests, and wasted a tremendous amount of my money for nothing! How can you dare to come before me and request payment for those few hours that you managed to get yourself to work?!"

The king was right, of course. The gardener's chutzpah was indeed beyond belief. But is this young man not a reflection of each and every one of us in a certain sense? God desires to grant us everlasting, boundless reward in the World to Come, and to that end He gave us the Torah to study and the mitzvos to keep. He gave us all the necessary tools to take advantage of this offer — health, intelligence, strength, talents, etc. But what do we do with all these gifts? We squander them on unimportant matters. We go to a *shiur* (Torah class) here and have a *chavrusah* (study partner) there, we cast a glance at a *sefer* every now and then — but for the most part we have failed to come anywhere near fulfilling the task for which we were put on this earth. And yet we expect that when our time comes to be judged before the heavenly throne, we will be granted reward for whatever few good deeds we did manage to put together. We are more like that gardener in the parable than we care to admit!

God, for His part, would be fully justified in reacting to the results of our meager efforts in the same manner as the king in the parable. But, fortunately for us, God is not like a flesh-and-blood king. With his great mercy, "He repays each man according to his deeds," for without the element of mercy such payment would not be granted at all.

It is for this reason that it is indeed appropriate to beseech God that He grant us a portion in the World to Come. We may have "earned" a certain share in the world of eternal reward, but, in light of our pitiful performance at our assignment, it is only through God's mercy that we can expect to receive the "payment" for these earnings.

וּלְחַיֵּי הָעוֹלָם הַבָּא
and the life of the World to Come.

An Otherwordly Person

There are several places in the Talmud where the Sages declare that if a person follows a certain virtuous course of action, "he has a portion in the World to Come" (lit., *he is a person of the World to Come*). For instance, "Anyone who studies halachos (points of Jewish law) every day has a portion in the World to Come" (*Niddah* 73a). **R' Shneur Kotler** explained that the Sages' intention with such statements was not that this person is guaranteed a place in the World to Come regardless of what else he does in the course of his lifetime. Rather, they mean to tell us that such a person is someone who, even while living in This World, shows that his life is based upon sublime, spiritual matters (matters of "the World to Come"), as opposed to being "a person of This World," whose life revolves around principles and ambitions that relate to the physical and materialistic sphere.

R' Shneur used this idea to explain a comment made by *Tosafos* in *Rosh Hashanah* (16b). The Talmud (ibid.) teaches that on Rosh Hashanah all the people of the world are divided into three categories and judged accordingly: The righteous are immediately sealed in the "Book of Life," the wicked in the "Book of Death," and judgment for the intermediate group is suspended until Yom Kippur. *Tosafos* interprets the Talmud's description of the judgment on Rosh Hashanah to be a judgment concerning not merely one's fate for the forthcoming year in This World, but rather a judgment for the World to Come. Taken at face value, this means that every year on Rosh Hashanah each individual's place in the World to Come is assessed, based on his deeds performed up to that Rosh Hashanah. But the question has been asked: Why should God make this judgment every year anew, being that this decision is applicable only once in a person's lifetime — namely, after his death? What is the point of reaching a verdict and then changing it year after year?

R' Shneur explained that *Tosafos* in fact does not mean to say that the judgment of Rosh Hashanah is to determine whether or to what extent a person is to merit a share in the World to Come. Rather, he means that God's judgment of man on Rosh Hashanah consists of His determination as to whether a particular individual is a "person of the World to Come" — i.e., one who builds the foundations of his life upon principles of spirituality and morality — or a "person of This World" — one whose sole principle in life is the pursuit of comfort, physical security, and self-gratification.

R' Shneur also used this concept to elucidate another saying of the Sages of the Talmud (*Kiddushin* 40b): "A person's judgment (after death) begins with the issue of Torah study. And just as his judgment (i.e., punishment) begins with this issue, so does his reward begin with it." The obvious question is: Since the individual is to be judged and held accountable for every single action he has taken throughout his life, what difference does it make which order God chooses to prosecute or reward him for these actions? What is the significance of the fact that He judges man for his dedication to Torah study before other matters?

The answer, R' Shneur explained, is that the outcome of this initial judgment of dedication to Torah study sheds light upon all the rest of a man's deeds. If his life was centered around Torah study (or another form of pursuit of spiritual achievement) this classifies him as a "person of the World to Come," and forms a basis for favorable judgment of the accomplishments of his life in general. If, however, a person is assessed as having failed in the realm of spiritual pursuits (as exemplified by his lack of Torah study), this fact negatively affects the evaluation of his other endeavors in life.

מַגְדִּיל יְשׁוּעוֹת מַלְכּוֹ וְעֹשֶׂה חֶסֶד לִמְשִׁיחוֹ לְדָוִד וּלְזַרְעוֹ עַד עוֹלָם.¹ עֹשֶׂה שָׁלוֹם בִּמְרוֹמָיו, הוּא יַעֲשֶׂה שָׁלוֹם עָלֵינוּ וְעַל כָּל יִשְׂרָאֵל. וְאִמְרוּ, אָמֵן.

יְראוּ אֶת יהוה קְדֹשָׁיו, כִּי אֵין מַחְסוֹר לִירֵאָיו. כְּפִירִים רָשׁוּ וְרָעֵבוּ, וְדֹרְשֵׁי יהוה לֹא יַחְסְרוּ כָל טוֹב.² הוֹדוּ לַיהוה כִּי טוֹב, כִּי לְעוֹלָם חַסְדּוֹ.³

יְראוּ אֶת ה' קְדֹשָׁיו, כִּי אֵין מַחְסוֹר לִירֵאָיו.
כְּפִירִים רָשׁוּ וְרָעֵבוּ, וְדֹרְשֵׁי ה' לֹא יַחְסְרוּ כָל טוֹב
Fear Hashem, you — His holy ones — for there is no deprivation for His reverent ones. Those who deny God may become poor and starve, but those who seek Hashem will not lack any good.

Coping   The assertion declared in these two verses is astounding. Is it really true that there is a general rule that those who fear God lack nothing? The problem of why many good people suffer misfortune and many wicked people prosper is one that has perplexed many wise men and prophets, such as Yirmiyahu (12:1), Chavakuk (1:13), and even the greatest of all prophets, Moshe (*Shemos* 33:13, see *Berachos* 7a). How can King David make such a sweeping statement that seems to contradict everyday human experience?

R' Zalman Sorotzkin offered an insight into this verse. The psalmist, he explained, is simply contrasting the reactions of the wicked and the righteous to situations of adversity. He who denies God becomes poor — and he starves as a result. He does not believe that there is some higher Power that has decreed, for some unknown, lofty reason that he should be deprived at this time. He therefore experiences great emotional — and even physical — suffering because of his deprivation. He who fears God, however, when undergoing the same exact type of deprivation and hardship, reassures himself that "Everything God does He does for a good purpose," and this enables him to be at peace with his unfortunate situation. Such people truly believe that they "do not lack anything good," for even if they are in dire poverty they realize that for some reason this is all that they are supposed to have at this particular time.

כִּי אֵין מַחְסוֹר לִירֵאָיו
for there is no deprivation for His reverent ones.

This Is Best for You   There have been many righteous, saintly men in history who lived lives of unspeakable poverty and privation — such as R' Chanina ben Dosa, whose sole weekly sustenance consisted of a *kav* (about 2 liters) of carob seeds, R' Elazar ben Pedas, Hillel, etc. How can we explain such a sweeping generalization that "there is nothing lacking to those who fear him"? The answer is, of course (see previous piece), that these people might have

He Who is a tower of salvations to His king and does kindness for His anointed, to David and to his descendants forever.[1] He Who makes peace in His heights, may He make peace upon us and upon all Israel. Now respond: Amen!

Fear HASHEM, you — His holy ones — for there is no deprivation for His reverent ones. Those who deny God may become poor and starve, but those who seek HASHEM will not lack any good.[2] Give thanks to God for He is good; His kindness endures forever.[3]

---

1. *II Shmuel* 22:51. 2. *Tehillim* 34:10-11. 3. Ibid., 136:1.

---

been dirt poor, but they indeed did not feel that they lacked anything, for they were satisfied with their meager lot and did not desire anything beyond it.

The **Chafetz Chaim** once offered a parable to illustrate the concept of being satisfied with one's portion in life:

There was once a poor carpenter who had to borrow money to make ends meet. He went to the town's moneylender to obtain the funds, and obligated himself to pay by a certain date. When the date arrived and the debt was not paid, the moneylender obtained a court order to seize the man's carpenters' plane as collateral.

The carpenter came to the moneylender the next day to plead his case. "When I borrowed the money I thought I would be able to earn enough through my trade to repay the loan by the specified date," he told him, with tears in his eyes. "Unfortunately, I did not have the expected amount of work available to me, and I was not able to meet the deadline. Just today I was offered an extensive, lucrative project, one which will enable me to pay you back with ease. But now that you have seized my plane, I cannot get *any* work done! It will be impossible for me to ever earn the money to pay you back now!"

The moneylender understood the man's argument, and agreed to return the plane to the poor carpenter. He went into his attic, where he stored dozens of items taken as collateral for all his outstanding loans. After a while he returned to the carpenter and said, "I can't seem to find your plane, but look what I came up with instead — a diamond polisher! It is worth ten times as much as your plane! Take this and be on your way."

"I beg you," appealed the carpenter. "Please search once again and try to find my plane."

"Fool that you are!" cried the moneylender. "I am offering you an object worth many times as much as the one you seek, and yet you insist on taking the less valuable item! Furthermore, what's the difference between a diamond polisher and a plane? They both do the same task — they smooth off the surface of the material they are applied to!"

"It is true that the diamond polisher is worth more than my plane," explained the

פּוֹתֵחַ אֶת יָדֶךָ, וּמַשְׂבִּיעַ לְכָל חַי רָצוֹן.[1] בָּרוּךְ הַגֶּבֶר אֲשֶׁר יִבְטַח בַּיהוה, וְהָיָה יהוה מִבְטַחוֹ.[2] נַעַר הָיִיתִי

poor man. "But as a carpenter, it is the plane that I need. The diamond polisher may be fine for a jeweler, but for me it is totally useless."

The lesson of the parable is that God knows the qualities and attributes of each man's soul — much better, in fact, than the man himself! He knows which goals are most suited for that soul and which sort of conditions that soul requires for its optimum accomplishment. "There is no man who is not put to trial by God," the Midrash tells us. But each man's trial is different from that of the next man. There are people who are tried by suffering pain or illness, to see how they are able to function under hardship. Others are tried with lives of riches and luxury, for this too is a sort of trial, to see if the person involved uses the money and power at his disposal in the proper manner, to help others and gain accomplishments for the benefit of mankind. Each soul receives the kind of trial that is most suited for it; if its situation would be altered — even to what appears outwardly to be a greatly improved lot in life — he will find himself in the same state as the carpenter with the diamond polisher. We must always remember that whatever God gives us in life is the best possible situation for us — and then we will realize that in fact "there is no deprivation for His reverent ones."

פּוֹתֵחַ אֶת יָדֶךָ, וּמַשְׂבִּיעַ לְכָל חַי רָצוֹן
You open up Your hand and satisfy every living thing with contentment.

Be Content; Be Happy

R' **Zalman Sorotzkin** noted that the verse does not say that God satisfies everyone "with money" or "with all their desires," but that He satisfies them with contentment. (This is the literal translation of the verse, although it is often rendered in different ways.) If a person has contentment, it is as if he has everything; if he is not content, whatever he has is pointless. As the Sages put it, "When someone has a *maneh* (a large amount of money), he wants two *manehs*!" Thus, the psalmist expresses in this verse the greatest possible blessing — the achievement of satisfaction with what one has.

R' Zalman illustrated this concept with a story told about the Ba'al Shem Tov. The Talmud records a disagreement among Tannaim as to when man is judged for his deeds in the course of his life. According to R' Meir a person is judged on Rosh Hashanah concerning what his fate is to be for the coming year; R' Yosi's opinion is that man is judged every single day of his life. The Ba'al Shem Tov's students once asked him if the positions of R' Yosi and R' Meir were irrevocably opposed to each other or if there might be some way of resolving the two sides. Rather than answer the question directly, the Ba'al Shem Tov went over to the window and waited there until he spotted an elderly Jewish water-carrier, lugging pails full of water down the street, delivering the buckets to his customers all over town, sometimes having to haul the water up several flights of stairs. The Ba'al Shem Tov asked his students to call the old man in to see him.

הגדה של פסח

You open up Your hand and satisfy every living thing with contentment.[1] Blessed is the man who trusts in Hashem, then Hashem will be his security.[2] I was a youth

1. *Tehillim* 145:16. 2. *Yirmiyahu* 17:7.

The water carrier came into the *beis midrash*. The Ba'al Shem Tov greeted him and asked him how he was doing.

The man replied bitterly, "Oy, Rebbe! I am not well at all! I am already seventy years old, and I have no strength left in me. Every day, in all kinds of weather — in the freezing winter and in the sweltering heat of summer — I have to *shlep* these heavy buckets of water all over town in order to eke out a living, and it is really too much for me to handle!"

The Ba'al Shem Tov thanked the man for coming in and bid him farewell. The students had no idea what the Rabbi was trying to prove to them with his conversation with the old Jew.

The next day the same man passed by the Ba'al Shem Tov's window again, and once more he had his students summon him. Once again the Ba'al Shem Tov asked the old man how he was doing.

"Very well, thank you," answered the water carrier. "Thank God in His infinite mercy that I still have the strength at the age of seventy to lug these buckets full of water, in all sorts of weather. He is so kind to me that He enables me to make a living for myself, and does not leave me at the mercy of charity!"

When the old man left, the Ba'al Shem Tov turned to his students and told them, "Now you have an answer to your question. There is no difference in this old water carrier's health or monetary situation between yesterday and today. The only thing that changed was the man's mood. Yesterday he was gloomy and depressed; today he is cheerful and optimistic, happy with his lot.

"You can apply this lesson to your question," the Ba'al Shem Tov concluded. "While it is true that God determines our fate on Rosh Hashanah, as R' Meir says, He does not determine in advance how we will be able to cope with that fate; that he decides on a day-by-day basis, as R' Yosi says."

It is true that God supplies us with all we need to survive, but even more important is the fact that He grants us the ability to appreciate what we have and to be content with it.

בָּרוּךְ הַגֶּבֶר אֲשֶׁר יִבְטַח בַּה'
Blessed is the man who trusts in Hashem,

Trust in Hashem — The Rambam, in his introduction to *Avos* writes, "We find that even prophets occasionally show imperfection [in their personal attributes], as was the case with Shmuel, who feared Shaul (*I Shmuel* 16:2), and Yaakov, who feared Esau (*Bereishis* 32:8) [and did not have absolute trust in God]." The Rambam seems to criticize these two great men for their lack of trust in God, for Yaakov had been explicitly guaranteed God's protection (*Bereishis* 28:15), and Shmuel was carrying out a mission from God (loc. cit.). The

גַּם זָקַנְתִּי, וְלֹא רָאִיתִי צַדִּיק נֶעֱזָב, וְזַרְעוֹ מְבַקֶּשׁ לָחֶם.[1] יהוה עֹז לְעַמּוֹ יִתֵּן, יהוה יְבָרֵךְ אֶת עַמּוֹ בַשָּׁלוֹם.[2]

---

commentator *Chesed L'Avraham* (ad loc.) poses a very strong question in relation to the Rambam's assertion: The Talmud (*Berachos* 4a) raises the issue of Yaakov's fear in the face of God's explicit promise of protection to him, and provides a clear explanation: Yaakov was afraid that he might have shown himself to be undeserving of God's benevolence because of some sin he might have committed. Elsewhere (*Pesachim* 8b) the Talmud asks a similar question in regard to Shmuel's apprehension despite the fact that he was being sent on a mission from God, in view of the principle that no harm befalls those who are engaged in the performance of a mitzvah, and once again gives an explicit answer: In a situation of clear danger there is no guarantee of protection for one who is performing a mitzvah. How, then, Chesed L'Avraham asks, can the Rambam call these two men to task for their conduct when their behavior seems to have been clearly vindicated by the Talmud?

R' Elchanan Wasserman offered an explanation for the Rambam's statement. It is true that the unique protection that is guaranteed for those who are carrying out a mitzvah and the particular guarantee of safety that had been offered to Yaakov may not have applied, for the reasons offered by the Talmud. However, even after these *specific* forms of protection are removed from the equation there is still a *general* attribute called "trust in God" (בִּטָּחוֹן), mentioned innumerable times in the *Tanach* (such as in our verse). Even when a person has no specific guarantee of safety it is inappropriate for him to show worry or distress at what might happen to him if he truly possesses this critical trait of "trust in God." It is for a small imperfection in this element of their faith that the Rambam criticizes the attitudes of Yaakov and Shmuel.

R' Elchanan notes, however, that we can understand Yaakov and Shmuel's fear without imputing their absolute faith. The trait of "trust in God," he explained, pertains not to God's Attribute of Strict Justice, but rather to His Attribute of Mercy. In other words, when we say that a person should place his trust in God, this does not mean that he is supposed to imagine that he really deserves that God should come to his salvation. Rather, he is supposed to believe that despite his unworthiness, God's trait of mercy is available to all who call on Him sincerely. This assertion is seen through many verses that connect the idea of "trust" with "mercy" — e.g., "And I trust in Your mercy" (*Tehillim* 13:6), "I trust in the mercy of God" (ibid., 52:10), "Let me hear Your kindness at dawn, for I trust in You" (ibid., 143:8).

R' Elchanan then quoted an interpretation of the *Shelah* of an *aggadata* in *Menachos* (29b). The Talmud tells us that when Moshe went up to Heaven to receive the Torah he was told that one day there would be a scholar named Akiva who would derive numerous halachos from each of the little marks found on the letters of the Torah. Moshe was even shown an excerpt from one of Rabbi Akiva's lectures. Most impressed with what he saw, Moshe then asked to be shown what R' Akiva's final reward would be. God thereupon showed him R' Akiva's end — the Romans flayed him alive and weighed out his flesh in the butcher's market. Astounded by the

and also have aged, and I have not seen a righteous man forsaken, with his children begging for bread.[1] HASHEM will give might to His people; HASHEM will bless His people with peace.[2]

---

1. *Tehillim* 37:25. 2. Ibid., 29:11.

---

seemingly unfair compensation for this saintly scholar's dedication to the Torah, Moshe exclaimed, "This is the Torah, and this is its reward?!" But God answered him, "Silence! This is how it entered My mind!"

How did God's response answer Moshe's question? It seems more like an evasion of the question rather than an answer! Furthermore, what did God mean when He said, "This is how it entered My mind"? If He meant to say that Moshe had no right to question His absolute judgment, He should have said something like, "This is My decision, and it is unfathomable."

The Shelah explains the passage based on a statement of the Sages, found in the Midrash. When the Torah (*Bereishis* 1) first describes the Creation of the Universe it uses only the Name of God denoting the Attribute of Strict Justice (אֱלֹהִים). But later (Chap. 2), when the Torah describes certain aspects of the Creation in more detail, this Name is supplemented by the four-letter Name, which connotes the Attribute of Mercy. The Midrash explains that at first it "entered God's mind" to create the Universe and conduct it according to the Attribute of Strict Justice, but He did not actually do so, because He realized that the world would not have a chance to survive under those conditions. He therefore injected the element of the Attribute of Mercy into the process of Creation.

When the Talmud depicts God as justifying the horrifying death of R' Akiva with the words, "This is how it entered My mind!" the Shelah explains, the Sages were alluding to this Midrashic statement. The reason God did not create the world solely on the basis of the Attribute of Strict Justice (as it had originally "entered His mind") is that it is impossible for man to be completely virtuous and without sin, and he would therefore be doomed to failure. In the history of the world, however, there are individuals who are on such a high spiritual plane that they are indeed capable of surviving even in a world that is conducted on the basis of the Attribute of Strict Justice, and such saintly individuals are indeed judged on that basis, according to the "original plan." R' Akiva was such a person. Thus, what God was telling Moshe was that the reason for R' Akiva's harsh fate was that he was being judged according to the initial plan of the Universe — "how it entered God's mind" originally — namely, solely through the Attribute of Strict Justice.

Now let us return to our original discussion of Shmuel and Yaakov. As explained above, trusting in God means having faith in the efficacy of His Attribute of Mercy. Great men, however, as the Shelah explained above, are not judged according to the Attribute of Mercy, but according to the Attribute of Strict Justice. The concept of "trusting in God" as an antidote to fear of danger, then, does not apply to such people, and Yaakov and Shmuel were thus entirely justified in their conduct.

Upon completion of *Bircas Hamazon* the blessing over wine is recited and the third cup is drunk while reclining on the left side. It is preferable to drink the entire cup, but at the very least, most of the cup should be drained.

Some recite the following before the third cup:

הִנְנִי מוּכָן וּמְזוּמָּן לְקַיֵּם מִצְוַת כּוֹס שְׁלִישִׁי שֶׁל אַרְבַּע כּוֹסוֹת. לְשֵׁם יִחוּד קוּדְשָׁא בְּרִיךְ הוּא וּשְׁכִינְתֵּיהּ, עַל יְדֵי הַהוּא טָמִיר וְנֶעְלָם, בְּשֵׁם כָּל יִשְׂרָאֵל. וִיהִי נֹעַם אֲדֹנָי אֱלֹהֵינוּ עָלֵינוּ, וּמַעֲשֵׂה יָדֵינוּ כּוֹנְנָה עָלֵינוּ, וּמַעֲשֵׂה יָדֵינוּ כּוֹנְנֵהוּ:

בָּרוּךְ אַתָּה יהוה אֱלֹהֵינוּ מֶלֶךְ הָעוֹלָם, בּוֹרֵא פְּרִי הַגָּפֶן.

The fourth cup is poured. According to most customs, the Cup of Eliyahu is poured at this point, after which the door is opened in accordance with the verse, "It is a guarded night." Then the following paragraph is recited.

שְׁפֹךְ חֲמָתְךָ אֶל הַגּוֹיִם אֲשֶׁר לֹא יְדָעוּךָ וְעַל מַמְלָכוֹת אֲשֶׁר בְּשִׁמְךָ לֹא קָרָאוּ. כִּי אָכַל אֶת יַעֲקֹב וְאֶת נָוֵהוּ הֵשַׁמּוּ.[1] שְׁפֹךְ עֲלֵיהֶם זַעְמֶךָ וַחֲרוֹן אַפְּךָ יַשִּׂיגֵם.[2] תִּרְדֹּף בְּאַף וְתַשְׁמִידֵם מִתַּחַת שְׁמֵי יהוה.[3]

שְׁפֹךְ חֲמָתְךָ אֶל הַגּוֹיִם אֲשֶׁר לֹא יְדָעוּךָ . . . כִּי אָכַל אֶת יַעֲקֹב
***Pour Your wrath upon the nations that do not
recognize You . . . For they have devoured Yaakov. . .***

The Chafetz Chaim's prayer   Towards the end of the First World War, when the czar was deposed, chaos and conflict reigned in the land. Groups of "reds" and "whites" roamed the countryside and the cities vying for power, their only common interest being hostility towards the Jews. At the time the **Chafetz Chaim** and his yeshivah were staying in a town called Shumiatz, where they had fled from Radin due to the war. They would gather in the village *beis midrash* and learn from morning to night. One day the door to the *beis midrash* was suddenly smashed down, and in marched a troop of "whites" with their commander.

"There they are!" shouted the commanding officer to his men. It seems they had just taken control of Shumiatz, and were searching for rival "reds," whom they sought to eradicate. Here was a large gathering of young, able-bodied men; they were not on the "white" side, so they must be "reds."

"We are not soldiers or fighters at all," the yeshivah students protested to the

הגדה של פסח   [224]

Upon completion of *Bircas Hamazon* the blessing over wine is recited and the third cup is drunk while reclining on the left side. It is preferable to drink the entire cup, but at the very least, most of the cup should be drained.

Some recite the following before the third cup:

Behold, I am prepared and ready to fulfill the mitzvah of the third of the Four Cups. For the sake of the unification of the Holy One, Blessed is He, and His presence, through Him Who is hidden and inscrutable — [I pray] in the name of all Israel. May the pleasantness of my Lord, our God, be upon us — may He establish our handiwork for us; our handiwork may He establish.

Blessed are You, Hashem, our God, King of the universe, Who creates the fruit of the vine.

The fourth cup is poured. According to most customs, the Cup of Eliyahu is poured at this point, after which the door is opened in accordance with the verse, "It is a guarded night." Then the following paragraph is recited.

Pour Your wrath upon the nations that do not recognize You and upon the kingdoms that do not invoke Your Name. For they have devoured Yaakov and destroyed His habitation.[1] Pour Your fury upon them and let Your fierce anger overtake them.[2] Pursue them with wrath and annihilate them from beneath the heavens of Hashem.[3]

---

1. *Tehillim* 79:6-7. 2. Ibid., 69:25. 3. *Eichah* 3:66.

---

commander. "This is a synagogue, and we are praying, that's all!" The *goy* would not understand what "sitting and learning" is about, but he surely must know what praying is!

"If this is a synagogue," the commander commented, "there must be a rabbi here!"

The Chafetz Chaim approached the soldier and said calmly, "I am the leader of these men. What is it that you want?"

"I would like to know what you are praying for," the man said, half-jokingly.

The Chafetz Chaim responded, "I have never told a lie in my life, and I will not do so now either." He went over to the shelf and took a siddur, which he opened up to the page before Shabbos *Mussaf* and showed to the army commander. "Here, you see, are two prayers. The first is a prayer for the local government under whose administration we live. The next prayer beseeches God to avenge the spilt blood of Jewish martyrs from those who murdered them. Now, sir, please tell me which prayer you would like to be recited concerning you!"

The commander was taken aback. "I'll take the first one, Rabbi!" he declared, and promptly told his men to leave the premises.

הַלֵּל – Hallel

הלל

The door is closed and the recitation of the Haggadah is continued.

לֹא לָנוּ יהוה לֹא לָנוּ, כִּי לְשִׁמְךָ תֵּן כָּבוֹד, עַל חַסְדְּךָ עַל אֲמִתֶּךָ. לָמָּה יֹאמְרוּ הַגּוֹיִם, אַיֵּה נָא אֱלֹהֵיהֶם. וֵאלֹהֵינוּ בַשָּׁמָיִם, כֹּל אֲשֶׁר חָפֵץ עָשָׂה. עֲצַבֵּיהֶם כֶּסֶף וְזָהָב, מַעֲשֵׂה יְדֵי אָדָם. פֶּה לָהֶם וְלֹא יְדַבֵּרוּ, עֵינַיִם לָהֶם וְלֹא יִרְאוּ. אָזְנַיִם לָהֶם וְלֹא יִשְׁמָעוּ, אַף לָהֶם וְלֹא יְרִיחוּן. יְדֵיהֶם וְלֹא יְמִישׁוּן, רַגְלֵיהֶם וְלֹא יְהַלֵּכוּ, לֹא יֶהְגּוּ בִּגְרוֹנָם. כְּמוֹהֶם יִהְיוּ עֹשֵׂיהֶם, כֹּל אֲשֶׁר בֹּטֵחַ בָּהֶם. יִשְׂרָאֵל בְּטַח בַּיהוה, עֶזְרָם וּמָגִנָּם הוּא. בֵּית אַהֲרֹן בִּטְחוּ בַיהוה, עֶזְרָם וּמָגִנָּם הוּא. יִרְאֵי יהוה בִּטְחוּ בַיהוה, עֶזְרָם וּמָגִנָּם הוּא.

יהוה זְכָרָנוּ יְבָרֵךְ, יְבָרֵךְ אֶת בֵּית יִשְׂרָאֵל, יְבָרֵךְ אֶת בֵּית אַהֲרֹן. יְבָרֵךְ יִרְאֵי יהוה, הַקְּטַנִּים עִם הַגְּדֹלִים. יֹסֵף יהוה עֲלֵיכֶם, עֲלֵיכֶם וְעַל בְּנֵיכֶם.

ה' זְכָרָנוּ יְבָרֵךְ יְבָרֵךְ אֶת בֵּית יִשְׂרָאֵל
Hashem Who has remembered us will bless — He will bless the House of Israel.

Hashem Remembers and Blesses

The Midrash (*Bereishis Rabbah, Vayeira*) teaches: "We find that whenever God remembers (mentions) the name of Israel He blesses them, as it says, 'Hashem Who has remembered us will bless.'" The inference, explained the **Netziv**, is from the phrasing of the verse. If the intent of the verse had been to say that on *some* occasions God sees fit to remember Israel for a blessing, it would have been more clearly expressed as, "Hashem remembered us to bless us." The fact that it says instead, "Hashem Who has remembered us will bless" implies that *whenever* He mentions Israel's name it is for the purpose of bestowing blessing upon them. The same thought is expressed in the *Sifrei* on the verse, "You will be remembered before Hashem and you will be saved from your enemies" (*Bamidbar* 10:9): "Whenever the remembrance of Israel is recalled before God it is for salvation."

This idea explains the deeper meaning of the verse, "And Aharon shall carry their names [engraved on the ephod's stones] before Hashem, on his two shoul-

HALLEL

The door is closed and the recitation of the Haggadah is continued.

Not for our sake, Hashem, not for our sake, but for Your Name's sake give glory, for the sake of Your kindness and Your truth! Why should the nations say: "Where is their God now?" Our God is in the heavens; whatever He pleases, He does! Their idols are silver and gold, the handiwork of man. They have a mouth, but cannot speak; they have eyes, but cannot see; they have ears, but cannot hear; they have a nose, but cannot smell; their hands — they cannot feel; their feet — they cannot walk; nor can they utter a sound with their throat. Those who make them should become like them, whoever trusts in them! O Israel! Trust in Hashem; He is their help and their shield! House of Aharon! Trust in Hashem! He is their help and their shield! You who fear Hashem — trust in Hashem, He is their help and their shield!

Hashem Who has remembered us will bless — He will bless the House of Israel; He will bless the House of Aharon; He will bless those who fear Hashem, the small as well as the great. May Hashem increase upon you, upon you and upon your children!

---

ders, for a remembrance" (*Shemos* 28:12). The intent of this verse is quite vague; the Torah does not specify what the nature of this remembrance is, or why it is necessary. According to the concept taught by the Midrash, the meaning of the phrase becomes clear: The stones were to seek God's blessing and beneficence for His people, for the word "remembrance" is always associated with "goodness."

Based on this Midrash the Netziv supplied an explanation for a difficult passage found in the festival prayers: "Hold up for us, Hashem, Your holiday blessing, as You consented and wished and said to bless us." Where, asked the Netziv, do we find any reference in the Torah or elsewhere to the fact that God "wished and said" to bless us on the festivals?

According to the Midrash, the Netziv wrote, the answer to this question is obvious. This passage refers to the verse cited above: "On the days of your joy and *festivals*... you shall blow the trumpets, and you will be *remembered* before Hashem." As the Midrash teaches, the remembrance of Israel coming before Hashem is always associated with God's blessing to them.

בְּרוּכִים אַתֶּם לַיהוה, עֹשֵׂה שָׁמַיִם וָאָרֶץ. הַשָּׁמַיִם שָׁמַיִם לַיהוה, וְהָאָרֶץ נָתַן לִבְנֵי אָדָם. לֹא הַמֵּתִים יְהַלְלוּ יָהּ, וְלֹא כָּל יֹרְדֵי דוּמָה. וַאֲנַחְנוּ נְבָרֵךְ יָהּ, מֵעַתָּה וְעַד עוֹלָם, הַלְלוּיָהּ.

אָהַבְתִּי, כִּי יִשְׁמַע יהוה אֶת קוֹלִי, תַּחֲנוּנָי. כִּי הִטָּה אָזְנוֹ לִי, וּבְיָמַי אֶקְרָא. אֲפָפוּנִי חֶבְלֵי מָוֶת, וּמְצָרֵי שְׁאוֹל מְצָאוּנִי, צָרָה וְיָגוֹן אֶמְצָא. וּבְשֵׁם יהוה אֶקְרָא, אָנָּה יהוה מַלְּטָה נַפְשִׁי. חַנּוּן יהוה וְצַדִּיק, וֵאלֹהֵינוּ מְרַחֵם. שֹׁמֵר פְּתָאיִם יהוה, דַּלּוֹתִי וְלִי יְהוֹשִׁיעַ. שׁוּבִי נַפְשִׁי

וְהָאָרֶץ נָתַן לִבְנֵי אָדָם. לֹא הַמֵּתִים יְהַלְלוּ יָהּ וכו'
but the earth He has given to mankind.
The dead cannot praise God....

Only the Living Can Praise Hashem — These two verses appear to be totally unrelated to each other, **R' Zalman Sorotzkin** noted. What is the connection between them?

R' Zalman explained that when we say that "the earth He has given to mankind," this can have two implications: to live on the land, or to be be interred *in* it. The Talmud (*Makkos* 11b), after all, interprets the phrase "to return, to dwell in the land" in *Bamidbar* 35:32 to mean "to be buried in the land." Therefore, after stating that God gave the land to the sons of man, the psalmist clarifies for which purpose he means to say that the land was given to man: "The dead cannot praise God"; the land is therefore better suited for being *on* it, not *in* it!

לֹא הַמֵּתִים יְהַלְלוּ יָהּ. . . . וַאֲנַחְנוּ נְבָרֵךְ יָהּ, מֵעַתָּה וְעַד עוֹלָם
The dead cannot praise God... but we will
bless God from this time and forever.

The Policeman May Still Come — If a person narrowly escapes harm in an accident or through illness, or if he has a close brush with death through any other tragedy from which he was saved, the **Chafetz Chaim** used to say, he should see to it that he dedicates the time granted to him from Heaven toward a good purpose. He should think, "If I were now thrown back into that grave situation, I would have been prepared to give anything to be extricated from danger. Now that I have been saved, how can I be ungrateful toward God for His kindness?"

The Chafetz Chaim drove the point home with a parable:

A warrant was was once put out for a certain man's arrest. A policeman arrived at his house armed with a club and handcuffs, to take the man off to jail. The

You are blessed of Hashem, Maker of heaven and earth. As for the heavens — the heavens are Hashem's, but the earth He has given to mankind. The dead cannot praise God, nor can any who descend into silence; but we will bless God from this time and forever. Halleluyah!

I love Him, for Hashem hears my voice, my supplications. For He has inclined His ear to me, so in my days shall I call. The ropes of death encircled me; the confines of the grave have found me; trouble and sorrow have I found. Then I called upon the Name of Hashem: "Please Hashem, save my soul." Gracious is Hashem and righteous, our God is merciful. Hashem protects the simple; I was brought low, but He saved me. Return, my soul,

---

accused man pulled out a hundred-dollar bill and "persuaded" the policeman to forget about his mission. The maneuver worked, and the policeman left the house.

The man was overjoyed, and the very next day he called together his family and friends to celebrate and rejoice. They had averted a nasty encounter with the authorities. Who knows what evils the courts would have in store for these charges!

But let us reflect on the man's conduct. How foolish he was! There were many more policemen where this one came from, and if he bribed one man, he surely must realize that he could not continue to do so forever. Eventually the law would catch up with him; he would sit in jail and face trial — and his hundred-dollar bills would all have been spent for nothing. Instead of wasting his time rejoicing and partying, the man should have used the time he had bought wisely, seeking legal counsel, approaching the authorities to convince them of his innocence or to plead for mercy, etc. In this manner the hundred dollars would have been a well-spent investment.

Similarly, if a man narrowly escapes from mortal danger, he should realize that God's Attribute of Strict Justice is poised against him. If he escapes once he will surely be faced with adversity again, if this is God's will. Instead of celebrating and rejoicing over his stroke of good fortune, he should spend his time and energy seeking favor in God's eyes and pray that he be forgiven for his sins. And there is no better way to find favor in God's eyes in such situations, the Chafetz Chaim concluded, than to devote some extra time to the study of Torah, for in this manner he can hope to have his "warrant" rescinded.

דַּלּוֹתִי וְלִי יְהוֹשִׁיעַ
I was brought low, but He saved me.

A Positive Outlook on Human Suffering

Suffering and deprivation themselves can sometimes actually prove to be the key to salvation.

The **Chafetz Chaim** related that one time the Vilna Gaon was telling his students about the unfathomable extent of punishment the soul experiences in Gehinnom, even for the slightest sin committed during one's lifetime.

[231] THE HAGGADAH OF THE ROSHEI YESHIVAH

לִמְנוּחָיְכִי, כִּי יהוה גָּמַל עָלָיְכִי. כִּי חִלַּצְתָּ נַפְשִׁי מִמָּוֶת, אֶת עֵינִי מִן דִּמְעָה, אֶת רַגְלִי מִדֶּחִי. אֶתְהַלֵּךְ

"All the books that describe such things," the Gaon cautioned, "are able to portray only a drop in the bucket of the true dimension of the unspeakable suffering there."

One of the students was so overwhelmed with terror at the Gaon's words that he literally took ill. The Gaon was told the next day about the young man's condition, and he went to see him as he lay in his sick bed. He told the student, "Everything I said yesterday was absolutely true. But you should know that when a person's sins are judged, the suffering and hardships that that individual underwent during his lifetime are also taken into account. A large portion of a person's sins are neutralized by such calculations. If not for pain and suffering we would have no hope at all in the World to Come!"

The Chafetz Chaim used to illustrate this idea by means of a parable that he told in the name of the Vilna Maggid:

There was once a Jew who rented an inn from a certain nobleman. For three hundred gold coins per month he was allowed to run the inn and earn a meager, but sufficient living. He paid his rent on time and had an excellent relationship with his landlord, who was a fair and decent man.

One day the nobleman had to travel abroad. He appointed his greedy manager to oversee all the affairs of his extensive land holdings in his absence. As soon as the nobleman departed the manager got to work. He approached the Jewish innkeeper and told him, "You are making a fortune in this inn, yet you pay a paltry sum to my master in rent! From now on you will pay double — six hundred gold pieces per month!"

The innkeeper was dumbfounded. "Believe me," he pleaded with the evil custodian. "The local farmers are dirt poor, and I sell them beer at almost no profit. I am just barely able to support my family with my earnings. If you double the rent, we will starve!"

But his words fell on deaf ears. "If you do not bring me six hundred gold pieces on the first of next month," he shouted back arrogantly, "you will be evicted immediately!"

The innkeeper saw that he had no choice but to comply. "I will have to borrow the money," he thought to himself. "When the duke comes back from his trip I will file a complaint about the outrageous behavior of the manager and perhaps he will refund the money to me."

He traveled to town and knocked on the doors of everyone he knew, borrowing a few coins here and another few there, until he had scrounged up 280 gold pieces out of the 300 extra that he needed. He went to the nobleman's manager and handed over the money. When the money was counted and found to be lacking 20 gold pieces, the manager was furious.

"How dare you bring me less than the required amount?" he demanded. "Now you must be punished for your lack of compliance!" And he ordered that the innkeeper be given twenty lashes, one for each missing gold piece.

to your rest; for HASHEM has been kind to you. You delivered my soul from death, my eyes from tears, my feet from stumbling. I shall walk before

---

It was not only this innkeeper who was suffering at the hands of the nobleman's manager, for all the tenants were being overcharged, with the extra money all going for the sole purpose of lining the man's crooked pockets. The manager soon made a fortune in this manner, and built himself a beautiful mansion with his ill-gotten profits.

Many months went by, and finally the nobleman returned to his estate. Many sighs of relief were heard across the countryside, and the innkeeper decided to go and tell the nobleman what had happened in his absence, hoping to retrieve all or some of the money extorted from him.

The nobleman was astounded to hear about the outrageous behavior of the man he had put in charge of his affairs. "I will have your money refunded doubly!" he promised the innkeeper.

The innkeeper saw that he was being received kindly, and he continued with his complaints. "Not only did he take my money, but he sentenced me to twenty lashes for underpaying him!"

The nobleman could not believe his ears. "Lashes?!" he exclaimed. "How dare he raise his hand against one of my tenants! He must be punished appropriately. I will award you half of his mansion as a compensation for your suffering and humiliation."

The duke had a certificate written up right then and there that bestowed upon the innkeeper immediate title to half the manager's splendid house.

When the man arrived home he greeted his wife, who could not help but notice a look of disappointment on his face. "Oh, no!" she cried out. "Don't tell me the duke turned down your request for a refund!"

"No, that's not it," the innkeeper reassured her. "He was actually quite understanding and offered me a generous compensation." He showed her the deed to half the manager's mansion.

"That's wonderful!" she exclaimed. "So why the glum look on your face?"

"Don't you understand?" the innkeeper replied. "If only the manager had whipped me with *forty* lashes I would have been awarded the entire mansion instead of just half!"

The lesson of the parable is that when a person is subjected to pain and adversity in life he sits back and grumbles in misery, bitter over his lot in life. But the time will come when he will get to the World to Come and see the extent of the reward granted to him in return for all his suffering. Then he will appreciate the suffering he had had to bear, and even wish that there had been more of it!

This message is conveyed by the Midrash as well, basing itself on the verse, "Remember the days of old (lit., *days of the world*)" (Devarim 32:7). The Midrash comments on this verse: "God said to [the Jewish people]: Whenever I bring suffering upon you in this world, just remember how much goodness and delight I am destined to bring you in the 'days of the World [to Come]!'"

לִפְנֵי יהוה, בְּאַרְצוֹת הַחַיִּים. הֶאֱמַנְתִּי כִּי אֲדַבֵּר, אֲנִי עָנִיתִי מְאֹד. אֲנִי אָמַרְתִּי בְחָפְזִי, כָּל הָאָדָם כֹּזֵב.

אֶתְהַלֵּךְ לִפְנֵי ה' בְּאַרְצוֹת הַחַיִּים
I shall walk before Hashem in the lands of the living.

The Many "Lands" of Olam Haba

The phrase "lands of the living" refers, according to some commentators, to the World to Come. Why, then, we may ask, is the plural (*lands*) used? How many "Worlds to Come" are there? We can learn the answer to this question from an explanation given by the **Chafetz Chaim** in another context.

The Sages (*Avos* 4:16) use an interesting analogy to describe the relationship between This World and the World to Come: "This World is comparable to an entrance hall, and the World to Come is comparable to a palace. Prepare yourself in the entrance hall in order to enter the palace." There seems to be something incongruous about this comparison, the Chafetz Chaim noted. When we think of waiting in an entrance hall before being admitted to see an important person, we think perhaps of preparing ourselves for a few minutes, or perhaps hours, to put our thoughts together and arrange our words carefully in order to ensure that we are able to express our intention clearly to the powerful person we are about to see. Perhaps, in the case of a king, we might spend several weeks buying the clothing and attaining the grooming necessary to make the proper impression, and seeking counsel from many different sources so that we are sure to present our case in the most convincing manner. But how can we understand a full seventy- or eighty-year period (man's life span) as nothing but a period of preparation for an experience beyond this?

The Chafetz Chaim explained that in fact the Sages do not mean to say that we should regard all the days of our lives as preparation for one single event — the World to Come. Rather, he explained, the "palace" of paradise consists of many "chambers" (as described in Kabbalistic works), and each and every mitzvah that we do in our lives enables us to be granted entry into one of those "chambers." Thus, we are not exhorted to view life as one long waiting period for "the next step," but to regard each moment of life as an opportunity to achieve yet another stake in the spiritual bliss of the World to Come.

Now we can understand why the psalmist uses the plural word *lands* when referring to the World to Come — for there are indeed many different "lands" that we aspire to traverse when the time comes for us to be called forth from the "vestibule" of this world.

אֶתְהַלֵּךְ לִפְנֵי ה' בְּאַרְצוֹת הַחַיִּים. הֶאֱמַנְתִּי כִּי אֲדַבֵּר, אֲנִי עָנִיתִי מְאֹד
I shall walk before Hashem in the lands of the living.
I kept faith although I say: "I suffer exceedingly."

Solace Through Hope

Even when one is suffering in the depths of disgrace and deprivation, he can take solace in the fact that ultimately the time will come when he will be granted a reprieve from his troubles and be able to "walk in the lands of the living."

HASHEM in the lands of the living. I kept faith although I say: "I suffer exceedingly." I said in my haste: "All mankind is deceitful."

The **Chafetz Chaim** elucidated this concept with a parable:

Once there was a wealthy jeweler who made a fortune trading in gems. One day he went on a business trip to a faraway land, taking 3000 rubles in cash to buy merchandise and another 400 rubles for traveling expenses — 200 for the trip there and another 200 for the return trip. He arrived at his destination, made some very good deals, and, when he had used up the 3000 rubles, packed his bags to head for home.

Just as he was leaving town, a mysterious man approached him and said, "I heard that you trade in gems."

The stranger did not appear to be particularly threatening. The merchant confirmed, "Yes, I deal in jewels."

"Well, you see, I have some very fine stones here with me, and I am willing to sell them to you at an unbelievably low price!" the man told him.

"I'm sorry," answered the jeweler. "I have already used up all my money buying merchandise. I cannot purchase any more."

"Perhaps you could just look at them for a moment," begged the stranger. "I think you will find them interesting."

"Very well, then," consented the merchant, who was growing rather curious to see what the man was so excited about.

The man opened his pouch and took out three stunning gems. The merchant, who was an expert in his field, had never seen anything like these stones before. They were truly treasures! "How much do you think they're worth?" asked the stranger.

The merchant thought for a moment and ventured his estimation of the stones' value. "I reckon the combined value of these gems is in the area of four thousand rubles."

"Listen to me," whispered the stranger. "I am in big trouble with the authorities, and I must leave the province immediately. I have no money whatsoever, and I am desperate to sell these gems for cash. I don't have much time. I'll take whatever you give me."

The jeweler was tantalized by the offer, for he knew that he could make a very handsome profit on such a deal. But he quickly remembered that he had no money, so there was nothing to talk about. "I'm sorry," he told the stranger with disappointment. "As I said, I'm afraid I have no more money to spend."

"Please, mister," pleaded the stranger. "I have no time to argue. If you give me even a few hundred rubles I will take them."

"A few hundred rubles!" thought the merchant to himself. "What a deal! I still have my traveling money with me — 200 rubles. But if I give him that money I will have no way of getting back home! On the other hand, how can I pass up this tremendous opportunity?"

"I will give you 180 rubles for the stones," offered the merchant, figuring that he could somehow manage to find a way home for 20 rubles if he tried.

"It's a deal!" agreed the stranger. "Hurry, please!"

מָה אָשִׁיב לַיהוה, כָּל תַּגְמוּלוֹהִי עָלָי. כּוֹס יְשׁוּעוֹת

The jeweler took the gems and gave the money to the stranger, who ran off immediately thereafter.

The merchant now turned his mind to the task of getting home with almost no money. Trains were out of the question. He stood at the side of the road and traveled from farm to farm by paying a few kopeks to traveling wagondrivers to allow him to ride in the back with the hay. In between farms he walked miles on foot, until his bones ached and his shoes began to tear. Towards evening he passed an inn, one of the establishments he was used to frequenting, and he thought to go in, but he realized that he would not be able to afford lodging at such a standard. If he would sell some of the private belongings in his suitcase he might be able to pull together enough cash to sleep in the basement, where the wagondrivers and waiters slept on piles of straw.

And so he traveled from town to town, day after day. One evening, as he was "checking in" to a basement of an inn not far from his hometown, a guest in the hotel cast a glance at him. The man couldn't believe his eyes. The merchant was wearing dirty, torn clothing, his shoes were tattered and his personal appearance was totally unkempt. He was heading down the back stairs to his "quarters."

"Why, aren't you Reb Yossel, the millionaire?" the guest asked in amazement.

"Yes, that's me," the man answered shamefacedly.

"What's become of you?" inquired the guest. "Have you suddenly run into financial difficulty?"

"On the contrary," replied the merchant. "I have never been so rich in my life!"

Now the guest was even more puzzled than before.

"Let me explain," offered the jeweler. "I have some very valuable jewels which I will soon sell for a huge profit. I might look like a beggar now, but very soon I will be more wealthy than ever!"

"I see," said the guest. "But tell me, Reb Yossele... How can a man such as yourself, accustomed to fine food and luxurious lodgings, bear to put up with such a deplorable standard of living?"

"I cannot deny that I have had moments of anguish and despair," answered the merchant candidly. "But whenever I begin to feel depressed I simply take out the pouch from my pocket and glance at the brilliant, sparkling gems that I am carrying with me. This gives me the encouragement to keep going!"

The Chafetz Chaim used this parable to describe the proper attitude towards dedication in studying the Torah. Man was put on this earth to apply himself to learning Torah and doing good deeds; these accomplishments are worth far more than precious stones. The Sages advise us (*Avos* 6:4) about the manner in which to go about acquiring Torah knowledge: "Eat bread with (only) salt, drink water sparingly, sleep on the ground, etc." The way of the Torah is to seek the minimum standard of living, and channel one's efforts to the acquisition of spiritual goals. Although this advice seems quite reasonable to the mind and spirit, man's physical desire for pleasure and comfort constantly steers him away from such sentiments,

> How can I repay (or respond to) HASHEM? All His benevolence is upon me! I will raise the cup of

for it finds it most difficult to bear the deprivation involved in such a minimal standard of living. But all one has to do is to ponder the great reward which will ultimately be his, and this will give him the encouragement and drive to put up with all the discomfort and carry out his sacred mission in life.

מָה אָשִׁיב לַה' כָּל תַּגְמוּלוֹהִי עָלָי
How can I repay (or respond to) Hashem?
All His benevolence is upon me!

King David's Debt to Hashem

What is meant by the strange expression, "All His benevolence is upon me," and how does this explain why the psalmist finds it so difficult to repay God? The **Chafetz Chaim** explained this verse through a parable:

Once there was a wealthy merchant who owned a jewelry company. He had hundreds of people in his employ, with whom he dealt fairly and honestly. One day he called in two of his buyers for a meeting; one of the men was an expert in diamonds and the other in sapphires. The boss told the men that he had heard that there was a new mine in a certain country where large quantities of precious stones had been found, and that there were great bargains to be had. The merchant wanted to send these men to that land to purchase as many gems as they could, for the potential for large profits was quite high. He would supply the buyers with large amounts of cash with which to make the purchases. Since diamonds are worth so much more than sapphires, he explained to them, the diamond expert would be given a hundred thousand rubles, while the sapphire expert would have only one thousand rubles to spend on the merchandise. In addition to this the men were given a small amount of spending money, and the promise of very handsome fees for their efforts upon their return. The two men eagerly accepted the attractive assignment.

They set off on their long journey in good spirits. Their buoyant mood enticed them to enjoy life while traveling. They stayed at the best hotels, ordered the best meals, and indulged in expensive entertainment in the evenings. Soon, of course, their traveling allowance ran out, and in order to keep up their standard of living the men had to "borrow" from the capital that they were supposed to use for purchasing jewels for their boss. The situation continued until they had pilfered quite a large sum from their employee's money. The diamond merchant had only 20,000 rubles left, and the sapphire buyer had only 400.

One night, after checking into a (luxury) hotel, the men went up to their room to set themselves up for the evening. "The bed next to the window is mine!" called the diamond expert.

But the sapphire expert also had his eyes on that bed. "Is that so?" he protested. "Actually, I would also like to take that bed. If you don't want to let me have it, we'll just have to draw lots to determine who gets his way!"

אֶשָּׂא, וּבְשֵׁם יהוה אֶקְרָא. נְדָרַי לַיהוה אֲשַׁלֵּם, נֶגְדָה נָּא לְכָל עַמּוֹ. יָקָר בְּעֵינֵי יהוה, הַמָּוְתָה לַחֲסִידָיו. אָנָּה יהוה כִּי אֲנִי עַבְדֶּךָ, אֲנִי עַבְדְּךָ, בֶּן אֲמָתֶךָ,

"Lots!?" cried the diamond expert. "What nerve! Aren't you the the 'proud pauper'! You know, I, as a diamond trader, am worth so much more than you are, and it is only right that *I* should have precedence in such matters!"

"You are mistaken!" the sapphire dealer shot back. "Your higher level of expertise should not be a cause for pride now! Quite the contrary is the case!"

"What do you mean by that?!" asked the diamond expert quizzically.

The sapphire buyer explained himself. "If the money we had in our possession would be our own, you would be entitled to conduct yourself with seniority. After all, you have much more money in your wallet than I do, and your buying power and earning power are that much more as well. But in fact it is not our own money that we have; it is the boss's funds that we are squandering, and we will eventually have to face the music and pay back every single penny of what we have spent! And then, *you* will have to pay back 80,000 rubles, while I will only have to come up with 600! Now tell me, which of us is the 'proud pauper'?!"

The diamond trader was humbled by his colleague's admonition, for he knew that every word was true.

David, the author of the psalms, had good reason to feel superior to all the other Jews in the kingdom. He was, after all, their king, and he was a well-known saint and wise man as well. Who could even compare himself to him? But in this verse he declares: If these accomplishments were of my own doing I would be within my rights to allow such astounding achievements to go to my head. But I acknowledge that in fact all that I have is a gift from God — and an *undeserved* gift at that. If sometimes I do not use these God-given abilities and powers in the best manner I will be held accountable for "mishandling" God's trust — and the punishment will, of course, be commensurate with the magnitude of the potential for good that was entrusted to me. It is precisely because all of God's benevolence is *upon* me (i.e., I am beholden to God for it), and because my debt is so great to Him that I have nothing to respond to Him when He calls me to task!

On another occasion the **Chafetz Chaim** explained this verse in a slightly different manner, offering the following parable:

Once there was a storeowner who would purchase his stock from a certain wholesaler. Every six months he would go to the wholesaler's establishment and place a large order on credit. He would then set the goods up on the shelves of his store and sell them at a profit, part of which went to pay back the wholesaler and the rest of which went towards supporting the retailer's family. Each time the storeowner would go to the wholesaler, then, he would pay off his outstanding debt — or most of it — and order new stock on credit.

A few years went by and the retailer's oldest daughter came of age. A match was found for her, but the groom's father insisted that the wedding plans could not

salvations and the Name of HASHEM I will invoke. My vows to HASHEM I will pay, in the presence, now, of His entire people. Precious in the eyes of HASHEM is the death of His devout ones. Please, HASHEM — for I am Your servant, I am Your servant, son of Your handmaid —

---

proceed unless a proper dowry was paid. The retailer had no extra money saved up, so he had no choice but to take all the profits from the store and save them up week after week until he could begin to meet the considerable payment that was demanded of him.

Meanwhile, the shelves of the store were steadily emptying out. The time for the retailer to make his biannual trip to the wholesaler had come. He went to the man's place of business and handed him his order list.

"And how do you intend to pay?" asked the wholesaler.

"As usual," the retailer answered. "I will take the merchandise on credit!"

"You know," argued the wholesaler, "half a year ago you took a huge load of goods from me, and you haven't yet paid for that order. How, then, do you expect me to give you yet further merchandise on credit?!"

The retailer could not answer this argument; he knew that the wholesaler was right. He bowed his head in shame and went on his way.

This, the Chafetz Chaim continued, is the meaning of our verse. God gives us so many blessings. How can we turn to Him and request yet more benevolence, when we have not even begun to repay Him for what he has already done for us? "What can I answer to God? All His benevolence is upon me (i.e., I owe Him for them)."

אֲנִי עַבְדְּךָ, בֶּן אֲמָתֶךָ
I am your servant, son of your handmaid.

Voluntary Punishment

The **Chafetz Chaim** was once asked to explain a story recounted in the Gemara (*Berachos* 5b):

R' Elazar fell ill, and R' Yochanan went to his house to visit him. The latter asked, "Do you like suffering?"

"I would prefer to have neither suffering nor its reward!"

R' Yochanan thereupon placed his hand upon him and healed him.

The question put to the Chafetz Chaim was: There are many sick people in the world who would agree with R' Elazar's statement that "I would prefer to have neither suffering nor its reward!" Why was this simple statement enough for him to be miraculously extricated from his illness?

The Chafetz Chaim replied with a parable:

Once there was a journalist who wanted to write a report on life among convicted criminals in prison. In order to learn all there was to know about the subject, he decided he would have to experience prison life firsthand for a while. He turned to the jail warden and told him of his request to be incarcerated along with the prisoners. The warden consented to the plan; he shaved the writer's head, gave him a prisoner's uniform, and locked his hands and feet in chains. He then threw him

פִּתַּחְתָּ לְמוֹסֵרָי. לְךָ אֶזְבַּח זֶבַח תּוֹדָה, וּבְשֵׁם יהוה אֶקְרָא. נְדָרַי לַיהוה אֲשַׁלֵּם, נֶגְדָה נָּא לְכָל עַמּוֹ. בְּחַצְרוֹת בֵּית יהוה, בְּתוֹכֵכִי יְרוּשָׁלָיִם הַלְלוּיָהּ.

into the dungeon with the most hardened criminals, who had their fun torturing and abusing the newcomer among them.

The next day the reporter was sent out with the other prisoners to a day at hard labor in the fields, where he was whipped and manhandled along with everyone else. When the day was done, the writer, whose back was already full of blisters from the taskmaster's whip, and whose body was completely broken from the harsh forced labor, decided he had learned quite enough. He called out for the warden and told him that he wished to go, and he immediately unlocked the chains and released him.

The other prisoners were astounded. "What's going on here?" they demanded. "We've been here much longer than he has! This guy came only yesterday, and just because he complains a little you let him go?!"

The jail warden explained the circumstances to them. "You can't compare your situation with his," he told them. "You are convicted criminals, and have sentences to serve. This man was an innocent citizen, who voluntarily had himself subjected to prison life in order to write a report for a newspaper. We put him into confinement upon his request, and we released him upon his request!"

R' Elazar's illness was not inflicted upon him as a result of some wrongdoing on his part. His suffering fell under the category of "suffering of love," which God inflicts upon certain righteous people in order to enlarge their share in the World to Come (see *Berachos* ibid.). Hence, it was only proper that when he declared that he desired neither the suffering nor its attendant reward, his suffering come to an end. This is, of course, far from the situation of most sick people, who are being punished for their sins.

David is expressing the same sentiments with these words: "I am Your faithful servant, the son of Your maidservant" and hence the sufferings I experience are surely nothing but "suffering of love," and not deserved as punishment for wrongdoing. Therefore, "You have released my bonds." Like the reporter in the parable and like R' Elazar in the Gemara's story I know that You will release me from my bonds when I can no longer bear the pain and suffering.

לְךָ אֶזְבַּח זֶבַח תּוֹדָה, וּבְשֵׁם ה' אֶקְרָא.
נְדָרַי לַיי אֲשַׁלֵּם, נֶגְדָה נָּא לְכָל עַמּוֹ
To you I will sacrifice thanksgiving offerings, and the Name of Hashem will I invoke. My vows to Hashem will I pay in the presence, now, of His entire people.

Public Thanks — Why does the psalmist say that he will fulfill his vows "in the presence of His entire people"? Is it not more proper for a person to carry out acts of righteousness and piety inconspicuously, or, as the prophet puts it, "to walk humbly with your God" (*Michah* 6:8)? The **Netziv** posed this question,

> You have released my bonds. To You I will sacrifice thanksgiving offerings, and the Name of HASHEM will I invoke. My vows to HASHEM will I pay in the presence, now, of His entire people. In the courtyards of the House of HASHEM, in your midst, O Yerushalayim, Halleluyah!

in addition to another one concerning the following verse: "In the courtyards of the House of Hashem, in your midst, O Yerushalayim, Halleluyah!" "The courtyards of the House of Hashem" are in the Temple, on the outskirts of Jerusalem; the second phrase of the sentence, "in your midst, O Yerushalayim," thus seems to be in contradiction to the first phrase of the verse.

To address these problems the Netziv began by examining the unique nature of the thanksgiving offering, the topic of the verses under discussion. This is the only individual offering in the entire Temple service that included leavened bread, in defiance of the general rule that "you shall not offer up before Me any leaven or honey" (*Vayikra* 2:11). What is the significance of this exception to the rule in the case of this particular sacrifice? Another question was asked by the Netziv in connection with this offering. The thanksgiving offering is classified as a type of peace offering (*Vayikra* 7:11-12), but it differs from the general peace offering in two main respects: It may be eaten only on the day it is offered, and not on the following day (ibid., 7:15); and it is accompanied by several loaves of bread (including the leavened loaves mentioned above), while the ordinary peace offering has no such accompaniment. What is the significance of these departures from the norm in the thanksgiving offering?

The main objective of the thanksgiving offering, the Netziv explained, is for the celebrant to relate the details of his particular experience of salvation from God. Unlike other offerings, the thanksgiving offering consisted of *two* major components — the sacrificial service itself, and the festive meal at which the meat and breads were consumed, for this was the forum at which the beneficiary of God's grace would publicize the miracles that had happened to him, thereby glorifying His name. This, suggested the Netziv, accounts for the peculiarities of the thanksgiving offering. The ordinary peace offering, which may be eaten for two days, can be totally consumed by oneself and one's extended family; half the meat can be eaten one day and the other half the next day. The eating of the thanksgiving offering, however, being limited to one day's consumption, would have to be accomplished through inviting a much larger circle of friends and guests, thus amplifying the scope of spreading the story of salvation that lay behind the thanksgiving offering. The accompaniment of forty loaves of bread clearly contributes to this goal of maximizing the number of participants in the festive meal as well. And furthermore, the Netziv wrote, it is in order to enhance the enjoyment of the food — and thus the rejoicing in the salvation of Hashem — at the thanksgiving meal that unleavened breads are served, for unleavened bread is known as "poor bread" (*Devarim* 16:3), indicating that it is somewhat difficult and unpleasant to eat (see *Tosafos* to *Zevachim* 75b).

הַלְלוּ אֶת יהוה, כָּל גּוֹיִם, שַׁבְּחוּהוּ כָּל הָאֻמִּים.
כִּי גָבַר עָלֵינוּ חַסְדּוֹ, וֶאֱמֶת יהוה לְעוֹלָם,
הַלְלוּיָהּ.

Returning to the three verses of *Hallel* that began this discussion, the Netziv explained that the psalmist refers to this dual nature of the thanksgiving offering — the sacrifice itself and the festive meal that followed, where the glory of God was proclaimed. "To You I will sacrifice thanksgiving offerings" — refers to the sacrifice itself; "and the Name of Hashem will I invoke" — upon the consumption, by myself and a large group of guests, of the sacrificial meat and breads. "My vows to Hashem will I pay" — that is, I will offer up the sacrifice that I had undertaken to bring in celebration of God's salvation; "in the presence, now, of His entire people" — the subsequent festive meal will take place in the presence of the largest possible assembly of people. It is not the fulfillment of the vow that will be carried out in public, for that would be more appropriately accomplished in a humble, private setting. Rather, it is the proclamation of God's grace and beneficence that will, most befittingly, be declared in as public a manner as possible. The next verse continues, "In the courtyards of the House of Hashem" — the location where the sacrifice is carried out; "in your midst, O Yerushalayim" — the area where the festive meal is held, for sacrificial meat (קָדָשִׁים קַלִּים) could be eaten anywhere within the city walls of Jerusalem, and holding the celebration in the *midst* of the city would be an opportunity to maximize the publicizing of the events of salvation being celebrated by the thanksgiving offering.

הַלְלוּ אֶת ה׳, כָּל גּוֹיִם . . . כִּי גָבַר עָלֵינוּ חַסְדּוֹ
*Praise Hashem, all nations. . . for
His kindness has overwhelmed us,*

Protecting the Nations From Themselves

The obvious question on this verse is posed already in the Talmud (*Pesachim* 118b): Why should the nations of the world praise God because His mercy has overwhelmed *us*, the Jewish people? It is *we* who should be called upon to sing His praises for the benevolence He has shown us — not the other nations of the world!

The **Chafetz Chaim** suggested an answer to this question, based on the following parable:

There was once a baron who had a Jewish manager who oversaw all his business affairs. He would sell the baron's produce from his landholdings for the best possible profit, all for the benefit of the baron. The Jew served the nobleman faithfully and selflessly, and the latter knew it. This did not, however, prevent the baron's jealous secretary from continuously trying to ruin the Jew's reputation by heaping upon him all sorts of accusations — all to no avail.

One day the baron had to travel to a distant land and he placed all responsibility

> Praise Hashem, all nations; extol Him, all the states! For His kindness has overwhelmed us, and the truth of Hashem is eternal, Halleluyah!

for his affairs in the hands of his evil secretary. The man lost no time in framing his Jewish nemesis, accused him of charging more for the wheat than he claimed and pocketing the difference. He had finally "exposed" the untrustworthiness of the Jew for all to see. The baron was mistaken by putting so much trust in him all these years! The Jewish manager protested, pointing out his complete innocence, but the secretary was not interested in hearing any "excuses." He decided to fine the manager 1000 golden pieces and to have him flogged with 200 lashes.

The secretary brought the "criminal" to the baron's court and told the law-enforcement officials of the sentence that he had decreed for the Jewish manager. But he was quite surprised at the reaction he experienced there!

"The baron has given orders that no one should be punished with more than 20 lashes or with more than 100 gold pieces, without his express consent!"

The secretary was bitterly disappointed, but he knew he had to accept the baron's rules. "All right, then," he responded begrudgingly. "Then give him 20 lashes meanwhile, and fine him 100 gold pieces. When the baron returns, this cheater will get the rest of his punishment!"

The punishments were carried out in accordance with the baron's limitations.

Some time later the baron returned. The secretary approached him and gave him a detailed account of all that had transpired in his absence. Among other things, he complained to the baron that he did not think it was proper for him to issue a ruling limiting the administration of corporal and monetary punishments in his absence. This hampered the handling of criminal offenses while the baron was away and was likely to lead to lawlessness, etc.

"How did you happen to hear about my rule of limitation of punishments?" the baron asked the secretary.

"Oh, it was when that Jewish manager was caught embezzling funds from your coffers. I was only able to have him flogged twenty times, and I could fine him only 100 gold pieces!"

The nobleman was take aback. How could his trusted manager, upon whom he had relied all these years, suddenly betray him? He called the Jew in and asked him to state his side of the story.

"The entire report is a fabrication, sir," he told him. "I can prove to you that I did not take one penny from your profits that was not coming to me!" The manager thereupon took out all his meticulously kept records and brought witnesses to corroborate his story. The nobleman was convinced of his innocence, and redirected his fury against his secretary, who had himself been dishonest.

"I decree," he pronounced, "that you yourself should be flogged exactly

[243]   THE HAGGADAH OF THE ROSHEI YESHIVAH

according to the number of lashes that you inflicted upon my innocent manager, and that you return the man's 100 gold pieces to him immediately."

The secretary motioned that he wanted to say something at that point.

"Yes, what is it?" asked the baron impatiently.

"I just want to thank you for issuing an order to the law-enforcement officers limiting the number of lashes permitted in your absence!"

Suddenly, when the tables were turned, the secretary thought that the baron's decree of limitation of punishment was a good idea!

The lesson of the parable is that ever since our exile from our land we have suffered at the hands of tormentors and enemies of all sorts. But even though God sometimes hides His countenance from us and allows these episodes of persecution to occur, eventually He steps in and prevents our enemies from totally annihilating us. And in the future, when God sees fit to redeem His people and usher in the Messianic age, there will come a time when "He will take vengeance against the nations and chastise the nationalities" (*Tehillim* 149:7). Each nation will be made to pay for every act of persecution that it has perpetrated against the Jewish people. At that point, they will suddenly feel that it was a good thing that God did not allow them to carry out their plans of destruction for the Jews to the fullest extent. The very same foiling of their plots of annihilation which so frustrated them at the time of its implementation will suddenly be a cause of great relief to them. They will then praise Hashem for having protected the Jews with His great mercy, for by doing so He brought about the mitigation of their own punishment as well.

On another occasion the **Chafetz Chaim** related a story in which another answer to the question posed above emerges.

The story involved Count Potocki, the famous nobleman who converted to Judaism in the time of the Vilna Gaon, and was condemned to death because of it.

One day the count, who had had to go into hiding far away from his home town in order to evade the authorities, was sitting in a *beis midrash* learning, when the son of the local tailor came in and began to speak with his friends in a foul manner, behaving in a way that was totally inappropriate to the sanctity of the place. The count muttered a quote from the Talmud, "If a person can show such impudence and disrespect, he must be a *mamzer*!" (*Kiddushin* 70a). The boy heard the comment and repeated it to his father. The tailor was furious and decided that he would inform on the count to the authorities. The count was arrested and sentenced to be burned at the stake. (It is said that the Vilna Gaon offered to have the count miraculously freed through a kabbalistic incantation, but the count, like Rabbi Akiva many centuries earlier, was genuinely pleased that he had the opportunity to perform the great mitzvah of dying for God's Name.)

When the count was brought out to be executed the tailor who had caused him to be arrested came before him, weeping in remorse and begging forgiveness for his actions. He pleaded with the count not to hold his behavior against him when he would arrive in the "World of Truth."

The count turned to the tailor and pronounced our verse: "Praise Hashem, all nations... for His kindness has overwhelmed us." He then posed the question that was noted above: Why should the *other nations* thank God for His benevolent treatment of the Jews? The count explained with a parable:

One time a very young prince, the son of the king, was playing with his friend in the sandbox. The prince built himself a splendid castle in the sand, and his friend decided, out of sheer meanness, to go up to the castle and kick it with all his might, totally destroying it in the process. The prince was completely devastated and ran home crying.

The years passed, and eventually the little prince from the sandbox was himself crowned king. At the coronation celebration, the new king looked up and saw someone he did not recognize standing before him. "Who are you?" he asked.

"I am your childhood friend," the man answered. "I came to ask your forgiveness for breaking your marvelous castle, and to beg you not to hold it against me now that you have risen to power!"

The king laughed. "Look around you," he told his friend. "Now I live in a *real* castle. I have hundreds of rooms to use, unlimited money at my disposal, and a staff of hundreds of servants waiting on me hand and foot. Everywhere I go people bow down to me and hail me. How could I possibly attach any significance whatsoever to a childhood spat in a sandbox at this point in my life?!"

Similarly, the count explained, the day will come when the Jews will return to their land and once again be granted God's grace and favored status. At that time, the nations of the world will become nervous and anxious over their own fates. Perhaps now that the Jews had risen to power they would retaliate for all the persecution that they had faced at the hands of the other nations! But the extent of God's mercy and grace toward us will be so great that it will be unimaginable for us to attach any significance to such "petty" matters as persecutions, pogroms, inquisitions, etc. For this the nations of the world will indeed be grateful!

"And now," the count concluded, "I am about to go to the World to Come. Our Sages tell us that a martyr who is killed for the sake of God's Name is awarded a special status in heaven, which no one else, no matter how righteous, can share. With such incomparable sublime honor and spiritual bliss, do you think I could possibly attach any importance to the injustice that you have done to me?"

The Chafetz Chaim used to conclude the story by mentioning that although the count himself forgave the tailor with a full heart, God Himself did not do so. As the Sages (*Berachos* 19a) tell us, God avenges the honor of Torah scholars. It happened that all the descendants of that tailor who studied the Torah died young, so that the merit of Torah study would not avail that family, as a punishment for having cut short the Torah study of the righteous convert Potocki.

[245]   THE HAGGADAH OF THE ROSHEI YESHIVAH

הוֹדוּ לַיהוה כִּי טוֹב,   כִּי לְעוֹלָם חַסְדּוֹ.
יֹאמַר נָא יִשְׂרָאֵל,   כִּי לְעוֹלָם חַסְדּוֹ.
יֹאמְרוּ נָא בֵית אַהֲרֹן,   כִּי לְעוֹלָם חַסְדּוֹ.
יֹאמְרוּ נָא יִרְאֵי יהוה,   כִּי לְעוֹלָם חַסְדּוֹ.

מִן הַמֵּצַר קָרָאתִי יָּהּ, עָנָנִי בַמֶּרְחָב יָהּ. יהוה לִי לֹא אִירָא, מַה יַּעֲשֶׂה לִי אָדָם. יהוה לִי בְּעֹזְרָי, וַאֲנִי אֶרְאֶה בְשֹׂנְאָי. טוֹב לַחֲסוֹת בַּיהוה, מִבְּטֹחַ בָּאָדָם. טוֹב לַחֲסוֹת בַּיהוה, מִבְּטֹחַ בִּנְדִיבִים. כָּל גּוֹיִם סְבָבוּנִי, בְּשֵׁם יהוה כִּי אֲמִילַם. סַבּוּנִי גַם סְבָבוּנִי, בְּשֵׁם יהוה כִּי אֲמִילַם. סַבּוּנִי כִדְבֹרִים דֹּעֲכוּ כְּאֵשׁ קוֹצִים, בְּשֵׁם יהוה כִּי אֲמִילַם. דָּחֹה דְחִיתַנִי לִנְפֹּל, וַיהוה עֲזָרָנִי. עָזִּי וְזִמְרָת יָהּ, וַיְהִי לִי לִישׁוּעָה. קוֹל רִנָּה וִישׁוּעָה, בְּאָהֳלֵי צַדִּיקִים, יְמִין יהוה עֹשָׂה חָיִל. יְמִין יהוה רוֹמֵמָה, יְמִין יהוה עֹשָׂה חָיִל. לֹא אָמוּת כִּי אֶחְיֶה, וַאֲסַפֵּר מַעֲשֵׂי יָהּ. יַסֹּר יִסְּרַנִי יָּהּ, וְלַמָּוֶת לֹא נְתָנָנִי.

יַסֹּר יִסְּרַנִי יָּהּ, וְלַמָּוֶת לֹא נְתָנָנִי
God chastised me exceedingly, but He did not let me die.

Warnings From Above

One of the prophecies proclaimed concerning the present period of history — the period of "the footsteps of the Messiah" — wrote **R' Elchanan Wasserman,** is the phenomenon that "I will cause the Egyptians to contend with their [fellow] Egyptians; everyone will fight against his brother and his neighbor — one city against the other city and one province against the other province" (*Isaiah* 19:2). We can see with our own eyes how the world has become like a vast jungle, with each nation waiting anxiously to devour the next. Even within each nation there are numerous mutually hostile parties, and within each party belligerent factions — all united in their disdain and hostility towards the Jews. [R' Elchanan wrote these words in the 1930's - ed.] The prophet warns us, "I said, 'Only fear Me and accept rebuke' " (*Tzefaniah* 3:7) — when God sends ominous signs against us it is to humble our hearts and turn them to our heavenly Father. This recognition that we are being chastised for our failings is itself enough to neutralize the evil decree against us. This is what the Sages meant when they explained the verse, "It happened that when Moshe raised his hand Israel prevailed and when he put down his hand Amalek prevailed" (*Shemos* 17:11), to mean, "When Israel would look upward and subjugate their hearts to their Father in Heaven they would prevail." When we look toward God and recognize Him as the

Give thanks to Hashem for He is good;
His kindness endures forever!
Let Israel say: His kindness endures forever!
Let the House of Aharon say:
His kindness endures forever!
Let those who fear Hashem say:
His kindness endures forever!

From the straits did I call to God; God answered me with expansiveness. Hashem is for me, I have no fear; how can man affect me? Hashem is for me through my helpers; therefore I can face my foes. It is better to take refuge in Hashem than to rely on man. It is better to take refuge in Hashem than to rely on princes. All the nations surround me; but in the Name of Hashem I cut them down! They encircle me; they surround me; but in the Name of Hashem I cut them down! They encircle me like bees, but they are extinguished as a fire does thorns; in the Name of Hashem I cut them down! You pushed me hard that I might fall, but Hashem assisted me. My strength and song is God. He became my salvation. The sound of rejoicing and salvation is in the tents of the righteous: "The right hand of Hashem does valiantly! The right hand of Hashem is raised triumphantly! The right hand of Hashem does valiantly!" I shall not die! But I shall live and relate the deeds of God. God chastened me exceedingly but He did not let me die.

Master of our destiny we are assured that we will survive and prevail. But if, on the other hand, we ignore God's signals and dismiss these momentous events as insignificant "mere coincidence," the Torah warns us, "If you go with Me in casualness, I shall also go with you in casualness." That is, "If you regard life as a series of casual coincidences, I too will abandon you to circumstance." It is thus of the utmost importance for us to read and understand the signs that God has sent us.

In truth, mere recognition of God's role in the chaotic upheavals that are taking place in the world is enough only to prevent the situation from deteriorating further. It is insufficient, however, to avert the decree that threatens us. This can be done only through intensifying our commitment to the study of Torah and to doing acts of kindness, as the Sages teach: "What can a person do in order to avoid the 'pains of the advent of the Messiah'? He should engage in Torah study and acts of kindness" (*Sanhedrin* 98b). This is only logical, for we cannot expect God to deal with us with mercy if we do not do so with our own fellow men.

פִּתְחוּ לִי שַׁעֲרֵי צֶדֶק, אָבֹא בָם אוֹדֶה יָהּ. זֶה הַשַּׁעַר לַיהוה, צַדִּיקִים יָבֹאוּ בוֹ. אוֹדְךָ כִּי עֲנִיתָנִי, וַתְּהִי לִי לִישׁוּעָה. אוֹדְךָ כִּי עֲנִיתָנִי, וַתְּהִי לִי לִישׁוּעָה. אֶבֶן מָאֲסוּ הַבּוֹנִים, הָיְתָה לְרֹאשׁ פִּנָּה. אֶבֶן מָאֲסוּ הַבּוֹנִים, הָיְתָה לְרֹאשׁ פִּנָּה. מֵאֵת יהוה הָיְתָה זֹּאת, הִיא נִפְלָאת בְּעֵינֵינוּ. מֵאֵת יהוה הָיְתָה זֹּאת, הִיא נִפְלָאת בְּעֵינֵינוּ. זֶה הַיּוֹם עָשָׂה יהוה, נָגִילָה וְנִשְׂמְחָה בוֹ. זֶה הַיּוֹם עָשָׂה יהוה, נָגִילָה וְנִשְׂמְחָה בוֹ.

אָנָּא יהוה הוֹשִׁיעָה נָּא.

אָנָּא יהוה הוֹשִׁיעָה נָּא.

אָנָּא יהוה הַצְלִיחָה נָּא.

אָנָּא יהוה הַצְלִיחָה נָּא.

בָּרוּךְ הַבָּא בְּשֵׁם יהוה, בֵּרַכְנוּכֶם מִבֵּית יהוה. בָּרוּךְ הַבָּא בְּשֵׁם יהוה, בֵּרַכְנוּכֶם מִבֵּית יהוה. אֵל יהוה וַיָּאֶר לָנוּ, אִסְרוּ חַג בַּעֲבֹתִים, עַד קַרְנוֹת הַמִּזְבֵּחַ. אֵל יהוה וַיָּאֶר לָנוּ, אִסְרוּ חַג בַּעֲבֹתִים, עַד קַרְנוֹת הַמִּזְבֵּחַ. אֵלִי אַתָּה וְאוֹדֶךָּ,

---

אוֹדְךָ כִּי עֲנִיתָנִי, וַתְּהִי לִי לִישׁוּעָה
I thank You for You answered me and became my salvation!

Necessary Surgery Many commentators interpret the word עֲנִיתָנִי in its other meaning of *You have afflicted me,* and translate the verse: "I thank You, for You have afflicted me, and You have become my salvation." The psalmist has just said, "God chastened me exceedingly, but He did not let me die." Then he declares, "Open for me the gates of righteousness; I will enter them and thank God." In our verse he clarifies what it is that he wishes to express his thanks for — not only for the salvation (*He did not let me die*), but also for the affliction itself: "I thank You for You have afflicted me."

We must not, wrote **R' Zalman Sorotzkin,** compare episodes of misfortune, to the doctor who tells a prospective patient that he wishes to break his foot and then heal it, to prove to him what a good physician he is (*Mo'ed Katan* 21b). Any sane

Open for me the gates of righteousness, I will enter them and thank God. This is the gate of Hashem; the righteous shall enter through it. I thank You for You answered me and became my salvation! I thank You for You answered me and became my salvation! The stone which the builders despised has become the cornerstone! The stone which the builders despised has become the cornerstone! This emanated from Hashem; it is wondrous in our eyes! This emanated from Hashem; it is wondrous in our eyes! This is the day Hashem has made; we will rejoice and be glad in Him! This is the day Hashem has made; we will rejoice and be glad in Him!

O, Hashem, please save us!
O, Hashem, please save us!
O, Hashem, please make us prosper!
O, Hashem, please make us prosper!

Blessed is he who comes in the Name of Hashem; we bless you from the House of Hashem. Blessed is he who comes in the Name of Hashem; we bless you from the House of Hashem. Hashem is God and He illuminated for us; bind the festival offering with cords to the corners of the Altar. Hashem is God and He illuminated for us; bind the festival offering with cords to the corners of the Altar. You are my God, and I shall thank You;

---

person would refuse the doctor's "kind" offer to perform such a demonstration. God controls all the events of our lives; why should we thank Him for extricating us from affliction when He could have prevented the affliction from coming upon us in the first place?! The answer to this question is that setbacks and episodes of misfortune, unpleasant though they may be to experience, are in fact good for the soul. They provide man's personality with a crucial injection of the critical elements of humility and awareness of one's limitations, without which he is incapable of achieving spirituality. Continuing the analogy to the doctor, we should compare it to a case where a surgeon amputates a diseased limb. The doctor is paid a large sum for his services and is likely to be rewarded as well with copious expressions of thanks on the part of his patient. When we undergo suffering we must remember that this, too, is ultimately for our own good, although it is upsetting when we experience it. It is for this reason that the psalmist in this verse expresses his thanks to God for both the affliction and the salvation from it.

אֱלֹהַי אֲרוֹמְמֶךָּ. אֵלִי אַתָּה וְאוֹדֶךָּ, אֱלֹהַי אֲרוֹמְמֶךָּ.
הוֹדוּ לַיהוה כִּי טוֹב, כִּי לְעוֹלָם חַסְדּוֹ. הוֹדוּ לַיהוה
כִּי טוֹב, כִּי לְעוֹלָם חַסְדּוֹ.

יְהַלְלוּךָ יהוה אֱלֹהֵינוּ כָּל מַעֲשֶׂיךָ, וַחֲסִידֶיךָ
צַדִּיקִים עוֹשֵׂי רְצוֹנֶךָ, וְכָל עַמְּךָ בֵּית
יִשְׂרָאֵל בְּרִנָּה יוֹדוּ וִיבָרְכוּ וִישַׁבְּחוּ וִיפָאֲרוּ וִירוֹמְמוּ
וְיַעֲרִיצוּ וְיַקְדִּישׁוּ וְיַמְלִיכוּ אֶת שִׁמְךָ מַלְכֵּנוּ, כִּי לְךָ
טוֹב לְהוֹדוֹת וּלְשִׁמְךָ נָאֶה לְזַמֵּר, כִּי מֵעוֹלָם וְעַד
עוֹלָם אַתָּה אֵל.

הוֹדוּ לַיהוה כִּי טוֹב   כִּי לְעוֹלָם חַסְדּוֹ.

הוֹדוּ לַה' כִּי טוֹב כִּי לְעוֹלָם חַסְדּוֹ
Give thanks to Hashem, for He is good;
His kindness endures forever.

The Great Dance — By saying "His kindness endures *forever*," the **Netziv** wrote, the psalmist means to convey the idea that even when it appears to us, with our limited mortal capacities, that God is being overly harsh, this is in fact a misconception, for He is *always* merciful, although often it is in some way that is unapparent to us. Even when tragedy or punishment is meted out it is for some ultimate good purpose.

The Netziv used this concept to explain an enigmatic passage in the Talmud (*Ta'anis* 31a):

> In the End of Days, God is going to arrange a circular dance for the righteous, who will point at Him with their fingers, as it says, "And they will say (or, *they said*) on that day, 'Behold, this is our God, to whom we hoped that He would save us. This is Hashem, to Whom we hoped; we will rejoice and be happy in His salvation.'"

The entire passage is shrouded in mystery. What is the point of this circular dance to be held in the End of Days? Can't the righteous behold God without dancing around Him? Furthermore, it is a fundamental principle of Judaism that God cannot be seen. The righteous' glimpse of God must therefore be understood as a metaphor — but a metaphor for what? Finally, the verse cited is difficult in that the second part of the verse (*Behold, this is our God, to Whom we hoped...*) seems to be a virtually exact duplicate of the first half (*This is Hashem, to Whom we hoped...*).

The Netziv explained the Talmudic excerpt as follows. In a circular dance each participant passes round about the center of the circle. At each stage of the dance he is exposed to a different angle of whatever object or person is in the center. In

my God, and I shall exalt You. You are my God, and I shall thank You; my God, and I shall exalt You. Give thanks to Hashem, for He is good; His kindness endures forever. Give thanks to Hashem, for He is good; His kindness endures forever!

They shall praise You, Hashem our God, for all Your works, along with Your pious followers, the righteous, who do Your will, and Your entire people, the House of Israel, with joy will thank, bless, praise, glorify, exalt, revere, sanctify, and coronate Your Name, our King! For to You it is fitting to give thanks, and unto Your Name it is proper to sing praises, for from eternity to eternity You are God.

Give thanks to Hashem, for He is good;
His kindness endures forever!

---

the dance of the End of Days, the Talmud tells us, God Himself will be at the center. The righteous who dance around in the circle will "see" God at many different angles. They will begin by "seeing" His back, which is a metaphorical reference to the fact that they will view the events of history without understanding how the hand of God was involved in those events; it will appear to them as if He was detached and unconcerned, as if He had "turned His back" on His people. But as the dance progresses they will gradually come to "see" God's face, meaning that they will come to the realization that in fact God had clearly been the driving force behind these incidents, as they will understand why these actions were undertaken with a specific, beneficial purpose in mind. He had never "turned His back" after all, they will realize; He was involved all along! The dance will then continue as the righteous consider yet another event in history, from which they begin by perceiving God's back only; this perception too will change as the circle comes around to the other side and the participants begin to "see" God's face again.

The verse adduced by the Talmud to support its assertion proves the point admirably. "They *said* on that day, 'Behold, this is our God, to whom we hoped that He would save us.' " *On that day,* when tragedy and misfortune beset the Jewish people, we called out in prayer to "our God" (אֱלֹהֵינוּ, the Name of God used to denote His Attribute of Strict Justice), hoping that "He would save us." In the future, however, when the righteous are granted the ability to clearly perceive God's role in history, they will exclaim, "This is *Hashem* (the Name of God used to denote His Attribute of Mercy), to Whom we hoped; we will rejoice and be happy in His salvation." They will realize that in fact all along He was the God of Mercy, and the misfortunes that befell us, which we perceived as unfair judgments, were in fact turned in the long run into "salvation."

הוֹדוּ לֵאלֹהֵי הָאֱלֹהִים	כִּי לְעוֹלָם חַסְדּוֹ.
הוֹדוּ לַאֲדֹנֵי הָאֲדֹנִים	כִּי לְעוֹלָם חַסְדּוֹ.
לְעֹשֵׂה נִפְלָאוֹת גְּדֹלוֹת לְבַדּוֹ	כִּי לְעוֹלָם חַסְדּוֹ.
לְעֹשֵׂה הַשָּׁמַיִם בִּתְבוּנָה	כִּי לְעוֹלָם חַסְדּוֹ.
לְרֹקַע הָאָרֶץ עַל הַמָּיִם	כִּי לְעוֹלָם חַסְדּוֹ.
לְעֹשֵׂה אוֹרִים גְּדֹלִים	כִּי לְעוֹלָם חַסְדּוֹ.

לְעֹשֵׂה נִפְלָאוֹת גְּדֹלוֹת לְבַדּוֹ כִּי לְעוֹלָם חַסְדּוֹ
[Give thanks] to Him Who alone does great wonders; His kindness endures forever.

Everyday Miracles   When we read this verse that speaks of the many great wonders that God performs, we begin to picture in our minds the ten plagues, the splitting of the Reed Sea and the Jordan, the manna, and other such miracles. But if this would be the intention of the psalmist, **R' Zalman Sorotzkin** noted, he would have placed this verse later in the psalm, in the section praising God for striking the Egyptian firstborn, for smiting Sichon and Og, for splitting the Sea, etc. Instead, he placed the verse here, as a prelude to the first half of the psalm, which deals with giving thanks to God for Creation — "to the One Who made the Heaven... Who stretched out the earth... Who makes the great luminaries... the sun... and the moon, etc."

We are accustomed to thinking of the occasion when God caused the sun to stand still for Yehoshua as a major miracle, but when we see the sun rise and set day after day and the seasons unfold year after year, we are unimpressed. If we would see an inanimate object, such as a rock, get up and walk across the room without any apparent source of motion we would be utterly astounded. Yet the sun and the other celestial bodies are also inanimate objects, and they continue to move in their set paths without interruption and without variation, allowing life on earth to go on as normal. The psalmist, in this verse, calls upon us to arouse ourselves from our tendency to apathetically ignore the "miracles that are with us every day and the wonders that are present all the time, evening, morning, and afternoon" (*Shemoneh Esrei* prayer), and to praise God even — or perhaps *especially* — for these constant miracles.

לְעֹשֵׂה אוֹרִים גְּדֹלִים כִּי לְעוֹלָם חַסְדּוֹ
[Give thanks] to Him Who makes great luminaries; His kindness endures forever!

A Missed Opportunity   It is noteworthy that the present tense ("Who *makes*") is employed in this verse, and not, as might be expected, the past tense. In the morning liturgy this point is adduced as a proof for the assertion that God "renews the process of Creation each day, constantly." We do not

> Give thanks to the God of gods;
> > His kindness endures forever!
> Give thanks to the Master of masters;
> > His kindness endures forever!
> To Him Who alone does great wonders;
> > His kindness endures forever!
> To Him Who makes the heaven with understanding;
> > His kindness endures forever!
> To Him Who stretched out the earth over the waters;
> > His kindness endures forever!
> To Him Who makes great luminaries;
> > His kindness endures forever!

believe that God created the Universe and provided it with basic natural laws, through which its existence and functioning automatically ensue; rather, the continuous operation of the Universe is due to an active renewal of God's will that the Universe should continue to exist each day and each moment. The fact that there are scientific laws that seem to predetermine natural events and cycles is only because God happens to want this situation to exist. "If God would remove His input from all the elements of Creation for even one moment," the *Nefesh Hachayim* writes, "everything in the world would immediately revert to the primeval state of nothingness and void (תֹּהוּ וָבֹהוּ)."

R' Shneur Kotler quoted the Alter of Slobodka as saying that man, too, must emulate God in this respect. For every accomplishment and deed that a person achieves, he must not rest on his laurels and become complacent with his lot in life. Rather, he must continue to strive, never resting for a second, perfecting and adding on to previous achievements. A person's spiritual state is a function of his deeds, and if one refrains from producing virtuous deeds, even for a moment, this affects his overall spiritual status.

R' Shneur mentioned that his father (R' Aharon Kotler) applied this concept to a passage in the Talmud (*Chagigah* 9b): " 'A misdeed that one cannot correct' (*Koheles* 1:15) — This applies to someone who missed saying *Shema* or missed his prayers." It would seem to us that if someone lived for eighty years and forgot one prayer or one *Shema* that this would not be such a calamity in the overall view of events of that man's life. Yet the Talmud calls it an irrevocable lapse. R' Aharon explained that just as the world, although it is one interlinked unit, consists of many individual parts, so too man's life, in addition to being a single entity, is composed of thousands and millions of individual, independent moments. If one of those moments is wasted it can never be regained, no matter how efficiently other moments might be spent. If one opportunity to accept upon oneself the yoke of Heaven by saying *Shema* is missed, this opportunity can never be recovered, and this failing remains forever.

R' Aharon explained a passage in the *Rambam* (*Hil. Talmud Torah* 3:13) in a

אֶת הַשֶּׁמֶשׁ לְמֶמְשֶׁלֶת בַּיּוֹם כִּי לְעוֹלָם חַסְדּוֹ.	
אֶת הַיָּרֵחַ וְכוֹכָבִים לְמֶמְשְׁלוֹת בַּלָּיְלָה	כִּי לְעוֹלָם חַסְדּוֹ.
לְמַכֵּה מִצְרַיִם בִּבְכוֹרֵיהֶם	כִּי לְעוֹלָם חַסְדּוֹ.
וַיּוֹצֵא יִשְׂרָאֵל מִתּוֹכָם	כִּי לְעוֹלָם חַסְדּוֹ.
בְּיָד חֲזָקָה וּבִזְרוֹעַ נְטוּיָה	כִּי לְעוֹלָם חַסְדּוֹ.
לְגֹזֵר יַם סוּף לִגְזָרִים	כִּי לְעוֹלָם חַסְדּוֹ.
וְהֶעֱבִיר יִשְׂרָאֵל בְּתוֹכוֹ	כִּי לְעוֹלָם חַסְדּוֹ.
וְנִעֵר פַּרְעֹה וְחֵילוֹ בְיַם סוּף	כִּי לְעוֹלָם חַסְדּוֹ.
לְמוֹלִיךְ עַמּוֹ בַּמִּדְבָּר	כִּי לְעוֹלָם חַסְדּוֹ.
לְמַכֵּה מְלָכִים גְּדֹלִים	כִּי לְעוֹלָם חַסְדּוֹ.
וַיַּהֲרֹג מְלָכִים אַדִּירִים	כִּי לְעוֹלָם חַסְדּוֹ.
לְסִיחוֹן מֶלֶךְ הָאֱמֹרִי	כִּי לְעוֹלָם חַסְדּוֹ.
וּלְעוֹג מֶלֶךְ הַבָּשָׁן	כִּי לְעוֹלָם חַסְדּוֹ.

similar manner: "Although it is a mitzvah to study the Torah by day and by night (equally), a person attains most of his wisdom at nights. Therefore if someone desires to achieve the 'crown of the Torah' he must be careful all of his nights, and should not lose even one of them to sleep, eating and drinking, idle conversation, etc." The Rambam does not suffice with writing that a person must devote his nights to the study of Torah; he insists that *even one night* must not be wasted. This is because, as explained above, each night of a person's life is an independent unit; if this opportunity for gaining Torah knowledge is squandered it is an irrevocable loss.

וְנִעֵר פַּרְעֹה וְחֵילוֹ בְיַם סוּף
And threw Pharaoh and his army into the Sea of Reeds.

To Your Word Be True   The punishment of the Egyptians at the Reed Sea was an example of how God punishes people in a manner which corresponds in some way to the sin committed (מִדָּה כְּנֶגֶד מִדָּה), **R' Zalman Sorotzkin** commented. Pharaoh had originally opened up his land to the sons of Yaakov, inviting them to come and settle in his land, but over the years the Egyptians gradually changed their minds in their attitude toward these foreigners in their midst, and they forced the Jews to remain in their country, submitting them to forced labor, as if they were prisoners. In a similar manner the Sea, which had opened itself up and allowed the Egyptians to enter into it, suddenly "changed its

The sun for the reign of the day;
> His kindness endures forever!

The moon and the stars for the reign of the night;
> His kindness endures forever!

To Him Who smote Egypt through their firstborn;
> His kindness endures forever!

And took Israel out from their midst;
> His kindness endures forever!

With strong hand and outstretched arm;
> His kindness endures forever!

To Him Who divided the Sea of Reeds into parts;
> His kindness endures forever!

And caused Israel to pass through it;
> His kindness endures forever!

And threw Pharaoh and his army into the Sea of Reeds;
> His kindness endures forever!

To Him Who led His people through the wilderness;
> His kindness endures forever!

To Him Who smote great kings;
> His kindness endures forever!

And slew mighty kings;
> His kindness endures forever!

Sichon, king of the Emorites;
> His kindness endures forever!

And Og, king of Bashan;
> His kindness endures forever!

---

mind" — וַיָּשָׁב הַיָּם (*Shemos* 14:27), *the sea turned back* (the word וַיָּשָׁב can also mean *to have a change of heart*) — and closed in on its "guests," trapping them in its midst. This punishment corresponded also to the sudden change of heart that Pharaoh and the Egyptians had, when they said, "What is this that we have done, that we have sent away Israel from serving us!"

It is perhaps for this reason, R' Zalman suggested, that when someone reneges on a monetary agreement after money has already been paid to clinch the deal, the Talmud tells us that although he is technically within his rights to do so, he is subject to a curse: "May He who punished . . . the Egyptians at the Reed Sea punish also people who do not keep their word!" (*Bava Metzia* 48a). The example of the Egyptians' fate at the Reed Sea is used because their punishment was a reflection of this very shortcoming — the failure to stand by one's word and not to uphold the terms of an agreement.

וְנָתַן אַרְצָם לְנַחֲלָה	כִּי לְעוֹלָם חַסְדּוֹ.
נַחֲלָה לְיִשְׂרָאֵל עַבְדּוֹ	כִּי לְעוֹלָם חַסְדּוֹ.
שֶׁבְּשִׁפְלֵנוּ זָכַר לָנוּ	כִּי לְעוֹלָם חַסְדּוֹ.
וַיִּפְרְקֵנוּ מִצָּרֵינוּ	כִּי לְעוֹלָם חַסְדּוֹ.
נֹתֵן לֶחֶם לְכָל בָּשָׂר	כִּי לְעוֹלָם חַסְדּוֹ.
הוֹדוּ לְאֵל הַשָּׁמָיִם	כִּי לְעוֹלָם חַסְדּוֹ.

נִשְׁמַת כָּל חַי תְּבָרֵךְ אֶת שִׁמְךָ יהוה אֱלֹהֵינוּ וְרוּחַ כָּל בָּשָׂר תְּפָאֵר וּתְרוֹמֵם זִכְרְךָ מַלְכֵּנוּ תָּמִיד. מִן הָעוֹלָם וְעַד הָעוֹלָם אַתָּה אֵל וּמִבַּלְעָדֶיךָ אֵין לָנוּ מֶלֶךְ גּוֹאֵל וּמוֹשִׁיעַ פּוֹדֶה וּמַצִּיל וּמְפַרְנֵס וּמְרַחֵם בְּכָל עֵת צָרָה וְצוּקָה. אֵין לָנוּ מֶלֶךְ אֶלָּא אָתָּה. אֱלֹהֵי הָרִאשׁוֹנִים וְהָאַחֲרוֹנִים אֱלוֹהַּ כָּל בְּרִיּוֹת אֲדוֹן כָּל תּוֹלָדוֹת

וְנָתַן אַרְצָם לְנַחֲלָה כִּי לְעוֹלָם חַסְדּוֹ. נַחֲלָה לְיִשְׂרָאֵל עַבְדּוֹ כִּי לְעוֹלָם חַסְדּוֹ
And (He) gave their land as an inheritance; His kindness endures forever.
An inheritance to Israel His servant; His kindness endures forever.

Two Acts of Kindness — The sentence appears to be disjointed. It would have been much smoother to have said, "He gave their land as an inheritance to Israel." Why, asked **R' Zalman Sorotzkin,** is the statement split into two?

R' Zalman proposed the following explanation. After the killing of Sichon, king of the Emorites, and Og, the king of Bashan, there was still the danger that the native Emorites, "whose height was like the height of cedars, and who were as mighty as oaks" (*Amos* 2:9), would recoup and appoint a new king over themselves, who would challenge Israel again. Thus, it was an act of kindness that God did for us when "He gave their land (of the Emorites) as an inheritance" — to someone, to anyone — which prevented the reemergence of the local populace as a serious threat to Israel. In addition to this, moreover, it was a further, separate act of kindness that that "someone" to whom the Emorites were handed over happened to be Israel, which certainly eliminated the possibility of these people posing a threat to them anymore in the future.

אֱלוֹהַּ כָּל בְּרִיּוֹת אֲדוֹן כָּל תּוֹלָדוֹת
God of all human beings, Master of all generations,

The Full Picture — One time a Jew who was in great distress came before the **Chafetz Chaim** to pour his heart out before him and seek his comfort. His business had failed, his wife had taken ill, and his children had all turned their backs on him. He complained to the Chafetz Chaim, "I am a believing

And gave their land as an inheritance;
> His kindness endures forever!

An inheritance to Israel His servant;
> His kindness endures forever!

Who remembered us in our lowliness;
> His kindness endures forever!

And released us from our foes;
> His kindness endures forever!

He gives food to all living creatures;
> His kindness endures forever!

Give thanks to God of heaven;
> His kindness endures forever!

The soul of every living being shall bless Your Name, HASHEM our God; the spirit of all flesh shall always glorify and exalt Your remembrance, our King. From eternity to eternity, You are God, and other than You we have no king, redeemer or savior. Liberator, Rescuer, Sustainer, and Merciful One in every time of trouble, and anguish, we have no king but You — God of the first and of the last, God of all human beings, Master of all generations,

---

Jew, Rebbe, and I accepts God's decrees with love and faith. But when I look at my neighbor — who violates the Sabbath, never goes to the synagogue except on Yom Kippur, and desecrates all that is holy — and see how successful he is and how happy and healthy his family is, I sometimes wonder: Where is justice? It just doesn't seem fair!"

The Chafetz Chaim tried to calm the man down. "If you seek a blessing from me that you should experience better times, my blessing is hereby given to you. But if it is to complain about the way God runs His world that you seek, let me tell you a story:

"One time there was a Jew who had to take a trip to a distant city. In the course of his travels he spent Shabbos in a certain town. He went to the main shul to *daven* and he was very pleased with the services. After *davening* he approached the *gabbai* and told him, 'I just loved your *davening* here! Those who led the prayers were very inspiring and pleasant, and the *ba'al korei* (Torah reader) did a superb job. Everything was executed so smoothly and with such careful organization! The decorum is wonderful, and the *davening* went without a hitch. But there is only one comment I have to make to you. The *aliyos* (the men called up to recite the *berachah* over the Torah reading) were chosen at random. The Kohen was called from the right side of the shul, the Levi from the left; the third person came from the west side of the synagogue and the fourth from the east — all without any order whatsoever.

הַמְהֻלָּל בָּרֹב הַתִּשְׁבָּחוֹת הַמְנַהֵג עוֹלָמוֹ בְּחֶסֶד וּבְרִיּוֹתָיו בְּרַחֲמִים וַיהוה לֹא יָנוּם וְלֹא יִישָׁן הַמְעוֹרֵר יְשֵׁנִים וְהַמֵּקִיץ נִרְדָּמִים וְהַמֵּשִׂיחַ אִלְּמִים וְהַמַּתִּיר אֲסוּרִים וְהַסּוֹמֵךְ נוֹפְלִים וְהַזּוֹקֵף כְּפוּפִים לְךָ לְבַדְּךָ אֲנַחְנוּ מוֹדִים. אִלּוּ פִינוּ מָלֵא שִׁירָה כַּיָּם וּלְשׁוֹנֵנוּ רִנָּה כַּהֲמוֹן גַּלָּיו וְשִׂפְתוֹתֵינוּ שֶׁבַח כְּמֶרְחֲבֵי רָקִיעַ וְעֵינֵינוּ מְאִירוֹת כַּשֶּׁמֶשׁ וְכַיָּרֵחַ וְיָדֵינוּ פְרוּשׂוֹת כְּנִשְׁרֵי שָׁמָיִם וְרַגְלֵינוּ קַלּוֹת כָּאַיָּלוֹת אֵין אֲנַחְנוּ מַסְפִּיקִים לְהוֹדוֹת לְךָ יהוה אֱלֹהֵינוּ וֵאלֹהֵי אֲבוֹתֵינוּ וּלְבָרֵךְ אֶת שְׁמֶךָ עַל אַחַת מֵאֶלֶף אֶלֶף אַלְפֵי אֲלָפִים וְרִבֵּי רְבָבוֹת פְּעָמִים הַטּוֹבוֹת (נִסִּים וְנִפְלָאוֹת) שֶׁעָשִׂיתָ עִם אֲבוֹתֵינוּ וְעִמָּנוּ. מִמִּצְרַיִם גְּאַלְתָּנוּ יהוה אֱלֹהֵינוּ וּמִבֵּית עֲבָדִים פְּדִיתָנוּ בְּרָעָב זַנְתָּנוּ וּבְשָׂבָע כִּלְכַּלְתָּנוּ מֵחֶרֶב הִצַּלְתָּנוּ וּמִדֶּבֶר מִלַּטְתָּנוּ וּמֵחֳלָיִם רָעִים וְנֶאֱמָנִים דִּלִּיתָנוּ. עַד הֵנָּה עֲזָרוּנוּ רַחֲמֶיךָ וְלֹא עֲזָבוּנוּ חֲסָדֶיךָ וְאַל תִּטְּשֵׁנוּ יהוה אֱלֹהֵינוּ לָנֶצַח. עַל כֵּן אֵבָרִים שֶׁפִּלַּגְתָּ בָּנוּ וְרוּחַ וּנְשָׁמָה שֶׁנָּפַחְתָּ בְּאַפֵּינוּ וְלָשׁוֹן אֲשֶׁר שַׂמְתָּ בְּפִינוּ הֵן הֵם יוֹדוּ וִיבָרְכוּ וִישַׁבְּחוּ וִיפָאֲרוּ וִירוֹמְמוּ וְיַעֲרִיצוּ וְיַקְדִּישׁוּ וְיַמְלִיכוּ אֶת שִׁמְךָ מַלְכֵּנוּ.

It would be much more in keeping with the superb organization of the shul to have the seven men called up according to the places where they sit!'

" 'Tell me,' asked the *gabbai,* somewhat taken aback. 'How long have you been *davening* here?'

" 'Oh, I am a guest,' the man explained. 'I am just passing through. This is my first and last Shabbos here!'

" 'And do you know the men who were called up for *aliyos*?' the *gabbai* asked.

" 'No, not really,' the traveler confessed.

" 'If so, how can you give me advice as to the organization of the *aliyos*?' asked the *gabbai* in amazement. 'How could you possibly know that this man has *yahrtzeit* this week, that one has just come out of the hospital, this one received an *aliyah* just last week, and that one needs to be called on next week! How can you express an opinion about a matter concerning that which you have no knowledge whatsoever?'

Who is extolled through a multitude of praises, Who guides His world with kindness and His creatures with mercy. Hashem neither slumbers nor sleeps; He rouses the sleepers and awakens the slumberers; He makes the mute speak and releases the bound; He supports the fallen and straightens the bent. To You alone we give thanks. Were our mouth as full of song as the sea, and our tongue as full of jubilation as its multitude of waves, and our lips as full of praise as the breadth of the heavens, and our eyes as brilliant as the sun and the moon, and our hands as outspread as eagles of the sky and our feet as swift as hinds — we still could not sufficiently thank You, Hashem our God and God of our forefathers, and to bless Your Name for even one of the thousands upon thousands, and myriads upon myriads of favors (miracles and wonders) that You performed for our ancestors and for us. You redeemed us from Egypt, Hashem our God, and liberated us from the house of bondage. In famine You nourished us and in plenty You sustained us. From sword You saved us; from plague You let us escape; and You spared us from severe and enduring diseases. Until now Your mercy has helped us, and Your kindness has not forsaken us. Do not abandon us, Hashem our God, to the ultimate end. Therefore, the limbs which You set within us, and the spirit and soul which You have breathed into our nostrils, and the tongue which You have placed in our mouth — they shall thank, bless, praise, glorify, exalt, revere, sanctify and do homage to Your Name, our King.

"You see," concluded the Chafetz Chaim, "it is the same for us. We are just 'visitors' on this earth; before we know it we will be traveling on. Only God knows what is in men's hearts and what they have done in their past. He has numerous calculations to make, and many, many factors to take into consideration — matters about which we have no clue whatsoever. So how can we come to God with complaints and suggestions as to how He runs the world? We must realize at all times that 'He is the God of all human beings,' and that all His ways are just and fair!"

כִּי כָל פֶּה לְךָ יוֹדֶה וְכָל לָשׁוֹן לְךָ תִשָּׁבַע וְכָל בֶּרֶךְ
לְךָ תִכְרַע וְכָל קוֹמָה לְפָנֶיךָ תִשְׁתַּחֲוֶה וְכָל לְבָבוֹת
יִירָאוּךָ וְכָל קֶרֶב וּכְלָיוֹת יְזַמְּרוּ לִשְׁמֶךָ. כַּדָּבָר
שֶׁכָּתוּב כָּל עַצְמֹתַי תֹּאמַרְנָה יהוה מִי כָמוֹךָ מַצִּיל
עָנִי מֵחָזָק מִמֶּנּוּ וְעָנִי וְאֶבְיוֹן מִגֹּזְלוֹ. מִי יִדְמֶה לָּךְ
וּמִי יִשְׁוֶה לָּךְ וּמִי יַעֲרָךְ לָךְ הָאֵל הַגָּדוֹל הַגִּבּוֹר
וְהַנּוֹרָא אֵל עֶלְיוֹן קֹנֵה שָׁמַיִם וָאָרֶץ. נְהַלֶּלְךָ
וּנְשַׁבֵּחֲךָ וּנְפָאֶרְךָ וּנְבָרֵךְ אֶת שֵׁם קָדְשֶׁךָ כָּאָמוּר
לְדָוִד בָּרְכִי נַפְשִׁי אֶת יהוה וְכָל קְרָבַי אֶת שֵׁם
קָדְשׁוֹ:

הָאֵל בְּתַעֲצֻמוֹת עֻזֶּךָ הַגָּדוֹל בִּכְבוֹד שְׁמֶךָ הַגִּבּוֹר
לָנֶצַח וְהַנּוֹרָא בְּנוֹרְאוֹתֶיךָ הַמֶּלֶךְ הַיּוֹשֵׁב עַל
כִּסֵּא רָם וְנִשָּׂא:

שׁוֹכֵן עַד מָרוֹם וְקָדוֹשׁ שְׁמוֹ. וְכָתוּב רַנְּנוּ צַדִּיקִים
בַּיהוה לַיְשָׁרִים נָאוָה תְהִלָּה: בְּפִי יְשָׁרִים
תִּתְהַלָּל וּבְדִבְרֵי צַדִּיקִים תִּתְבָּרַךְ וּבִלְשׁוֹן חֲסִידִים
תִּתְרוֹמָם וּבְקֶרֶב קְדוֹשִׁים תִּתְקַדָּשׁ:

וּבְמַקְהֲלוֹת רִבְבוֹת עַמְּךָ בֵּית יִשְׂרָאֵל בְּרִנָּה
יִתְפָּאֵר שִׁמְךָ מַלְכֵּנוּ בְּכָל דּוֹר וָדוֹר
שֶׁכֵּן חוֹבַת כָּל הַיְצוּרִים לְפָנֶיךָ יהוה אֱלֹהֵינוּ וֵאלֹהֵי
אֲבוֹתֵינוּ לְהוֹדוֹת לְהַלֵּל לְשַׁבֵּחַ לְפָאֵר לְרוֹמֵם לְהַדֵּר
לְבָרֵךְ לְעַלֵּה וּלְקַלֵּס עַל כָּל דִּבְרֵי שִׁירוֹת וְתִשְׁבְּחוֹת
דָּוִד בֶּן יִשַׁי עַבְדְּךָ מְשִׁיחֶךָ.

יִשְׁתַּבַּח שִׁמְךָ לָעַד מַלְכֵּנוּ הָאֵל הַמֶּלֶךְ הַגָּדוֹל
וְהַקָּדוֹשׁ בַּשָּׁמַיִם וּבָאָרֶץ כִּי לְךָ נָאֶה יהוה
אֱלֹהֵינוּ וֵאלֹהֵי אֲבוֹתֵינוּ שִׁיר וּשְׁבָחָה הַלֵּל וְזִמְרָה עֹז
וּמֶמְשָׁלָה נֶצַח גְּדֻלָּה וּגְבוּרָה תְּהִלָּה וְתִפְאֶרֶת קְדֻשָּׁה

For every mouth shall offer thanks to You; every tongue shall vow allegiance to You; every knee shall bend to You; all who stand erect shall bow before You; all hearts shall fear You, and all men's innermost feelings and thoughts shall sing praises to Your Name, as it is written: "All my bones declare: 'Hashem, who is like You?' You save the poor man from one stronger than he, the poor and destitute from one who would rob him." Who is like unto You? Who is equal to You? Who can be compared to You? O great, mighty, and awesome God, supreme God, Maker of heaven and earth. We shall praise, acclaim, and glorify You and bless Your holy Name, as it is said "Of David: Bless Hashem, O my soul, and let all my innermost being bless His holy Name!"

O God, in the omnipotence of Your strength, great in the honor of Your Name, powerful forever and awesome through Your awesome deeds, O King enthroned upon a high and lofty throne!

He Who abides forever, exalted and holy is His Name. And it is written: "Rejoice in Hashem, you righteous; for the upright, praise is fitting.' By the mouth of the upright You shall be lauded; by the words of the righteous You shall be praised; by the tongue of the pious You shall be exalted; and amid the holy You shall be sanctified.

And in the assemblies of the myriads of Your people, the House of Israel, with jubilation shall Your Name, our King, be glorified, in every generation. For such is the duty of all creatures — before You, Hashem, our God, and God of our forefathers, to thank, praise, laud, glorify, exalt, adore, bless, raise high, and sing praises — even beyond all expressions of the songs and praises of David the son of Yishai, Your servant, Your anointed.

May Your Name be praised forever, our King, the God, and King Who is great and holy in heaven and on earth; for to You, Hashem, our God, and the God of our forefathers, it is fitting to render song and praise, lauding and hymns, power and dominion, triumph, greatness and strength, praise and splendor, holiness

וּמַלְכֻיוֹת בְּרָכוֹת וְהוֹדָאוֹת מֵעַתָּה וְעַד עוֹלָם: בָּרוּךְ אַתָּה יהוה אֵל מֶלֶךְ גָּדוֹל בַּתִּשְׁבָּחוֹת אֵל הַהוֹדָאוֹת אֲדוֹן הַנִּפְלָאוֹת הַבּוֹחֵר בְּשִׁירֵי זִמְרָה מֶלֶךְ אֵל חֵי הָעוֹלָמִים.

The blessing over wine is recited and the fourth cup is drunk while reclining to the left side. It is preferable that the entire cup be drunk.

Some recite the following before the fourth cup:

הִנְנִי מוּכָן וּמְזוּמָּן לְקַיֵּם מִצְוַת כּוֹס רְבִיעִי שֶׁל אַרְבַּע כּוֹסוֹת. לְשֵׁם יִחוּד קֻדְשָׁא בְּרִיךְ הוּא וּשְׁכִינְתֵּיהּ, עַל יְדֵי הַהוּא טָמִיר וְנֶעְלָם, בְּשֵׁם כָּל יִשְׂרָאֵל. וִיהִי נֹעַם אֲדֹנָי אֱלֹהֵינוּ עָלֵינוּ, וּמַעֲשֵׂה יָדֵינוּ כּוֹנְנָה עָלֵינוּ, וּמַעֲשֵׂה יָדֵינוּ כּוֹנְנֵהוּ:

בָּרוּךְ אַתָּה יהוה אֱלֹהֵינוּ מֶלֶךְ הָעוֹלָם בּוֹרֵא פְּרִי הַגָּפֶן:

After drinking the fourth cup, the concluding blessing is recited.
On Shabbos include the passage in parentheses.

בָּרוּךְ אַתָּה יהוה אֱלֹהֵינוּ מֶלֶךְ הָעוֹלָם עַל הַגֶּפֶן וְעַל פְּרִי הַגֶּפֶן וְעַל תְּנוּבַת הַשָּׂדֶה וְעַל אֶרֶץ חֶמְדָּה טוֹבָה וּרְחָבָה שֶׁרָצִיתָ וְהִנְחַלְתָּ לַאֲבוֹתֵינוּ לֶאֱכוֹל מִפִּרְיָהּ וְלִשְׂבּוֹעַ מִטּוּבָהּ. רַחֵם נָא יהוה אֱלֹהֵינוּ עַל יִשְׂרָאֵל עַמֶּךָ וְעַל יְרוּשָׁלַיִם עִירֶךָ וְעַל צִיּוֹן מִשְׁכַּן כְּבוֹדֶךָ וְעַל מִזְבְּחֶךָ וְעַל הֵיכָלֶךָ. וּבְנֵה יְרוּשָׁלַיִם עִיר הַקֹּדֶשׁ בִּמְהֵרָה בְיָמֵינוּ וְהַעֲלֵנוּ לְתוֹכָהּ וְשַׂמְּחֵנוּ בְּבִנְיָנָהּ, וְנֹאכַל מִפִּרְיָהּ וְנִשְׂבַּע מִטּוּבָהּ וּנְבָרֶכְךָ עָלֶיהָ בִּקְדֻשָּׁה וּבְטָהֳרָה. [וּרְצֵה וְהַחֲלִיצֵנוּ בְּיוֹם הַשַּׁבָּת הַזֶּה] וְשַׂמְּחֵנוּ בְּיוֹם חַג הַמַּצּוֹת הַזֶּה. כִּי אַתָּה יהוה טוֹב וּמֵטִיב לַכֹּל וְנוֹדֶה לְךָ עַל הָאָרֶץ וְעַל פְּרִי הַגֶּפֶן: בָּרוּךְ אַתָּה יהוה עַל הָאָרֶץ וְעַל פְּרִי הַגֶּפֶן:

and sovereignty, blessings and thanksgivings from now and forever. Blessed are You, Hashem, God, King, great in praises, God of thanksgivings, Master of wonders, Who favors songs of praise — King, God, Life-giver of the world.

The blessing over wine is recited and the fourth cup is drunk while reclining to the left side. It is preferable that the entire cup be drunk.

Some recite the following before the fourth cup:

Behold, I am prepared and ready to fulfill the mitzvah of the fourth of the Four Cups. For the sake of the unification of the Holy One, Blessed is He, and His Presence, through Him Who is hidden and inscrutable — [I pray] in the name of all Israel. May the pleasantness of my Lord, our God, be upon us — may He establish our handiwork for us; our handiwork may He establish.

Blessed are You, Hashem, our God, King of the universe, Who creates the fruit of the vine.

After drinking the fourth cup, the concluding blessing is recited. On Shabbos include the passage in parentheses.

Blessed are You, Hashem, our God, King of the universe, for the vine and the fruit of the vine, and for the produce of the field. For the desirable, good, and spacious land that You were pleased to give our forefathers as a heritage, to eat of its fruit and to be satisfied with its goodness. Have mercy, we beg You, Hashem, our God, on Israel Your people; on Yerushalayim, Your city; on Tziyon, resting place of Your glory; Your Altar, and Your Temple. Rebuild Yerushalayim the city of holiness, speedily in our days. Bring us up into it and gladden us in its rebuilding, and let us eat from its fruit and be satisfied with its goodness and bless You upon it in holiness and purity. (Favor us and strengthen us on this Shabbos day) and grant us happiness on this Festival of Matzos; for You, Hashem, are good and do good to all, and we thank You for the land and for the fruit of the vine. Blessed are You, Hashem, for the land and for the fruit of the vine.

נִרְצָה – Nirtzah

נִרְצָה

חֲסַל סִדּוּר פֶּסַח כְּהִלְכָתוֹ. כְּכָל מִשְׁפָּטוֹ וְחֻקָּתוֹ. כַּאֲשֶׁר זָכִינוּ לְסַדֵּר אוֹתוֹ. כֵּן נִזְכֶּה לַעֲשׂוֹתוֹ: זָךְ שׁוֹכֵן מְעוֹנָה. קוֹמֵם קְהַל עֲדַת מִי מָנָה. בְּקָרוֹב נַהֵל נִטְעֵי כַנָּה. פְּדוּיִם לְצִיּוֹן בְּרִנָּה:

לְשָׁנָה הַבָּאָה בִּירוּשָׁלָיִם:

On the first night recite the following.
On the second night continue on page 270.

וּבְכֵן וַיְהִי בַּחֲצִי הַלַּיְלָה:

אָז רוֹב נִסִּים הִפְלֵאתָ בַּלַּיְלָה.
בְּרֹאשׁ אַשְׁמוֹרֶת זֶה הַלַּיְלָה.
גֵּר צֶדֶק נִצַּחְתּוֹ כְּנֶחֱלַק לוֹ לַיְלָה.
וַיְהִי בַּחֲצִי הַלַּיְלָה.

דַּנְתָּ מֶלֶךְ גְּרָר בַּחֲלוֹם הַלַּיְלָה.
הִפְחַדְתָּ אֲרַמִּי בְּאֶמֶשׁ לַיְלָה.
וַיָּשַׂר יִשְׂרָאֵל לְמַלְאָךְ וַיּוּכַל לוֹ לַיְלָה.
וַיְהִי בַּחֲצִי הַלַּיְלָה.

וַיָּשַׂר יִשְׂרָאֵל לְמַלְאָךְ
Israel fought with an angel

Satan's Assault — This angel was, as Rashi (on *Bereishis* 32:25) tells us, the guardian angel of Esav, who is none other than Satan himself, the personification of man's Evil Inclination (the *Yetzer Hara*). Israel's (Yaakov's) prevailing over the angel thus represents the triumph of the forces of good over those of evil. Why, **R' Elchanan Wasserman** wondered, did the *Yetzer Hara* wait for this time to attack? Yaakov was antedated by two equally righteous and saintly predecessors — Avraham and Yitzchak. Why did the *Yetzer Hara* not seek to destroy *them* as he did Yaakov?

To answer this question, R' Elchanan began by citing the well-known Midrash (from the Introduction to *Eichah Rabbah*):

> God was willing to overlook the sins of idolatry, sexual immorality, and murder, but not the sin of neglecting Torah study, as it says, "For what reason did the land perish. . .? Because they forsook My Torah" (*Yirmiyahu* 9:11-12). [The implication of the verse is:] It would have been better had they forsaken Me but kept My Torah, for the light of the Torah would have returned them to the proper path.

NIRTZAH

The Seder is now concluded in accordance with its laws, with all its ordinances and statutes. Just as we were privileged to arrange it, so may we merit to perform it. O Pure One, Who dwells on high, raise up the countless congregation, soon guide the offshoots of Your plants, redeemed to Tziyon with glad song.

NEXT YEAR IN YERUSHALAYIM

On the first night recite the following.
On the second night continue on page 271.

It came to pass at midnight.

You have, of old, performed many wonders by night.
At the head of the watches of this night.
To the righteous convert (Avraham),
 You gave triumph by dividing for him the night.
It came to pass at midnight.
You judged the king of Gerar (Avimelech),
 in a dream by night.
You frightened the Aramean (Lavan), in the dark of night.
Israel (Yaakov) fought with an angel
 and overcame him by night.
It came to pass at midnight.

The assertion of this Midrash seems astounding. How can the study of Torah be given priority over all other mitzvos, and even the three cardinal sins? R' Elchanan explained the Midrash as follows. When a war is being waged between two nations, even if one side wins a battle over the other this does not mean the war has come to an end. One side scores a victory today and the other tomorrow; this is the nature of war. But when one of the belligerents manages to disarm the other side and thus render it defenseless, the war has been decisively concluded; one cannot continue to fight without weapons.

Man is engaged in constant warfare with his *Yetzer Hara;* he continuously finds himself faced with temptations and difficult decisions with which he must struggle in order to build up the moral fortitude to do what he knows is proper. But the Sages tell us (*Kiddushin* 30b) that when God created the *Yetzer Hara* He also created a potent antidote for it — the study of the Torah: "As long as you involve yourselves with Torah study you will not be defeated by him!" There is no other alternative for overcoming the *Yetzer Hara* besides Torah study, as *Mesillas Yesharim* discusses at

זֶרַע בְּכוֹרֵי פַתְרוֹס מָחַצְתָּ בַּחֲצִי הַלַּיְלָה.
חֵילָם לֹא מָצְאוּ בְּקוּמָם בַּלַּיְלָה.
טִיסַת נְגִיד חֲרוֹשֶׁת סִלִּיתָ בְּכוֹכְבֵי לַיְלָה.
וַיְהִי בַּחֲצִי הַלַּיְלָה.

יָעַץ מְחָרֵף לְנוֹפֵף אִוּוּי הוֹבַשְׁתָּ פְגָרָיו בַּלַּיְלָה.
כָּרַע בֵּל וּמַצָּבוֹ בְּאִישׁוֹן לַיְלָה.
לְאִישׁ חֲמוּדוֹת נִגְלָה רָז חֲזוֹת לַיְלָה.
וַיְהִי בַּחֲצִי הַלַּיְלָה.

מִשְׁתַּכֵּר בִּכְלֵי קֹדֶשׁ נֶהֱרַג בּוֹ בַּלַּיְלָה.
נוֹשַׁע מִבּוֹר אֲרָיוֹת פּוֹתֵר בִּעֲתוּתֵי לַיְלָה.
שִׂנְאָה נָטַר אֲגָגִי וְכָתַב סְפָרִים בַּלַּיְלָה.
וַיְהִי בַּחֲצִי הַלַּיְלָה.

עוֹרַרְתָּ נִצְחֲךָ עָלָיו בְּנֶדֶד שְׁנַת לַיְלָה.
פּוּרָה תִדְרוֹךְ לְשׁוֹמֵר מַה מִלַּיְלָה.
צָרַח כַּשּׁוֹמֵר וְשָׂח אָתָא בֹקֶר וְגַם לַיְלָה.
וַיְהִי בַּחֲצִי הַלַּיְלָה.

---

length. R' Elchanan quoted the Chafetz Chaim as having said, "The *Yetzer Hara* doesn't care if a person fasts and cries and prays all day long — as long as he doesn't learn Torah!" Thus, if the Jewish people break all the other laws of the Torah, even the most serious, this can still be regarded as a mere setback, which can be offset by future victories ("the light of the Torah would return them to the proper path"), as with the analogy of actual warfare discussed above. But if Torah study is neglected, this represents the loss of the only weapon available for combating the *Yetzer Hara*, and the war has been lost.

The three patriarchs, although all paragons of spiritual achievement, each specialized in perfecting one particular area of the human spirit. Avraham perfected the trait of *kindness* towards fellow human beings (חֶסֶד); Yitzchak cultivated *service* to God. Yaakov was known as the pillar of Torah. Thus, the *Yetzer Hara* had no urgent need to attack the first two patriarchs, for, as saintly as they may have been, they did not represent a direct threat to him. But Yaakov, the bearer of the Torah, possessed the only weapon that could be directed against the *Yetzer Hara*, and it was for this reason that he found it necessary to attack him.

Although the angel was not able to overpower Yaakov, he did manage to wound

Egypt's firstborn You crushed at midnight.
Their host they found not upon arising at night.
The army of the prince of Charoshes (Sisera)
 You swept away with stars of the night.
  It came to pass at midnight.

The blasphemer (Sancheriv) planned to raise his hand against Yerushalayim —
 but You withered his corpses by night.
Bel was overturned with its pedestal,
 in the darkness of night.
To the man of Your delights (Daniel)
 was revealed the mystery of the visions of night.
  It came to pass at midnight.

He (Belshazzar) who caroused from the holy vessels
 was killed that very night.
From the lions' den was rescued he (Daniel)
 who interpreted the "terrors" of the night.
The Agagite (Haman) nursed hatred
 and wrote decrees at night.
  It came to pass at midnight.

You began Your triumph over him
 when You disturbed (Achashverosh's) sleep
  at night.
Trample the wine-press to help those who ask the watchman, "What of the long night?"
He will shout, like a watchman, and say:
"Morning shall come after night."
  It came to pass at midnight.

---

him in his thigh. This injury is fraught with symbolism, as the Midrashim and commentators discuss at length. According to some the thigh symbolizes the pillar ("leg") upon which the Torah stands — those who support Torah study with their money and efforts. Others say that the thigh represents one's children (see *Bereishis* 46:26, *Shemos* 1:5). It seems, R' Elchanan noted, that nowadays, both of these interpretations have materialized, for monetary support for Torah learning has dwindled pitifully and the number of children who do not receive any amount of Torah education is appallingly high — all in accordance with the portent delivered to Yaakov by Esav's angel.

קָרֵב יוֹם אֲשֶׁר הוּא לֹא יוֹם וְלֹא לַיְלָה.
רָם הוֹדַע כִּי לְךָ הַיּוֹם אַף לְךָ הַלַּיְלָה.
שׁוֹמְרִים הַפְקֵד לְעִירְךָ כָּל הַיּוֹם וְכָל הַלַּיְלָה.
תָּאִיר כְּאוֹר יוֹם חֶשְׁכַּת לַיְלָה.
וַיְהִי בַּחֲצִי הַלַּיְלָה.

On the second night recite the following.
On the first night continue on page 276.

וּבְכֵן וַאֲמַרְתֶּם זֶבַח פֶּסַח:

אֹמֶץ גְּבוּרוֹתֶיךָ הִפְלֵאתָ בַּפֶּסַח.
בְּרֹאשׁ כָּל מוֹעֲדוֹת נִשֵּׂאתָ פֶּסַח.

תָּאִיר כְּאוֹר יוֹם חֶשְׁכַּת לַיְלָה
Brighten like the light of day the darkness of night.

Don't Be Caught When the Lights Go On

"Night" and "day" are often used as metaphors for the gloomy distress of exile and the radiant joy of the future redemption, respectively. The **Chafetz Chaim** once told a poignant parable using this imagery.

Once there was a peasant farmer who decided he wanted to see what the big city was like. He had never ventured very far from his village, but he heard many stories and he was filled with curiosity as to what went on in a real metropolis. He scraped together some money and bought a ticket for the train ride to the city. As he boarded the train he was fascinated by what he saw — the locomotive, the huge cars, the smoke from the engine — these were all things he had never beheld before. Then, as the train began to speed through the woods and farmlands, he watched in amazement as one landscape after another appeared in the window and then vanished to make room for the next.

There were some young troublemakers in the car with him, and they decided to make as much fun as possible out of this naive country bumpkin who was obviously on a train for the first time in his life. They approached him and struck up a conversation with him.

"So where are you headed, mister?" they asked him, pretending to be interested in the man's travel plans.

"To the city," he replied innocently. "I want to see the wonders of big city life!"

The young rascals shook their heads in mock disapproval. "You can't go to the city in farmer's clothes like that!" they warned him. "You will be a laughingstock."

"Well, I have some holiday clothes with me, packed in my bag. I was planning on changing into them after arriving in the city, when I am already checked into the hotel."

"I don't think you will be able to get anyone to rent you a room looking like

Hasten the day (of Mashiach),
 that is neither day nor night.
Most High — make known that Yours
 are day and night.
Appoint guards for Your city,
 all the day and all the night.
Brighten like the light of day
 the darkness of night.
It came to pass at midnight.

<small>On the second night recite the following.
On the first night continue on page 277.</small>

And you shall say: This is the feast of Pesach.

You displayed wondrously Your mighty powers
 on Pesach.
Above all festivals You elevated Pesach.

---

that," one of the youngsters advised him. His friends all nodded in consent.

The farmer began to feel uneasy. He did not want to look foolish in the big city. But he was glad he had met such wonderful, helpful friends on the train. Surely they would help him figure out what to do!

"I have an idea," said the ringleader suddenly. The peasant's face lit up. "In a few minutes the train will go through an underground passage called a 'tunnel.' At that time the cars of the train will become completely darkened for at least ten minutes. You can use that opportunity to quickly take your farmer's clothes off and change into your holiday clothing!"

The farmer thought that was a splendid idea, and he thanked his "friend" for his advice. Sure enough, five minutes later the train pulled into a tunnel and he began to remove his peasant clothes. But suddenly, after only a few moments, the train left the tunnel into broad daylight, with the farmer standing in the middle of the car completely undressed! The youngsters had the laugh of their life, while the poor, naive farmer stood there in total humiliation!

The message of the parable for us, the Chafetz Chaim explained, is that we now live in a period of the "darkness" of exile. But soon — very soon, we hope — we will suddenly find ourselves exposed in the bright light of Messianic redemption, after which time it will be too late to change our ways. We always think that we have plenty of time in our "tunnel" to change out of our "farmer's clothes" and change our ways, to repent and become the kind of person we know we should be, to achieve our goals in Torah knowledge and spiritual development. But what will we do when suddenly the light of day will shine on us and our "nakedness" and imperfections will be exposed? How foolish and embarrassed we will feel at that time! Therefore, we should waste no time and prepare ourselves now for this event, and not allow ourselves to be caught unprepared.

פֶּסַח.	גִּלִּיתָ לְאֶזְרָחִי חֲצוֹת לֵיל
	וַאֲמַרְתֶּם זֶבַח פֶּסַח.
בַּפֶּסַח.	דְּלָתָיו דָּפַקְתָּ כְּחֹם הַיּוֹם
בַּפֶּסַח.	הִסְעִיד נוֹצְצִים עֻגוֹת מַצּוֹת
פֶּסַח.	וְאֶל הַבָּקָר רָץ זֵכֶר לְשׁוֹר עֵרֶךְ
	וַאֲמַרְתֶּם זֶבַח פֶּסַח.

הִסְעִיד נוֹצְצִים עֻגוֹת מַצּוֹת בַּפֶּסַח
He satiated the angels with matzah-cakes on Pesach.

The Pre-Pesach Meal   The poet refers to Avraham, who fed cakes to his three "guests," who were actually — unbeknown to him — angels (*Bereishis* 18:6). It is a well-known dictum of the Sages (see Mishnah, *Kiddushin* 82a) that Avraham (and indeed all three patriarchs) upheld all the mitzvos of the Torah — and even the future enactments of the Sages (*Yoma* 28b) — although they were not to be officially ordained for many centuries to come. Thus, the Midrash tells us that the day when the angels came to visit Avraham was Pesach (see *Rashi* to *Bereishis* 18:10) and the "cakes" that Avraham served were actually unleavened cakes, or matzos. Indeed, that very evening the angels went to Sodom and went to lodge in Lot's house, where he served them matzos (*Bereishis* 19:3). Rashi (ad loc.) relates this to the fact that it was Pesach time when this occurred.

It is interesting to note, **R' Zalman Sorotzkin** wrote, the difference in terminology that the Torah uses in the two cases: Concerning Avraham it is written that he served "cakes" (which, according to the Midrash, were unleavened), while in connection with Lot the Torah writes that he gave them "matzos." What, asked R' Zalman, is the significance of this difference in description?

R' Zalman suggested that the night when the angels appeared in Sodom was actually the first night of Pesach, and their visit to Avraham (which was "during the heat of the day" — *Bereishis* 18:1) was thus not on the Pesach holiday itself, but on the fourteenth of Nisan, which we call *Erev Pesach* (although in the Torah [*Vayikra* 23:5, *Bamidbar* 28:16, etc.] it is in fact *this* day that is referred to as "Pesach"). (The assertion that the angels' visit to Avraham took place on the *eve* of Pesach was actually mentioned by some of the Midrash commentators as well. Incidentally, there is support for this position from our poem itself, for the next line states that the ox that Avraham ran to get on that same day [*Bereishis* 18:7] was a commemoration of the *pesach* sacrifice — which took place, of course, on the *fourteenth* of Nisan — ed.) It is forbidden (Biblically) to eat *chametz* on *Erev Pesach* after noon as well as on Pesach, and it was for this reason that Avraham could not give his guests leavened bread, for it was already "the heat of the day" (i.e., noontime). On the other hand, it is forbidden rabbinically to eat actual matzah on *Erev Pesach*

> To the Oriental (Avraham) You revealed
> the future midnight of Pesach.
> And you shall say: This is the feast of Pesach.
>
> At his door You knocked in the heat of the day
> on Pesach;
> He satiated the angels with matzah-cakes
> on Pesach.
> And he ran to the herd — symbolic of
> the sacrificial beast of Pesach.
> And you shall say: This is the feast of Pesach.

(*Yerushalmi Pesachim* 10:1). He therefore could not serve his guests actual matzos either. Hence, he gave them "unleavened *cakes*" — meaning unleavened baked goods containing flavorings and ingredients other than just flour and water (מַצָּה עֲשִׂירָה), as we read in *I Melachim* 17:12-13: " 'I have... a spoonful of flour... and a bit of oil...' And he said, 'Make me a cake from it.' " Lot, on the other hand, was able to serve his guests actual matzos, for it was already Pesach night when they came to his house. This is why the Torah speaks of "[unleavened] cakes" in the case of Avraham, but of "matzos" when speaking of Lot.

Based on this explanation, R' Zalman continued, we can answer several other questions that are asked in connection with the Torah's description of the angels' visit to Avraham and Lot. The Torah refers several times to Avraham's haste in his preparation of the food for his guests: "And he hurried" (18:6); "Hurry!" (ibid.); "And Avraham *ran* to the cattle" (18:7). Avraham knew that the "guests" were not that hungry, for they had originally appeared to be hesitant about troubling him to take them into his house altogether (see *Rashi*). What, then, was the reason for all this rushing? R' Zalman explained that the halachah forbids eating *any* form of matzah product (even "cakes") in the later part of the afternoon of *Erev Pesach*. Since the angels arrived when it was already after noon (see above), Avraham was afraid that by the time the meal was prepared it would already be too late for him to serve any cakes at all. This is why he rushed so much to get the food ready for the guests.

As Rashi notes, when the Torah describes how Avraham actually served the food (as opposed to how he prepared it), the meat is mentioned, but the cakes are not. Apparently there was some reason that prevented him from serving the cakes. Rashi explains that Sarah became menstrually unclean at that very time, and the dough became ritually disqualified through contact with her. But the question remains: Why could Avraham not have had another batch of dough prepared — by another person — after this happened? Why did he have to abandon the idea of serving cake altogether? According to the theory we have advanced, the answer is, of course, that it was already too late to bake cakes, for they would not have been ready until the latter part of the afternoon, when they could not be eaten anyway.

Another question is: The Torah tells us that Lot served the angels a מִשְׁתֶּה, which

זוֹעֲמוּ סְדוֹמִים וְלוֹהֲטוּ בָּאֵשׁ	בַּפֶּסַח.
חֻלַּץ לוֹט מֵהֶם וּמַצּוֹת אָפָה בְּקֵץ	פֶּסַח.
טִאטֵאתָ אַדְמַת מוֹף וְנוֹף בְּעָבְרְךָ	בַּפֶּסַח.
וַאֲמַרְתֶּם זֶבַח פֶּסַח.	
יָהּ רֹאשׁ כָּל אוֹן מָחַצְתָּ בְּלֵיל שִׁמּוּר	פֶּסַח.
כַּבִּיר עַל בֵּן בְּכוֹר פָּסַחְתָּ בְּדַם	פֶּסַח.
לְבִלְתִּי תֵּת מַשְׁחִית לָבֹא בִּפְתָחַי	בַּפֶּסַח.
וַאֲמַרְתֶּם זֶבַח פֶּסַח.	
מְסֻגֶּרֶת סֻגָּרָה בְּעִתּוֹתֵי	פֶּסַח.
נִשְׁמְדָה מִדְיָן בִּצְלִיל שְׂעוֹרֵי עֹמֶר	פֶּסַח.
שֹׂרְפוּ מִשְׁמַנֵּי פּוּל וְלוּד בִּיקַד יְקוֹד	פֶּסַח.
וַאֲמַרְתֶּם זֶבַח פֶּסַח.	
עוֹד הַיּוֹם בְּנֹב לַעֲמוֹד עַד גָּעָה עוֹנַת	פֶּסַח.
פַּס יָד כָּתְבָה לְקַעֲקֵעַ צוּל	בַּפֶּסַח.
צָפֹה הַצָּפִית עָרוֹךְ הַשֻּׁלְחָן	בַּפֶּסַח.
וַאֲמַרְתֶּם זֶבַח פֶּסַח.	
קָהָל כִּנְּסָה הֲדַסָּה צוֹם לְשַׁלֵּשׁ	בַּפֶּסַח.
רֹאשׁ מִבֵּית רָשָׁע מָחַצְתָּ בְּעֵץ חֲמִשִּׁים	בַּפֶּסַח.
שְׁתֵּי אֵלֶּה רֶגַע תָּבִיא לְעוּצִית	בַּפֶּסַח.
תָּעֹז יָדְךָ וְתָרוּם יְמִינְךָ כְּלֵיל הִתְקַדֶּשׁ חַג פֶּסַח.	
וַאֲמַרְתֶּם זֶבַח פֶּסַח.	

---

refers to a meal in which wine is served, while in connection with Avraham's feeding of the angels this word is not used. R' Zalman answered, in accordance with his theory, that Lot, who was in effect observing the Pesach Seder, served his guests much wine because four cups of wine are supposed to be drunk at the Seder. Avraham, on the other hand, who was serving his meal on *Erev Pesach*, did not give any wine at all, for the halachah states that it is forbidden to drink wine in the late afternoon of *Erev Pesach*, which, as we have established above, is when Avraham served his meal to the angels.

The Sodomites provoked (God) and were devoured
  by fire   on Pesach;
Lot was withdrawn from them — he had baked
  matzos at the time   of Pesach.
You swept clean the soil of Mof and Nof (in Egypt)
  when You passed through   on Pesach.
  And you shall say: This is the feast of Pesach.

God, You crushed every firstborn of On (in Egypt)
  on the watchful night   of Pesach.
But Master — Your own firstborn, You skipped
  by merit of the blood   of Pesach,
Not to allow the Destroyer to enter my doors
                                               on Pesach.
  And you shall say: This is the feast of Pesach.

The beleaguered (Yericho) was besieged   on Pesach.
Midyan was destroyed with a barley cake,
  from the Omer   of Pesach.
The mighty nobles of Pul and Lud (Assyria) were
  consumed in a great conflagration   on Pesach.
  And you shall say: This is the feast of Pesach.

He (Sancheriv) would have stood that day at Nob,
  but for the advent   of Pesach.
A hand inscribed the destruction of Tzul (Babylon)
                                               on Pesach.
As the watch was set, and the royal table decked
                                               on Pesach.
  And you shall say: This is the feast of Pesach.

Hadassah (Esther) gathered a congregation
  for a three-day fast   on Pesach.
You caused the head of the evil clan (Haman) to be
  hanged on a fifty-cubit gallows   on Pesach.
Doubly, will You bring in an instant
  upon Utzis (Edom)   on Pesach.
Let Your hand be strong, and Your right arm exalted,
  as on that night when You hallowed the festival
                                               of Pesach.
  And you shall say: This is the feast of Pesach.

On both nights continue here:

כִּי לוֹ נָאֶה, כִּי לוֹ יָאֶה:

אַדִּיר בִּמְלוּכָה, בָּחוּר כַּהֲלָכָה, גְּדוּדָיו יֹאמְרוּ לוֹ, לְךָ וּלְךָ, לְךָ כִּי לְךָ, לְךָ אַף לְךָ, לְךָ יהוה הַמַּמְלָכָה, כִּי לוֹ נָאֶה, כִּי לוֹ יָאֶה.

דָּגוּל בִּמְלוּכָה, הָדוּר כַּהֲלָכָה, וָתִיקָיו יֹאמְרוּ לוֹ, לְךָ וּלְךָ, לְךָ כִּי לְךָ, לְךָ אַף לְךָ, לְךָ יהוה הַמַּמְלָכָה, כִּי לוֹ נָאֶה, כִּי לוֹ יָאֶה.

זַכַּאי בִּמְלוּכָה, חָסִין כַּהֲלָכָה, טַפְסְרָיו יֹאמְרוּ לוֹ, לְךָ וּלְךָ, לְךָ כִּי לְךָ, לְךָ אַף לְךָ, לְךָ יהוה הַמַּמְלָכָה, כִּי לוֹ נָאֶה, כִּי לוֹ יָאֶה.

יָחִיד בִּמְלוּכָה, כַּבִּיר כַּהֲלָכָה, לִמּוּדָיו יֹאמְרוּ לוֹ, לְךָ וּלְךָ, לְךָ כִּי לְךָ, לְךָ אַף לְךָ, לְךָ יהוה הַמַּמְלָכָה, כִּי לוֹ נָאֶה, כִּי לוֹ יָאֶה.

מוֹשֵׁל בִּמְלוּכָה, נוֹרָא כַּהֲלָכָה, סְבִיבָיו יֹאמְרוּ לוֹ, לְךָ וּלְךָ, לְךָ כִּי לְךָ, לְךָ אַף לְךָ, לְךָ יהוה הַמַּמְלָכָה, כִּי לוֹ נָאֶה, כִּי לוֹ יָאֶה.

עָנָיו בִּמְלוּכָה, פּוֹדֶה כַּהֲלָכָה, צַדִּיקָיו יֹאמְרוּ לוֹ, לְךָ וּלְךָ, לְךָ כִּי לְךָ, לְךָ אַף לְךָ, לְךָ יהוה הַמַּמְלָכָה, כִּי לוֹ נָאֶה, כִּי לוֹ יָאֶה.

עָנָיו בִּמְלוּכָה
Modest in Dominion

Feelings and Actions

In this song, in which the attributes of God are listed according to the letters of the alphabet, the letter ע is used to spell עָנָיו, *modest*. It is interesting to contrast this depiction with that of the following song (אַדִּיר הוּא), where the attribute of the letter ע is listed as עִזּוּז (*mighty*, with an overtone of *harshness*). These traits seem to stand in opposition to each other. A similar observation may be made in the famous poem הָאַדֶּרֶת וְהָאֱמוּנָה (in the Yom Kippur liturgy), where the two praises for God used for the letter ע are הָעֹז וְהָעֲנָוָה, *might and modesty*.

We are enjoined to strive to emulate God's attributes in our own lives, as the

On both nights continue here:

To Him praise is due! To Him praise is fitting!

Mighty in majesty, perfectly distinguished, His companies of angels say to Him: Yours and only Yours; Yours, yes Yours; Yours, surely Yours; Yours, Hashem, is the sovereignty. To Him praise is due! To Him praise is fitting!

Supreme in kingship, perfectly glorious, His faithful say to Him: Yours and only Yours; Yours, yes Yours; Yours, surely Yours; Yours, Hashem, is the sovereignty. To Him praise is due! To Him praise is fitting!

Pure in kingship, perfectly mighty, His angels say to Him: Yours and only Yours; Yours, yes Yours; Yours, surely Yours; Yours, Hashem, is the sovereignty. To Him praise is due! To Him praise is fitting!

Alone in kingship, perfectly omnipotent, His scholars say to Him: Yours and only Yours; Yours, yes Yours; Yours, surely Yours; Yours, Hashem, is the sovereignty. To Him praise is due! To Him praise is fitting!

Commanding in kingship, perfectly wondrous, His surrounding (angels) say to Him: Yours and only Yours; Yours, yes Yours; Yours, surely Yours; Yours, Hashem, is the sovereignty. To Him praise is due! To Him praise is fitting!

Modest in dominion, perfectly the Redeemer, His righteous say to Him: Yours and only Yours; Yours, yes Yours; Yours, surely Yours; Yours, Hashem, is the sovereignty. To Him praise is due! To Him praise is fitting!

Sages tell us: "Just as He is gracious and compassionate, so should you be gracious and compassionate" (*Shabbos* 132b)." "Just as He clothes the naked, so should you; just as He visits the sick, so should you; just as He buries the dead, so should you" (*Sotah* 14a). Here, **R' Shneur Kotler** noted, we are faced with a dilemma: God is described with two diametrically opposed attributes. Which one is appropriate for us to emulate in our daily lives? Should we act with modesty and humility, or should we comport ourselves with unyielding toughness?

קָדוֹשׁ בִּמְלוּכָה, רַחוּם כַּהֲלָכָה, שִׁנְאַנָּיו יֹאמְרוּ לוֹ, לְךָ וּלְךָ, לְךָ כִּי לְךָ, לְךָ אַף לְךָ, לְךָ יהוה הַמַּמְלָכָה, כִּי לוֹ נָאֶה, כִּי לוֹ יָאֶה.

In dealing with this question R' Shneur began with an analysis of the words of the Rambam, who writes in *Hil. De'os* (1:4-5):

> The two extremes of any character trait are not good.... A person should follow the ... "straight path," consisting of the middle position of each trait.... For instance, one should not be an irritable person, who is easily angered, nor should he be like a corpse that has no feelings at all. Rather, he should be in the middle — allowing himself to be angry only over a major matter, where it is appropriate to do so.... He should also not covet many possessions, but only the necessities of life.... He should also not be a "workaholic," but should toil only to achieve those things that are necessary. He should not be too stingy nor extravagantly generous.... He should not be too jovial nor too morose.... This approach is the way of the wise; if all of a person's character traits are intermediate in this manner, he is called a "wise person."
>
> If a person is even more strict with himself and removes himself from the middle position toward one side or another, he is called a "righteous person." For instance, if a person distances himself totally from haughtiness, to the furthermost extreme... he is called a "righteous person." If he achieves only the middle position, however, he is called merely a "wise person" (as in the previous paragraph).... And similarly with all other character traits.

To sum up the Rambam's stance: A person should strive to achieve the middle position of each character trait, including temper, covetousness, economy, and modesty. If he accomplishes this goal he is called a "wise man"; if he goes beyond this he is a "righteous man."

This presentation seems to stand in contradiction with the Rambam's own words, in the very next chapter of *Hil. De'os* (2:6ff):

> There are some traits concerning which it is forbidden to act according to the middle position; rather, one must go to the extreme position. I refer to the trait of haughtiness. It is not sufficient for a person to simply be somewhat modest; he must be of exceedingly humble spirit... The same is true of anger. A person should distance himself from this trait and go to the opposite extreme, and he should train himself not to become angry even over something which rightfully deserves an angry reaction.

As the *Lechem Mishneh* points out, the Rambam seems to contradict himself on several points in this passage: In Chap. 1 he writes that a "wise man" is one who comports himself according to the middle ground of each trait, including modesty, while in Chap. 2 he asserts that "it is forbidden to act according to the middle

> Holy in kingship, perfectly merciful, His troops of angels say to Him: Yours and only Yours; Yours, yes Yours; Yours, surely Yours; Yours, HASHEM, is the sovereignty. To Him praise is due! To Him praise is fitting.

position" of this particular trait. Furthermore, in Chap. 1 the Rambam specifically used the example of anger to demonstrate how a person should not go to either extreme ("one should not be an irritable person, who is easily angered, nor should he be like a corpse that has no feelings at all"), while in Chap. 2 he tells us that when it comes to the trait of anger one must strive to reach the extreme and not settle for the middle ground. These are formidable difficulties indeed! How can we account for such incongruities in the Rambam's statements in such close proximity to each other?

R' Shneur quoted a resolution to these problems from *Even Ha'azel*, a commentary on the Rambam written by his grandfather, R' Isser Zalman Meltzer. The Rambam is addressing two completely different issues in the two passages, R' Isser Zalman explains. In Chap. 1 he speaks about how a person should build his personality — how he should feel about life's various situations and how he should perceive them. In Chapter 2, however, he speaks of how a person should *act* outwardly in reaction to a given situation. When it comes to one's innermost feelings and his attitude, for instance, he should adopt the middle position, even when it comes to modesty versus pride. However, when it comes to action he must behave in a manner that exhibits modesty in the extreme. Similarly with anger — he should allow himself to be internally upset by things that are truly upsetting, yet in his actions he should never allow himself to lose his temper, but practice extreme moderation instead.

R' Shneur offered a support to R' Isser Zalman's theory from a passage in the Talmud (*Ta'anis* 4a):

> R' Ashi said: Any Torah scholar who is not as firm as iron is not a true Torah scholar.... Ravina said: Nevertheless, a person must conduct himself with forbearance.

Ravina apparently agreed with R' Ashi's assertion that a Torah scholar must possess the trait of toughness, meaning that he must be firm and uncompromising in his attitudes and opinions. He merely added that despite this inner attribute of firmness, the scholar must *conduct himself* with forbearance and patience. As R' Isser Zalman explained, how one trains himself to feel and how he trains himself to act are two completely different issues.

Now let us return to our original question. If we are supposed to adopt God's attributes as the guiding forces in our own lives, how are we to deal with a situation where contradictory attributes are assigned to Him — namely, *firmness* and *modesty* (הָעֹז וְהָעֲנָוָה)? The answer is that we should adopt *both* traits simultaneously — one trait (firmness) with which to build our inner sensitivities and the other (modesty) as a guide for our actions.

תַּקִּיף בִּמְלוּכָה, תּוֹמֵךְ כַּהֲלָכָה, תְּמִימָיו יֹאמְרוּ לוֹ, לְךָ וּלְךָ, לְךָ כִּי לְךָ, לְךָ אַף לְךָ, לְךָ יהוה הַמַּמְלָכָה, כִּי לוֹ נָאֶה, כִּי לוֹ יָאֶה.

אַדִּיר הוּא יִבְנֶה בֵיתוֹ בְּקָרוֹב, בִּמְהֵרָה, בִּמְהֵרָה, בְּיָמֵינוּ בְּקָרוֹב. אֵל בְּנֵה, אֵל בְּנֵה, בְּנֵה בֵיתְךָ בְּקָרוֹב.

בָּחוּר הוּא. גָּדוֹל הוּא. דָּגוּל הוּא. יִבְנֶה בֵיתוֹ בְּקָרוֹב, בִּמְהֵרָה, בִּמְהֵרָה, בְּיָמֵינוּ בְּקָרוֹב. אֵל בְּנֵה, אֵל בְּנֵה, בְּנֵה בֵיתְךָ בְּקָרוֹב.

הָדוּר הוּא. וָתִיק הוּא. זַכַּאי הוּא. חָסִיד הוּא. יִבְנֶה בֵיתוֹ בְּקָרוֹב, בִּמְהֵרָה, בִּמְהֵרָה, בְּיָמֵינוּ בְּקָרוֹב. אֵל בְּנֵה, אֵל בְּנֵה, בְּנֵה בֵיתְךָ בְּקָרוֹב.

טָהוֹר הוּא. יָחִיד הוּא. כַּבִּיר הוּא. לָמוּד הוּא. מֶלֶךְ הוּא. נוֹרָא הוּא. סַגִּיב הוּא. עִזּוּז הוּא. פּוֹדֶה הוּא.

בְּנֵה בֵיתְךָ בְּקָרוֹב
rebuild Your House soon.

Be Prepared for the Quest — Dozens of times a day we beseech God to rebuild His Temple in Jerusalem. What would happen, mused the **Chafetz Chaim**, if God would suddenly heed our pleas and provide us with the Temple we so fervently desire? There would be an urgent need for Kohanim to officiate at the sacrificial service — Kohanim who are experts in the relevant fields of halachah. How foolish we would feel if we were faced with a beautiful, fully equipped Temple and could find no one with the slightest idea of what to do with it! Such a situation would only serve as an indication that all of our prayers throughout the ages were insincere, hollow pronouncements uttered out of force of habit. For if someone truly yearns for something and expects to get it he prepares himself for the eventuality of the realization of his desire.

The Chafetz Chaim illustrated the point with a parable. A man was planning a bar mitzvah celebration for his son. He sent out invitations to all his friends and relatives, specifying the date and time — 9 a.m. — of the party, which was to be held in his house.

The designated morning came around, and the guests began to arrive one by one. But what they found there astonished them. The lights in the house were out; the door was locked. They knocked on the door several times, until their host,

Almighty in kingship, perfectly sustaining, His perfect ones say to Him: Yours and only Yours; Yours, yes Yours; Yours, surely Yours; Yours, Hashem, is the sovereignty. To Him praise is due! To Him praise is fitting!

He is most mighty. May He soon rebuild His House, speedily, yes speedily, in our days, soon. God, rebuild, God, rebuild, rebuild Your House soon!

He is distinguished, He is great, He is exalted. May He soon rebuild His House, speedily, yes speedily, in our days, soon. God, rebuild, God, rebuild, rebuild Your House soon!

He is all glorious, He is faithful, He is faultless, He is righteous. May He soon rebuild His House, speedily, yes speedily, in our days, soon. God, rebuild, God, rebuild, rebuild Your House soon!

He is pure, He is unique, He is powerful, He is all-wise, He is King, He is awesome, He is sublime, He is all-powerful, He is the Redeemer,

---

dressed in his nightgown and rubbing his eyes sleepily, finally opened the door. When he saw the guests, dressed in their finest, assembled outside his front door, he said to them, "Come in! Come in! Please grab a seat wherever you find one. In a few minutes I intend to begin preparing the food!"

Would the guests in such a situation not be totally amazed and shocked at the inappropriate behavior of this host? How rude it is to invite someone — and especially a large group of people — to a meal without bothering to undergo any preparation whatsoever in advance!

Yet this is precisely the situation we ourselves are likely to face. Every *Shemoneh Esrei*, every *Bircas Hamazon*, practically every Shabbos *zemirah* contains one or more petitions for God to have mercy on us and rebuild the Temple. Yet we sit back and do not make the slightest effort to prepare ourselves for the realization of this "invitation." We imagine that we will begin to organize ourselves only after the *Mashiach* has already arrived and the Temple is standing idle before us!

(For this reason the Chafetz Chaim [who was himself a Kohen] encouraged Torah scholars, and Kohanim in particular, to engage in the study of the parts of the Talmud that pertain to the Temple service, and he himself formed a *"Kollel Kodashim"* where this was the topic of study. He also wrote an authoritative, extensive halachic compendium called *Likkutei Halachos,* patterned after the Rif's *Halachos,* in which he extracted and presented the practical halachos of the Temple service from the extensive Talmudic discussions of these issues.)

צַדִּיק הוּא. יִבְנֶה בֵיתוֹ בְּקָרוֹב, בִּמְהֵרָה, בִּמְהֵרָה, בְּיָמֵינוּ בְּקָרוֹב. אֵל בְּנֵה, אֵל בְּנֵה, בְּנֵה בֵיתְךָ בְּקָרוֹב.

קָדוֹשׁ הוּא. רַחוּם הוּא. שַׁדַּי הוּא. תַּקִּיף הוּא. יִבְנֶה בֵיתוֹ בְּקָרוֹב, בִּמְהֵרָה, בִּמְהֵרָה, בְּיָמֵינוּ בְּקָרוֹב. אֵל בְּנֵה, אֵל בְּנֵה, בְּנֵה בֵיתְךָ בְּקָרוֹב.

אֶחָד מִי יוֹדֵעַ? אֶחָד אֲנִי יוֹדֵעַ. אֶחָד אֱלֹהֵינוּ שֶׁבַּשָּׁמַיִם וּבָאָרֶץ.

שְׁנַיִם מִי יוֹדֵעַ? שְׁנַיִם אֲנִי יוֹדֵעַ. שְׁנֵי לֻחוֹת הַבְּרִית, אֶחָד אֱלֹהֵינוּ שֶׁבַּשָּׁמַיִם וּבָאָרֶץ.

שְׁלֹשָׁה מִי יוֹדֵעַ? שְׁלֹשָׁה אֲנִי יוֹדֵעַ. שְׁלֹשָׁה אָבוֹת, שְׁנֵי לֻחוֹת הַבְּרִית, אֶחָד אֱלֹהֵינוּ שֶׁבַּשָּׁמַיִם וּבָאָרֶץ.

אַרְבַּע מִי יוֹדֵעַ? אַרְבַּע אֲנִי יוֹדֵעַ. אַרְבַּע אִמָּהוֹת, שְׁלֹשָׁה אָבוֹת, שְׁנֵי לֻחוֹת הַבְּרִית, אֶחָד אֱלֹהֵינוּ שֶׁבַּשָּׁמַיִם וּבָאָרֶץ.

חֲמִשָּׁה מִי יוֹדֵעַ? חֲמִשָּׁה אֲנִי יוֹדֵעַ. חֲמִשָּׁה חֻמְשֵׁי תוֹרָה, אַרְבַּע אִמָּהוֹת, שְׁלֹשָׁה אָבוֹת, שְׁנֵי לֻחוֹת הַבְּרִית, אֶחָד אֱלֹהֵינוּ שֶׁבַּשָּׁמַיִם וּבָאָרֶץ.

שִׁשָּׁה מִי יוֹדֵעַ? שִׁשָּׁה אֲנִי יוֹדֵעַ. שִׁשָּׁה סִדְרֵי מִשְׁנָה, חֲמִשָּׁה חֻמְשֵׁי תוֹרָה, אַרְבַּע אִמָּהוֹת, שְׁלֹשָׁה אָבוֹת, שְׁנֵי לֻחוֹת הַבְּרִית, אֶחָד אֱלֹהֵינוּ שֶׁבַּשָּׁמַיִם וּבָאָרֶץ.

שִׁבְעָה מִי יוֹדֵעַ? שִׁבְעָה אֲנִי יוֹדֵעַ. שִׁבְעָה יְמֵי שַׁבַּתָּא,

---

שִׁבְעָה יְמֵי שַׁבַּתָּא
seven are the days of the week;

Shabbos Also Has a Partner

The Midrash (*Bereishis Rabbah* 11:9) tells us that the Shabbos approached God with the following complaint: "All the other days of the week have a partner; only I have no partner!" But God assuaged the Sabbath's concern, and answered, "The congregation of Israel will be your partner!"

What did the Shabbos mean when it said that all the other days of the week had a partner? The way this passage is usually explained is that Sunday is paired up with Monday, Tuesday with Wednesday, and Thursday goes together with Friday. Only Shabbos is left without a mate. **R' Gedaliah Schorr**, however, disagreed with this inter-

He is the all-righteous. May He soon rebuild His House, speedily, yes speedily, in our days, soon. God, rebuild, God, rebuild, rebuild Your House soon!

He is holy, He is compassionate, He is Almighty, He is omnipotent. May He soon rebuild His House, speedily, yes speedily, in our days, soon. God, rebuild, God, rebuild, rebuild Your House soon!

Who knows one? I know one: One is our God, in heaven and on earth.

Who knows two? I know two: two are the Tablets of the Covenant; One is our God, in heaven and on earth.

Who knows three? I know three: three are the Patriarchs; two are the Tablets of the Covenant; One is our God, in heaven and on earth.

Who knows four? I know four: four are the Matriarchs; three are the Patriarchs; two are the Tablets of the Covenant; One is our God, in heaven and on earth.

Who knows five? I know five: five are the Books of Torah; four are the Matriarchs; three are the Patriarchs; two are the Tablets of the Covenant; One is our God, in heaven and on earth.

Who knows six? I know six: six are the Orders of the Mishnah; five are the Books of the Torah; four are the Matriarchs; three are the Patriarchs; two are the Tablets of the Covenant; One is our God, in heaven and on earth.

Who knows seven? I know seven: seven are the days

---

pretation, for there is no logical basis to pair up the days of the week in this manner, leaving Shabbos by itself. One could just as easily make different pairs, counting Shabbos in and leaving another day of the week out on its own! For this reason R' Gedaliah suggested an entirely different explanation for the words of the Midrash, as follows.

Each day of the very first week of time saw the creation of a different facet of the universe — on Sunday light was created, on Monday the firmament, etc. Each facet of creation, which was brought into creation on its particular day, continues to have a relationship with its day of the week. We find (*Tamid* 33b) that each day of the week had a certain psalm associated with it, which was sung in the Temple on that day. Each day's psalm, the Talmud (*Rosh Hashanah* 31a) tells us, reflects on the theme of that day's creation. This shows that there is an ongoing connection between a particular day of the week and that which was created on it. On Sundays, God's glory is revealed through light, on Mondays through the firmament, on Tuesdays through the heavenly bodies, etc. This is what the Midrash means when it says that each day of the

שִׁשָּׁה סִדְרֵי מִשְׁנָה, חֲמִשָּׁה חֻמְשֵׁי תוֹרָה, אַרְבַּע אִמָּהוֹת, שְׁלשָׁה אָבוֹת, שְׁנֵי לֻחוֹת הַבְּרִית, אֶחָד אֱלֹהֵינוּ שֶׁבַּשָּׁמַיִם וּבָאָרֶץ.

שְׁמוֹנָה מִי יוֹדֵעַ? שְׁמוֹנָה אֲנִי יוֹדֵעַ. שְׁמוֹנָה יְמֵי מִילָה, שִׁבְעָה יְמֵי שַׁבַּתָּא, שִׁשָּׁה סִדְרֵי מִשְׁנָה, חֲמִשָּׁה חֻמְשֵׁי תוֹרָה, אַרְבַּע אִמָּהוֹת, שְׁלשָׁה אָבוֹת, שְׁנֵי לֻחוֹת הַבְּרִית, אֶחָד אֱלֹהֵינוּ שֶׁבַּשָּׁמַיִם וּבָאָרֶץ.

תִּשְׁעָה מִי יוֹדֵעַ? תִּשְׁעָה אֲנִי יוֹדֵעַ. תִּשְׁעָה יַרְחֵי לֵדָה, שְׁמוֹנָה יְמֵי מִילָה, שִׁבְעָה יְמֵי שַׁבַּתָּא, שִׁשָּׁה סִדְרֵי מִשְׁנָה, חֲמִשָּׁה חֻמְשֵׁי תוֹרָה, אַרְבַּע אִמָּהוֹת, שְׁלשָׁה אָבוֹת, שְׁנֵי לֻחוֹת הַבְּרִית, אֶחָד אֱלֹהֵינוּ שֶׁבַּשָּׁמַיִם וּבָאָרֶץ.

עֲשָׂרָה מִי יוֹדֵעַ? עֲשָׂרָה אֲנִי יוֹדֵעַ. עֲשָׂרָה דִבְּרַיָּא, תִּשְׁעָה יַרְחֵי לֵדָה, שְׁמוֹנָה יְמֵי מִילָה, שִׁבְעָה יְמֵי שַׁבַּתָּא,

---

week has a partner — Sunday has the light, through which it is able to achieve the glorification of God's Name, Monday the firmament, etc. But Shabbos has no such partner, for nothing was created on that day! How would Shabbos be able to serve as a medium to the revelation of God's glory? This was the complaint that the Sabbath day brought before God.

In response to this complaint God reassured Shabbos that it would indeed have a role — and a crucial role, at that — to play in the glorification of God. This would be achieved through the people of Israel. The other nations of the world have no part in the sanctity of Shabbos; it is totally inapplicable to them. "God did not give it (the Sabbath) to the nations of the lands... nor can the uncircumcised partake in its rest" (Shabbos liturgy). The Sabbath day is set aside for spiritual purification, for reflection upon the greatness of God's creation: "You have brought me joy with Your works... How great are Your deeds, Hashem; Your thoughts are exceedingly deep..." (*Tehillim* 92, the "Psalm for the Sabbath day"). It is through Israel that Shabbos is able to participate in the process of the glorification of Hashem's Name.

עֲשָׂרָה אֲנִי יוֹדֵעַ. עֲשָׂרָה דִבְּרַיָּא
I know ten: ten are the Ten Commandments;

The Positive of the Negative

The *Mechilta* tells us that after the Jews heard the Ten Commandments pronounced at Mount Sinai they enthusiastically voiced their acceptance of each precept. But there is a dispute as to exactly how their endorsement was formulated. According to R' Yishmael, when they heard a positive commandment (such as "Remember the Sabbath day")

of the week; six are the Orders of the Mishnah; five are the Books of the Torah; four are the Matriarchs; three are the Patriarchs; two are the Tablets of the Covenant; One is our God, in heaven and on earth.

Who knows eight? I know eight: eight are the days of circumcision; seven are the days of the week; six are the Orders of the Mishnah; five are the Books of the Torah; four are the Matriarchs; three are the Patriarchs; two are the Tablets of the Covenant; One is our God, in heaven and on earth.

Who knows nine? I know nine: nine are the months of pregnancy; eight are the days of circumcision; seven are the days of the week; six are the Orders of the Mishnah; five are the Books of the Torah; four are the Matriarchs; three are the Patriarchs; two are the Tablets of the Covenant; One is our God, in heaven and on earth.

Who knows ten? I know ten: ten are the Ten Commandments; nine are the months of pregnancy; eight are the days of circumcision; seven are the days of the week;

---

they proclaimed, "Yes!" while after a negative commandment (such as, "You shall not steal") they called out, "No!" R' Akiva, on the other hand, is of the opinion that the response to both the positive and negative commandments was, "Yes!"

R' Akiva's position seems a bit puzzling. It appears to be totally inappropriate for one to respond "Yes!" after hearing "You shall not steal," if his intention is to accept that command.

R' Gedaliah Schorr explained R' Akiva's opinion as follows. When the commandment not to kill was proclaimed by God, it was more than simply a directive not to commit actual murder; it went much further than that. It imbued the people with a sense of brotherhood and compassion for one another to the extent that the thought of taking another man's life became totally foreign to their minds. Even those deeds that the Sages compare to the shedding of blood — such as causing a person to blush with embarrassment — became completely rejected in their minds. This, then, is what the people meant when they answered "Yes" to the commandment of "You shall not kill" — "Yes, we will conduct ourselves according to the highest standards of brotherly love and mutual respect, to the extent that killing someone will be totally out of the realm of possibility." The same idea applies to all the other negative commandments as well.

The experience of receiving the Torah implanted these conceptions within the Jewish soul for all time, and even today each of us has the ability to achieve such lofty perspectives, if we but strive to allow the potential powers of the spirit within us to materialize and express themselves in our everyday actions, when we will be able to exclaim with all sincerity, "I know ten!"

שִׁשָּׁה סִדְרֵי מִשְׁנָה, חֲמִשָּׁה חֻמְשֵׁי תוֹרָה, אַרְבַּע אִמָּהוֹת, שְׁלֹשָׁה אָבוֹת, שְׁנֵי לֻחוֹת הַבְּרִית, אֶחָד אֱלֹהֵינוּ שֶׁבַּשָּׁמַיִם וּבָאָרֶץ.

אַחַד עָשָׂר מִי יוֹדֵעַ? אַחַד עָשָׂר אֲנִי יוֹדֵעַ. אַחַד עָשָׂר כּוֹכְבַיָּא, עֲשָׂרָה דִבְּרַיָּא, תִּשְׁעָה יַרְחֵי לֵדָה, שְׁמוֹנָה יְמֵי מִילָה, שִׁבְעָה יְמֵי שַׁבְּתָא, שִׁשָּׁה סִדְרֵי מִשְׁנָה, חֲמִשָּׁה חֻמְשֵׁי תוֹרָה, אַרְבַּע אִמָּהוֹת, שְׁלֹשָׁה אָבוֹת, שְׁנֵי לֻחוֹת הַבְּרִית, אֶחָד אֱלֹהֵינוּ שֶׁבַּשָּׁמַיִם וּבָאָרֶץ.

שְׁנֵים עָשָׂר מִי יוֹדֵעַ? שְׁנֵים עָשָׂר אֲנִי יוֹדֵעַ. שְׁנֵים עָשָׂר שִׁבְטַיָּא, אַחַד עָשָׂר כּוֹכְבַיָּא, עֲשָׂרָה דִבְּרַיָּא, תִּשְׁעָה יַרְחֵי לֵדָה, שְׁמוֹנָה יְמֵי מִילָה, שִׁבְעָה יְמֵי שַׁבְּתָא, שִׁשָּׁה סִדְרֵי מִשְׁנָה, חֲמִשָּׁה חֻמְשֵׁי תוֹרָה, אַרְבַּע אִמָּהוֹת, שְׁלֹשָׁה אָבוֹת, שְׁנֵי לֻחוֹת הַבְּרִית, אֶחָד אֱלֹהֵינוּ שֶׁבַּשָּׁמַיִם וּבָאָרֶץ.

שְׁנֵים עָשָׂר שִׁבְטַיָּא
twelve are the tribes;

Parts of A Whole — Each item on this song's list represents an entity that consists of several parts, yet is in actuality a single unit, **R' Gedaliah Schorr** explained. For instance, although there were two tablets, it is obvious that all ten commandments that were engraved on them are viewed as a single, unified entity. The same may be said of the three patriarchs, the four matriarchs, etc. And the same concept should be applied to the twelve tribes. Although the people of Israel are divided into twelve distinct groupings, each with its unique capabilities and characteristics, it must always be borne in mind that these twelve divisions are in fact components of a single unit, and are meant to blend their various attributes together to form a unified whole. The twelve tribes have been compared to the twelve months of the year; just as it is self-evident that although each month exists independently of the other they must join forces in order to form a year, so it is with the twelve tribes.

Thus, we find that after Yaakov gave each of his sons his individual blessings, the Torah writes, "Each one according to his blessing he blessed them" (*Bereishis* 49:28). Rashi notes that good grammar would have dictated that the Torah should have said, "Each one according to his blessing he blessed *him,*" not "*them.*" The reason for the use of the plural, Rashi explains, is as follows: "Because Yaakov ascribed the might of the lion to Yehudah and the plunder of the wolf to Binyamin

six are the Orders of the Mishnah; five are the Books of the Torah; four are the Matriarchs; three are the Patriarchs; two are the Tablets of the Covenant; One is our God, in heaven and on earth.

Who knows eleven? I know eleven: eleven are the stars (in Yosef's dream); ten are the Ten Commandments; nine are the months of pregnancy; eight are the days of circumcision; seven are the days of the week; six are the Orders of the Mishnah; five are the Books of the Torah; four are the Matriarchs; three are the Patriarchs; two are the Tablets of the Covenant; One is our God, in heaven and on earth.

Who knows twelve? I know twelve: twelve are the tribes; eleven are the stars (in Yosef's dream); ten are the Ten Commandments; nine are the months of pregnancy; eight are the days of circumcision; seven are the days of the week; six are the Orders of the Mishnah; five are the Books of the Torah; four are the Matriarchs; three are the Patriarchs; two are the Tablets of the Covenant; One is our God, in heaven and on earth.

---

and the swiftness of the deer to Naftali — one might think that he did not include all the tribes in each other's blessings. Therefore the Torah says, 'he blessed *them.*' " The idea behind Rashi's explanation is that, as established above, although each tribe has its unique strengths and abilities, these individual attributes are supposed to be channeled for the benefit of the community of Israel as a whole, so that the individual strengths are shared by all alike.

This is also the idea that lies behind the familiar Midrash that accounts for the discrepancy between two verses in connection with the stones that Yaakov used to place under his head on the first night of his trip to Aram. According to one verse (*Bereishis* 28:11) he took "some of the stones" upon which to lay his head, while another verse writes that "Yaakov took *the stone* (singular) that he had placed at his head" (ibid., 28:18). The Midrash explains that at first Yaakov had taken twelve stones to lie on, but the stones began quarreling with each other for the privilege of having Yaakov's head rest on it, until miraculously the twelve stones became a single stone. This Aggadic explanation is found in the Talmud, and is quoted in *Rashi,* but the Midrash (*Pirkei D'Rabbi Eliezer*) adds: "This intimated to him that all twelve tribes were destined to become one single nation in the land." In other words, the essence of the twelve tribes is to unite into a single unified entity. The concept discussed above is thus depicted by the Midrash allegorically.

שְׁלֹשָׁה עָשָׂר מִי יוֹדֵעַ? שְׁלֹשָׁה עָשָׂר אֲנִי יוֹדֵעַ. שְׁלֹשָׁה עָשָׂר מִדַּיָּא, שְׁנֵים עָשָׂר שִׁבְטַיָּא, אַחַד עָשָׂר כּוֹכְבַיָּא, עֲשָׂרָה דִבְּרַיָּא, תִּשְׁעָה יַרְחֵי לֵדָה, שְׁמוֹנָה יְמֵי מִילָה, שִׁבְעָה יְמֵי שַׁבַּתָּא, שִׁשָּׁה סִדְרֵי מִשְׁנָה, חֲמִשָּׁה חֻמְשֵׁי תוֹרָה, אַרְבַּע אִמָּהוֹת, שְׁלֹשָׁה אָבוֹת, שְׁנֵי לֻחוֹת הַבְּרִית, אֶחָד אֱלֹהֵינוּ שֶׁבַּשָּׁמַיִם וּבָאָרֶץ.

חַד גַּדְיָא, חַד גַּדְיָא, דְּזַבִּין אַבָּא בִּתְרֵי זוּזֵי, חַד גַּדְיָא חַד גַּדְיָא.

וְאָתָא **שׁוּנְרָא** וְאָכְלָה לְגַדְיָא, דְּזַבִּין אַבָּא בִּתְרֵי זוּזֵי, חַד גַּדְיָא חַד גַּדְיָא.

וְאָתָא **כַלְבָּא** וְנָשַׁךְ לְשׁוּנְרָא, דְּאָכְלָא לְגַדְיָא, דְּזַבִּין אַבָּא בִּתְרֵי זוּזֵי, חַד גַּדְיָא חַד גַּדְיָא.

וְאָתָא **חוּטְרָא** וְהִכָּה לְכַלְבָּא, דְּנָשַׁךְ לְשׁוּנְרָא, דְּאָכְלָה לְגַדְיָא, דְּזַבִּין אַבָּא בִּתְרֵי זוּזֵי, חַד גַּדְיָא חַד גַּדְיָא.

וְאָתָא **נוּרָא** וְשָׂרַף לְחוּטְרָא, דְּהִכָּה לְכַלְבָּא, דְּנָשַׁךְ לְשׁוּנְרָא, דְּאָכְלָה לְגַדְיָא, דְּזַבִּין אַבָּא בִּתְרֵי זוּזֵי, חַד גַּדְיָא חַד גַּדְיָא.

וְאָתָא **מַיָּא** וְכָבָה לְנוּרָא, דְּשָׂרַף לְחוּטְרָא, דְּהִכָּה לְכַלְבָּא, דְּנָשַׁךְ לְשׁוּנְרָא, דְּאָכְלָה לְגַדְיָא, דְּזַבִּין אַבָּא בִּתְרֵי זוּזֵי, חַד גַּדְיָא חַד גַּדְיָא.

וְאָתָא **תוֹרָא** וְשָׁתָה לְמַיָּא, דְּכָבָה לְנוּרָא, דְּשָׂרַף לְחוּטְרָא, דְּהִכָּה לְכַלְבָּא, דְּנָשַׁךְ לְשׁוּנְרָא, דְּאָכְלָה לְגַדְיָא, דְּזַבִּין אַבָּא בִּתְרֵי זוּזֵי, חַד גַּדְיָא חַד גַּדְיָא.

וְאָתָא **הַשּׁוֹחֵט** וְשָׁחַט לְתוֹרָא, דְּשָׁתָא לְמַיָּא, דְּכָבָה לְנוּרָא, דְּשָׂרַף לְחוּטְרָא, דְּהִכָּה לְכַלְבָּא, דְּנָשַׁךְ לְשׁוּנְרָא, דְּאָכְלָה לְגַדְיָא, דְּזַבִּין אַבָּא בִּתְרֵי זוּזֵי, חַד גַּדְיָא חַד גַּדְיָא.

וְאָתָא **מַלְאַךְ הַמָּוֶת** וְשָׁחַט לְשׁוֹחֵט, דְּשָׁחַט לְתוֹרָא, דְּשָׁתָה לְמַיָּא, דְּכָבָה לְנוּרָא, דְּשָׂרַף לְחוּטְרָא, דְּהִכָּה לְכַלְבָּא, דְּנָשַׁךְ לְשׁוּנְרָא, דְּאָכְלָה לְגַדְיָא, דְּזַבִּין אַבָּא

Who knows thirteen? I know thirteen: thirteen are the attributes of God; twelve are the tribes; eleven are the stars (in Yosef's dream); ten are the Ten Commandments; nine are the months of pregnancy; eight are the days of circumcision; seven are the days of the week; six are the Orders of the Mishnah; five are the Books of the Torah; four are the Matriarchs; three are the Patriarchs; two are the Tablets of the Covenant; One is our God, in heaven and on earth.

A kid, a kid, that father bought for two zuzim, a kid, a kid.

A cat then came and devoured the kid that father bought for two zuzim, a kid, a kid.

A dog then came and bit the cat, that devoured the kid that father bought for two zuzim, a kid, a kid.

A stick then came and beat the dog, that bit the cat, that devoured the kid that father bought for two zuzim, a kid, a kid.

A fire then came and burnt the stick, that beat the dog, that bit the cat, that devoured the kid that father bought for two zuzim, a kid, a kid.

Water then came and quenched the fire, that burnt the stick, that beat the dog, that bit the cat, that devoured the kid that father bought for two zuzim, a kid, a kid.

An ox then came and drank the water, that quenched the fire, that burnt the stick, that beat the dog, that bit the cat, that devoured the kid that father bought for two zuzim, a kid, a kid.

A slaughterer then came and slaughtered the ox, that drank the water, that quenched the fire, that burnt the stick, that beat the dog, that bit the cat, that devoured the kid that father bought for two zuzim, a kid, a kid.

The angel of death then came and killed the slaughterer, who slaughtered the ox, that drank the water, that quenched the fire, that burnt the stick, that beat the dog, that bit the cat, that devoured the kid that father

בִּתְרֵי זוּזֵי, חַד גַּדְיָא חַד גַּדְיָא.
וְאָתָא הַקָּדוֹשׁ בָּרוּךְ הוּא וְשָׁחַט לְמַלְאַךְ הַמָּוֶת,
דְּשָׁחַט לְשׁוֹחֵט, דְּשָׁחַט לְתוֹרָא, דְּשָׁתָה לְמַיָּא,
דְּכָבָה לְנוּרָא, דְּשָׂרַף לְחוּטְרָא, דְּהִכָּה לְכַלְבָּא,
דְּנָשַׁךְ לְשׁוּנְרָא, דְּאָכְלָה לְגַדְיָא, דְּזַבִּין אַבָּא
בִּתְרֵי זוּזֵי, חַד גַּדְיָא חַד גַּדְיָא.

Although the Haggadah formally ends at this point, one should continue to occupy himself with the story of the Exodus, and the laws of Pesach, until sleep overtakes him.

bought for two zuzim, a kid, a kid.

The Holy One, Blessed is He, then came and slew the angel of death, who killed the slaughterer, who slaughtered the ox, that drank the water, that quenched the fire, that burnt the stick, that beat the dog, that bit the cat, that devoured the kid that father bought for two zuzim, a kid, a kid.

> Although the Haggadah formally ends at this point, one should continue to occupy himself with the story of the Exodus, and the laws of Pesach, until sleep overtakes him.

שִׁיר הַשִּׁירִים
Shir HaShirim

שיר השירים

Many recite שִׁיר הַשִּׁירִים, *Song of Songs,* after the Haggadah.

א

א **שִׁיר הַשִּׁירִים** אֲשֶׁר לִשְׁלֹמֹה. ב יִשָּׁקֵנִי מִנְּשִׁיקוֹת פִּיהוּ, כִּי טוֹבִים דֹּדֶיךָ מִיָּיִן. ג לְרֵיחַ שְׁמָנֶיךָ טוֹבִים, שֶׁמֶן תּוּרַק שְׁמֶךָ, עַל כֵּן עֲלָמוֹת אֲהֵבוּךָ. ד מָשְׁכֵנִי אַחֲרֶיךָ נָּרוּצָה, הֱבִיאַנִי הַמֶּלֶךְ חֲדָרָיו, נָגִילָה וְנִשְׂמְחָה בָּךְ. נַזְכִּירָה דֹדֶיךָ מִיַּיִן, מֵישָׁרִים אֲהֵבוּךָ. ה שְׁחוֹרָה אֲנִי וְנָאוָה, בְּנוֹת יְרוּשָׁלָיִם, כְּאָהֳלֵי קֵדָר, כִּירִיעוֹת שְׁלֹמֹה. ו אַל תִּרְאוּנִי שֶׁאֲנִי שְׁחַרְחֹרֶת, שֶׁשְּׁזָפַתְנִי הַשָּׁמֶשׁ, בְּנֵי אִמִּי נִחֲרוּ בִי, שָׂמֻנִי נֹטֵרָה אֶת הַכְּרָמִים, כַּרְמִי שֶׁלִּי לֹא נָטָרְתִּי. ז הַגִּידָה לִּי, שֶׁאָהֲבָה נַפְשִׁי, אֵיכָה תִרְעֶה, אֵיכָה תַּרְבִּיץ בַּצָּהֳרָיִם, שַׁלָּמָה אֶהְיֶה כְּעֹטְיָה עַל עֶדְרֵי חֲבֵרֶיךָ. ח אִם לֹא תֵדְעִי לָךְ, הַיָּפָה בַּנָּשִׁים, צְאִי לָךְ בְּעִקְבֵי הַצֹּאן, וּרְעִי אֶת גְּדִיֹּתַיִךְ עַל מִשְׁכְּנוֹת הָרֹעִים. ט לְסֻסָתִי בְּרִכְבֵי פַרְעֹה דִּמִּיתִיךְ, רַעְיָתִי. י נָאווּ לְחָיַיִךְ בַּתֹּרִים, צַוָּארֵךְ בַּחֲרוּזִים. יא תּוֹרֵי זָהָב נַעֲשֶׂה לָּךְ, עִם נְקֻדּוֹת הַכָּסֶף. יב עַד שֶׁהַמֶּלֶךְ בִּמְסִבּוֹ, נִרְדִּי נָתַן רֵיחוֹ. יג צְרוֹר הַמֹּר דּוֹדִי לִי, בֵּין שָׁדַי יָלִין. יד אֶשְׁכֹּל הַכֹּפֶר דּוֹדִי לִי, בְּכַרְמֵי עֵין גֶּדִי. טו הִנָּךְ יָפָה, רַעְיָתִי, הִנָּךְ יָפָה, עֵינַיִךְ יוֹנִים. טז הִנְּךָ יָפֶה, דוֹדִי, אַף נָעִים, אַף עַרְשֵׂנוּ רַעֲנָנָה. יז קֹרוֹת בָּתֵּינוּ אֲרָזִים, רַהִיטֵנוּ בְּרוֹתִים.

ב

א אֲנִי חֲבַצֶּלֶת הַשָּׁרוֹן, שׁוֹשַׁנַּת הָעֲמָקִים. ב כְּשׁוֹשַׁנָּה בֵּין הַחוֹחִים, כֵּן רַעְיָתִי בֵּין הַבָּנוֹת. ג כְּתַפּוּחַ בַּעֲצֵי הַיַּעַר, כֵּן דּוֹדִי בֵּין הַבָּנִים, בְּצִלּוֹ חִמַּדְתִּי וְיָשַׁבְתִּי, וּפִרְיוֹ מָתוֹק לְחִכִּי. ד הֱבִיאַנִי אֶל בֵּית הַיָּיִן, וְדִגְלוֹ עָלַי אַהֲבָה. ה סַמְּכוּנִי בָּאֲשִׁישׁוֹת, רַפְּדוּנִי בַּתַּפּוּחִים, כִּי חוֹלַת אַהֲבָה אָנִי. ו שְׂמֹאלוֹ תַּחַת לְרֹאשִׁי, וִימִינוֹ

תְּחַבְּקֵנִי. ז הִשְׁבַּעְתִּי אֶתְכֶם, בְּנוֹת יְרוּשָׁלָיִם, בִּצְבָאוֹת אוֹ בְּאַיְלוֹת הַשָּׂדֶה, אִם תָּעִירוּ וְאִם תְּעוֹרְרוּ אֶת הָאַהֲבָה עַד שֶׁתֶּחְפָּץ. ח קוֹל דּוֹדִי הִנֵּה זֶה בָּא, מְדַלֵּג עַל הֶהָרִים, מְקַפֵּץ עַל הַגְּבָעוֹת. ט דּוֹמֶה דוֹדִי לִצְבִי, אוֹ לְעֹפֶר הָאַיָּלִים, הִנֵּה זֶה עוֹמֵד אַחַר כָּתְלֵנוּ, מַשְׁגִּיחַ מִן הַחַלֹּנוֹת, מֵצִיץ מִן הַחֲרַכִּים. י עָנָה דוֹדִי וְאָמַר לִי, קוּמִי לָךְ, רַעְיָתִי, יָפָתִי, וּלְכִי לָךְ. יא כִּי הִנֵּה הַסְּתָו עָבָר, הַגֶּשֶׁם חָלַף הָלַךְ לוֹ. יב הַנִּצָּנִים נִרְאוּ בָאָרֶץ, עֵת הַזָּמִיר הִגִּיעַ, וְקוֹל הַתּוֹר נִשְׁמַע בְּאַרְצֵנוּ. יג הַתְּאֵנָה חָנְטָה פַגֶּיהָ, וְהַגְּפָנִים סְמָדַר נָתְנוּ רֵיחַ, קוּמִי לָךְ, רַעְיָתִי, יָפָתִי, וּלְכִי לָךְ. יד יוֹנָתִי, בְּחַגְוֵי הַסֶּלַע, בְּסֵתֶר הַמַּדְרֵגָה, הַרְאִינִי אֶת מַרְאַיִךְ, הַשְׁמִיעִנִי אֶת קוֹלֵךְ, כִּי קוֹלֵךְ עָרֵב, וּמַרְאֵיךְ נָאוֶה. טו אֶחֱזוּ לָנוּ שׁוּעָלִים, שׁוּעָלִים קְטַנִּים, מְחַבְּלִים כְּרָמִים, וּכְרָמֵינוּ סְמָדַר. טז דּוֹדִי לִי, וַאֲנִי לוֹ, הָרֹעֶה בַּשּׁוֹשַׁנִּים. יז עַד שֶׁיָּפוּחַ הַיּוֹם, וְנָסוּ הַצְּלָלִים, סֹב דְּמֵה לְךָ, דוֹדִי, לִצְבִי אוֹ לְעֹפֶר הָאַיָּלִים, עַל הָרֵי בָתֶר.

ג

א עַל מִשְׁכָּבִי בַּלֵּילוֹת בִּקַּשְׁתִּי אֵת שֶׁאָהֲבָה נַפְשִׁי, בִּקַּשְׁתִּיו וְלֹא מְצָאתִיו. ב אָקוּמָה נָּא וַאֲסוֹבְבָה בָעִיר, בַּשְּׁוָקִים וּבָרְחֹבוֹת, אֲבַקְשָׁה אֵת שֶׁאָהֲבָה נַפְשִׁי, בִּקַּשְׁתִּיו וְלֹא מְצָאתִיו. ג מְצָאוּנִי הַשֹּׁמְרִים הַסֹּבְבִים בָּעִיר, אֵת שֶׁאָהֲבָה נַפְשִׁי רְאִיתֶם. ד כִּמְעַט שֶׁעָבַרְתִּי מֵהֶם, עַד שֶׁמָּצָאתִי אֵת שֶׁאָהֲבָה נַפְשִׁי, אֲחַזְתִּיו וְלֹא אַרְפֶּנּוּ, עַד שֶׁהֲבֵיאתִיו אֶל בֵּית אִמִּי, וְאֶל חֶדֶר הוֹרָתִי. ה הִשְׁבַּעְתִּי אֶתְכֶם, בְּנוֹת יְרוּשָׁלָיִם, בִּצְבָאוֹת אוֹ בְּאַיְלוֹת הַשָּׂדֶה, אִם תָּעִירוּ וְאִם תְּעוֹרְרוּ אֶת הָאַהֲבָה עַד שֶׁתֶּחְפָּץ. ו מִי זֹאת עֹלָה מִן הַמִּדְבָּר, כְּתִימֲרוֹת עָשָׁן, מְקֻטֶּרֶת מֹר וּלְבוֹנָה, מִכֹּל אַבְקַת רוֹכֵל. ז הִנֵּה מִטָּתוֹ שֶׁלִּשְׁלֹמֹה, שִׁשִּׁים גִּבֹּרִים סָבִיב לָהּ, מִגִּבֹּרֵי יִשְׂרָאֵל.

ח כֻּלָּם אֲחֻזֵי חֶרֶב, מְלֻמְּדֵי מִלְחָמָה, אִישׁ חַרְבּוֹ עַל יְרֵכוֹ, מִפַּחַד בַּלֵּילוֹת. ט אַפִּרְיוֹן עָשָׂה לוֹ הַמֶּלֶךְ שְׁלֹמֹה מֵעֲצֵי הַלְּבָנוֹן. י עַמּוּדָיו עָשָׂה כֶסֶף, רְפִידָתוֹ זָהָב, מֶרְכָּבוֹ אַרְגָּמָן, תּוֹכוֹ רָצוּף אַהֲבָה מִבְּנוֹת יְרוּשָׁלָיִם. יא צְאֶינָה וּרְאֶינָה, בְּנוֹת צִיּוֹן, בַּמֶּלֶךְ שְׁלֹמֹה, בָּעֲטָרָה שֶׁעִטְּרָה לּוֹ אִמּוֹ, בְּיוֹם חֲתֻנָּתוֹ, וּבְיוֹם שִׂמְחַת לִבּוֹ.

ד

א הִנָּךְ יָפָה, רַעְיָתִי, הִנָּךְ יָפָה, עֵינַיִךְ יוֹנִים, מִבַּעַד לְצַמָּתֵךְ, שַׂעְרֵךְ כְּעֵדֶר הָעִזִּים, שֶׁגָּלְשׁוּ מֵהַר גִּלְעָד. ב שִׁנַּיִךְ כְּעֵדֶר הַקְּצוּבוֹת שֶׁעָלוּ מִן הָרַחְצָה, שֶׁכֻּלָּם מַתְאִימוֹת, וְשַׁכֻּלָה אֵין בָּהֶם. ג כְּחוּט הַשָּׁנִי שִׂפְתוֹתַיִךְ, וּמִדְבָּרֵךְ נָאוֶה, כְּפֶלַח הָרִמּוֹן רַקָּתֵךְ, מִבַּעַד לְצַמָּתֵךְ. ד כְּמִגְדַּל דָּוִיד צַוָּארֵךְ, בָּנוּי לְתַלְפִּיּוֹת, אֶלֶף הַמָּגֵן תָּלוּי עָלָיו, כֹּל שִׁלְטֵי הַגִּבּוֹרִים. ה שְׁנֵי שָׁדַיִךְ כִּשְׁנֵי עֳפָרִים, תְּאוֹמֵי צְבִיָּה, הָרוֹעִים בַּשּׁוֹשַׁנִּים. ו עַד שֶׁיָּפוּחַ הַיּוֹם, וְנָסוּ הַצְּלָלִים, אֵלֶךְ לִי אֶל הַר הַמּוֹר, וְאֶל גִּבְעַת הַלְּבוֹנָה. ז כֻּלָּךְ יָפָה, רַעְיָתִי, וּמוּם אֵין בָּךְ. ח אִתִּי מִלְּבָנוֹן, כַּלָּה, אִתִּי מִלְּבָנוֹן תָּבוֹאִי, תָּשׁוּרִי מֵרֹאשׁ אֲמָנָה, מֵרֹאשׁ שְׂנִיר וְחֶרְמוֹן, מִמְּעֹנוֹת אֲרָיוֹת, מֵהַרְרֵי נְמֵרִים. ט לִבַּבְתִּנִי, אֲחוֹתִי כַלָּה, לִבַּבְתִּנִי בְּאַחַת מֵעֵינַיִךְ, בְּאַחַד עֲנָק מִצַּוְּרֹנָיִךְ. י מַה יָּפוּ דֹדַיִךְ, אֲחֹתִי כַלָּה, מַה טֹּבוּ דֹדַיִךְ מִיַּיִן, וְרֵיחַ שְׁמָנַיִךְ מִכָּל בְּשָׂמִים. יא נֹפֶת תִּטֹּפְנָה שִׂפְתוֹתַיִךְ, כַּלָּה, דְּבַשׁ וְחָלָב תַּחַת לְשׁוֹנֵךְ, וְרֵיחַ שַׂלְמֹתַיִךְ כְּרֵיחַ לְבָנוֹן. יב גַּן נָעוּל אֲחֹתִי כַלָּה, גַּל נָעוּל, מַעְיָן חָתוּם. יג שְׁלָחַיִךְ פַּרְדֵּס רִמּוֹנִים, עִם פְּרִי מְגָדִים, כְּפָרִים עִם נְרָדִים. יד נֵרְדְּ וְכַרְכֹּם, קָנֶה וְקִנָּמוֹן, עִם כָּל עֲצֵי לְבוֹנָה, מֹר וַאֲהָלוֹת, עִם כָּל רָאשֵׁי בְשָׂמִים. טו מַעְיַן גַּנִּים, בְּאֵר מַיִם חַיִּים, וְנֹזְלִים מִן לְבָנוֹן. טז עוּרִי צָפוֹן, וּבוֹאִי תֵימָן, הָפִיחִי גַנִּי, יִזְּלוּ בְשָׂמָיו, יָבֹא דוֹדִי לְגַנּוֹ, וְיֹאכַל פְּרִי מְגָדָיו.

ה

א בָּאתִי לְגַנִּי, אֲחֹתִי כַלָּה, אָרִיתִי מוֹרִי עִם בְּשָׂמִי, אָכַלְתִּי יַעְרִי עִם דִּבְשִׁי, שָׁתִיתִי יֵינִי עִם חֲלָבִי, אִכְלוּ רֵעִים, שְׁתוּ וְשִׁכְרוּ דּוֹדִים. ב אֲנִי יְשֵׁנָה וְלִבִּי עֵר, קוֹל דּוֹדִי דוֹפֵק, פִּתְחִי לִי, אֲחֹתִי, רַעְיָתִי, יוֹנָתִי, תַמָּתִי, שֶׁרֹּאשִׁי נִמְלָא טָל, קְוֻצּוֹתַי רְסִיסֵי לָיְלָה. ג פָּשַׁטְתִּי אֶת כֻּתָּנְתִּי, אֵיכָכָה אֶלְבָּשֶׁנָּה, רָחַצְתִּי אֶת רַגְלַי, אֵיכָכָה אֲטַנְּפֵם. ד דּוֹדִי שָׁלַח יָדוֹ מִן הַחוֹר, וּמֵעַי הָמוּ עָלָיו. ה קַמְתִּי אֲנִי לִפְתֹּחַ לְדוֹדִי, וְיָדַי נָטְפוּ מוֹר, וְאֶצְבְּעֹתַי מוֹר עֹבֵר, עַל כַּפּוֹת הַמַּנְעוּל. ו פָּתַחְתִּי אֲנִי לְדוֹדִי, וְדוֹדִי חָמַק עָבָר, נַפְשִׁי יָצְאָה בְדַבְּרוֹ, בִּקַּשְׁתִּיהוּ וְלֹא מְצָאתִיהוּ, קְרָאתִיו וְלֹא עָנָנִי. ז מְצָאֻנִי הַשֹּׁמְרִים הַסֹּבְבִים בָּעִיר, הִכּוּנִי פְצָעוּנִי, נָשְׂאוּ אֶת רְדִידִי מֵעָלַי שֹׁמְרֵי הַחֹמוֹת. ח הִשְׁבַּעְתִּי אֶתְכֶם, בְּנוֹת יְרוּשָׁלָיִם, אִם תִּמְצְאוּ אֶת דּוֹדִי, מַה תַּגִּידוּ לוֹ שֶׁחוֹלַת אַהֲבָה אָנִי. ט מַה דּוֹדֵךְ מִדּוֹד, הַיָּפָה בַּנָּשִׁים, מַה דּוֹדֵךְ מִדּוֹד, שֶׁכָּכָה הִשְׁבַּעְתָּנוּ. י דּוֹדִי צַח וְאָדוֹם, דָּגוּל מֵרְבָבָה. יא רֹאשׁוֹ כֶּתֶם פָּז, קְוֻצּוֹתָיו תַּלְתַּלִּים, שְׁחֹרוֹת כָּעוֹרֵב. יב עֵינָיו כְּיוֹנִים עַל אֲפִיקֵי מָיִם, רֹחֲצוֹת בֶּחָלָב, יֹשְׁבוֹת עַל מִלֵּאת. יג לְחָיָו כַּעֲרוּגַת הַבֹּשֶׂם, מִגְדְּלוֹת מֶרְקָחִים, שִׂפְתוֹתָיו שׁוֹשַׁנִּים, נֹטְפוֹת מוֹר עֹבֵר. יד יָדָיו גְּלִילֵי זָהָב, מְמֻלָּאִים בַּתַּרְשִׁישׁ, מֵעָיו עֶשֶׁת שֵׁן, מְעֻלֶּפֶת סַפִּירִים. טו שׁוֹקָיו עַמּוּדֵי שֵׁשׁ, מְיֻסָּדִים עַל אַדְנֵי פָז, מַרְאֵהוּ כַּלְּבָנוֹן, בָּחוּר כָּאֲרָזִים. טז חִכּוֹ מַמְתַקִּים, וְכֻלּוֹ מַחֲמַדִּים, זֶה דוֹדִי וְזֶה רֵעִי, בְּנוֹת יְרוּשָׁלָיִם.

ו

א אָנָה הָלַךְ דּוֹדֵךְ, הַיָּפָה בַּנָּשִׁים, אָנָה פָּנָה דוֹדֵךְ, וּנְבַקְשֶׁנּוּ עִמָּךְ. ב דּוֹדִי יָרַד לְגַנּוֹ, לַעֲרוּגוֹת הַבֹּשֶׂם, לִרְעוֹת בַּגַּנִּים וְלִלְקֹט שׁוֹשַׁנִּים. ג אֲנִי לְדוֹדִי, וְדוֹדִי לִי,

הָרוֹעֶה בַּשּׁוֹשַׁנִּים. ד יָפָה אַתְּ רַעְיָתִי כְּתִרְצָה, נָאוָה כִּירוּשָׁלָיִם, אֲיֻמָּה כַּנִּדְגָּלוֹת. ה הָסֵבִּי עֵינַיִךְ מִנֶּגְדִּי, שֶׁהֵם הִרְהִיבֻנִי, שַׂעְרֵךְ כְּעֵדֶר הָעִזִּים, שֶׁגָּלְשׁוּ מִן הַגִּלְעָד. ו שִׁנַּיִךְ כְּעֵדֶר הָרְחֵלִים, שֶׁעָלוּ מִן הָרַחְצָה, שֶׁכֻּלָּם מַתְאִימוֹת, וְשַׁכֻּלָה אֵין בָּהֶם. ז כְּפֶלַח הָרִמּוֹן רַקָּתֵךְ, מִבַּעַד לְצַמָּתֵךְ. ח שִׁשִּׁים הֵמָּה מְלָכוֹת, וּשְׁמֹנִים פִּילַגְשִׁים, וַעֲלָמוֹת אֵין מִסְפָּר. ט אַחַת הִיא יוֹנָתִי תַמָּתִי, אַחַת הִיא לְאִמָּהּ, בָּרָה הִיא לְיוֹלַדְתָּהּ, רָאוּהָ בָנוֹת וַיְאַשְּׁרוּהָ, מְלָכוֹת וּפִילַגְשִׁים, וַיְהַלְלוּהָ. י מִי זֹאת הַנִּשְׁקָפָה כְּמוֹ שָׁחַר, יָפָה כַלְּבָנָה, בָּרָה כַּחַמָּה, אֲיֻמָּה כַּנִּדְגָּלוֹת. יא אֶל גִּנַּת אֱגוֹז יָרַדְתִּי לִרְאוֹת בְּאִבֵּי הַנָּחַל, לִרְאוֹת הֲפָרְחָה הַגֶּפֶן, הֵנֵצוּ הָרִמֹּנִים. יב לֹא יָדַעְתִּי, נַפְשִׁי שָׂמַתְנִי, מַרְכְּבוֹת עַמִּי נָדִיב.

ז

א שׁוּבִי שׁוּבִי, הַשּׁוּלַמִּית, שׁוּבִי שׁוּבִי וְנֶחֱזֶה בָּךְ, מַה תֶּחֱזוּ בַּשּׁוּלַמִּית, כִּמְחֹלַת הַמַּחֲנָיִם. ב מַה יָּפוּ פְעָמַיִךְ בַּנְּעָלִים, בַּת נָדִיב, חַמּוּקֵי יְרֵכַיִךְ כְּמוֹ חֲלָאִים, מַעֲשֵׂה יְדֵי אָמָּן. ג שָׁרְרֵךְ אַגַּן הַסַּהַר, אַל יֶחְסַר הַמָּזֶג, בִּטְנֵךְ עֲרֵמַת חִטִּים, סוּגָה בַּשּׁוֹשַׁנִּים. ד שְׁנֵי שָׁדַיִךְ כִּשְׁנֵי עֳפָרִים, תָּאֳמֵי צְבִיָּה. ה צַוָּארֵךְ כְּמִגְדַּל הַשֵּׁן, עֵינַיִךְ בְּרֵכוֹת בְּחֶשְׁבּוֹן, עַל שַׁעַר בַּת רַבִּים, אַפֵּךְ כְּמִגְדַּל הַלְּבָנוֹן, צוֹפֶה פְּנֵי דַמָּשֶׂק. ו רֹאשֵׁךְ עָלַיִךְ כַּכַּרְמֶל, וְדַלַּת רֹאשֵׁךְ כָּאַרְגָּמָן, מֶלֶךְ אָסוּר בָּרְהָטִים. ז מַה יָּפִית וּמַה נָּעַמְתְּ, אַהֲבָה בַּתַּעֲנוּגִים. ח זֹאת קוֹמָתֵךְ דָּמְתָה לְתָמָר, וְשָׁדַיִךְ לְאַשְׁכֹּלוֹת. ט אָמַרְתִּי, אֶעֱלֶה בְתָמָר, אֹחֲזָה בְּסַנְסִנָּיו, וְיִהְיוּ נָא שָׁדַיִךְ כְּאֶשְׁכְּלוֹת הַגֶּפֶן, וְרֵיחַ אַפֵּךְ כַּתַּפּוּחִים. י וְחִכֵּךְ כְּיֵין הַטּוֹב, הוֹלֵךְ לְדוֹדִי לְמֵישָׁרִים, דּוֹבֵב שִׂפְתֵי יְשֵׁנִים. יא אֲנִי לְדוֹדִי, וְעָלַי

תְּשׁוּקָתוֹ. יב לְכָה דוֹדִי, נֵצֵא הַשָּׂדֶה, נָלִינָה בַּכְּפָרִים. יג נַשְׁכִּימָה לַכְּרָמִים, נִרְאֶה אִם פָּרְחָה הַגֶּפֶן, פִּתַּח הַסְּמָדַר, הֵנֵצוּ הָרִמּוֹנִים, שָׁם אֶתֵּן אֶת דֹּדַי לָךְ. יד הַדּוּדָאִים נָתְנוּ רֵיחַ, וְעַל פְּתָחֵינוּ כָּל מְגָדִים, חֲדָשִׁים גַּם יְשָׁנִים, דּוֹדִי, צָפַנְתִּי לָךְ.

ח

א מִי יִתֶּנְךָ כְּאָח לִי, יוֹנֵק שְׁדֵי אִמִּי, אֶמְצָאֲךָ בַחוּץ אֶשָּׁקְךָ, גַּם לֹא יָבוּזוּ לִי. ב אֶנְהָגְךָ, אֲבִיאֲךָ אֶל בֵּית אִמִּי, תְּלַמְּדֵנִי, אַשְׁקְךָ מִיַּיִן הָרֶקַח, מֵעֲסִיס רִמֹּנִי. ג שְׂמֹאלוֹ תַּחַת רֹאשִׁי, וִימִינוֹ תְּחַבְּקֵנִי. ד הִשְׁבַּעְתִּי אֶתְכֶם, בְּנוֹת יְרוּשָׁלִָם, מַה תָּעִירוּ וּמַה תְּעֹרְרוּ אֶת הָאַהֲבָה עַד שֶׁתֶּחְפָּץ. ה מִי זֹאת עֹלָה מִן הַמִּדְבָּר, מִתְרַפֶּקֶת עַל דּוֹדָהּ, תַּחַת הַתַּפּוּחַ עוֹרַרְתִּיךָ, שָׁמָּה חִבְּלַתְךָ אִמֶּךָ, שָׁמָּה חִבְּלָה יְלָדַתְךָ. ו שִׂימֵנִי כַחוֹתָם עַל לִבֶּךָ, כַּחוֹתָם עַל זְרוֹעֶךָ, כִּי עַזָּה כַמָּוֶת אַהֲבָה, קָשָׁה כִשְׁאוֹל קִנְאָה, רְשָׁפֶיהָ רִשְׁפֵּי אֵשׁ, שַׁלְהֶבֶתְיָה. ז מַיִם רַבִּים לֹא יוּכְלוּ לְכַבּוֹת אֶת הָאַהֲבָה, וּנְהָרוֹת לֹא יִשְׁטְפוּהָ, אִם יִתֵּן אִישׁ אֶת כָּל הוֹן בֵּיתוֹ בָּאַהֲבָה, בּוֹז יָבוּזוּ לוֹ. ח אָחוֹת לָנוּ קְטַנָּה, וְשָׁדַיִם אֵין לָהּ, מַה נַּעֲשֶׂה לַאֲחוֹתֵנוּ בַּיּוֹם שֶׁיְּדֻבַּר בָּהּ. ט אִם חוֹמָה הִיא, נִבְנֶה עָלֶיהָ טִירַת כָּסֶף, וְאִם דֶּלֶת הִיא, נָצוּר עָלֶיהָ לוּחַ אָרֶז. י אֲנִי חוֹמָה, וְשָׁדַי כַּמִּגְדָּלוֹת, אָז הָיִיתִי בְעֵינָיו כְּמוֹצְאֵת שָׁלוֹם. יא כֶּרֶם הָיָה לִשְׁלֹמֹה בְּבַעַל הָמוֹן, נָתַן אֶת הַכֶּרֶם לַנֹּטְרִים, אִישׁ יָבִא בְּפִרְיוֹ אֶלֶף כָּסֶף. יב כַּרְמִי שֶׁלִּי לְפָנָי, הָאֶלֶף לְךָ שְׁלֹמֹה, וּמָאתַיִם לְנֹטְרִים אֶת פִּרְיוֹ. יג הַיּוֹשֶׁבֶת בַּגַּנִּים, חֲבֵרִים מַקְשִׁיבִים לְקוֹלֵךְ, הַשְׁמִיעִנִי. יד בְּרַח דּוֹדִי, וּדְמֵה לְךָ לִצְבִי, אוֹ לְעֹפֶר הָאַיָּלִים, עַל הָרֵי בְשָׂמִים.

This volume is part of
THE ARTSCROLL SERIES®
an ongoing project of
translations, commentaries and expositions
on Scripture, Mishnah, Talmud, Halachah,
liturgy, history, the classic Rabbinic writings,
biographies and thought.

For a brochure of current publications
visit your local Hebrew bookseller
or contact the publisher:

Mesorah Publications, ltd
4401 Second Avenue
Brooklyn, New York 11232
(718) 921-9000